Lecture Notes in Artificial Intelligence 13546

Subseries of Lecture Notes in Computer Science

Series Editors

Randy Goebel
University of Alberta, Edmonton, Canada

Wolfgang Wahlster
DFKI, Berlin, Germany

Zhi-Hua Zhou
Nanjing University, Nanjing, China

Founding Editor

Jörg Siekmann
DFKI and Saarland University, Saarbrücken, Germany

More information about this subseries at https://link.springer.com/bookseries/1244

Salvador Pacheco-Gutierrez · Alice Cryer ·
Ipek Caliskanelli · Harun Tugal ·
Robert Skilton (Eds.)

Towards Autonomous
Robotic Systems

23rd Annual Conference, TAROS 2022
Culham, UK, September 7–9, 2022
Proceedings

 Springer

Editors
Salvador Pacheco-Gutierrez (ID)
UKAEA's RACE
Abindgon, UK

Alice Cryer (ID)
UKAEA's RACE
Abingdon, UK

Ipek Caliskanelli (ID)
UKAEA's RACE
Abingdon, UK

Harun Tugal (ID)
UKAEA's RACE
Abingdon, UK

Robert Skilton (ID)
UKAEA's RACE
Abingdon, UK

ISSN 0302-9743 ISSN 1611-3349 (electronic)
Lecture Notes in Artificial Intelligence
ISBN 978-3-031-15907-7 ISBN 978-3-031-15908-4 (eBook)
https://doi.org/10.1007/978-3-031-15908-4

LNCS Sublibrary: SL7 – Artificial Intelligence

This Springer imprint is published by the registered company Springer Nature Switzerland AG
The registered company address is: Gewerbestrasse 11, 6330 Cham, Switzerland

Preface

This volume contains the papers presented at TAROS 2022, the 23rd Towards Autonomous Robotic Systems (TAROS) Conference, held at Culham Science Centre by the Remote Applications in Challenging Environments (RACE) Department of the UK Atomic Energy Authority (UKAEA), Abingdon, UK, during September 7–9, 2022 (https://ukaeaevents.com/23rd-taros/).

TAROS is the longest running UK-hosted international conference on robotics and autonomous systems (RAS), which is aimed at the presentation and discussion of the latest results and methods in autonomous robotics research and applications. The conference offers a friendly environment for robotics researchers and industry to take stock and plan future progress. It welcomes senior researchers and research students alike, and specifically provides opportunities for research students and young research scientists to present their work to the scientific community.

TAROS 2022 was held in the Culham Science Centre, home of the UK Atomic Energy Authority, including the Remote Applications in Challenging Environments (RACE) facility, and the Joint European Torus (JET) fusion energy experiment. The papers in this volume were selected from 38 submissions, which were sent for single-blind peer review. Out of these, 14 full papers and 10 short papers were selected for the conference, which is a 63% acceptance rate. The conference programme included an academic conference, industry exhibitions, robot demonstrations, a tour of JET and the robotics facilities supporting its remote handling, and a conference dinner. The program covered robotic systems, human–robot interaction, robot navigation and planning, robot control, and industrial robots, and highlights included

- Keynote lectures by world-leading experts in robotics, including lectures by Paul Newman from the University of Oxford, UK, and Luc Jaulin from ENSTA Bretagne, France,
- An IET-sponsored evening lecture by Rob Buckingham, co-founder of OC Robotics and current head of the RACE department within UKAEA,
- Poster presentations, covering various topics of robotics, mobile robots and vehicles, robot design and testing, detection and recognition, learning and adaptive behaviors, human–robot and robot–robot interaction, and
- Industrial and academic exhibition stands.

The TAROS 2022 Organizing Committee would like to thank all the authors, reviewers, and the conference sponsors, including the UK Atomic Energy Authority, IET, and Springer for their support to the conference.

September 2022

Alice Cryer
Salvador Pacheco-Gutierrez
Ipek Caliskanelli
Harun Tugal
Robert Skilton

Organization

General Chair

Robert Skilton   RACE-UKAEA, UK

Program Chairs

Alice Cryer   RACE-UKAEA, UK
Salvador Pacheco-Gutierrez   RACE-UKAEA, UK
Ipek Caliskanelli   RACE-UKAEA, UK
Harun Tugal   RACE-UKAEA, UK

Web Chair

Sam Wainwright   RACE-UKAEA, UK

Steering Committee

Manuel Giuliani   University of the West of England, UK
Chris Melhuish   University of the West of England, UK
Mark Witkowski   Imperial College London, UK

Organizing Committee

Radhika Nath   RACE-UKAEA, UK
Bechir Tabia   RACE-UKAEA, UK
Ozan Tokatli   RACE-UKAEA, UK
Kate Conway   RACE-UKAEA, UK
Guy Burroughes   RACE-UKAEA, UK
Kaiqiang Zhang   RACE-UKAEA, UK

Invited Speakers

Rob Buckingham   RACE-UKAEA, UK
Luc Jaulin   ENSTA Bretagne, France
Paul Newman   University of Oxford, UK

Additional Reviewers

Jonathan Aitken	University of Sheffield, UK
Omar Aldughayem	Mobily Telecomunications, Saudi Arabia
Joaquin Carrasco-Gomez	University of Manchester, UK
Kamil Cetin	Izmir Katip Celebi University, Turkey
Gautham Das	University of Lincoln, UK
Maurice Fallon	University of Oxford, UK
Ildar Farkhatdinov	Queen Mary University of London, UK
Alessandro Giusti	Istituto Dalle Molle di Studi sull'Intelligenza Artificiale, Switzerland
Gunay Gultekin	RACE-UKAEA, UK
William Harwin	University of Reading, UK
Esra Icer	Technical University of Munich, Germany
Balazs Janko	RACE-UKAEA, UK
Emil Jonasson	RACE-UKAEA, UK
Hasan Kivrak	University of Manchester, UK
Ibrahim Kucukdemiral	Glasgow Caledonian University, UK
Henry Lau	RACE-UKAEA, UK
Pengcheng Liu	University of York, UK
Erwin Lopez	University of Manchester, UK
Mario Martinez-Guerrero	University of Manchester, UK
Nando Milella	RACE-UKAEA, UK
Alan Millard	University of York, UK
Christopher Peers	University of Leeds, UK
Can Pehlivanturk	RACE-UKAEA, UK
Nikola Petkov	RACE-UKAEA, UK
Alexandros Plianos	RACE-UKAEA, UK
Roger Powell	RACE-UKAEA, UK
Vijaykumar Rajasekaran	RACE-UKAEA, UK
Robert Richardson	Univeristy of Leeds, UK
Sohabe Richyal	RACE-UKAEA, UK
Tomoki Sakaue	TEPCO, Japan
Enver Salkim	Mus Alparslan University, Turkey
Wataru Sato	TEPCO, Japan
Onder Tutsoy	Adana Alparslan Turkes Science and Technology University, Turkey
Mingfeng Wang	University of Nottingham, UK
Lushan Weerasooriya	RACE-UKAEA, UK
Andrew West	University of Manchester, UK
Andika Yudha	RACE-UKAEA, UK
Kaiqiang Zhang	RACE-UKAEA, UK
Ioannis Zoulias	RACE-UKAEA, UK

Contents

Robotic Learning, Mapping and Planning

Robotic Systems and Applications

Robotic Grippers and Manipulation

Robotic Cooperation and Multiplication

A Distributed Approach to Haptic Simulation

Dan Norman[1]([✉]) [iD], William Harwin[1,2] [iD], and Faustina Hwang[1] [iD]

[1] University of Reading, RG6 6AY Reading, UK
d.j.norman@pgr.reading.ac.uk, {w.s.harwin,f.hwang}@reading.ac.uk
[2] RACE UK Atomic Energy Authority, Culham Science Centre, Abingdon, UK

Abstract. The quality of the physical haptic interaction and the need to link the haptic device or devices to high quality computer simulations in a time critical way are two key problems in modern haptic rendering.

Additionally, in large simulation environments, the need to update the dynamic state of every object is required, even if the objects are not involved in haptic feedback. This can result in a decreasing haptic update rate for increasing simulation complexity.

A possible way to address these conflicting requirements is to consider control structures that operate at differing loop times and consider issues such as stability in the context of these loop times. This paper therefore, outlines a flexible rendering architecture to manage the conflicting requirements of simulation quality and simulation speed across multiple devices.

Keywords: Distributed systems · Haptics · Multi-finger · Bi-manual

1 Introduction

One hurdle towards securing sustained interest for higher quality devices is the high cost of the haptic device and difficulty when adapting bespoke haptic devices to a specific task. Considering applications as a distribution of hardware and software may allow a more universal consideration of haptic based simulators and could also lead to the establishment of standards for haptic simulators.

This paper considers the above dilemma from the perspective of haptics as a distributed system. Distributed systems can be applied to haptics in two ways, physical distribution and control distribution. Physical distribution of the haptic hardware is considered as a potential method to create re-configurable multi-point haptic devices. Control distribution refers to the process of creating control software that has capabilities ranging from allowing physical distribution to function to increasing simulation stability in complex environments by limiting the number of objects handled in the haptic update, and therefore reducing the delay in the system [3].

Distributed control is widely used in the process industry and research on swarm robotics [10], where each robot can be considered a node in the control

© The Author(s), under exclusive license to Springer Nature Switzerland AG 2022
S. Pacheco-Gutierrez et al. (Eds.): TAROS 2022, LNAI 13546, pp. 3–13, 2022.
https://doi.org/10.1007/978-3-031-15908-4_1

network. However, the bandwidth of the communication channels tends to be a limiting factor in distributed systems. Therefore, there have been attempts to reduce the amount of data needing to be sent. One example is a system that uses state estimators [15] to predict what the other nodes are outputting rather than having each node sending an update to over the whole network.

2 Physical Distribution

Physical distribution refers to how the haptic devices in a multi device setup are connected to each other, and the hardware that runs the control software. One of the simplest types of physical distribution is a pair of devices that have been connected to the same controller board to allow for two point haptic interaction, for example a two finger grasp [2].

The inputs and outputs of both devices are sent to the same controller board, which is connected to a computer and uses a control software library that expects two devices regardless of configuration. As such these two devices, which are approximating a single multi-point device can be reconfigured without needing any changes to the base level controller.

An alternative concept for implementing physical distribution is to create a system that consists of multiple device control boards connected by communication channels to the same simulation.

This can be used to create a system of devices with mixed locality, where some devices are connected directly to the machine running the simulation environment and others are connected indirectly. This concept has been partly implemented on a test-bed haptic environment developed at the University of Reading and is shown in Fig. 1. The test-bed haptic environment (colloquially known as the Matrix) consists of two pairs of devices and their two corresponding control boards. Two control boards are used as each board can only have two devices connected to it. One of the boards is connected directly to the computer running the simulation while the other is connected indirectly via a secondary computer using an Ethernet cable. Communication over the Ethernet cable was handled by the communications protocol called UDP. The CHAI3D simulation framework [4], using the bullet physics module, is being used to test the effect of remote (indirectly connected) devices on simulation performance. The experiment consists of a pick and place task where the local pair represent one hand and the remote pair the other. The initial results from this experiment suggest that UDP over Ethernet could be a viable method for physical distribution, as the simulation remains stable and runs at least 1 kHz even when all four virtual end effectors are contacting the simulated cube and returning a force.

If the communication channels between the simulation (host) computer and the peripheral computers do not significantly increase the delay in the system it will not be necessary to have a device control board located within the computer running the simulation. The choice of communication channel and communication protocol types will impact system delay as each channel has constraints on capacity and speed. Additionally there is often a trade off between speed and

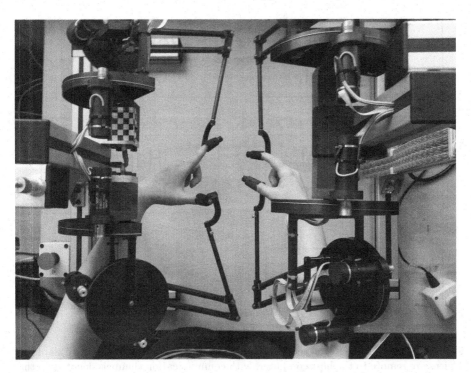

Fig. 1. The University of Reading bi-manual test-bed, comprising of 4 devices that are based on the phantom [7], arranged in pairs with one pair having a direct connection to the simulation environment and the other an indirect UDP based connection.

reliability in communication protocols. For example, UDP type communication is fast with less computing overheads but receipt of the data is not guaranteed, whereas TCP type communication is slower but guaranteed to deliver data and packet order can be reconstructed [1].

Figure 2 provides an example of a generalised configuration of the hardware where the devices are connected to a control board, which is within a peripheral computer/machine, with the encoder and motor values being sent via a communications channel. This configuration has the advantage of functioning as a plug-and-play type system where the number of devices is controlled by the number of peripheral machines. In addition, the peripheral machines can vary in complexity based off of whether they are intended to do any of the processing for the simulation or simply act as data relay stations.

A consideration when working with multiple nodes (e.g. multiple haptic devices, the virtual environment and other sensors such as the Vicon (vicon.com) for movement tracking) is the need to agree to a common coordinate frame. In the absence of a well defined relationship between these different coordinate frames, a least squares calibration can be used. Consider two sets of Cartesian data of the same point $\vec{s}$ moving in the workspace. If $^{f}S = \begin{bmatrix} ^{f}\vec{s}_1 & ^{f}\vec{s}_2 & ... \end{bmatrix}$ is collected from

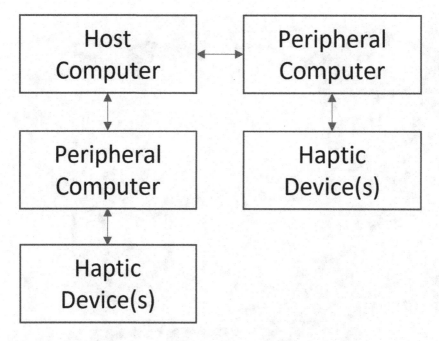

Fig. 2. Diagram displaying a generalised configuration of the hardware, where all of the devices are remote to the host computer, with communication channels denoted by the blue arrows. This configuration presents a plug-and-play type solution with peripheral machines of a lesser complexity than the host computer. (Color figure online)

the fiducial device while $^cS = \begin{bmatrix} ^c\vec{s}_1 & ^c\vec{s}_2 & ... \end{bmatrix}$ represents the same positions but collected in the coordinate frame of the device to be calibrated then, in a linear workspace we can assume

$$^cS = {}^c_fT \; {}^fS$$

where ^c_fT is a 4×4 homogeneous transform matrix linking the two spaces. A least squares solution to this equation is straight forward, e.g. Moore-Penrose inverse. Leading to the solution

$$^c_fT = ({}^fS^T \; {}^fS)^{-1f}S^T \; {}^cS$$

This technique was used in the University of Reading test-bed using the Vicon as the fiducial device for calibration.

3   Control Distribution

Control distribution can be considered from two perspectives: distribution of the physics simulation and distribution of the underlying computational process. Physics simulation distribution pertains to the question of how collision detection and physics update calculations should be implemented within the simulation code. Whereas, process distribution refers to the code functionality that allows for physical distribution and the code that allows the distributed physics to interface with the rest of the program.

In haptics it is often assumed that having a physics engine that can handle all objects in the environment at a minimum update rate of 1 kHz is a necessity. In practice haptic interactions can be stable at much lower update rates, and there are other factors that influence the limit cycles [11]. Currently there seems to be two main concepts of implementing physics in haptic simulations: First, having a single physics update loop that handles all objects in the simulation or second, having multiple physics update loops to enable graphical and haptic physics to update at different speeds. Chai3D [4] is an example of the first approach. An example of the second approach is Toia from Generic robotics[1], which uses a commercial physics engine 'Carbon' running on the multi-core CPU to compute the haptic physics, and the PhysX engine running on the GPU to update the physics of non-haptic objects at a speed suitable for stereoscopic computer graphics rendering[2].

Having multiple physics loops is likely to be preferable in complex multi-contact point haptic simulations since this will allow high loop times for individual haptic devices and complex physics on objects that are only needed for graphical rendering. The overhead for this approach is that the location of haptic objects must passed to the graphics render engine, and that it may be necessary to interchange objects between the haptics and graphics physics programmes. The benefit is that in large complex environments objects that don't need to be handled at haptic speeds can be handled in a separate "graphics" physics loop. Thus more haptic objects and points of contact can be computed in large and complex simulated environments before performance starts to degrade and instabilities start to appear.

3.1 Physics Engines and Haptics

The potential of using multiple physics engines in a simulation requires consideration into what physics engines are suitable for use in haptics and which are only suitable for the graphical rendering of non-haptic objects. The main consideration when choosing a physics engine for haptic, and robotic limb, simulation is the trade off between simulation speed and physical accuracy [5]. Table 1 lists some contemporary physics engine libraries with what type of dynamics they use, as well as their licence and primary application types.

Of the engines listed in Table 1 most of them were created with the purpose simulating physics for computer games and as such are designed with more emphasis on ensuring the results create a visually pleasing result when graphically rendered, often at the cost of an accurate portrayal of the underlying physical system. This is because, of the three types of dynamics used in physics

---

[1] https://www.genericrobotics.com/.
[2] Information from personal correspondence.

engines, force based dynamics are considered to be the slowest and most accurate whereas position based dynamics are considered to be the fastest, but with the most deviation from the physical system it is simulating [8].

Impulse based dynamics are assumed to lie between force based dynamics and position based dynamics in terms of speed and accuracy. An approach to rendering both solids and fluids using a point based physics is also possible in a haptics context, but is computationally expensive requiring GPU hardware to achieve haptic rendering speeds [13].

Both ODE and Bullet are used by Chai3D [4], which is evidence that impulse based dynamics can be suitable for haptics though additional code needs to be generated by the haptic handler to calculate forces from outputs of the physics engines. Though the work by Erez et al. [5] would suggest that MuJoCo would be better suited.

Table 1. Table to list a variety of Physics engine libraries and provide information useful for determining if they are suitable for haptics. Primary dynamics type is supplied when known explicitly, developers own terms used otherwise.

Engine	Dynamics	Licence	Primary applications	Source
ODE	Impulse	Open source	Gaming	ODE[a]
Havok	Constraint based	Commercial	Gaming	Havok[b]
PhysX	Position	Open source	Gaming	NVIDIA PhysX[c]
Box2D	Impulse	Open source	Gaming	Box2D[d]
Bullet	Impulse	Open source	Gaming and robotics	PyBullet[e]
Carbon	Constraint based	Commercial	Gaming and animation	Numerion software[f]
MuJoCo	Impulse	Open source	Robotics	MuJoCo [12]
Dart	Constraint based	Open source	Robotics	Dartsim[g]
Simbody	Constraint based	Open source	Bio-simulation and gaming	SimTK: Simbody [9]

[a] https://www.ode.org/
[b] https://www.havok.com/havok-physics/
[c] https://developer.nvidia.com/physx-sdk
[d] https://box2d.org/
[e] https://pybullet.org/wordpress/
[f] https://www.numerion-software.com
[g] https://dartsim.github.io/index.html

However, regardless of the engine chosen to handle haptics, a second process is needed to handle the non haptic objects. This second process can either be the same physics engine as that used for computing haptic response to physical encounters, or like Toia it could be a different physics engine. If the object representation is different for the two engines then conversion between object representation would be needed across the functionality of objects rendered in these physics engines.

3.2   Transferring Objects Between Physics Engines

A simulator that has the functionality of changing which of the physics engines an object is handled by is theorised to allow for further increases to the complexity of the simulation environment without decreasing haptic refresh rate to a point that causes instability.

The theory is based on the fact that objects that are not involved in haptics do not need to be computed as fast as objects that are involved in haptic feedback. Therefore, in order to keep the haptic refresh rate as high as possible only the objects currently involved in the calculation of the feedback force to be generated should be dynamically simulated at haptic speeds.

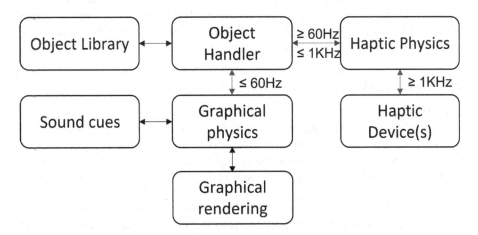

Fig. 3. Diagram displaying a configuration of the physics engines and object handler for a haptic simulator that can change which physics engine handles a particular object at each iteration. Object library contains all material, shape and location details at the beginning of the simulation. While the simulation is running these objects will be passed between the library and the local device haptic physics nodes. The object handler brokers these exchanges. This allows high speed update of objects that have a direct or semi direct contact with the individual haptic device. Two approximate channel capacities are shown. Blue channels are of the order of 60 kHz, red channels are notional haptic speeds of > 1 kHz (Color figure online)

In order to achieve a haptic simulator that can change which physics engine an object is handled by an object library that is accessible by both physics engines and an object handler function, that determines which engine has access to what objects, would be required.

Because the system would now be comprised of three elements, each with their own data and refresh rate requirements, the distribution of the control software can considered in terms of the capacity and speed of communication between the elements.

The diagram in Fig. 3 provides an example of how the two physics engines could interface with the object library via the handler and other elements necessary for simulation. It also illustrates the potential communication speeds between the elements, based off of the refresh rate of their internal loops.

As the object handler controls which of the objects are handled by the haptics physics it needs to be able to determine when to assign the objects. In addition the handler needs to make these assignments in regards to every connected haptic device and as such needs to happen at fast loop speeds, preferably the same speed as the haptic physics loop.

Therefore it is proposed that a method based on broad phase collision detection be used in the handler to determine which objects in the environment are to be handled by haptics physics. This is because broad phase collision detection methods are designed to operate quickly over all objects in the scene in order to ensure only objects that might be colliding are passed to the next phases of collision detection and resolution [6].

3.3 Multiple Haptics Physics Engines Approach

While Fig. 3 describes a system that uses two physics engines, one for graphical objects and one for haptic objects, it would be possible to expand the framework to work with more than two physics engines. When using three or more physics engines for example, one of them would handle the graphical physics and the others would handle the physics for a subset of objects across the set of haptic devices.

In such a system each device or device group can be considered to be part of an inner closed loop system (Fig. 4), within the larger system, with impedance provided by the human user and object information being exchanged with the object handler.

Figure 4 shows a possible node for one part of the arrangement described above. Stability of this type of structure is relatively well understood for simple physics. For example Colgate and Schenkel [3] show a stability condition for Fig. 4 where the collision detector is a 'relop' function and the collision response is a PD controller of the form

$$H(z) = K + B\frac{1 - z^{-1}}{T}$$

where K is the proportional gain of the digital controller, B is the differential gain and T is the sampling time of the control loop. The haptic device is assumed to have an implicit damping b in which case Colgate and Schenkel stability requires

$$b > \frac{KT}{2} + |B|$$

Additionally, the variables J and J^T in the control loop are generalised transforms from Cartesian space to joint space and back again, and are not necessarily Jacobian matrices.

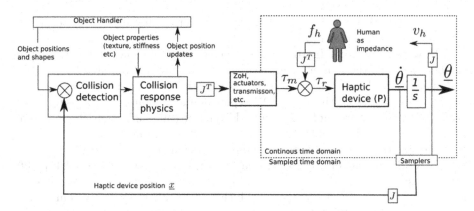

Fig. 4. Block diagram of haptic device showing a generalised inner closed loop with human interactions considered as an impedance and haptic physics and exchange of information with object handler. (Color figure online)

This type of controller assumes a backdrivable type of haptic device. Devices with an admittance control allow the forces from the human f_h to be included in the control loop. The controller is necessarily a mixture of continuous time elements (amplifiers, actuators, linkages) and discrete time elements (digital computer with sampler and zero order holds (ZoH)).

Because the object handler as well as physics engines on other nodes will have a lower update time contact instability will be possible. However, passing the control of an object to a haptic device that is local to the persons space should enable these instabilities to be better managed. This would also lend itself to collaborative simulations where the two users can come into contact with the same objects or each other. This is due to the fact that until the users come into close proximity, or indirect contact, their respective devices are not impacted by the feedback forces caused by the other user. Though when in close proximity or contact, the two physics loops will either need to communicate or be superseded by another physics loop that is included to handle these situations.

Additional benefits of a system that uses multiple haptic physics loops are that it would be tolerant of individual node failures since all haptic devices run their own version of the physics, and that the devices being connected and their physics engine do not have to be of the same type. For example, a simulation could be run where one of the devices is a device like the phantom [7] and the other could be a planar device like the haply 2diy [14].

4   Conclusions and Further Work

This research sought to determine if viewing haptics simulation in terms of a distributed system would have the potential to improve performance by addressing the problems of requiring high quality physical haptic interaction in complex environments and the need to link devices to high quality computer simulations in a time critical way. This was done by considering distribution in terms of physical and control distribution.

The work on physical distribution has shown that stable physical distribution can be achieved if the communication channels used have the required bandwidth and speed. Initial experiments using the university of Reading haptic test-bed (Fig. 1) have suggested that the UDP type communication protocol using Ethernet cables are an example of a suitable type of communication channel and protocol for producing stable simulations. However, more work needs to be done to determine the best choice for communication channel and protocol.

The work on control distribution has shown how expanding on the type of control distribution used in Toia allows for the system to be considered a closed loop with many inner closed loops. Which in turn allows for a system to be proposed that takes Toia's approach to reducing computation at haptic speeds even further (Fig. 3), by varying the number of objects in the haptic physics every loop.

Following on from this research, work focusing on developing the object handler functionality, it's associated simulation control structure (Fig. 3) and testing its performance in large, complex, and collaborative environments to determine if it does provide a better alternative to a single powerful physics engine and computer running all the haptic objects will be carried out.

References

1. AL-Dhief, F.T., et al.: Performance comparison between TCP and UDP protocols in different simulation scenarios. Int. J. Eng. Technol. **7**(4.36), 172–176 (2018)
2. Barrow, A., Harwin, W.: Design and analysis of a haptic device design for large and fast movements. Machines **4**(1), 8 (2016)
3. Colgate, J., Schenkel, G.: Passivity of a class of sampled-data systems: application to haptic interfaces. J. Robot. Syst. **14**(1), 37–47 (1997)
4. Conti, F., et al.: The chai libraries. In: Proceedings of Eurohaptics 2003, pp. 496–500. Dublin, Ireland (2003)
5. Erez, T., Tassa, Y., Todorov, E.: Simulation tools for model-based robotics: Comparison of Bullet, Havok, MuJoCo, ode and PhysX. In: 2015 IEEE international conference on robotics and automation (ICRA). pp. 4397–4404. IEEE (2015)
6. Luque, R.G., Comba, J.L., Freitas, C.M.: Broad-phase collision detection using semi-adjusting BSP-trees. In: Proceedings of the 2005 symposium on Interactive 3D graphics and games, pp. 179–186 (2005)
7. Massie, T.H., Salisbury, J.K., et al.: The phantom haptic interface: a device for probing virtual objects. In: Proceedings of the ASME Winter Annual Meeting, Symposium on Haptic Interfaces for Virtual Environment and Teleoperator Systems, vol. 55, pp. 295–300. Citeseer (1994)
8. Müller, M., Heidelberger, B., Hennix, M., Ratcliff, J.: Position based dynamics. J. Vis. Commun. Image Represent. **18**(2), 109–118 (2007). https://www.sciencedirect.com/science/article/pii/S1047320307000065
9. Sherman, M.A., Seth, A., Delp, S.L.: Simbody: multibody dynamics for biomedical research. Procedia IUTAM **2**, 241–261 (2011). https://www.sciencedirect.com/science/article/pii/S2210983811000241, iUTAM Symposium on Human Body Dynamics

10. Spears, W.M., Spears, D.F., Hamann, J.C., Heil, R.: Distributed, physics-based control of swarms of vehicles. Auton. Robot. **17**(2), 137–162 (2004)

11. Swaidani, L., Steele, L., Harwin, W.: Motor shaft vibrations may have a negative effect on ability to implement a stiff haptic wall. In: Prattichizzo, D., Shinoda, H., Tan, H.Z., Ruffaldi, E., Frisoli, A. (eds.) EuroHaptics 2018. LNCS, vol. 10894, pp. 252–263. Springer, Cham (2018). https://doi.org/10.1007/978-3-319-93399-3_23

12. Todorov, E., Erez, T., Tassa, Y.: Mujoco: a physics engine for model-based control. In: 2012 IEEE/RSJ International Conference on Intelligent Robots and Systems, pp. 5026–5033. IEEE (2012)

13. Tse, B., Barrow, A., Quinn, B., Harwin, W.S.: A smoothed particle hydrodynamics algorithm for haptic rendering of dental filling materials. In: 2015 IEEE World Haptics Conference (WHC), pp. 321–326. IEEE (2015)

14. Weill-Duflos, A., Ong, N., Desourdy, F., Delbos, B., Ding, S., Gallacher, C.: Haply 2diy: an accessible haptic platform suitable for remote learning. In: Proceedings of the 2021 International Conference on Multimodal Interaction, pp. 839–840 (2021)

15. Yook, J., Tilbury, D., Soparkar, N.: Trading computation for bandwidth: reducing communication in distributed control systems using state estimators. IEEE Trans. Control Syst. Technol. **10**(4), 503–518 (2002)

A Novel Two-Hand-Inspired Hybrid Robotic End-Effector Fabricated Using 3D Printing

Benjamin Marsh(ID) and Pengcheng Liu(✉)(ID)

Department of Computer Science, University of York, York YO10 5DD, UK
pengcheng.liu@york.ac.uk

Abstract. The field of soft robotics aims to improve on limitations of traditional rigid robots by using naturally compliant materials. This work designed a novel robotic end-effector, inspired by two-handed human grasping and fabricated using 3D printing, that is capable of lifting target objects without exerting large forces. The end-effector is a hybrid of rigid and soft materials, and aims to be simple, low-cost, and fabricated using a reliable process. Grasp tests were performed on a wide range of target objects and the success of the design is evaluated in terms of grasping capability and fabrication process. Results show the capability of the novel design to lift a range of target objects, and highlight improved grasping performance over other types of gripper. Material costs and fabrication/assembly time of the 3D printed components are also presented.

Keywords: Soft robotics · Robotic grasping · 3D printing

1 Introduction

Soft robotic grippers used for grasping and pick-and-place operations have many advantages over traditional rigid designs. They also present challenges, requiring different methods of design, fabrication, actuation, and control. One such challenge is that soft robots are more structurally vulnerable [17]; [14] suggests that some soft materials are "not suitable for manipulating heavy objects". Hybrid robots that combine hard and soft materials, such as the designs presented in [1] and [21], can therefore leverage the strengths of both approaches [20].

Many soft robots are biologically inspired due to the soft bodies of animals providing abilities such as conforming to surfaces, adapting to changing environments, and damping impact forces, influencing soft robots to be equipped with capabilities based in material properties, rather than complex control systems [18]. There are also challenges in building bio-inspired soft robots; without a skeleton soft animals cannot support much weight [18], and there is no mechanical equivalent to animals' complex muscle structures [14] with comparable size and performance [11] so alternative actuation methods are required.

Supported by The University of York.

A specific biological influence is the human hand (e.g. [4,5]), a popular source of design inspiration due to its ability to manipulate objects of various shapes, sizes, and materials [2]. However, robotic hands that attempt to mimic human capabilities are often expensive, difficult to design, and require complex sensing and control [5]. Many designs use just the idea of how human fingers are used to grasp objects, such as [6–9,12–14,21,25], which demonstrate a wide range of finger-based designs, suggesting that fingers are a good source of inspiration, with much variation possible based on the same structure. While hand-based designs have superior dexterity and can perform a wider range of motion, finger-based designs are much simpler in design, construction, and control, while still exhibiting successful grasping of target objects.

Actuation is an important consideration and challenge in soft robots, particularly due to their compliant structures that require under-actuation and cannot support heavy actuators. Whereas rigid robots typically use an electric motor in every joint [24], the compliant and flexible material of soft robots must move unrestrained by rigid joints, and controlling the shape and tip position of a continuum-like structure is more challenging [22,24]. Pneumatic actuation is a popular method [22], and has been successfully used in many soft robots [5,7,8,12,14,21,25]. Advantages include rapid actuation [14], robustness to impact [5,8], and actuation of multiple fingers simultaneously [12]. Pneumatic actuators also have many limitations; they can rupture [22], easily be cut or pierced [5], and require extensive additional pressure infrastructure [20] which is usually big, bulky, and inefficient [8,22]. Another common method of actuation is tendon-driven actuation [22], also used in many soft robot designs [3,4,6,9–11,13,16,19] and chosen due to advantageous properties such as tendon cables' light weight, flexibility, and possibility of miniaturization [19] and ability to bend a soft structure with a single cable [3,6]. [13] used tendon-driven actuation as it was low cost, compact, and required simple controls, and highlighted how it allowed for an under-actuated mechanism requiring only a single motor and cable to control three soft fingers. Tendon-driven actuation can also provide an under-actuated adaptive grasp, where a robot can conform to an uneven or unexpected object shape [4,16]. Tendon-driven actuation does have some limitations, such as the possibility of tendon derailment – often specifically accounted for [11,15,16] – and reliability and lifetime of the system – often not considered but discussed extensively in [17]. Despite these limitations, tendon-driven actuation is a very promising technique for the actuation of soft robots.

One of the main benefits of soft robots is their potential to interact with unknown and irregular target objects, however grasping capabilities are often not tested on a wide range of objects, making it difficult to be confident in the grasping capability of existing soft robots. Another factor is the level of human assistance required to achieve a stable grasp. The soft gripper designed in [7] was intended for use with fragile target objects and shows the ability to gently grasp a tomato, but no other objects are reported to have been tested, while the gripper in [25] is stated to be able to hold various objects but provides little evidence of this. Only one target object grasp was attempted in [6] and three in [9]. The robotic hand designed in [5] was tested extensively with 33 different grasps and disturbance forces, showing impressive grasping capabilities, however the grasps are achieved with human assistance. The robot developed in [10] was specifically intended to grasp large or irregularly shaped objects and was tested on some but not many such objects, while the soft gripper in [14] demonstrated grasping and lifting an uncooked egg, an anaesthetized mouse, and plastic spheres with increasing diameter and weight. The under-actuated soft gripper designed in [13] was tested on target objects of varying size, shape, and material, but could only grasp with human assistance, the grasp is supported from beneath by the fixed parts of the gripper, and there is no evidence of the gripper being used to lift objects. Finally, the tests in [12] are some of the most extensive, showing the gripper's ability to grasp and lift a large variety of different objects, varying in size, shape, weight, and material, more convincingly demonstrating the ability and versatility of the gripper.

Fabrication is another key consideration in soft robotic design. Most designers fabricate their own custom parts, as standardized components are not available [20], limiting the techniques that can be used. [22] identifies that for soft robots to deliver on their full potential, rapid design tools and fabrication recipes for low-cost soft robots are needed, and this is still a challenge in this field. Curing silicone rubber is the most common technique for fabricating soft grippers, popular due to the low forces needed to cause high strain deformations and the convenience of a room-temperature vulcanizing process [18]. Cured silicone rubber has been used in many soft robots [1,3–5,8,12–14] due to benefits such as the low cost of materials [8,14], ease to acquire and work with [14], suitable elastic modulus [3], and ability to directly embed actuation components into the material [13]. Often, the molds used to cure the silicone rubber are 3D printed [5,8,12,25], as this technology is becoming affordable to users outside of industry [8] and allows rapid iterative fabrication [12]. Another fabrication technique is shape deposition manufacturing (SDM), used in [6] to embed sensing and actuation components during fabrication. Silicone curing and SDM share a common limitation: they are both manually involved processes, requiring human time and limiting scalability and consistency. 3D printing has been used to directly print final components of robots, such as the links and pulleys in [10] and the rigid base support in [12]. However, in both of these cases the 3D printed parts were hard and non-compliant. The scaffold in the robotic hand designed in [5] was also 3D printed using solid material, but in such a way that it was deformable. [23] used microstructures to 3D print a deformable object using rigid material, and created a simple gripper using this technique to prove its applicability to the field of soft robotics, suggesting their method could be an "important step towards a design tool for printable soft robots". Another option for 3D printing soft structures is to use flexible material. [1] used multi-material 3D printing to manufacture a robot body that employed a stiffness gradient, while [7] directly 3D printed a soft gripper without the need for molds and curing. Direct 3D printing is more accurate and consistent than multi-stage curing processes [7], requires fewer assembly steps, and does not require creating multiple complex molds for constantly evolving prototype designs [1].

In this paper, a novel design of robotic end-effector, inspired by the use of two human hands and combining hard and soft materials, is firstly evaluated based on its ability to manipulate a range of target objects of varying size, shape, weight, material, and fragility. Evaluation will focus particularly on the range of target objects that can be grasped and the benefits of the novel two-handed design. Secondly, 3D printing is evaluated as a fabrication technique for soft robots, based on its feasibility, consistency, repeatability, and manual involvement, as well as cost, time, and quality of fabricated parts. The rest of this paper is organised as follows. Section 2 will explore in depth the design of this work, the methods used, and the procedures used to test the design and evaluate its success. Section 3 will present the results of testing and evaluate the strengths and limitations of the design and fabrication process. Section 4 will summarise the findings, consider the extent to which this work has met its initial aims, and discuss potential future research.

2   Design and Methods

2.1   High-Level Design and Methods

The robotic end-effector presented is a hybrid design combining a rigid base lifting plate and soft fingers, inspired by two human hands lifting objects with one hand supporting from beneath and the other hand grasping the sides gently. The addition of the base lifting plate reduces the force needed by the fingers to grasp objects, allowing fragile objects to be handled more gently without causing deformation. This end-effector could be combined with a robotic arm for pick-and-place tasks, so size and weight are minimised to reduce the strain that would be put on an arm. The end-effector works by gently grasping an object with the fingers and rotating the base lifting plate underneath the object. All components are designed using 3D CAD software and are 3D printed. An iterative design, prototyping, and evaluation process was used, where parts were first designed and improved in 3D CAD software to eliminate some issues before fabrication. Parts were then printed individually, evaluated, and improved and re-printed where necessary. This iterative process enabled parts to be produced to a high standard while minimising fabrication time and material use.

The 3D printing process involves designing a component in CAD software, slicing the 3D model with appropriate parameters for the component, and printing. The choice of material is important to obtain the desired mechanical properties of components. Rigid components were printed from PLA, an easy to print, inexpensive, environmentally friendly, and strong material. PLA components have a good surface quality and can withstand reasonable force. Soft components were printed from NinjaFlex, a flexible filament that is compliant after printing, producing parts that can bend, stretch, and absorb forces. Flexible materials are more challenging to print with, so the design and print parameters are even more important.

2.2 Base Lifting Plate

The CAD model of the base lifting plate is shown in Fig. 1. This component lifts target objects from beneath and so must be strong and rigid. The plate is thin at its edges so that it can slide under objects with minimal resistance and thicker in the middle to bear weight without bending. The design of the plate with an attached arm, similar to a hand on the end of an arm, allows the base lifting plate to be rotated around the main body. The base lifting plate was printed from PLA with 100% infill density (the amount of material inside a part) for maximum strength and minimum flexibility. A high resolution layer height (0.1 mm) was used to create smooth slopes on the edges of the plate, resulting in less resistance when sliding under objects.

Fig. 1. CAD model of base lifting plate

2.3 Fingers

Figure 2 and Fig. 3 show the standard finger and extended finger that were designed. The standard finger was inspired by [13] and is similarly constructed from a soft material, actuated by tendons, and features three phalanges similar to the human finger. However, unlike the finger in [13], all three phalanges are actuated. Also, the maximum angular displacement between phalanges is 70°, chosen as a balance between sufficient bending at each joint while reducing the tendon force needed and increasing the surface area of each phalange. [13] recognised that their phalanges bend together when it is desirable for proximal phalanges to bend before distal phalanges, a behaviour demonstrated in [6] by varying joint stiffness. Here, this behaviour is achieved by increasing joint thickness from proximal to distal; thinner joints bend more easily so bend first. Tendon-driven actuation was chosen for the fingers due to its light weight, small size, simplicity, low cost, low power requirements, simple control, and adaptive grasp capabilities. Each finger has square channels for rounded tendon cables, as square channels are simpler to 3D print and reduce friction against the rounded cable. The channel openings in the finger base feature slopes rather than sharp edges, also to reduce friction. These design features are shown in Fig. 2.

Fingers are 3D printed from NinjaFlex, allowing the fingers to bend easily and the phalanges to passively comply to target objects for a gentle adaptive grasp. The fingers were printed with 20% "Lightning" infill (Fig. 4), reducing material

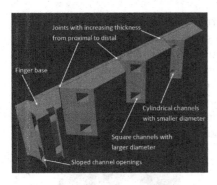

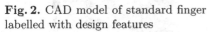

Fig. 2. CAD model of standard finger labelled with design features

Fig. 3. CAD model of extended finger

use and increasing compliance of the fingers, while the finger base was printed with 100% infill to provide a rigid and stable mounting. The wall thickness and top/bottom thickness were reduced, increasing finger compliance for gentle grasping and passive adaptation to target objects. NinjaFlex, being a flexible material, is more prone to "stringing", so print speed was reduced to increase quality.

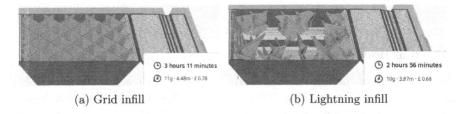

(a) Grid infill   (b) Lightning infill

Fig. 4. Infill and its effect on material usage

The extended finger is identical to the standard finger except the phalanges are extended such that when the finger is mounted in the main body of the end-effector, the finger can grasp objects vertically below it – this can be seen more clearly in Sect. 2.5 and Fig. 12. The extended fingers were designed as the mounting of the fingers in the main body must be some distance higher than the base lifting plate, and therefore the standard fingers would be unable to grasp small objects.

2.4 Tendon Cables

The tendon cables used for actuation are 3D printed from NinjaFlex, meaning cables need not be specially acquired; they are instead fabricated using the same material and process used for the fingers. The NinjaFlex cables designed have the benefits of being flexible but with some rigidity and not too stretchy, with a slight limitation that they are not perfectly smooth. Cables can also be printed to the perfect length, and different lengths are used for different fingers. Figure 5 shows a cable inserted into a finger. These cables feature a thin section at the end of each cable (Fig. 6) which provides an easy mechanism for attachment to the winding spool, as shown in Fig. 7. The cables were printed solid (no internal space) to reduce elasticity and with high resolution 0.1 mm layer height to achieve a smoother finish, reducing friction when sliding through the finger channels.

Fig. 5. Printed finger with cable inserted

Fig. 6. Thin end sections of printed cable

Fig. 7. CAD model showing cable-to-spool attachment mechanism

2.5   Main Body

The main body of the end-effector (Fig. 8) provides the housing for the motors and the mounting for the base lifting plate and fingers. The design is highly modular; all parts fit together with non-permanent attachments, allowing parts, such as a larger base lifting plate or different fingers, to be easily swapped out. Tightly interlocking parts can be fabricated easily using 3D printing where complexity comes at almost no cost and high accuracy components can be fabricated consistently. Components can be printed with mostly default settings, except the main body housing which was printed with supports in the cut-out sections.

The base lifting plate is mounted in the main body using interlocking blocks and rings, allowing it to rotate within the main body, using parts that are all held together tightly using just friction and gravity. The fingers are mounted in the main body using sliding attachments (Fig. 9). The positions of the slots were chosen such that the fingers could grasp reasonably wide and reasonably small objects. The main body can hold up to four fingers (two on each side) but can also hold just two bottom fingers or just two top fingers.

Each component actuated by a motor features a plate with a recess, allowing the motor blade to fit tightly and rotate without slipping (Fig. 11). The spool used to pull the tendon cables is shown in Fig. 10. No slack-enabling mechanism [11,15,16] was used as this would increase complexity and initial prototypes

Fig. 8. CAD model of main body

Fig. 9. CAD model showing attachment of finger to main body

suggested that the flexible fingers naturally return to full extension when cable tension is released. Figure 12 shows the complete assembled end-effector with base lifting plate, two standard fingers, and two extended fingers.

Fig. 10. Winding spool and mechanism

Fig. 11. Motor blade recess of components actuated by a motor

2.6   Experimental Design

Tests were carried out on a range of objects of varying size, shape, weight, and material to evaluate the capabilities of the end-effector, particularly the usefulness of the novel base lifting plate design. The testing procedure involved grasping an object, lifting the end-effector to show stable grasping, and releasing the object. The testing procedure was repeated for three configurations of the end-effector for all objects: using two extended fingers and the base lifting plate; using two extended fingers, two standard fingers, and the base lifting plate; and using just two extended fingers without the base lifting plate. Ideally the end-effector can grasp objects with no assistance, but this can be problematic for heavy objects and the low strength motors used, as the base lifting plate can struggle to slide underneath the object while it is flat on a surface. All target objects

(a)   (b)

Fig. 12. Assembled end-effector; (a) CAD model, (b) Real fabrication

were first tested without any assistance, but for any objects that encountered this problem the object was manually lifted slightly while the base lifting plate rotated underneath ("assisted grasp"), to test the ability of the end-effector to stably grasp even if acquiring the grasp without assistance was unsuccessful. 31 target objects were tested and are listed in Sect. 3. The results of the grasp tests can also be used to determine the quality of the 3D printed components of the end-effector. To evaluate cost and time of fabrication and assembly, the material cost of and time taken to print every 3D printed component was recorded during fabrication, and the time taken to assemble the end-effector was measured.

3   Results and Discussion

3.1   Grasp Tests

The testing procedure described in Sect. 2.6 was performed for all objects and repeated for the configurations described. The results are shown in Table 1, and some objects successfully grasped in the two finger configuration are shown in Fig. 13.

Fig. 13. Some objects successfully grasped with two fingers unassisted

Table 1 shows that 20 of the 31 objects tested were successfully grasped in the two finger configuration. These objects varied in shape, size, weight, and material. Furthermore, most (16 out of 20) of the objects successfully grasped using the base lifting plate could not be grasped without it (two fingers only),

Table 1. Test results for all objects and all configurations, with approximate dimensions and mass of objects

Object	Size (cm)	Mass (g)	Two fingers	Four fingers	Two fingers only	Assisted grasp
Glass pepper grinder	13 × 4 × 4	150	✓	✗	✗	–
Packet of tissues	11 × 5 × 3	25	✓	✓	✓	–
Bicycle light	10 × 4 × 3	100	✓	✗	✗	–
Torch	13 × 3 × 3	160	✗	✗	✗	✓
Set of keys	N/A	100	✓	✗	✗	–
Wallet	9 × 11 × 3	250	✗	✗	✗	✓
Aerosol can	14 × 5 × 5	130	✓	✗	✗	–
Kiwi fruit	5 × 7 × 5	75	✓	✗	✗	–
Pen	15 × 1 × 1	5	✓	✓	✓	–
Large plastic box	16 × 10 × 5	50	✗	✗	✗	✗
Small plastic box	8 × 8 × 3	25	✓	✓	✗	–
Compact disc	12 × 12 × 0.1	15	✗	✗	✗	✓
Small rubber duck	2 × 2 × 2	10	✓	✓	✗	–
Spray bottle	19 × 9 × 9	270	✓	✗	✗	–
Plastic bottle (empty)	15 × 7 × 7	20	✓	✓	✓	–
Plastic bottle (half full)	15 × 7 × 7	270	✓	✗	✗	–
Plastic bottle (full)	15 × 7 × 7	520	✗	✗	✗	✓
Egg holder	10 × 4 × 0.2	70	✗	✗	✗	✓
Drinking glass	11 × 5 × 5	250	✓	✗	✗	–
Large potato	9 × 7 × 6	250	✗	✗	✗	✓
Small potato	7 × 5 × 4	100	✓	✗	✗	–
Mango	9 × 7 × 7	350	✗	✗	✗	✓
Small tomato	3 × 3 × 3	10	✓	✓	✗	–
Raw egg	5 × 4 × 4	60	✓	✗	✗	–
Light bulb	11 × 6 × 6	70	✓	✗	✗	–
Paper cup (empty)	8 × 5 × 5	15	✓	✓	✓	–
Paper cup (half full)	8 × 5 × 5	100	✗	✗	✗	✓
Paper cup (full)	8 × 5 × 5	180	✗	✗	✗	✓
Packet of crisps	15 × 11 × 4	35	✓	✗	✗	–
Bottle of golden syrup	18 × 9 × 6	600	✗	✗	✗	✓
Bag of salad	10 × 10 × 4	120	✓	✗	✗	–

proving that the base lifting plate improves grasping capability. The objects successfully grasped without the base lifting plate were among the lightest tested, supporting the expectation that the base lifting plate would allow heavier objects to be grasped. Some of the most interesting successfully grasped objects are: the small rubber duck, which could not be grasped by the fingers alone due to its small size but was easily grasped using the base lifting plate; the spray bottle, which was too heavy for the fingers alone to grasp and larger than the base lifting plate but could be grasped by the combination of the two; and the bag of salad, which must be handled gently and was much larger than the base lifting plate but could be grasped without causing damage.

Despite the idea that more fingers would provide a more supported grasp, four fingers successfully grasped only 7 of the 31 objects. During testing the reason for this was clear; adding more fingers increases strain on the motor, and the small motor used was unable to pull the tendon cables as much, resulting in reduced bending in the fingers and providing a weaker grasp. It is expected that with a stronger motor, four fingers would perform similarly to two fingers. However, the results obtained show no advantage to using four fingers; taller objects such as the plastic bottle could be grasped using two fingers. Further investigation using a stronger motor is needed to establish any benefits of using extra fingers.

Only one object that was tested using the assisted grasp failed. The large plastic box could not be grasped as too much weight extended too far beyond the base lifting plate. Using a larger base lifting plate may yield a successful grasp – this could be investigated in future work. This potential solution highlights the strength of the modular design; a larger base lifting plate could easily be fabricated and installed. All other objects that could not be grasped in the two finger configuration were grasped using the assisted grasp, most of which were the larger, heavier objects. These could not be grasped unassisted as the base lifting plate was unable to slide underneath the object without pushing it out of the fingers' grasp, due to the weight and shape of the base of the object. The strength of the motors is again a likely contributor; stronger motors should provide a stronger stable grasp from the fingers and rotate the base lifting plate under heavier objects. However, the success of the assisted grasps demonstrates the capability of the end-effector to hold larger and heavier objects, even if it struggles to acquire the grasp, and showcases the ability of the base lifting plate design to hold objects that could not be held by the fingers alone.

Direct comparisons can be made for objects also tested on previous gripper designs. The gripper designed in [13], which inspired the fingers designed here, grasped a cylinder, box, and egg, similar to the aerosol can and egg grasped here. However, the gripper in [13] was only capable of an assisted grasp, whereas the end-effector designed here grasped many objects unassisted. The grippers here and in [12] both grasped a pen, compact disc, raw egg, and keys. The gripper in [12] grasped a large plastic box where the one designed here could not. On the other hand, it is unclear how much assistance was provided to achieve the grasps in [12] – the compact disc at least suggests assistance as it could not stand up by itself for unassisted grasping. These comparisons suggest that the end-effector designed here is similarly capable to previous designs, and more capable at unassisted grasping. The wider range of objects tested here also increases confidence in its capability and versatility.

The success of the end-effector in the two finger and assisted grasp configurations proves the strength of the design, the suitability of 3D printing to fabricate both hard and soft components for robotic grippers, and the quality of the fabricated components. The hard PLA components provide strength and rigidity and the flexible fingers and tendon cables grasp delicate objects gently and passively adapt to different shapes and sizes. The end-effector has a mass of 90 g in the two-finger configuration and 102 g in the four finger configuration, including the motors, so it can also be seen that the gripper can lift objects heavier than itself. However, there is room for improvement. Figure 14 shows the stages of grasping and releasing and it can be seen that the fingers do not always fully open when cable tension is released. The reason for this could be due to a number of factors; friction between the tendon cable and finger, angle at which the tendon cable is wound on the spool, and/or lack of cable tension when unwinding the spool. Further investigation is needed to improve this mechanism, but apart from this, the components all work well.

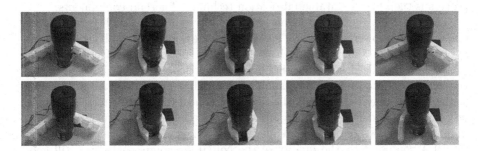

Fig. 14. Stages of grasping and releasing, performed twice. Sometimes the fingers do not fully open when the object is released.

This work did not aim to incorporate sensing or feedback control, however, sensing could be integrated in future work so that the performance of the end-effector during grasping could be characterised quantitatively. Application of the approach used in [7] to the design presented in this work would be particularly interesting, further utilising 3D printing to also integrate sensing directly into the fabricated components.

3.2 Fabrication and Assembly

All components can be fabricated using 54 g of PLA and 48 g of NinjaFlex (£4.44) and in 22 h (four-finger configuration), or 54 g of PLA and 30 g of NinjaFlex (£3.12) and in 16 h (two-finger configuration). Assembly of either configuration takes 5 min or less. This low cost design makes the end-effector economical, and fast fabrication and assembly allow for rapid prototyping of new design ideas. Optimisations for faster printing were made but more optimisation is possible to further reduce fabrication times. Also, no components depend on any other being fabricated first, so components can be fabricated simultaneously using multiple 3D printers.

Material cost and fabrication/assembly time is difficult to compare to previous designs as these factors are rarely reported. However, for their simplified gripper, [8] reported a cost of approximately $10 (£7.85) per student for a classroom of 30. Similarly, the end-effector designed in this work could be simplified, removing the cost of the motors and microcontroller, making the total cost (excluding the one-time overhead of a 3D printer) the material cost as detailed above. The full system with the motors and microcontroller adds around £20, still low-cost for an electronically actuated system. Fabrication of the gripper in

[8] may be faster than the one here (though print time of 3D molds is not given), but the silicone curing process is inherently serial, whereas the components used in this work could be fabricated simultaneously with multiple 3D printers.

The rigid PLA components are consistently fabricated to a very high standard. Throughout development, PLA components never failed due to a flaw in their fabrication, and components always fit together accurately. The 3D printing process is therefore a suitable fabrication technique for rigid components.

The soft NinjaFlex components are generally fabricated slightly less consistently and to a lower standard. This is due to the additional challenges of printing with a flexible material, such as reduced structural integrity, longer time to set, and increased stringing. Stringing in particular was an issue in all fingers produced, requiring some manual cleanup after printing. The lower quality of the fingers may be partially due to design and print parameters; they must be compliant and flexible, and parameters that achieve this, such as reduced wall thickness, also reduce the quality. Nevertheless, despite lower quality than the PLA components, the quality of the NinjaFlex components was still good and did not affect their operation. Further experimentation with tuning print parameters may also further improve quality.

3D printing the components does not require any manual involvement except starting prints, removing printed components, and cleaning up the stringing on the NinjaFlex fingers. Components could be combined into one print, reducing the number of times that prints must be started and components removed, and as mentioned above it may be possible to reduce stringing. Compared to the silicone curing process used in most other soft robotic designs, a manual process which can produce inconsistent and even non-functional results if not performed correctly and carefully, 3D printing requires little manual involvement and produces mostly consistent, high quality, and functional components.

4   Conclusion

This work aimed to evaluate a novel design of robotic end-effector, inspired by two-handed human grasping, comprised of rigid and soft materials, and fabricated using 3D printing. Grasp tests were performed on a wide range of objects to evaluate grasping capability, and results were discussed and compared to previous soft robotic gripper designs. The grasp tests show that the base lifting plate design allows the end-effector to successfully grasp many target objects that could not be grasped using only the fingers. All but one of the objects tested could be held by the end-effector, for many of which the grasp could be acquired without any assistance. The material costs and fabrication/assembly time of the 3D printed components were also discussed. Strengths and limitations of the design, as well as advantages of the fabrication process and opportunities for improvement, were highlighted, and avenues for further related work have been identified. The benefits of the novel design presented, and the successful application of 3D printing to a hybrid hard/soft robotic gripper, create new opportunities for this field, presenting innovative ideas that can be further explored and applied in future research.

References

1. Bartlett, N.W., et al.: A 3D-printed, functionally graded soft robot powered by combustion. Science **349**(6244), 161–165 (2015). https://doi.org/10.1126/science.aab0129
2. Billard, A., Kragic, D.: Trends and challenges in robot manipulation. Science **364**(6446) (2019). https://doi.org/10.1126/science.aat8414
3. Calisti, M., Giorelli, M., Levy, G., Mazzolai, B., Hochner, B., Laschi, C., Dario, P.: An octopus-bioinspired solution to movement and manipulation for soft robots. Bioinspir. Biomimet. **6**(3), 036002 (2011). https://doi.org/10.1088/1748-3182/6/3/036002
4. Carrozza, M.C., et al.: A cosmetic prosthetic hand with tendon driven under-actuated mechanism and compliant joints: ongoing research and preliminary results. In: Proceedings of the 2005 IEEE International Conference on Robotics and Automation, pp. 2661–2666. IEEE (2005). https://doi.org/10.1109/ROBOT.2005.1570515
5. Deimel, R., Brock, O.: A novel type of compliant and underactuated robotic hand for dexterous grasping. Int. J. Robot. Res. **35**(1–3), 161–185 (2016). https://doi.org/10.1177/0278364915592961
6. Dollar, A.M., Howe, R.D.: A robust compliant grasper via shape deposition manufacturing. IEEE/ASME Trans. Mechatron. **11**(2), 154–161 (2006). https://doi.org/10.1109/TMECH.2006.871090
7. Elgeneidy, K., Liu, P., Pearson, S., Lohse, N., Neumann, G., et al.: Printable soft grippers with integrated bend sensing for handling of crops. In: 19th Annual Conference Towards Autonomous Robotic Systems, vol. 10965, pp. 479–480 (2018). https://doi.org/10.1007/978-3-319-96728-8
8. Finio, B., Shepherd, R., Lipson, H.: Air-powered soft robots for k-12 classrooms. In: 2013 IEEE Integrated STEM Education Conference (ISEC), pp. 1–6. IEEE (2013). https://doi.org/10.1109/ISECon.2013.6525198
9. Firouzeh, A., Paik, J.: An under-actuated origami gripper with adjustable stiffness joints for multiple grasp modes. Smart Mater. Struct. **26**(5), 055035 (2017). https://doi.org/10.1088/1361-665X/aa67fd
10. Glick, P.E., Van Crey, N., Tolley, M.T., Ruffatto, D.: Robust capture of unknown objects with a highly under-actuated gripper. In: 2020 IEEE International Conference on Robotics and Automation (ICRA), pp. 3996–4002. IEEE (2020). https://doi.org/10.1109/ICRA40945.2020.9197100
11. Hannan, M.W., Walker, I.D.: Analysis and experiments with an elephant's trunk robot. Adv. Robot. **15**(8), 847–858 (2001). https://doi.org/10.1163/156855301317198160
12. Hao, Y., et al.: Universal soft pneumatic robotic gripper with variable effective length. In: 2016 35th Chinese Control Conference (CCC), pp. 6109–6114. IEEE (2016). https://doi.org/10.1109/ChiCC.2016.7554316
13. Hassan, T., Manti, M., Passetti, G., d'Elia, N., Cianchetti, M., Laschi, C.: Design and development of a bio-inspired, under-actuated soft gripper. In: 2015 37th Annual International Conference of the IEEE Engineering in Medicine and Biology Society (EMBC), pp. 3619–3622. IEEE (2015). https://doi.org/10.1109/EMBC.2015.7319176
14. Ilievski, F., Mazzeo, A.D., Shepherd, R.F., Chen, X., Whitesides, G.M.: Soft robotics for chemists. Angew. Chem. **123**(8), 1930–1935 (2011). https://doi.org/10.1002/ange.201006464

15. In, H., Jeong, U., Lee, H., Cho, K.J.: A novel slack-enabling tendon drive that improves efficiency, size, and safety in soft wearable robots. IEEE/ASME Trans. Mechatron. **22**(1), 59–70 (2016). https://doi.org/10.1109/TMECH.2016.2606574

16. In, H., Kang, B.B., Sin, M., Cho, K.J.: Exo-glove: a wearable robot for the hand with a soft tendon routing system. IEEE Robot. Autom. Mag. **22**(1), 97–105 (2015). https://doi.org/10.1109/MRA.2014.2362863

17. Jeong, U., Kim, K., Kim, S.H., Choi, H., Youn, B.D., Cho, K.J.: Reliability analysis of a tendon-driven actuation for soft robots. Int. J. Robot. Res. **40**(1), 494–511 (2021). https://doi.org/10.1177/0278364920907151

18. Kim, S., Laschi, C., Trimmer, B.: Soft robotics: a bioinspired evolution in robotics. Trends Biotechnol. **31**(5), 287–294 (2013). https://doi.org/10.1016/j.tibtech.2013.03.002

19. Laschi, C., Cianchetti, M., Mazzolai, B., Margheri, L., Follador, M., Dario, P.: Soft robot arm inspired by the octopus. Adv. Robot. **26**(7), 709–727 (2012). https://doi.org/10.1163/156855312X626343

20. Lipson, H.: Challenges and opportunities for design, simulation, and fabrication of soft robots. Soft Rob. **1**(1), 21–27 (2014). https://doi.org/10.1089/soro.2013.0007

21. McKenzie, R.M., Barraclough, T.W., Stokes, A.A.: Integrating soft robotics with the robot operating system: a hybrid pick and place arm. Front. Robot. AI **4**, 39 (2017). https://doi.org/10.3389/frobt.2017.00039, https://www.frontiersin.org/article/10.3389/frobt.2017.00039

22. Rus, D., Tolley, M.T.: Design, fabrication and control of soft robots. Nature **521**(7553), 467–475 (2015). https://doi.org/10.1038/nature14543

23. Schumacher, C., Bickel, B., Rys, J., Marschner, S., Daraio, C., Gross, M.: Microstructures to control elasticity in 3D printing. ACM Trans. Graph. (TOG) **34**(4), 1–13 (2015). https://doi.org/10.1145/2766926

24. Trivedi, D., Rahn, C.D., Kier, W.M., Walker, I.D.: Soft robotics: biological inspiration, state of the art, and future research. Appl. Bionics Biomech. **5**(3), 99–117 (2008). https://doi.org/10.1080/11762320802557865

25. Vamsi, P.B., Rao, V.R.: Design and fabrication of soft gripper using 3D printer. In: IOP Conference Series: Materials Science and Engineering, vol. 402, p. 012026. IOP Publishing (2018). https://doi.org/10.1088/1757-899X/402/1/012026

Investigating the Relationship Between Posture and Safety in Teleoperational Tasks: A Pilot Study in Improved Operational Safety Through Enhanced Human-Machine Interaction

Thomas Piercy[1]([⊠])(iD), Guido Herrmann[1](iD), Robert Skilton[2],
Angelo Cangelosi[1], Marta Romeo[1], and Erwin Jose Lopez Pulgarin[1]

[1] The University of Manchester, Manchester, UK
thomas.piercy@manchester.ac.uk
[2] UKAEA-RACE, Culham, UK
https://www.eee.manchester.ac.uk/research/,
https://race.ukaea.uk/

Abstract. This study seeks to investigate ways in which teleoperational safety can be improved though contemporary human interfacing techniques. This paper describes a pilot study investigating the relationship between posture metrics and task load across differing teleoperation task difficulties. Task load was operationalised through the NASA-TLX scale and a relative posture quality (lean and spine curvature) was estimated through skeletal position estimation and analysis. Associations between relative posture quality and task load were analysed to provide pilot information for the full study. The findings from this pilot study suggest that pose-based quantitative measures may be statistically related to self-reports of task load. Task load is a known indicator of performance, and therefore may be an appropriate indicator to estimate operational safety. Further study is required to produce statistically richer data that may be used to further explore the links between upper body skeletal position and teleoperational safety.

Keywords: Teleoperation · HMI · Safety · Task load

1 Introduction

1.1 Overview

MASCOT [1], first developed in 1958, is a 1:1 local-remote two-armed bilateral homogeneous telemanipulator with the remote side inside the reaction vessel of the Joint European Torus (JET) fusion reactor and the local in an on-site control room. The MASCOT system is operated by the physical manipulation of

Supported by The University of Manchester and UKAEA RACE.

S. Pacheco-Gutierrez et al. (Eds.): TAROS 2022, LNAI 13546, pp. 29–39, 2022.
https://doi.org/10.1007/978-3-031-15908-4_3

the local side, and the remote side exactly mirrors the movements. This type of remote handling solution with minimal artificial agency is common within the nuclear industry due to its reliability and low chance of mishap in hazardous environments [2–4]. However, human error is the primary cause of accidents in the nuclear sector [5], and therefore human factors must be considered. In this context, HMI (Human Machine Interaction) is the interactions between the telemanipulator operator, and the local telemanipulation device. The specific HMI considerations of MASCOT are the 1:1 design and the bilateral nature of the control. These factors mean that, compared to a joystick input or smaller surgical teleoperations, there are whole arm and sometimes whole body movements required to operate MASCOT.

This study aims to trial and prototype the use of skeletal tracking as a tool to improve HMI for telemanipulation. The notion of using Skeletal tracking for HMI investigations is reasonably well studied [6–8], though the specific use of skeletal tracking for telemanipulator operation is not. It is therefore desirable to investigate and prototype the use of this tool for human-telemanipulator interaction. This research forms part of a larger body of work, seeking to investigate tools and techniques for improved operator prediction and operational safety in the context of the MASCOT [1] telemanipulator and other similar systems.

1.2   Skeletal Tracking

Skeletal tracking is the process of estimating the 3D position and orientation of key points representing limbs of human body to describe a human's pose. One method of skeletal tracking is using RGBD (Red, Green, Blue, and Depth) cameras to inform a data-driven AI estimation of skeletal pose [9]. This methodology has the advantage of being a commercially available, simple and relatively cheap solution [10]. The limitations of this technique are a reliance on suitable lighting conditions, and some areas of the 3D camera field of view have a more accurate tracking capability than others [11].

Skeletal tracking can be used as a meaningful sensory input to an AI for action estimation [6,7], and can also be used for human action prediction [12]. This prediction mechanism could allow for AI intervention to prevent or mitigate driver accidents. Some methods of skeletal tracking do not require any worn sensors [13] and are therefore a non-intrusive method of operator data gathering. In this context, non-invasive human monitoring is desirable so as not to interfere with teleoperation.

The readings from skeletal tracking are often prone to errors such as jitter and subject loss due to occlusion, which can cause erroneous measurements. This can be mitigated in some ways, for example by using stable lighting, minimal occlusion and minimising sensor noise. One solution to further minimise error is to use a smoothing filter such as a Kalman filter [14]. Double exponential smoothing [15] is optimised for tracking, and can provide similar error reduction results to a Kalman filter at a much faster rate.

1.3   Task Load

'Task load' is a catch-all term used to describe the mental and physical demands of a task [16]. One validated measure of task load is the NASA-TLX (North American Space Agency - Task Load Index) [17]. The NASA-TLX is a quantitative questionnaire assessing experienced mental, physical, and temporal demand as well as performance, effort and frustration felt. This questionnaire has been used in a number of studies, and is widely regarded as a useful tool for indicating experienced task load [18]. However, the definitions of the NASA-TLX categories are ambiguous, and scores could be the result of a number of factors that are not measured. It is important to consider that self reported questionnaires are prone to socially desirable biases, but they will still provide meaningful data [19].

2   Methodology

This study asked participants to complete a teleoperation task while they had their estimated skeletal position recorded. Posture measurements (spine lean and spine curve) were then derived from the skeletal position during the task. The participants were then asked to complete a questionnaire to indicate their perceived task-load. This process was conducted for a second time on a more complex task to induce a higher perceived task load. The results from the task load questionnaire were then compared with the derived posture measurements as part of a relationship analysis.

Experimental Design. The independent variable is task difficulty, having two levels: simple and complex. The dependent variables are NASA-TLX [17] outputs and posture. NASA-TLX outputs a self-reported measure of mental, physical and temporal demand as well as performance, effort and frustration. Posture is a derived pair of values from skeletal estimation - spine curvature and upper body lean, the derivation of this is described in Sect. 2.2.

Participants. The only inclusion criteria for participants was that they are trained for MASCOT use, there is no exclusion criteria. Participants will also be asked their hours of teleoperational experience, for any prior knowledge of tasks and their handedness. In this pilot study, three participants were used.

2.1   Experimental Setup

Below is a list of the materials used, as well as a description of the experimental setup.

- MASCOT telemanipulator
- Simple task: This task involved wrapping a wire around pegs on a board in a fixed path
- Complex task: This task involved mounting a panel to the wall of JET

- NASA-TLX questionnaire - a set of scaled questions to evaluate perceived task load
- Demographic questionnaire (handedness, teleoperational experience, prior knowledge of tasks)
- Microsoft Azure Kinect RGBD camera and mounting equipment
- Laptop with GPU for data processing
- Python programming language for data processing

The Study was conducted in the MASCOT control room at UKAEA-RACE. Within the control room is the MASCOT local input manipulator, this is mounted on a height-adjustable platform and so can be adjusted to not influence posture. The operator sits on a standard office chair underneath this platform in order to operate MASCOT (see Fig. 1).

Fig. 1. MASCOT operator area

The RGBD sensor was positioned approximately 2.5 m to the front and 2 m right of the operator, and was mounted on a tripod, raising it 1.6 m from the ground. The sensor was pointed at the operator so that no part of the operator was out of the field of view of the sensor during the recording. The RGBD sensor was used to record a estimated skeletal position of a MASCOT operator as they completed two telemanipulation training tasks - the simple and complex task. This position was recorded and stored as a series of Cartesian coordinates - an X, Y, and Z for each joint at a variable rate of an average 3.2 Hz. A visual representation of this can be seen in Fig. 2, where it is mapped onto a 3D image.

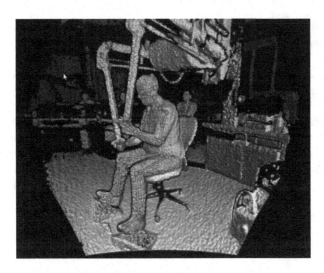

Fig. 2. 3D image of MASCOT operator with skeleton position estimation overlay

The simple task was to wrap a insulated wire around a series of pegs stuck into a board in a fixed pattern. The complex task was a panel mounting and dismounting exercise that required a tool change and performing complicated procedures with both hands. These are both standard training exercises for operators. Please note that more rich and controlled tasks will be used for the full study with standardised instructions. The tasks used here were taken ad-hoc from existing training tasks used for MASCOT. The operators were not given any specific instructions on how to complete the tasks, but they were familiar with MASCOT operation and the tasks.

2.2 Experimental Procedure

Participant Actions

- Participant was asked to complete the demographic questionnaire
- Participant was asked to complete task 1 - the simple task. During this task, the participant was recorded using the RGBD camera
- The participant was asked to complete NASA-TLX questionnaire for task 1.
- Participant was asked to complete task 2 - the complex task. During this task, the participant was recorded using the RGBD camera
- The participant was asked to complete NASA-TLX questionnaire for task 2.

Data Gathering. The demographic questionnaire was given to the participants before starting any tasks. Recordings were started before an operator started each task, and ended after they had completed each task. The NASA-TLX questionnaire was completed by the participant as soon as practicable after completing each task.

Data Processing. The skeletal position was analysed over a time series. A computer-assisted observational analysis was used to identify occlusion, loss of tracking, and drift. This step involved watching the operation along with the skeletal overlay, and noting the times when those errors occurred. A double exponential smoothing filter [15] was applied to all readings.

Posture was examined by isolating the spine position estimates: Pelvis, spine navel, spine chest, and neck. These label points were analysed trigonometrically to determine their relative displacements from the pelvis, and those relative positions were used to determine lean and curve. Lean was determined as a measure of the total angle of deflection from upright between pelvis and neck, normalised to be between 0 and 1 for a lean of 0 to 0.5π radians (0 to 90°):

$$height\ of\ neck = z_{disp} = z_{neck}$$

$$Planar\ displacement = p = \sqrt{(x_{neck}^2 + y_{neck}^2)}$$

$$Lean = L = tan^{-1}(\frac{p}{z_{disp}})$$

$$Normalised\ Lean = L_{norm} = \frac{L}{0.5\pi}$$

Spine curve is derived by measuring the cumulative total angle of deflection between pelvis and neck normalised to between 0 and 1 - It is the normalised sum of the magnitude of angle of deflection from each joint to the next (from pelvis to neck):

$$Height\ of\ link = \Delta z = z_n - z_{n-1}$$

$$Link\ planar\ displacement = p_n = \sqrt{(x_n - x_{n-1})^2 + (y_n - y_{n-1})^2}$$

$$Deflection = d_n = tan^{-1}(\frac{p_n}{\Delta z})$$

$$Total\ curve = C_{total} = \sum_{n=pelvis}^{neck} d_n$$

$$Normalised\ curve = C_{norm} = \frac{C_{total}}{0.5\pi}$$

Ultimately there is not enough data here to investigate correlations with a sufficient statistical power as the sample size and the testing ranges are both too small. However a simple comparison of data is demonstrated in the results section.

3   Results

Figure 3 and Fig. 4 present the average scores of all participants in the NASA-TLX categories, and average Spine Lean and Spine Curves during each task.

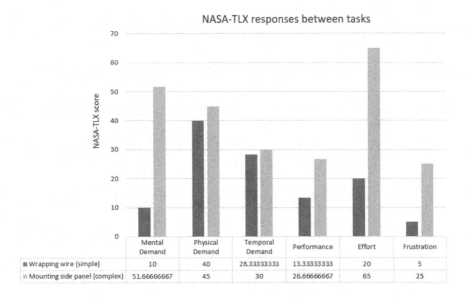

Fig. 3. Combined figure comparing average NASA-TLX response scores for each task

The results presented in Fig. 3 show the average NASA-TLX scores for each task. For these scores, a higher result equates to a higher report of the category, with the exception of performance, where a low score indicates a good performance. The maximum possible score in each of these categories is 100, the minimum is 0. All scores of the wire wrapping (simple) task are lower than the mounting side panel (complex) task. Effort and mental demand showed the most change between tasks ($\Delta > 30$), frustration and performance showed moderate change between tasks ($30 < \Delta > 10$) and physical demand and temporal demand showed the least change between tasks ($10 < \Delta$).

The results presented in Fig. 4 show the average posture metrics for each task. A greater value for lean indicates a sharper lean from upright - where 0 would mean that the neck is directly above the pelvis, and 1 would mean that the neck and pelvis are on the same horizontal plane. A greater value for curve indicates a more curved spine - a curve of 0 would indicate that each joint is exactly in line with the next, and a curve of 1 would indicate that the neck is at 90° relative to the pelvis.

Below are presented a series of observational notes regarding the quality of recorded data.

- Tracking appears to be accurate to approximately 50 mm, any discovered tracking errors greater than this are noted
- Tracking will usually not fail unless there is an occlusion
- Tracking is sometimes sensitive to clothing types - specifically struggling with sharp colour changes caused by short sleeves etc.
- Of the 38976 total estimated skeletal positions, 10913 had significant errors due to occlusion (approximately 28% of frames)

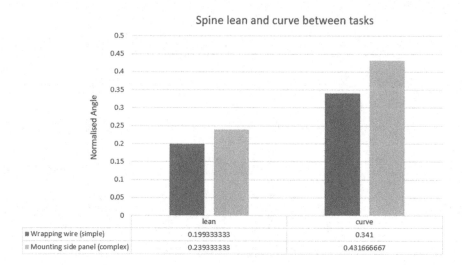

Fig. 4. Combined figure comparing average posture scores for each task

– Only 286 frames had other significant tracking errors (approximately 0.73% of frames).

4 Discussion

This was the first study to our knowledge to examine associations between posture and task demand, in the context of informing teleoperational safety using MASCOT. Overall, the skeletal estimation recording was robust and reliable but sensitive to occlusion. The tracking was accurate to an estimated 50 mm, with clear indicators when a loss of tracking does occur. Kurillo et al. [20] found an the Azure Kinect accuracy to be under 24 mm in all axes, suggesting this is a reliable measure of spine position for use in a larger scale study. Results suggest posture metrics could be a predictor of task load, which could be used to inform safety. If the planned full study confirms these findings, this could have significant impact on safety for teleoperation. The overall rate of recording was 3.2 Hz. This recording rate was sufficient for movement analysis, but it is likely that some information was lost. The real-time position estimation was useful for preliminary study, but will likely not be used for further data-gathering exercises as the images can be processed afterwards to produce a much higher capture rate. In general, there was very little drift, however, the relative twist and incline of the hips was subject to a slow drift that did not match with the visually recorded data. It is suspected that this is due to the self-occlusion of the hips that is caused by a seated position.

These initial results suggest a relationship between skeletal pose estimation measures and self-reported task demand; however, a major limitation is a sample size of only three participants. Such a small sample limits the power of statistical analysis. It is possible that the types of tasks conducted dictate the posture and that this is a false correlation, posture itself is also heavily influenced by individual factors (e.g. height, weight). A study with more participants and tasks with a more varied range of difficulty levels could be used to explore both the personal and interpersonal differences. In the planned full study, a correlational analysis will be conducted to test for statistical significance.

The results of the NASA-TLX questions indicate that the complex task is more mentally and physically demanding and requires more effort. This supports the suitability of these tasks in eliciting differences in task load, which may influence posture. However, it is possible that these results are due to other unmeasured factors - such as fatigue. Therefore, it may be desirable to cross-validate these results with other task-load measures.

The specific problems arising from studying the MASCOT are the seated positions causing self-occlusion, some errors in skeletal pose estimation and the occlusion caused by the MASCOT arms. Generally the tracking estimation was robust to occlusion and would only lose tracking accuracy if the hand or elbow were covered, which happened for approximately 28% of the total frames - specifically where the operator's left hand or elbow was occluded. This inaccuracy was limited to the occluded limbs. There were some other significant errors in tracking, accounting for 0.73% of the frames. It is possible these were from a computational failure in skeletal position estimation, or may have been caused by transient objects such as dust in front of the sensor.

To further validate this study another sensor system could be used alongside the kinect such as a Vicon tracking system. The findings of this study could be compared to other teleoperational safety methodologies to confirm internal validity.

5 Conclusion

This study demonstrated a potential association between posture-based measures and factors predicting teleoperational safety (i.e. perceived task load). One conclusion of this study is that skeletal position estimation can be used to estimate posture during the teleoperation of MASCOT; this is a known factor of performance in other teleoperated robots and is therefore likely to be a good indicator of performance for nuclear telemanipulation. Results of data analysis show possible links between upper body posture and task load. Overall, further study is warranted as these techniques suggest a potential link that could improve teleoperational safety. The further study will use more varied task complexity and methods such as counterbalancing to improve validity, and a larger sample size of operators will provide more statistical power.

References

1. Skilton, R., Hamilton, N., Howell, R., Lamb, C., Rodriguez, J.: MASCOT 6: achieving high dexterity tele-manipulation with a modern architectural design for fusion remote maintenance. Robotics **10**(3) (2021)
2. Tokatli, O., et al.: Robot-assisted glovebox teleoperation for nuclear industry. Robotics **10**(3), 85 (2021)
3. Seward, D., Bakari, M.J.: The use of robotics and automation in nuclear decommissioning. In: 22nd International Symposium on Automation and Robotics in Construction (2005)
4. Melchiorri, C.: Robotic telemanipulation systems: an overview on control aspects. IFAC Proc. Vol. **36**(17), 21–30 (2003). https://doi.org/10.1016/S1474-6670(17)33365-7, https://www.sciencedirect.com/science/article/pii/S1474667017333657. ISSN 1474–6670, 7th IFAC Symposium on Robot Control (SYROCO 2003), Wroclaw, Poland, 1–3 September 2003
5. Swaton, E., Neboyan, V., Lederman, L.: Human factors in the operation of nuclear power plants. IAEA Bull. **29**, 27–30 (1987)
6. Li, C., Yang, C., Wan, J., Annamalai, A., Cangelosi, A.: Neural learning and Kalman filtering enhanced teaching by demonstration for a baxter robot. In: 23rd International Conference on Automation and Computing (ICAC) (2017)
7. Roitberg, A., Perzylo, A., Somani, N., Giuliani, M., Rickert, M., Knoll, A.: Human activity recognition in the context of industrial human-robot interaction. In: 2014 Asia-Pacific Signal and Information Processing Association Annual Summit and Conference (APSIPA), pp. 1–10 (2014). https://doi.org/10.1109/APSIPA.2014.7041588
8. Roth, P. M., Mauthner, T., Khan, I., Bischof, H.: Efficient human action recognition by cascaded linear classifcation. In: 2009 IEEE 12th International Conference on Computer Vision Workshops, ICCV Workshops, pp. 546–553 (2009). https://doi.org/10.1109/ICCVW.2009.5457655
9. Papadopoulos, G.T., Axenopoulos, A., Daras, P.: Real-time skeleton-tracking-based human action recognition using kinect data. In: Gurrin, C., Hopfgartner, F., Hurst, W., Johansen, H., Lee, H., O'Connor, N. (eds.) MMM 2014. LNCS, vol. 8325, pp. 473–483. Springer, Cham (2014). https://doi.org/10.1007/978-3-319-04114-8_40. ISBN 978-3-319-04114-8
10. Clark, R.A., Mentiplay, B.F., Hough, E., Pua, Y.H.: Three-dimensional cameras and skeleton pose tracking for physical function assessment: a review of uses, validity, current developments and kinect alternatives. Gait Posture **68**, 193–200 (2019). https://doi.org/10.1016/j.gaitpost.2018.11.029, https://www.sciencedirect.com/science/article/pii/S0966636218311913. ISSN 0966–6362
11. Schlagenhauf, F., Sreeram, S., Singhose, W.: Comparison of kinect and vicon motion capture of upper-body joint angle tracking. In: 2018 IEEE 14th International Conference on Control and Automation (ICCA), pp. 674–679 (2018). https://doi.org/10.1109/ICCA.2018.8444349
12. Pulgarin, E.J.L., Herrmann, G., Leonards, U.: Drivers' manoeuvre prediction for safe HRI. In: 2018 IEEE/RSJ International Conference on Intelligent Robots and Systems (IROS) (2018)
13. Kar, A.: Skeletal tracking using Microsoft kinect. Methodology **1**, 11 (2010)
14. Kalman, R.E.: A new approach to linear filtering and prediction problems. J. Basic Eng. **82**(1), 35–45 (1960). https://doi.org/10.1115/1.3662552. ISSN 0021-9223

15. LaViola, J.J.: Double exponential smoothing: an alternative to Kalman filter-based predictive tracking. In: Proceedings of the Workshop on Virtual Environments 2003, EGVE 2003, pp. 199–206. Association for Computing Machinery, New York (2003). https://doi.org/10.1145/769953.769976. ISBN 1581136862

16. Zimmerman, M.E.: Task load. In: Kreutzer, J.S., DeLuca, J., Caplan, B. (eds.) Encyclopedia of Clinical Neuropsychology, pp. 2469–2470. Springer, New York (2011). https://doi.org/10.1007/978-0-387-79948-3_1256. ISBN 978-0-387-79948-3

17. Hart, S.G., Staveland, L.E.: Development of NASA-TLX (task load index): results of empirical and theoretical research. In: Hancock, P.A., Meshkati, N. (eds.) Human Mental Workload. Advances in Psychology, vol. 52, pp. 139–183. North-Holland (1988). https://doi.org/10.1016/S0166-4115(08)62386-9, https://www.sciencedirect.com/science/article/pii/S0166411508623869

18. Hart, S.G.: Nasa-task load index (NASA-TLX); 20 years later. In: Proceedings of the Human Factors and Ergonomics Society Annual Meeting, vol. 50, no. 9, pp. 904–908 (2006). https://doi.org/10.1177/154193120605000909

19. McKendrick, R.D., Cherry, E.: A deeper look at the NASA TLX and where it falls short. In: Proceedings of the Human Factors and Ergonomics Society Annual Meeting, vol. 62, no. 1, pp. 44–48 (2018). https://doi.org/10.1177/1541931218621010

20. Kurillo, G., Hemingway, E., Cheng, M.-L., Cheng, L.: Evaluating the accuracy of the azure kinect and kinect V2. Sensors (Basel) 22(7), 2469 (2022)

Design and Analysis of an End Effector Using the Fin Ray Structure for Integrated Limb Mechanisms

Jack Pledger and Mingfeng Wang$^{(\boxtimes)}$ (iD)

Department of Mechanical and Aerospace Engineering, Brunel University London, London UB8 3PH, UK
{1820772,mingfeng.wang}@brunel.ac.uk

Abstract. This paper presents the design and analysis of a novel end effector used in the integrated limb mechanism that enables manipulation and locomotion tasks to be performed with a single limb. A Fin Ray structure-based two-finger gripper design is incorporated into the end effector with a novel flexible tendon design that wraps around the base of each finger. A Finite Element Analysis (FEA) study was performed to optimize the Fin Ray structure-based finger design by varying its physical parameters and quantifying its performance. Simulation results were discussed with several trends to be used to design the structure for specific tasks. A preliminary prototype was developed, and a range of experimental tests were carried out to validate the FEA study.

Keywords: Integrated limb mechanism · End-effector design · Fin Ray structure · FEA analysis

1 Introduction

An integrated limb mechanism (ILM) is a system which combines the function of an arm and leg into one limb, reducing the number of unique appendages needed for a legged robot and increasing its versatility [1]. The design of such a limb and its adjoined end effector depends on its intended use: whether it is biased towards manipulation [2] or locomotion [3], the capability for single or multi-limb manipulation and the type of objects being manipulated. Inspiration can be taken from nature, mimicking the simple limbs of an insect [4] to the structure of a primate's arm, although little work has been shown at this level of complexity. Much of the design challenge lies with the end effector, which must be dexterous to interact with small objects while remaining robust for locomotion. As such, many previous examples show a traditional foot with the capability of multi-limb manipulation [2] or additional grabber attachment [4]. An optimal design could include both aspects in a single mechanism.

© The Author(s), under exclusive license to Springer Nature Switzerland AG 2022
S. Pacheco-Gutierrez et al. (Eds.): TAROS 2022, LNAI 13546, pp. 40–49, 2022.
https://doi.org/10.1007/978-3-031-15908-4_4

The requirement for higher adaptability and work in cooperation with humans has led to an area of research into compliant structures, or soft robotics [5]. These are mechanisms which rely on soft, deformable materials, often mimicking natural structures. Using compliant materials has additional benefits, including reduction in mechanism complexity and improved handling of soft objects [5]. The level of compliance can range from replacing traditional rigid fingers with soft structures [6], to robots composed almost entirely of soft materials [7]. An ILM end effector could make use of compliant structures to conform to objects or terrain and increase resilience to shock loading or environmental effects [8].

One structure suited to robot grippers is that of the Fin Ray® Effect, which mimics the anatomy of fish fins and can deform around objects when force is applied [9]. The first commercial use of a Fin Ray gripper is that of Festo, with their adaptive gripper fingers available for use in industrial robots [10]. Several works have looked at the optimal design for the Fin Ray structure, altering physical parameters to improve its gripping performance through simulation or physical experiments. Many of these are based on the dimensions of the original Festo finger and alter values of rib density and angle [11] or wall thickness and rib geometry [12], along with others of similar design [6]. The effects of object position and size have also been studied [13]. Fingers which differ significantly from the Festo design have not been widely studied and changing aspect ratio (the ratio of finger length to base width) or overall scale could provide increased object variability. Further study can also be performed on object size and position, giving a more real-world demonstration of the structure's performance in different scenarios. Various methods have been shown to produce compliant parts with differing cost and capabilities, including material casting [7], Fused Deposition Modeling (FDM) printing [11], and multi-material jetting [14].

In this paper, a novel end-effector is proposed based on the Fin Ray structure for an integrated limb mechanism. In Sect. 2, the design of the end effector is presented with consideration of compliant structures and 3D printing techniques. In Sect. 3, an FEA analysis on the Fin Ray structure is performed in ANSYS® software to study how rib parameters affect the structure, as well as the effect of object position. Furthermore, the simulation results are compared with experimental tests to validate their accuracy. Discussion and conclusion are presented in Sect. 4.

2 Design

In this section, a novel design for the ILM end effector is introduced, including the basic mechanical principle and design of compliant parts. Then, the 3D printing technique for the Fin Ray Effect finger is demonstrated.

2.1   End Effector Design

The proposed end effector can function as a foot or a gripper with a single actuation method, as shown in Fig. 1. It uses a two-finger design, allowing for enveloping and pinching grasp modes to increase object variability. The key principle is the use of compliant fingers which can rotate more than 180°, allowing them to be fully retracted during locomotion tasks. In Fig. 1(b), four typical modes of the gripper have been illustrated, with retracted and flat plane configurations for stable ground contact, and both methods of grasping.

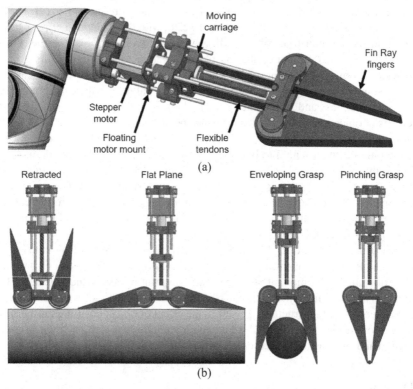

Fig. 1. CAD design of the proposed end-effector: (a) overview mounted to UR5 collaborative arm and (b) demonstration of the end effector functions.

The entire end-effector is actuated by a single stepper motor, coupled directly to a leadscrew and nut. A carriage is driven by the nut, moving linearly, and supported by four rods with linear bearings (see Fig. 1(a)). These rods also form the main structure, creating a stiff frame for both ground contacting and object grasping. Different from conventional tendon-driven methods (e.g., cable-driven), the novel flexible tendon design wraps around the base of each finger. This allows a bi-directional operation, namely pulling while grasping and pushing when releasing grasping and reconfiguring for ground contact. The lead screw can create a large mechanical reduction, multiplying the torque of the motor to increase maximum gripping force and positional accuracy of the fingers. The motor mount can move freely along the direction of the leadscrew, relieving all axial load which is transferred to a thrust bearing to allow unimpeded operation of the motor (see Fig. 1(a)). The design is made from a combination of metal hardware and 3D printed parts, with PLA and TPU materials being used for stiff and compliant parts respectively. The design incorporates a mounting surface to interface with the UR5 collaborative robot arm, which facilitates physical testing of the end effector. However, this can be reconfigured for any mounting solution, as well as for integration into a full ILM.

2.2 Compliant Design and Manufacturing

The compliant parts used in the design are printed as a single monolithic structure, incorporating the Fin Ray finger, attachment base and actuator tendon, as shown in Fig. 2. This significantly decreases the complexity of the mechanism and removes stress concentrations at joints. The tendon is pre-shaped around the finger base, creating an additional restoring force on retraction to compensate for the lack of stiffness in compression. This is also aided by a rubber band mechanism. A T-shaped attachment point provides a strong fixture for force transmission. The Fin Ray finger has a length of 117 mm from the first rib to the tip, with a base of width 36 mm, giving it a higher aspect ratio and larger size than the original Festo design and many mentioned in Sect. 1. This aims to increase the maximum size of object that can be gripped, while remaining compact in a retracted state.

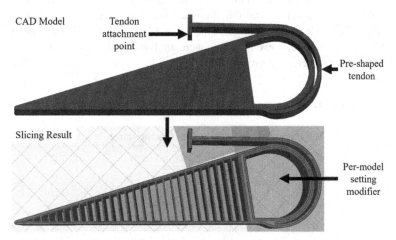

Fig. 2. Design of Fin Ray finger in CAD (top) and outcome from the Cura slicing software (bottom). Techniques used are highlighted.

The compliant parts were printed using RS PRO TPU filament from RS Components, with a Shore hardness of 98 A [15]. This is higher than that used in previously mentioned works [7] (30D) and [8] (85 A), but the higher aspect ratio of the fingers results in larger forces being generated, requiring higher stiffness to prevent failure of the structure. The CAD model contains features necessary for the function of the mechanism, as well as a solid prism in place of the Fin Ray structure. The ribs are generated according to infill settings in the Cura slicing software using the 'Lines' pattern, such as line distance, line direction and line width, as well as outer wall thickness (see Fig. 2). This procedure was demonstrated in [8] and allows fast iteration of designs with an optimized nozzle path to increase print quality. Additional settings have been modified using overlapping volumes and per-model settings, allowing the attached tendon and base to be printed as solid with no infill cavities, increasing strength and uniformity. All printing was performed on a modified Anycubic Mega S FDM printer.

The chosen material leaves a smooth, glossy surface after printing which is not ideal for grasping. Consequently, rubber strips were adhered to the contact surface to greatly increase friction without impeding deformation.

3   Finite Element Analysis (FEA) of the Fin Ray Structure

In this section, an FEA analysis is performed in ANSYS® software to study the effects of various sets of rib parameters on the stiffness of the Fin Ray finger structure. Furthermore, the results are compared to a physical model for validation.

3.1   Analysis Setup

A 2D static structural analysis within ANSYS® software was utilized to develop the geometry of the gripper finger. Thickness, spacing, and angle of the internal ribs was varied while object contact area and total contact force were measured with the object at points spaced 20 mm along the finger. This captured the fingertip, base and a range of points in between. In total, eleven designs were analysed with a range of values being tested for each parameter, as shown in Table 1.

Table 1. Tested variations of the Fin Ray finger with parameters

Variation No.	Rib thickness (mm)	Rib spacing (mm)	Rib angle (°)
Ref	0.8	3.2	0
1	1.2	3.2	0
2	1.6	3.2	0
3	2	3.2	0
4	0.8	2	0
5	0.8	4.4	0
6	0.8	5.6	0
7	0.8	3.2	−30
8	0.8	3.2	−15
9	0.8	3.2	15
10	0.8	3.2	30

The simulation was configured to mimic the mechanical model shown in Sect. 2, with a 1 Nm torque applied to the finger base reacting against a rigid object of diameter 80 mm. The object position was varied in increments of 20 mm up to a maximum of 80 mm to determine the change in response along the structure (see Fig. 3). The material applied to the finger was selected to match the 98 A shore hardness TPU used in the physical design. While a datasheet for this material was available [15], it did not specify every parameter required for a complete simulation. Consequently, the in-built ANSYS® material *'Rubber, TPU (Ester, aromatic, Shore A85/D35)'* from the Granta Design materials database was modified to provide the missing properties. Specifically, the Youngs Modulus was increased from 33.7 MPa to 150 MPa, and the ultimate tensile strength was increased from 43.3 MPa to 50 MPa.

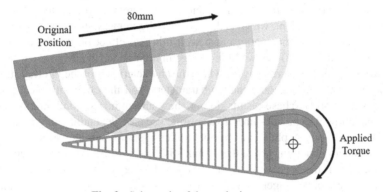

Fig. 3. Schematic of the analysis geometry

3.2 Analysis Results

General Observations. Figure 4 shows the results gathered from the study. For the purpose of explanation, the fingertip is defined as 0 mm of displacement and the finger base is at 80 mm of displacement. In all cases, contact area and contact force increase as the object moves towards the base of the finger, with a maximum of 426% increased contact area shown in variation 9. This highlights how greatly the characteristics of the Fin Ray structure vary along its length, allowing it to support fingertip and enveloping grasp modes.

Effect of Varying Rib Thickness. Figure 4(a) and 4(a) indicate that a higher rib thickness results in a lower overall contact area, with an average decrease of 38% between the reference finger and variation 3. This shows that the overall stiffness of the structure has been increased. Contact area at the fingertip is affected the least due to the naturally higher stiffness in this region. Conversely, a higher rib thickness results in a larger total contact force, especially towards the base of the finger, showing an increase of 41% at 80 mm of object displacement. Additionally, the increase in contact force between subsequent thickness values becomes smaller, indicating that the force will reach an upper limit. This will occur when rib thickness is equal to rib spacing, resulting in a solid structure.

Effect of Varying Rib Spacing. Figure 4(c) and (d) show how the measured values were affected by varying the rib spacing. Some values have been omitted due to the simulation failing to converge at higher rib spacings. This may have been caused by buckling of the structure due to the stiffness becoming too low. The large variance in contact area is likely due to the object coming into contact on or between ribs, locally changing the stiffness. It is difficult to draw a conclusion for this reason. For a more successful study, lower values of rib spacing would be tested. Contact force displays a trend opposite to that seen in Fig. 4(b), showing that rib thickness and rib spacing have a similar effect and can be referred to in combination as rib density.

Effect of Varying Rib Angle. Figure 4(e) shows an increasing gradient as angle decreases and becomes negative, corresponding to higher variation across the length of the finger. Negative rib angle has not been tested in previous literature and produces the lines of steepest gradient, which is desirable for the Fin Ray structure as it increases the effectiveness of the enveloping grasp with minimal effect on the fingertip grasp. Contact force (see Fig. 4(f)) shows little change in relation to rib angle.

These results show several ways in which the characteristics of the Fin Ray structure can be altered through changing the rib parameters, and the effect of object position on the gripping ability. These results do not show an optimized configuration for the structure but allow it to be fine-tuned to a specific use case depending on type of object or the actuation force. A phenomenon not explicitly shown through simulation is the finger experiencing buckling when the overall stiffness becomes too low to support the reaction force. This has been explicitly observed in physical testing (Fig. 6) and limits the minimum stiffness of the finger, as it can fail to create adequate gripping force. Although not tested, it is theorized that this effect becomes more pronounced as the aspect ratio of the structure increases due to the higher moment being supported by a smaller base.

3.3 Physical Validation

Following the analysis, a 3D printed model of the reference finger design was tested to verify the results. The gripper was actuated using approximately 1 Nm of moment to match the simulation, and the deformation was observed with a range of object positions. Figure 5 shows the results compared side by side. The analysis and physical deformation are very similar, giving credibility to the validity of the results.

Figure 6 shows the buckling phenomenon seen on the physical finger and implied by the simulation results. It occurs at the base of the finger where the moment due to object contact is highest and is a result of the opposite wall deforming inwards with a simultaneous separation of the ribs. The structure shows much lower resistance to further deformation beyond this point. This creates a limit on the maximum force the finger can exert and will cause a grasp to fail. The way in which parameters affect the maximum buckling load has not been studied.

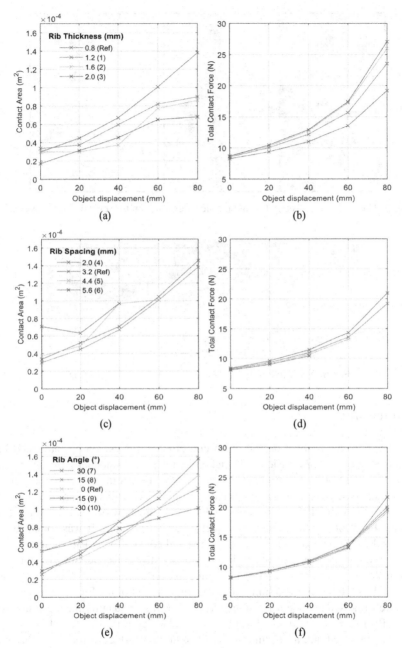

Fig. 4. Simulation results for the three tested parameters. Contact area and total contact force are displayed side by side. Variation No. From Table 1 is shown.

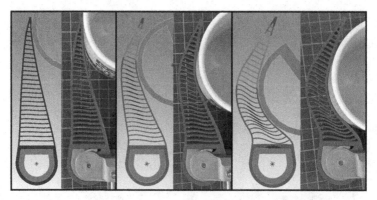

Fig. 5. Comparison between FEA and physical deformation for several object positions.

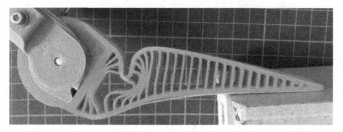

Fig. 6. Buckling of the Fin Ray structure due to overloading.

4   Conclusions

This paper presents a novel design of an end effector for use on an integrated limb mechanism along with the basic mechanical principle, accommodating locomotion and manipulation. 3D printed compliant structures have been utilized, with the Fin Ray Effect acting as a gripper finger for enhanced object versatility, actuated via flexible tendons. An FEA simulation was performed to determine how rib parameters affect the grasping ability of the finger and the effect of object position. It was found that rib density is directly related to object contact area and contact force. Rib angle also has a large effect on the deformation of the finger, with negative rib angles showing increased variation along its length. A buckling effect due to overloading of the structure has been highlighted and this presents a limit on the maximum load of the Fin Ray finger.

Future work will include performing physical testing to quantify the performance of the end effector, e.g., maximum object payload and leg carrying capacity. Eventually, it will be incorporated into a full limb mechanism and multi-legged robot. Furthermore, additional study into the Fin Ray structure can be conducted, namely the effects of aspect ratio and overall scale for use with mechanisms of varying design. As required gripping forces increase, the buckling effect may become more relevant and mitigating changes can be found to decrease the likelihood of failure.

References

1. Koyachi, N., Arai, T., Adachi, H., Asami, K., Itoh, Y.: Hexapod with integrated limb mechanism of leg and arm. In: Proceedings of 1995 IEEE International Conference on Robotics and Automation, vol. 2, pp. 1952–1957 (1995)
2. Deng, H., Xin, G., Zhong, G., Mistry, M.: Object carrying of hexapod robots with integrated mechanism of leg and arm. Robot. Comput.-Integr. Manuf. **54**, 145–155 (2018)
3. Camacho-Arreguin, J., Wang, M., Dong, X., Axinte, D.: A novel class of reconfigurable parallel kinematic manipulators: concepts and fourier-based singularity analysis. Mech. Mach. Theor. **153**, 103993 (2020)
4. Rönnau, A., Heppner, G., Nowicki, M., Dillmann, R.: LAURON V: a versatile six-legged walking robot with advanced maneuverability. In: 2014 IEEE/ASME International Conference on Advanced Intelligent Mechatronics, pp. 82–87 (2014)
5. Rus, D., Tolley, M.T.: Design, fabrication and control of soft robots. Nature **521**(7553), 467–475 (2015)
6. Lee, L.Y., Nurzaman, S.G., Tan, C.P.: Design and analysis of a gripper with interchangeable soft fingers for ungrounded mobile robots. In: 2019 IEEE International Conference on Cybernetics and Intelligent Systems (CIS) and Robotics, Automation and Mechatronics (RAM), pp. 221–226 (2019)
7. Fras, J., Noh, Y., Macias, M., Wurdemann, H., Althoefer, K.: Bio-inspired octopus robot based on novel soft fluidic actuator. In: 2018 IEEE International Conference on Robotics and Automation (ICRA), pp. 1583–1588 (2018)
8. Tolley, M., Shepherd, R., Galloway, K., Wood, R., Whitesides, G.: A resilient, untethered soft robot. Soft Rob. **1**(3), 213–223 (2014)
9. Pfaff, O., Simeonov, S., Cirovic, I., Stano, P.: Application of fin ray effect approach for production process automation. Ann. DAAAM Proc. **22**(1), 1247–1249 (2011)
10. Festo: Adaptive gripper fingers DHAS. https://www.festo.com/cat/en-gb_gb/data/doc_ENGB/PDF/EN/DHAS_EN.PDF. Accessed 03 May 2022
11. Elgeneidy, K., Lightbody, P., Pearson, S., Neumann, G.: Characterising 3D-printed soft fin ray robotic fingers with layer jamming capability for delicate grasping. In: 2019 2nd IEEE International Conference on Soft Robotics (RoboSoft), pp. 143–148 (2019)
12. Suder, J., Bobovský, Z., Mlotek, J., Vocetka, M., Oščádal, P., Zeman, Z.: Structural optimization method of a FinRay finger for the best wrapping of object. Appl. Sci. **11**(9), 3858 (2021)
13. Shan, X., Birglen, L.: Modeling and analysis of soft robotic fingers using the fin ray effect. Int. J. Robot. Res. **39**(14), 1686–1705 (2020)
14. Crooks, W., Vukasin, G., O'Sullivan, M., Messner, W., Rogers, C.: Fin ray® effect inspired soft robotic gripper: From the robosoft grand challenge toward optimization. Front. Robot. AI **3**(1), 70 (2016)
15. RS Components FLEX PRO 98. https://docs.rs-online.com/9bb7/0900766b81697e93.pdf. Accessed 03 May 2022

Trigger-Assisted Ambidextrous Control Framework for Teleoperation of Two Legged Manipulators

Christopher Peers[1], Joseph Humphreys[1], Yuhui Wan[1], Jun Li[1,2], Jingcheng Sun[1], Robert Richardson[1], and Chengxu Zhou[1(✉)]

[1] School of Mechanical Engineering, University of Leeds, Leeds, UK
c.x.zhou@leeds.ac.uk
[2] State Key Laboratory of Robotics and System, Harbin Institute of Technology, Harbin, China

Abstract. This paper presents a motion-capture based control framework for the purpose of effectively teleoperating two legged manipulators without significant delays caused by the switching of controllers. The control framework generates high-level trajectories in 6 degrees of freedom and uses finger gesture detection to act as triggers in selecting which robot to control as well as toggling various aspects of control such as yaw rotation of the quadruped platform. The functionality and ease of use of the control framework are demonstrated through a real-life experiment where the operator controls two quadrupedal manipulator robots to open a spray can. The experiment was successfully accomplished by the proposed teleoperation framework.

Keywords: Teleoperation · Legged robots · Manipulation

1 Introduction

Teleoperation has become an important part of robotic control, as an increasing number of robotic systems are being used for operations in locations that would be considered hazardous or remote. In the past, robots were merely used as platforms for collecting data in these environments, but more recently, an ever-increasing number of robotic systems are beginning to implement additional manipulation devices to allow them to also undertake physical manipulation tasks in the field [22]. However, if the robot becomes more complex, the teleoperation system must also improve and provide the teleoperator with the capabilities to control the robot effectively. With the increasing number of hybrid robots, namely robots consisting of multiple systems that would typically

This work was supported by the Engineering and Physical Sciences Research Council [grant numbers EP/R513258/1-2441459, EP/V026801/2], the Advanced Machinery and Productivity Institute [Innovate UK project number 84646] and the China Scholarship Council [grant number (2020)06120186].

S. Pacheco-Gutierrez et al. (Eds.): TAROS 2022, LNAI 13546, pp. 50–62, 2022.
https://doi.org/10.1007/978-3-031-15908-4_5

require their own controller [14], current teleoperation control systems lack the capability to control both aspects of these robots simultaneously, allowing for a wider range of motions and intuitive and natural control.

Traditionally, joystick control has been the most common method of high-level command generation for robots, however as presented in [2], it is seen that via this method, only one system could be controlled at once. Joysticks have been used to successfully teleoperate hybrid robotic systems, such as in that presented by [4] where an aerial manipulator was teleoperated through the use of a whole body controller and a joystick. However, the teleoperation is limited by the joystick having only 2 degrees of freedom (DoF) and consequently the trajectory generated by the joystick is only within a 2-dimensional plane.

Implementing a generic whole-body controller (WBC) [21] in these systems, would enable the teleoperator to utilise the full redundancy of the robot while only providing one input reference trajectory. This is achieved in [7] through the development of a WBC-teleoperation framework, however, this framework neither realises locomotion tasks nor offers the ability to control multiple robots. Furthermore, this also requires a teleoperation controller to generate feasible input trajectories. Alternative methods of teleoperation have thus been developed, such as the use of haptic controllers alongside whole body control [20] as well as semi-autonomous systems [3]. Many of these haptic controllers employ bilateral control through the use of a compliant master device, but the range of movement is limited to the hardware workspace, which may interfere in some teleoperative tasks [6]. Target-object-orientated methods such as that presented by [9] illustrate the use of physical devices to assist in teleoperation. However, when compared to a wearable motion capture suit, the hardware used in this study does not allow for manipulation of compliant objects nor does it enable accurate manipulation of objects of a different geometry than a cuboid.

Others utilised motion as a method of high-level command generation for hybrid manipulator systems, for example, [17] presents a method using body tilt to generate acceleration and velocity commands for a bipedal wheeled robot. The manipulator in this case is controlled via an arm-mounted motion capture linkage [16]. However, the hardware limits the freedom of the teleoperator in this case.

In contrast, motion capture suits are being used at an increasing rate due to being a lightweight and cost-effective method to extract human joint data. In addition, many motion capture suits are wireless, meaning that the teleoperator is not constrained to the hardware space. Body tilt is also used by [18], in a scenario where a teleoperator uses a motion capture suit to detect the pitch of the human, this method however lacks the force feedback implemented by [19]. This method employs a mode switching trigger used to determine whether commands are sent to the base or the manipulator [18]. This issue of being unable to control both base and manipulator simultaneously is answered through the use of a whole body controller to couple the two systems, however, this method lacks control in specific DoFs [19]. As many motion capture applications in robot teleoperation focus on using the operator's upper-body motion, there are limited studies that

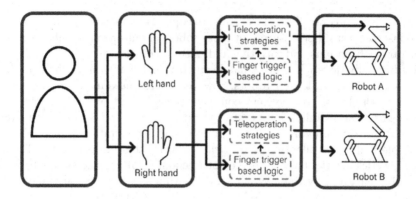

Fig. 1. Overview of the proposed teleoperation framework.

utilise the human operator's lower-body motion. Although one of which is [10] which is also an example of precise mapping from the user's movement to the robot's pose.

To improve the dynamic performance of humanoid robots, Ishiguro et al. introduced a real-time dynamic control method to both the upper and lower body of a humanoid robot [8]. The methods could implement dynamic whole-body movements, including kicking and hitting a ball. However, it still has difficulties in applying to complex movements, for example, running and rough terrain locomotion. [5] presented a method using whole-body control as well as joint mapping to control a humanoid robot. This method would however only work with robots that are kinematically similar to a human, and could not be applied to any robot that is not a biped. Motion capture suits have been paired with joystick controllers to achieve both low-level joint mapping and high-level motion commands, however, the joint mapping is limited to a robot of humanoid structure [13]. Furthermore, although the joystick suits this method as using motion tracking to generate high-level commands would interfere with the joint mapping [13]. The combination of joystick and motion capture suit works particularly well when the joystick is used to control a 2-DoF system, such as a quadruped, and the motion capture suit is used for higher-DoF systems such as robotic arms [15]. Motion capture suits have also been used in motion imitation control, where a wheeled manipulator would mimic the teleoperator's movements [1]. However, this work only utilises the use of one of the teleoperator's arms and only works for robots that have a similar kinematic structure to a human, limiting the potential for a highly functional control framework.

In this paper, we propose a teleoperation control framework, based upon our previous work [21], that uses a wireless inertia-based motion capture suit to generate high-level commands for simultaneous control of two legged manipulators (Fig. 1). With the use of finger-detection, gesture controls are implemented to allow the teleoperator to enable and disable certain axis of movement for ease of control and switch between control of the robot's manipulator and quadrupedal base seamlessly.

The paper is structured as follows: Section 2 contains an overview of the control system as well as its formulation. Section 3 covers the experiment design, Sect. 4 analyses the results obtained from the experiment, and Sect. 5 discusses the conclusions and future work.

2   Control Framework Overview

In the control framework, coordinate frames are obtained from the inertia-based motion capture suit, Perception Neuron. In our previous work, we showcased a framework using the entirety of the motion capture suit, however, due to this framework only making use of the upper body, the lower half of the motion capture suit is not used and therefore not necessary for the teleoperator to wear [12]. This decision comes from multiple factors, from the ability to prepare to teleoperate faster as there is less preparation and to focus more on where humans are more naturally dexterous, their hands and arms rather than their legs.

Thus, in the control framework, a single hand is used to control several parts of a single robot system, in this example, the framework is used to control a quadruped platform and a robotic arm. As this is implemented on both hands, the total number of systems that are able to be controlled increases as well as enabling the possibility of controlling two separate systems simultaneously. In order to select which system to control, finger triggers are utilised allowing for the teleoperator to close and open specific fingers to send commands to a selected system.

Using the fingers as triggers is made possible with the motion capture suit being able to output coordinate frames of each of the fingers. This allows for the linking of each finger to a function, however, to make it easier for the teleoperator, a trigger is activated when either both the index and middle finger or the ring and pinky finger are closed. Trajectories are generated by the framework by first setting a reference point in the world frame by closing a hand. Cartesian positions and Euler angles of each hand are calculated, of which are then translated into high-level commands for the end effector of the robot arm or base of the platform.

2.1   Finger-Based Trigger System

Firstly, when both hands are open, no commands are sent to the robots and the teleoperator can move freely without controlling either robot. To begin controlling the robot, the teleoperator must close either hand, the trigger used to detect this is the closure of the ring and pinky finger. As the goal is to control multiple robots with a distinct platform and manipulator, each hand controls a different robot, in this scenario the left-hand controls the A1 system and the right controls the Aliengo system.

The thumb is used to toggle control between either the quadruped base or the robotic arm. Another trigger, the index and middle finger, is used to determine whether the teleoperator controls linear movement in the Cartesian x or y axis or rotational movement in the yaw axis for the quadruped platform if used when the thumb trigger is not active. If the thumb trigger is active, this trigger then determines the closure state of the end-effector gripper. These triggers and their respective functions are outlined in Fig. 2.

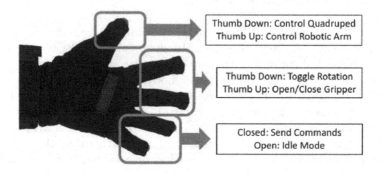

Fig. 2. Triggers and their functions assigned to each group of fingers, the triggers on the respective fingers are the same for both hands.

2.2   Teleoperation Algorithm

Whilst the Cartesian position of the hand is taken with respect to the world frame, the orientation cannot as it would also incorporate aspects of the human body tilt into the output. Therefore, to avoid this, the relative orientation of the hand is instead taken with respect to the forearm link origin, located at the elbow.

To generate trajectories, an origin point in the world frame is created when the hand is closed and the relative position of the hand in the world frame to this origin point is used to determine the direction and magnitude of motion of the respective device. This is formulated as:

$$\boldsymbol{x}^t_{sd} = \boldsymbol{x}^0_{sd} + \boldsymbol{\mu}(\boldsymbol{x}^t_m - \boldsymbol{x}^0_m), \tag{1}$$

where $\boldsymbol{x}$ refers to the vector $\boldsymbol{x} = [x, y, z, \theta_{\text{roll}}, \theta_{\text{pitch}}, \theta_{\text{yaw}}]$ of which represents displacements in the Cartesian and rotations in the Euler axes respectively. Subscripts "m" refers to the master device, "s" refers to the slave device, and "d" to the desired value. Superscript "0" refers to the initial time when the hand is closed. μ are the gains used to scale motion between the operator and robot.

Due to the motion capture suit not being constrained to a set location, the human teleoperator is free to rotate and move around their environment. However, if the relative position of the hand to the world frame is not corrected for the yaw of the teleoperator in the world frame, then the output trajectories are orientated towards the location where the motion capture suit was first initialised. Therefore, the yaw from the central backlink is used to determine the direction the operator is facing and offset the yaw generated from turning. This is formulated as

$$h_{\text{local}} = R_{\text{yaw}}^{-1} \cdot h, \tag{2}$$

where $h \in \mathbb{R}^{3 \times 1}$ represents the position vector of the hand link with respect to the world frame. h_{local} refers to the position vector where the yaw of the operator's body has been offset. $R_{\text{yaw}} \in \mathbb{R}^{3 \times 3}$ is a rotation matrix constructed using the yaw orientation of the central spine line.

Multiple triggers are used in the framework through the action of opening and closing the thumb and fingers. To detect finger closure, the framework checks the distances between the end of each finger to the link in the centre of the hand. Once each distance is below a tuned threshold, the finger is considered closed. This is formulated as

$$r_{\text{finger}} \geq s_{\text{finger threshold}}, \tag{3}$$

where $r \in \mathbb{R}^{4 \times 1}$ represents the distance of each finger to the central hand link and $s \in \mathbb{R}^{4 \times 1}$ represents the threshold distance values for each finger set to detect the closure of each finger. Subscripts "f" and "h" refer to the finger end link and hand link respectively. Where the finger triggers could be detected through gauging the distance between two points, the thumb however is different as there as many locations that could be considered a closed thumb, however, a "thumbs up" position is discreet with little ambiguity, therefore the trigger is based around whether the thumb is in this position. The formulation for this is

$$w_{\text{thumb}} \geq s_{\text{thumb threshold}}, \tag{4}$$

where $w \in \mathbb{R}^{3 \times 1}$ represents the Euler angles in the of the end link of the thumb with respect to the base link of the thumb and $b \in \mathbb{R}^{3 \times 1}$ represents the threshold values in each rotational axis set to detect the thumb closure.

2.3   Hardware Implementation

The quadrupeds used are the Unitree Aliengo and A1, each with a mounted robotic arm on top. They each carry a ViperX 300 5-DoF robotic arm and a PhantomX Pincher 4-DoF robotic arm respectively. Each robotic arm is mounted on the top side of the trunk of the quadruped. Robot Operating System (ROS) is used to connect the two robots over a 5 GHz wireless network to a Ubuntu computer, which acts as the ROS master. The motion capture suit data is retrieved from the suit via the Perceptron Neuron dedicated software on a Windows computer, which is then sent to the Ubuntu computer via ROS serial. This data is then converted into standard ROS TF format, which is then input into the teleoperation algorithm that allows for the high-level commands for either robot to be computed. A flag is used in the command message to differentiate which command goes to which robot. A complete system diagram is presented in Fig. 3.

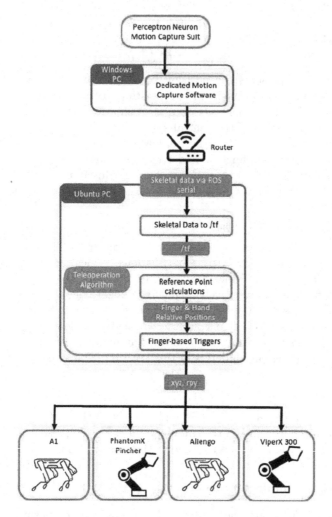

Fig. 3. A complete system diagram of the teleoperation framework, illustrating the flow of information from the motion capture suit to the robots.

3   Experiment Design

To demonstrate the capabilities of the control framework, a real-life experiment was conducted through the use of two quadrupedal manipulators. In the experiment, the operator must control both robots to perform the task of removing the cap of a spray can. The cap removal task is split into several steps; firstly, the two robots are placed approximately 1.5 m on either side of the water bottle, which is located in the centre of the testing area. Secondly, the smaller robot with the lower DoF robotic arm, the A1 system, will travel forward, rotate as needed and pick up the spray can from a flat surface and then move into an open area. Next, the Aliengo system will approach the A1 system and then both robots will be orientated to allow the Aliengo's robotic arm to proceed in removing the cap of the spray can, at which point the experiment ends[1].

In the experiment, the PhantomX Pincher's end-effector is redesigned to be more effective at grasping cylindrical objects. The experiment is performed with the operator in line of sight of the robot however in the future, the possibilities of using two robots to act as a 3rd person view for teleoperation will be investigated.

4   Experiment Results

In the experiment, the operator first closes their left hand to send linear velocities to the A1 quadruped in order to move it towards the spray can's location, which is achieved by having the operator move their left hand forward when in this state. Then, the index and middle finger of the operator is opened to initiate the yaw control state of the A1, due to this being a different trigger, the reference is generated again from the moment the index and middle fingers are opened. In this state, rolling the left hand will result in a corresponding yaw velocity in the A1. The operator then opens their left hand to reset the reference point and then closes their left hand excluding the thumb to activate arm control. The arm is then manoeuvred using the left hand to grasp the spray can with the teleoperator opening their index and middle finger to toggle the gripper closure state, picking up the spray can.

Following this stage, the operator initiates yaw control of the A1 again and rotates it so that it is facing the Aliengo. The operator then closes their index and middle fingers in order to move the A1 sideways until within range of the ViperX 300 robotic arm that is mounted on the Aliengo. The operator now keeps their left-hand open to prevent any commands from being sent to the A1 system, and the right-hand excluding the thumb closes to control the ViperX 300. First, the right hand is moved in the y-axis to send a yaw position to the robot arm before guiding the end-effector around the cap of the spray can and opening the right hand's index and middle finger to close the end-effector. The operator then guides the robot arm to lift the cap away and opens their right hand before closing it again, thumb included, to generate a sideways velocity so the Aliengo moves out of the path of the A1. After this is complete, the right hand opens to prevent commands from being sent to the Aliengo system and the left-hand closes to move the A1 forward past the Aliengo, concluding the experiment.

A time-lapse of the experiment is illustrated in Fig. 4. Figures 5, 6, 7, 8, 9 and 10, representing respectively (b), (c), (d), (f), (i) and (l) in Fig. 4, illustrate the relationship between the references generated by the teleoperation framework and the finger-based trigger system with the velocity and position feedback of the quadrupeds and robotic arms. The references consist of the velocity and position commands generated by the teleoperation framework post-gain. The feedback values are obtained from the IMU of the quadruped and the joint positions of the robotic arm. As can be seen in Figs. 5, 6, 7, 8, 9 and 10, the feedback values

---

[1] The experiment video can be found at https://youtu.be/TApk6XrgYhY.

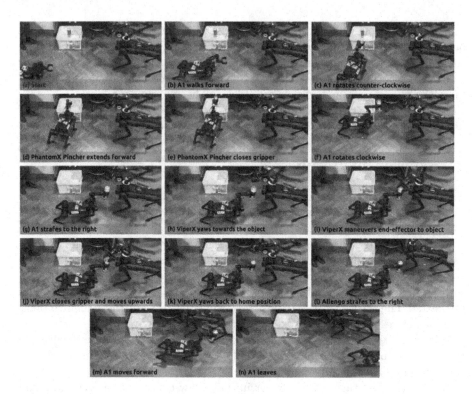

Fig. 4. Time-lapse showing each stage of the experiment. The experiment is performed in the line of sight of the teleoperator.

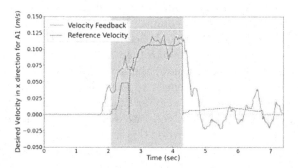

Fig. 5. Chart illustrating the forward velocity feedback of the A1 quadruped in reaction to the provided reference in the x-axis from the teleoperation framework. The shaded area represents when the teleoperation trigger for linear velocity control of the A1 is active.

from the quadruped and robotic arms do not respond to the change in reference values unless the teleoperation trigger, represented by the shaded area, is active. Upon the release of the teleoperation trigger, represented by non-shaded areas,

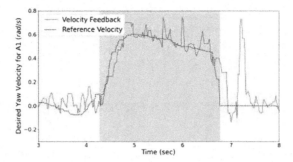

Fig. 6. Chart illustrating the yaw velocity feedback of the A1 quadruped in reaction to the provided reference in the roll-axis from the teleoperation framework. The shaded area represents when the teleoperation trigger for rotational control of the A1 quadruped is active.

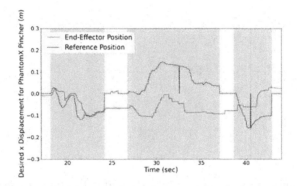

Fig. 7. Chart illustrating the end-effector location of the PhantomX Pincher in reaction to the provided reference in the x-axis from the teleoperation framework. The shaded area represents when the teleoperation trigger for controlling the robotic arm on the left hand is active.

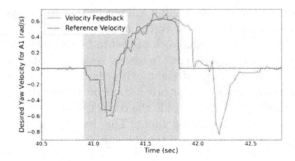

Fig. 8. Chart illustrating the yaw velocity feedback of the A1 quadruped in reaction to the provided reference in the roll-axis from the teleoperation framework. The shaded area represents when the teleoperation trigger for rotational control of the A1 quadruped is active.

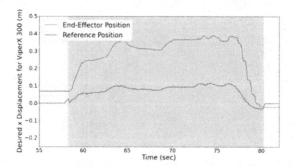

Fig. 9. Chart illustrating the end-effector location of the ViperX 300 robotic arm in reaction to the provided reference in the x-axis from the teleoperation framework. The shaded area represents when the teleoperation trigger for controlling the robotic arm on the right hand is active.

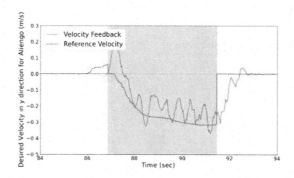

Fig. 10. Chart illustrating the sideways velocity feedback of the Aliengo quadruped in reaction to the provided reference in the y-axis from the teleoperation framework. The shaded area represents when the teleoperation trigger for linear velocity control of the Aliengo is active.

no further changes in the reference value will not be sent to the system until the respective teleoperation trigger is activated again.

Overall, the teleoperation framework proved to be successful as it completed the task outlined in the experiment. However, some difficulty came from the teleoperation being in the line of sight, with the velocity references for the quadrupeds being respective to the orientation of the quadruped itself. This then required the teleoperator to decide the correct direction of travel based on the yaw rotation of the commanded robot. This issue could be tackled in the future by adding a camera to each of the robots.

5   Conclusions

In this study, a teleoperation framework, that is highly versatile yet trivial to operate, has been developed. Through utilising both hands of the motion capture suit and a range of triggers bound to the fingers of the suit's gloves, two robots have been simultaneously controlled to complete a complex cooperative task, where two robots work together to remove a cap from a spray can. It is also postulated that this framework could be applied to control a pair of a wide range of different robots, from wheeled manipulators to humanoids, due to its independence from the kinematic structure of the robots it is controlling. Future work to further develop this framework will be to integrate a whole-body controller within it and add a mobile third-person camera, with gaze control [11], to allow for reliable visual feedback during teleoperation scenarios. In addition, to further enable the manipulation and control capabilities, sensors allowing the localisation of the two robots could be implemented.

References

1. Arduengo, M., Arduengo, A., Colome, A., Lobo-Prat, J., Torras, C.: Human to robot whole-body motion transfer. In: IEEE-RAS International Conference on Humanoid Robots, pp. 299–305 (07 2021). https://doi.org/10.1109/HUMANOIDS47582.2021.9555769

2. Bellicoso, C.D., et al.: Alma - articulated locomotion and manipulation for a torque-controllable robot. In: International Conference on Robotics and Automation, pp. 8477–8483 (2019). https://doi.org/10.1109/ICRA.2019.8794273

3. Brosque, C., Herrero, E., Chen, Y., Joshi, R., Khatib, O., Fischer, M.: Collaborative welding and joint sealing robots with haptic feedback. In: International Symposium on Automation and Robotics in Construction, vol. 38, pp. 1–8 (2021). https://doi.org/10.22260/ISARC2021/0003

4. Coelho, A., et al.: Whole-body teleoperation and shared control of redundant robots with applications to aerial manipulation. J. Intell. Robot. Syst. **102**(1), 1–22 (2021). https://doi.org/10.1007/s10846-021-01365-7

5. Dalin, E., Bergonzani, I., Anne, T., Ivaldi, S., Mouret, J.B.: Whole-body teleoperation of the Talos humanoid robot: preliminary results. In: ICRA Workshop on Teleoperation of Dynamic Legged Robots in Real Scenarios. Xi'an, China (2021). https://hal.inria.fr/hal-03245005

6. Farkhatdinov, I., Ryu, J.H.: Hybrid position-position and position-speed command strategy for the bilateral teleoperation of a mobile robot. In: International Conference on Control, Automation and Systems, pp. 2442–2447 (2007). https://doi.org/10.1109/ICCAS.2007.4406773

7. Humphreys, J., Peers, C., Wan, Y., Richardson, R., Zhou, C.: Teleoperation of a legged manipulator for item disposal. In: UK Robotics and Autonomous Systems Conference (2022)

8. Ishiguro, Y., et al.: High speed whole body dynamic motion experiment with real time master-slave humanoid robot system. In: IEEE International Conference on Robotics and Automation, pp. 5835–5841 (2018). https://doi.org/10.1109/ICRA.2018.8461207

9. Kitagawa, S., Hasegawa, S., Yamaguchi, N., Okada, K., Inaba, M.: Miniature tangible cube: concept and design of target-object-oriented user interface for dual-arm telemanipulation. IEEE Robot. Autom. Lett. **6**(4), 6977–6984 (2021). https://doi.org/10.1109/LRA.2021.3096475

10. Koenemann, J., Burget, F., Bennewitz, M.: Real-time imitation of human whole-body motions by humanoids. In: IEEE International Conference on Robotics and Automation, pp. 2806–2812 (2014). https://doi.org/10.1109/ICRA.2014.6907261
11. Peers, C., Kanoulas, D., Kaddouh, B., Richardson, R., Zhou, C.: Dynamic camera usage in mobile teleoperation system for buzz wire task. In: UK Robotics and Autonomous Systems Conference (2022)
12. Peers, C., Motawei, M., Richardson, R., Zhou, C.: Development of a teleoperative quadrupedal manipulator. In: UK Robotics and Autonomous Systems Conference, pp. 17–18. Hatfield, UK (June 2 2021). https://doi.org/10.31256/Hy7Sf7G
13. Penco, L., Scianca, N., Modugno, V., Lanari, L., Oriolo, G., Ivaldi, S.: A multimode teleoperation framework for humanoid loco-manipulation: an application for the icub robot. IEEE Robot. Autom. Mag. **26**(4), 73–82 (2019). https://doi.org/10.1109/MRA.2019.2941245
14. Ur Rehman, B., Focchi, M., Lee, J., Dallali, H., Caldwell, D., Semini, C.: Towards a multi-legged mobile manipulator. In: 2016 IEEE International Conference on Robotics and Automation (ICRA), pp. 3618–3624 (05 2016). https://doi.org/10.1109/ICRA.2016.7487545
15. Wan, Y., Sun, J., Peers, C., Humphreys, J., Kanoulas, D., Zhou, C.: Performance and usability evaluation scheme for mobile manipulator teleoperation (2022)
16. Wang, S., Murphy, K., Kenney, D., Ramos, J.: A comparison between joint space and task space mappings for dynamic teleoperation of an anthropomorphic robotic arm in reaction tests (2020)
17. Wang, S., Ramos, J.: Dynamic locomotion teleoperation of a wheeled humanoid robot reduced model with a whole-body human-machine interface (2021)
18. Wu, Y., Balatti, P., Lorenzini, M., Zhao, F., Kim, W., Ajoudani, A.: A teleoperation interface for loco-manipulation control of mobile collaborative robotic assistant. IEEE Robot. Autom. Lett. **4**(4), 3593–3600 (2019). https://doi.org/10.1109/LRA.2019.2928757
19. Wu, Y., Lamon, E., Zhao, F., Kim, W., Ajoudani, A.: Unified approach for hybrid motion control of moca based on weighted whole-body cartesian impedance formulation. IEEE Robotics and Automation Letters **6**(2), 3505–3512 (2021). https://doi.org/10.1109/LRA.2021.3062316
20. Xin, G., Smith, J., Rytz, D., Wolfslag, W., Lin, H.C., Mistry, M.: Bounded haptic teleoperation of a quadruped robot's foot posture for sensing and manipulation. In: IEEE International Conference on Robotics and Automation, pp. 1431–1437 (2020). https://doi.org/10.1109/ICRA40945.2020.9197501
21. Zhou, C., Fang, C., Wang, X., Li, Z., Tsagarakis, N.: A generic optimization-based framework for reactive collision avoidance in bipedal locomotion. In: IEEE International Conference on Automation Science and Engineering, pp. 1026–1033 (2016). https://doi.org/10.1109/COASE.2016.7743516
22. Zimmermann, S., Poranne, R., Coros, S.: Go fetch! - dynamic grasps using Boston dynamics spot with external robotic arm. In: IEEE International Conference on Robotics and Automation, pp. 4488–4494 (2021)

Teleoperating a Legged Manipulator Through Whole-Body Control

Joseph Humphreys[1], Christopher Peers[1], Jun Li[1,2], Yuhui Wan[1], Jingcheng Sun[1], Robert Richardson[1], and Chengxu Zhou[1(✉)]

[1] School of Mechanical Engineering, University of Leeds, Leeds, UK
`c.x.zhou@leeds.ac.uk`
[2] State Key Laboratory of Robotics and System, Harbin Institute of Technology, Harbin, China

Abstract. In this work, we present a highly functional teleoperation system, that integrates a full-body inertia-based motion capture suit and three intuitive teleoperation strategies with a Whole-Body Control (WBC) framework, for quadrupedal legged manipulators. This enables the realisation of commands from the teleoperator that would otherwise not be possible, as the framework is able to utilise DoF redundancy to meet several objectives simultaneously, such as locking the gripper frame in position while the trunk completes a task. This is achieved through the WBC framework featuring a defined optimisation problem that solves a range of Cartesian and joint space tasks, while subject to a set of constraints (e.g. halt constraints). These tasks and constraints are highly modular and can be configured dynamically, allowing the teleoperator to switch between teleoperation strategies seamlessly. The overall system has been tested and validated through a physics-based simulation and a hardware test, demonstrating all functionality of the system, which in turn has been used to evaluate its effectiveness.

Keywords: Teleoperation · Legged robots · Whole-body control

1 Introduction

Within many areas of industry, people put their lives at risk while working in hazardous environments such as nuclear waste decommission, disaster response and explosive ordinance disposal. Environments such as these have given rise to one of the driving factors behind recent innovation within the field of robotics; replacing humans with robots in these environments, mitigating risk to human lives. The quadrupedal legged manipulator shows great potential for this application due to its proficiency in traversing over rough terrain and its ability to interact

This work was supported by the Engineering and Physical Sciences Research Council [grant numbers EP/R513258/1-2441459, EP/V026801/2], the Advanced Machinery and Productivity Institute [Innovate UK project number 84646] and the China Scholarship Council [grant number (2020)06120186].

S. Pacheco-Gutierrez et al. (Eds.): TAROS 2022, LNAI 13546, pp. 63–77, 2022.
https://doi.org/10.1007/978-3-031-15908-4_6

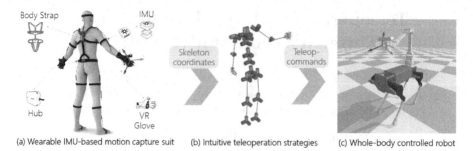

(a) Wearable IMU-based motion capture suit   (b) Intuitive teleoperation strategies   (c) Whole-body controlled robot

Fig. 1. System overview of the teleoperated legged manipulator.

with its environment. However, these robots are highly redundant systems and therefore require an effective control framework to utilise this redundancy. The favoured method within research of maximising the efficiency of these robots is whole-body control (WBC) through optimisation as this method is able to leverage this high redundancy to achieve multiple tasks simultaneously, with all elements of the robot working cooperatively.

In the literature, WBC frameworks are normally formulated as either an inverse dynamics (ID) [6,13,18] or an inverse kinematics (IK) [2,7,19] based optimisation problem. An ID-based WBC framework, utilising a weighted QP problem, is developed in [18] and paired with model predictive control (MPC) for humanoid locomotion. This WBC-MPC pairing is also utilised in [13] to enable quadrupedal legged manipulator to execute a range of gaits and manipulation tasks by optimising for joint torques. To improve control over how tasks are realised by these WBCs for whole-body motion tracking, [6] produced an advanced task prioritisation method. These types of frameworks offer impressive results in tackling real-world obstacles, such as spring-loaded doors [9]. While joint level torque control is not possible, IK-based WBC frameworks are preferable for position-controlled robots. An IK-based WBC is developed in [2] which ensures the stability of wheeled quadruped robots, although it has not been tested while completing a gait. To enhance the robustness of IK-based WBCs, [7] introduces specialised adaptability tasks, but its proficiency is dependent on wheeled locomotion. In the effort of improving the safety of humanoid robots, a generic WBC framework is designed in [19] for collision avoidance, however, it has yet to be expanded for use in robots with five limbs.

Moreover, jobs in hazardous environments are typically too complex for robots to autonomously perform. Therefore, robust and effective teleoperation controllers have been developed for real-life scenarios. Motion capture suits have been seen previously to control robots, such as in [5], but not in such an application where direct joint mapping is not optimal. IMU-based motion capture devices have been used to control a 7 Degree-of-Freedom (DoF) robotic arm [17]. The use of foot position and stance estimation tracking of the teleoperator allows a bipedal robot to mimic walking action [8], though walking delays arose due to imperfect motion recognition.

It is natural to combine WBC and teleoperation strategies together to give people more control authority over the robot, as complex tasks in hazardous environments require redundant whole-body motions and prompt human interventions. An aerial manipulator was controlled using a WBC teleoperation framework designed for use in scenarios with input delay and connection issues [3], however, using a joystick to align the robot with an object makes teleoperation more difficult. A wheeled manipulator was teleoperated through the use of a 3D motion tracking device and monitoring the teleoperator's muscle activity [15]. The robot is however limited to wheeled locomotion, decreasing the overall mobility of the system. Two control methods are shown utilising both joysticks and a wearable motion capture suit for the low- and high-level control of a bipedal robot [12], however, this method can only be used for robots that are kinematically similar to humans. A teleoperation system is described through the use of a haptic feedback device to control the arms of a bipedal robot [1]. The system, however, does not allow the robot to locomote with the use of gaits. The whole-body motion capture suit with an IK retargeting method is shown in [5] to control multiple humanoid robots, but the centre of mass (CoM) trajectories cannot be directly controlled through this method, limiting its functionality. A joystick-controlled quadrupedal robot is shown to use WBC to perform basic manipulation and depth sensing tasks [16]. Xsens body sensors were used in the WBC of a simulated bipedal robot with direct kinematic mapping between the teleoperator and robot [4], however, strategies that could improve teleoperation such as fixing a robot's frame were not shown.

Therefore, the contributions presented in this paper are twofold. The first is a set of intuitive teleoperation strategies that enable the inertia-based motion capture suit to control different frames of the quadrupedal legged manipulator. The second is the further development of our WBC previously developed in [19] to tailor it specifically for teleoperation applications through designing specific constraints to aid the teleoperator, namely halt and CoM constraints. This in turn enables the teleoperator to fully utilise robot redundancy for task completion, which was not possible in our previous framework [11].

This paper is organised as follows. Section 2 describes the hardware used for the robot platform and the teleoperation control device. Section 3 outlines the WBC framework, optimisation tasks and constraints. In Sect. 4, three teleoperation strategies using the motion capture suit are described. Section 5 details the simulation tests performed using the WBC framework with the proposed teleoperation strategies, while Sect. 6 covers these tests again but carried out using real-life hardware. In Sect. 7, the research is summarised and discussed.

2   System Description

This system consists of the Laikago quadrupedal robot, the ViperX 300 robotic arm and, for teleoperation, the Noitom Perception Neuron motion capture suit. Laikago is a lightweight quadrupedal robot capable of holding a payload of 5 kg. Mounted on the top of the Laikago is the 5 DoF ViperX 300 robotic arm. The arm had previously been redesigned with carbon fibre rods in place of the aluminium box section [11], to alleviate additional mass from the Laikago. Controlling this system is the inertia-based wearable motion capture suit, consisting of 16 IMU devices on each link of the human body. The suit collects skeleton data, allowing for control algorithms to make use of human body motion. This system has also been used over a more basic controller, such as a gamepad with joysticks, as they are better suited for end-effector control tasks, as demonstrated in [14]. Connecting these devices together involves the use of a Windows computer for the motion capture suit, a Ubuntu computer for the robot and a 5 GHz Wi-Fi router to communicate between them. The entire system is illustrated in Fig. 1.

3   Whole-Body Control Framework

3.1   Formulation of Optimisation Problem

To set up the WBC optimisation problem, a Quadratic Programming (QP) problem is formulated using the IK cost function to optimise for joint velocities $\dot{\boldsymbol{\theta}}$, while subject to a range of constraints. The QP problem takes the form of

$$\min_{\dot{\theta}} \quad \frac{1}{2}\dot{\boldsymbol{\theta}}^T \boldsymbol{A}^T \boldsymbol{A}\dot{\boldsymbol{\theta}} - \boldsymbol{b}^T \boldsymbol{A}\dot{\boldsymbol{\theta}} \tag{1}$$

$$\text{s.t.} \quad \boldsymbol{C}_{\text{lb}} \leq \boldsymbol{J}_{CoM}\dot{\boldsymbol{\theta}} \leq \boldsymbol{C}_{\text{ub}} , \tag{2}$$

$$\boldsymbol{J}_{\text{halt}}\dot{\boldsymbol{\theta}} = 0 , \tag{3}$$

$$\dot{\boldsymbol{\theta}}_{\text{lb}} \geq \dot{\boldsymbol{\theta}} \geq \dot{\boldsymbol{\theta}}_{\text{ub}} , \tag{4}$$

$$\boldsymbol{\theta}_{\text{lb}} \geq \boldsymbol{\theta} \geq \boldsymbol{\theta}_{\text{ub}} , \tag{5}$$

in which the problem is subject to CoM (2), halt (3), joint velocity (4) and joint position (5) constraints, who's specifics are covered in later sections.

To implement the Cartesian and joint tasks of the WBC, $\boldsymbol{A}$ and $\boldsymbol{b}$ of (1) are formed as

$$\boldsymbol{A} = \begin{bmatrix} \alpha_{\text{Cart}}\boldsymbol{A}_{\text{Cart}} \\ \alpha_{\text{Jnt}}\boldsymbol{A}_{\text{Jnt}} \end{bmatrix} \in \mathbb{R}^{(6m+n)\times d}, \boldsymbol{b} = \begin{bmatrix} \alpha_{\text{Cart}}\boldsymbol{b}_{\text{Cart}} \\ \alpha_{\text{Jnt}}\boldsymbol{b}_{\text{Jnt}} \end{bmatrix} \in \mathbb{R}^{6m+n} , \tag{6}$$

so that the QP problem can solve for tasks simultaneously. $n = 12 + 5$ is the number of joints of the legged manipulator, $d = 23$ is the number of DoF of the legged manipulator, $m = 5 + 1$ is the number of Cartesian tasks, and α_{Cart} and α_{Jnt} are the tasks weights used to prioritise critical tasks over others based on the application. This task weighting method has been used as opposed to a hierarchical method as it has a lower computational cost due to only one QP problem being solved per time step compared to solving several sequential problems, resulting in a computational time for each QP solve being within 1 ms. The details of the tasks stacked in (6) are outlined in the following sections.

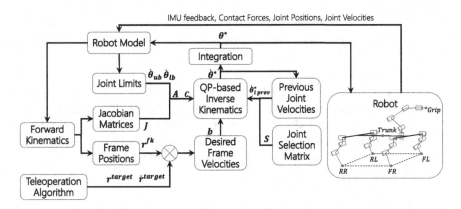

Fig. 2. Block diagram of the WBC framework, built around the QP problem.

Cartesian Tasks. Cartesian tasks are used to reduce the residual between a reference Cartesian trajectory and the current Cartesian configuration of a frame of the robot. To achieve a high level of utility, this task will be applied to all end-effector frames and the trunk frame, in accordance with Fig. 2, making a wide variety of movements and tasks to be feasible. This task is realised by applying the Jacobian matrix of the frame, which maps Cartesian velocity to joint velocities, causing it to experience a velocity that moves it through the trajectory. This task is implemented within $\boldsymbol{A}$ and $\boldsymbol{b}$ as

$$\boldsymbol{A}_{\text{Cart}} = \boldsymbol{W}\boldsymbol{J} \in \mathbb{R}^{6m \times d}, \quad \boldsymbol{b}_{\text{Cart}} = [\dot{\boldsymbol{r}}_1^T \cdots \dot{\boldsymbol{r}}_m^T] \in \mathbb{R}^{6m}, \tag{7}$$

where $\boldsymbol{J} = [\boldsymbol{J}_1^T \cdots \boldsymbol{J}_m^T]^T$, $\boldsymbol{J}_i \in \mathbb{R}^{6 \times n}$ is the combined Jacobian matrix of all controlled frames, $\boldsymbol{W} \in \mathbb{R}^{6m \times 6m}$ is a diagonal weight matrix used to scale the degree to which the frame is allowed to deviate from the reference trajectory; a higher weight increases strictness. The target Cartesian task frame velocity

$$\dot{\boldsymbol{r}}_i = \dot{\boldsymbol{r}}_i^{\text{target}} + \boldsymbol{K}_{\text{Cart}}(\boldsymbol{r}_i^{\text{target}} - \boldsymbol{r}_i^{\text{fk}}) \tag{8}$$

describes the required target velocity for a frame to execute a reference trajectory using the velocity control law presented in [10], where $\boldsymbol{r}_i^{\text{fk}} \in \mathbb{R}^6$ is the current frame configuration calculated through forward kinematics, $\boldsymbol{r}_i^{\text{target}} \in \mathbb{R}^6$ is the target frame configuration, $\dot{\boldsymbol{r}}_i^{\text{target}} \in \mathbb{R}^6$ is the target frame velocity, and $\boldsymbol{K}_{\text{Cart}}$ is the task gain. It should be noted that all configuration orientations are described in Euler angles.

Joint Tasks. To enforce specific characteristics on each joint of the robot, joint tasks are added to the QP problem. In this framework, the joint damping task is added for all joints of the robot to reduce high-frequency oscillations, caused by the overshoot of the Cartesian tasks, to improve stability. Aligning with (6), these joint tasks take the following form,

$$\boldsymbol{A}_{\text{Jnt}} = \boldsymbol{S}, \quad \boldsymbol{b}_{\text{Jnt}} = \dot{\boldsymbol{\theta}}_{i\,\text{prev}}^*, \tag{9}$$

$S \in \mathbb{R}^{n \times n}$ and $\dot{\boldsymbol{\theta}}^*_{i\,\text{prev}} \in \mathbb{R}^n$ are the damping joint task weight, selection matrix, and optimised joint velocities for the last time step respectively. Further joint tasks could be used within (9), see [19] for details of these tasks.

Constraints. Constraints are used within the QP problem to refine the solution space. To improve the stability of the robot, the CoM stability constraint (2) utilises the CoM Jacobian $\boldsymbol{J}_{\text{CoM}}$ to force the CoM to lie within the support polygon, based on the position of the feet in contact with the ground. Within (2), the lower and upper bounds of the inequality constraint are

$$\boldsymbol{C}_{\text{lb}} = \frac{(\boldsymbol{r}_{\text{lb}} - \boldsymbol{r}^{\text{fk}}_{\text{CoM}})}{\delta t} \,, \quad \boldsymbol{C}_{\text{ub}} = \frac{(\boldsymbol{r}_{\text{ub}} - \boldsymbol{r}^{\text{fk}}_{\text{CoM}})}{\delta t} \,, \tag{10}$$

where $\boldsymbol{r}_{\text{lb}}$ and $\boldsymbol{r}_{\text{ub}}$ are the lower and upper bounds of the support polygon respectively, $\boldsymbol{r}^{\text{fk}}_{\text{CoM}}$ is the current position of the CoM, $\boldsymbol{J}_{\text{CoM}}$ is the CoM Jacobian, and δt is the time step.

The halt equality constraint (3) has also been applied to the QP problem, in which $\boldsymbol{J}_{\text{halt}} = [\boldsymbol{J}^T_1 \cdots \boldsymbol{J}^T_c]^T$, where $\boldsymbol{J}_i \in \mathbb{R}^{6 \times n}$ is the Jacobian of the frame to be constrained, and c is the number of these constraints. Adding this constraint to a frame ensures it has zero velocity. Hence, this constraint proves critical when a non-slip condition is required at the feet of the robot, or when the gripper is to remain static in either its position, orientation or both during manipulation tasks.

The final constraints, (4) and (5), ensure that the solutions of the QP problem respect the joint limits of the robot, where $\dot{\boldsymbol{\theta}}_{\text{lb}}$ and $\dot{\boldsymbol{\theta}}_{\text{ub}}$ are the joint upper and lower velocity limits, and $\boldsymbol{\theta}_{\text{lb}}$ and $\boldsymbol{\theta}_{\text{ub}}$ are the upper and lower joint position limits.

4   Teleoperation Strategies

The human body and the quadrupedal robot and manipulator are kinematically dissimilar, therefore direct mapping of the teleoperator's body to the robot is not viable. Thus, three teleoperation strategies (TS) are developed to intuitively teleoperate the legged manipulator via WBC, which use both hands of the motion capture suit to select the TS and the right hand to generate a reference trajectory. The proposed three strategies are as follows with the specific had poses detailed in Fig. 3,

- *TS0*: no reference is sent to the robot, acting as a safety feature.
- *TS1*: the relative teleoperator's arm movement is sent to control the pose of the gripper.
- *TS2*: the relative teleoperator's arm movement is sent to control the pose of the trunk.
- *TS3*: the gripper is locked in both position and orientation, and the relative teleoperator's arm movement is sent to control the pose of the trunk.

TS0	TS1	TS2	TS3

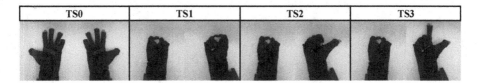

Fig. 3. The corresponding hand poses to activate each TS.

When one strategy is activated, the current pose of the right hand in the world frame is extracted from the motion capture suit and taken as the origin of the trajectory reference, with any subsequent movements being compiled and passed to the WBC framework. A relative scaled pose relationship is developed to map motions between the teleoperator and the robot, where at time t, the pose of the robot's frame of interest is modelled as

$$\boldsymbol{h}^t_{sd} = \boldsymbol{h}^0_{sd} + \boldsymbol{\mu}(\boldsymbol{h}^t_m - \boldsymbol{h}^0_m) \tag{11}$$

where $\boldsymbol{h} = [x; z; y; r; p; y]$ represents the displacements in the sagittal (x), lateral (y) and vertical (z) directions and the rotations in the roll (r), pitch (p) and yaw (y) directions. Subscript m refers to the master, s to the slave, d to a desired value and 0 refers to the initial timing when the hand is closed. $\boldsymbol{\mu}$ is the scaling factor for motions between the master and the robot. Orientation is not scaled by the scaling factor, therefore $\mu_r, \mu_p, \mu_y = 1$.

5 Simulations

To validate the effectiveness of the teleoperation system paired with the WBC framework, a physics-based PyBullet simulation was completed using the Laikago quadruped and ViperX 300 arm robots. During the simulation, three case studies were completed to test all three teleoperation strategies. During each study, a reference is generated by the teleoperation algorithm from the inertia-based motion capture suit, running at 500 Hz, and sent to the WBC framework, also running at 500 Hz.

For teleoperation strategies TS1, TS2, and TS3, tests were completed to validate the WBC framework's ability to track the input reference. Between each case study, the posture of the teleoperator's hand is used to switch between teleoperation strategies, as outlined in Sect. 4. It should be noted that all other references that were not being controlled through teleoperation were kept constant from their initial positions. For all studies that do not require the feet frames to move, halt constraints were added for these frames, as outlined in (3), keeping them locked in position. For the following case studies and the data presented in Fig. 4, the trunk frame is aligned with the world frame at the beginning of the first test, TS1.1. The world frame was set so that the $+x$ axis was in the direction the robot is facing, $+y$ was to the left of the robot, and $+z$ was in the upwards vertical direction. Furthermore, within Fig. 4 the Cartesian positions

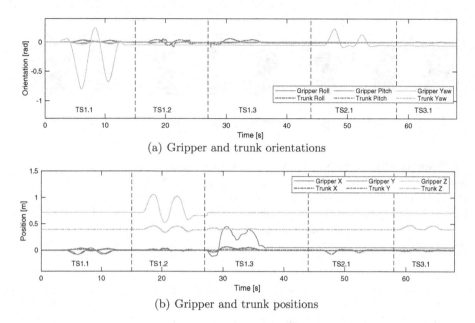

(a) Gripper and trunk orientations

(b) Gripper and trunk positions

Fig. 4. The WBC framework output of (a) orientations and (b) positions for the gripper and trunk frames covering all five tests.

and orientations are estimated through completing forward kinematics using the joint positions output by the WBC.

Across the case studies, three different types of movement from the tele-operator were used. This is a sweeping movement to the right (M1), a central vertical movement (M2), and a central thrusting movement forward (M3), with each movement type being completed twice sequentially. This was to explicitly demonstrate the capabilities of the WBC framework. For each test within these studies, references were input into the Cartesian task for either the gripper or trunk frame, with negligible latency being observed between these input references and robot motion generated by the WBC. For the frame that is being controlled, its task weight was set relatively high within the QP problem so that optimisation prioritised this task. A video of all proceeding simulations and testing is available online[1].

5.1 TS1 Case Study

For the case study of TS1, all three different types of movement from the teleoperator were used. This being M1, M2, and M3 to supply references for tests TS1.1, TS1.2, and TS1.3 respectively. Distinct WBC characteristics were observed in all three tests, where the robot adjusted to aid in the gripper frame to meet its target trajectory. These characteristics are portrayed in Fig. 4, where the position

---

[1] https://youtu.be/lhmZucVthc4.

and orientation of the gripper and trunk frame, for all studies, are presented. Within these graphs, for TS1.2 the trunk's z position and pitch angle can be seen to increase, and for TS1.3, the trunk's z position, x position, and pitch angle increase. This demonstrates how the WBC utilises the trunk frame to realise the gripper frame's Cartesian task. Furthermore, in TS1.1, WBC characteristics can be seen as whilst the gripper frame follows a yaw angle reference trajectory, the trunk can be seen to utilise many of its redundant DoF (x, y, roll, pitch, and yaw) to aid in realising the gripper's trajectory. This is further demonstrated in Fig. 4 and 5.

The effectiveness of the WBC framework is further emphasised in TS1.3, as shown in Fig. 6, where in the top row the WBC is disabled, and in the bottom row it is enabled. Without the WBC, the manipulator was observed to be unable to reach the desired position and a singularity was reached. Whilst with WBC enabled, the desired position was met and no singularities were observed. Therefore, this demonstrates how the WBC framework is able to take a teleoperation input reference and utilise all DoF of the robot to realise it.

5.2   TS2 Case Study

Test TS2.1 utilised the teleoperation strategy TS2. During this case study, the gripper frame was locked in place in terms of position using (3). The frame being controlled by the teleoperator switched to the trunk frame. For this test, M1 was used to send a y reference to the trunk Cartesian task within the WBC framework. As presented in Fig. 7, this resulted in the translation of the trunk frame in the y direction while the gripper frame remained in a constant position, but its orientation moved freely. This is supported by Fig. 4, where the position of the gripper frame remains constant throughout the test, whilst its orientation rotates in the roll and yaw axis. Simultaneously, the trunk frame can be seen to translate in the y direction. This demonstrates the effectiveness of the WBC framework in keeping the gripper frame locked in position whilst the trunk

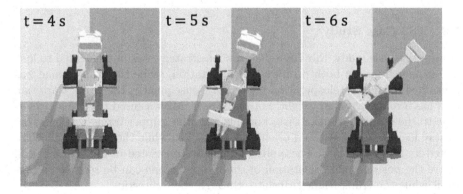

Fig. 5. Snapshots of the gripper frame rotating in the yaw axis during TS1.1.

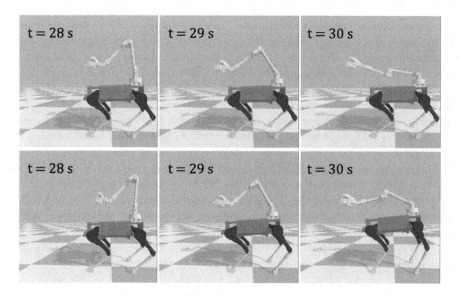

Fig. 6. Snapshots comparing the gripper frame moving through the x-axis driven by data from the motion capture suit during TS1.3 with the WBC disabled (top row), and enabled (bottom row).

exploits the system's redundancy to change its posture. Applying this constraint to only positions can aid in the robot realising tasks for other frames. This is because it increases the solution space of the QP, as a wider range of robot configurations are valid while satisfying the constraint. During this test, the CoM moves significantly due to the movement of the trunk which could potentially affect the robot's stability. However, it is evident from Fig. 8 that in not only this test but across all tests the centre of pressure (CoP) remains within the stability limits defined by the position of the feet. In turn, this suggests that the CoM constraint, defined in (2) aids in preserving stability.

5.3   TS3 Case Study

During this case study, the TS3 teleoperation strategy was implemented to lock the gripper frame in both position and orientation, while the trunk frame was controlled using the teleoperation reference. Consequently, the trunk Cartesian task has a relatively high weight. For test TS3.1, M2 was used to send a z reference to the trunk Cartesian task. For this test, the gripper frame was observed to stay locked in position and orientation using (3), while the trunk frame completed its trajectory in z. These observations are presented in Fig. 4 and Fig. 9, where the position and orientation of the gripper frame can be seen to be constant while the trunk frame translates through the z direction.

Although all other components of the input reference for the trunk frame's Cartesian task were constant, translation in x was observed, as detailed in Fig. 4.

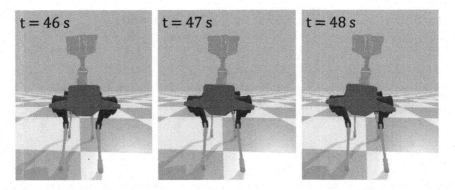

Fig. 7. Snapshots of the trunk frame translating in the y direction with the gripper constrained in position during TS2.1.

This observation was caused by the reduced solution space that fully constrains the gripper frame, in both position and orientation, results in. Therefore, due to this reduced solution space, the QP problem within the WBC framework had to sacrifice the strictness at which the trunk Cartesian task is tracked.

6   Hardware Experiments

The same series of studies presented in Sect. 5 were tested using real-life hardware, to analyse the overall framework's effectiveness in realising input teleoperation references. Regarding hardware, the A1, ViperX 300 arm, and Noitom Perception Neuron motion capture suit are set up as detailed in Sect. 2, with exception of using an A1 quadruped instead of a Laikago to demonstrate the proposed framework's generality, and the addition of the Ubuntu computer being connected to the A1 via Ethernet connection and the ViperX 300 arm via USB.

From completing this series of studies, it has been observed that the performance of the robot exhibits all whole-body motion characteristics as presented in Sect. 5, which can be shown in Fig. 10. Furthermore, very little latency

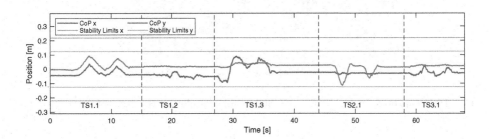

Fig. 8. Centre of pressure across all five tests.

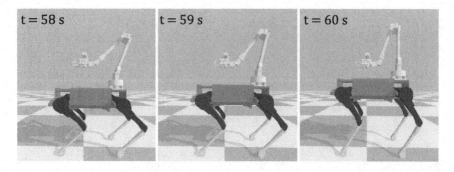

Fig. 9. Snapshots of the trunk translating in the z direction with the gripper constrained in position and orientation in TS3.1.

is observed between the A1 and ViperX 300, resulting in effective cooperative motion between the two robot systems. Consequently, not only does this demonstrate this framework's ability to be deployed onto hardware successfully, but also its modularity by successfully completing tests using the A1 and Laikago quadrupeds. This has served as preliminary testing, further analysis and more complex tests will be carried out in future work.

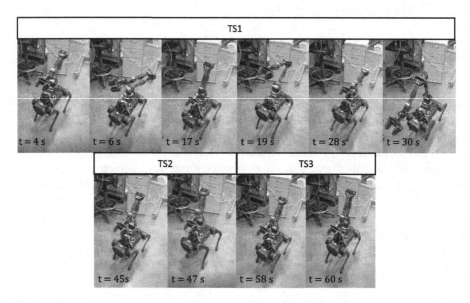

Fig. 10. Snapshots of the A1 ViperX 300 robot completing the tests of the different case studies.

7   Conclusion

In this paper, a highly functional teleoperation system that integrates a wearable inertia-based motion capture suit, three intuitive teleoperation strategies and a WBC framework to control quadrupedal legged manipulators has been proposed. By implementing a range of modular tasks and constraints within a QP optimisation problem, the teleoperation system can take input references and utilise WBC control to realise them through applying a teleoperation strategy, based on the application. The proficiency of the WBC framework to utilise the different teleoperation strategies was demonstrated, through simulation and preliminary hardware testing, in which it was used to complete a range of frame control tasks.

Future work will include expanding the teleoperation strategy functionality and full experimental validation of this teleoperation system on the real robot. Other future work could involve broadening the teleoperation strategies to use other elements of the inertia-based motion capture suit, implementing a method of dynamically weighting tasks, and integrating a wider range of gaits the teleoperator could use. To aid in the aforementioned further development of the teleoperation strategies, an index of performance will be created to analyse their effectiveness.

References

1. Abi-Farrajl, F., Henze, B., Werner, A., Panzirsch, M., Ott, C., Roa, M.A.: Humanoid teleoperation using task-relevant haptic feedback. In: IEEE/RSJ International Conference on Intelligent Robots and Systems, pp. 5010–5017 (2018). https://doi.org/10.1109/IROS.2018.8593521
2. Castano, J.A., Hoffman, E.M., Laurenzi, A., Muratore, L., Karnedula, M., Tsagarakis, N.G.: A whole body attitude stabilizer for hybrid wheeled-legged quadruped robots. In: IEEE International Conference on Robotics and Automation, pp. 706–712 (2018). https://doi.org/10.1109/ICRA.2018.8462875
3. Coelho, A., et al.: Whole-body teleoperation and shared control of redundant robots with applications to aerial manipulation. J. Intell. Robot. Syst. **102**(1), 1–22 (2021). https://doi.org/10.1007/s10846-021-01365-7
4. Dalin, E., Bergonzani, I., Anne, T., Ivaldi, S., Mouret, J.B.: Whole-body teleoperation of the Talos humanoid robot: preliminary results. In: ICRA Workshop on Teleoperation of Dynamic Legged Robots in Real Scenarios (2021)
5. Darvish, K., et al.: Whole-body geometric retargeting for humanoid robots. In: IEEE-RAS International Conference on Humanoid Robots, pp. 679–686 (2019). https://doi.org/10.1109/Humanoids43949.2019.9035059
6. Du, W., Fnadi, M., Benamar, F.: Whole-body motion tracking for a quadruped-on-wheel robot via a compact-form controller with improved prioritized optimization. IEEE Robot. Autom. Lett. **5**(2), 516–523 (2020). https://doi.org/10.1109/LRA.2019.2963822
7. Heins, A., Jakob, M., Schoellig, A.P.: Mobile manipulation in unknown environments with differential inverse kinematics control. In: 2021 18th Conference on Robots and Vision (CRV), pp. 64–71 (2021). https://doi.org/10.1109/CRV52889.2021.00017

8. Kim, S.K., Hong, S., Kim, D.: A walking motion imitation framework of a humanoid robot by human walking recognition from IMU motion data. In: IEEE-RAS International Journal of Humanoid Robotics, pp. 343–348 (2009). https://doi.org/10.1109/ICHR.2009.5379552

9. Li, J., Peers, C., Xin, S., Zhou, C.: Opening a spring-loaded door with a legged manipulator. In: UK RAS Conference (2022)

10. Nakanishi, J., Cory, R., Mistry, M., Peters, J., Schaal, S.: Operational space control: a theoretical and empirical comparison. Int. J. Robot. Res. **27**(6), 737–757 (2008). https://doi.org/10.1177/0278364908091463

11. Peers, C., Motawei, M., Richardson, R., Zhou, C.: Development of a teleoperative quadrupedal manipulator. In: UK-RAS Conference, pp. 17–18. Hatfield, UK, 2 June 2021. https://doi.org/10.31256/Hy7Sf7G

12. Penco, L., Scianca, N., Modugno, V., Lanari, L., Oriolo, G., Ivaldi, S.: A multimode teleoperation framework for humanoid loco-manipulation: an application for the ICUB robot. IEEE Robot. Autom. Mag. **26**(4), 73–82 (2019). https://doi.org/10.1109/MRA.2019.2941245

13. Sleiman, J.P., Farshidian, F., Minniti, M.V., Hutter, M.: A unified MPC framework for whole-body dynamic locomotion and manipulation. IEEE Robot. Autom. Lett. **6**(3), 4688–4695 (2021). https://doi.org/10.1109/LRA.2021.3068908

14. Wan, Y., Sun, J., Peers, C., Humphreys, J., Kanoulas, D., Zhou, C.: Performance and usability evaluation scheme for mobile manipulator teleoperation, under review 2022

15. Wu, Y., Balatti, P., Lorenzini, M., Zhao, F., Kim, W., Ajoudani, A.: A teleoperation interface for loco-manipulation control of mobile collaborative robotic assistant. IEEE Robot. Autom. Lett. **4**(4), 3593–3600 (2019). https://doi.org/10.1109/LRA.2019.2928757

16. Xin, G., Smith, J., Rytz, D., Wolfslag, W., Lin, H.C., Mistry, M.: Bounded haptic teleoperation of a quadruped robot's foot posture for sensing and manipulation. In: IEEE International Conference on Robotics and Automation, pp. 1431–1437 (2020). https://doi.org/10.1109/ICRA40945.2020.9197501

17. Yang, C., Chen, J., Chen, F.: Neural learning enhanced teleoperation control of Baxter robot using IMU based motion capture. In: International Conference on Automation and Computing, pp. 389–394 (2016). https://doi.org/10.1109/IConAC.2016.7604951

18. You, Y., Xin, S., Zhou, C., Tsagarakis, N.: Straight leg walking strategy for torque-controlled humanoid robots. In: IEEE International Conference on Robotics and Biomimetics, pp. 2014–2019. Qingdao, China, 3–7 December 2016). https://doi.org/10.1109/ROBIO.2016.7866625

19. Zhou, C., Fang, C., Wang, X., Li, Z., Tsagarakis, N.: A generic optimization-based framework for reactive collision avoidance in bipedal locomotion. In: IEEE International Conference on Automation Science and Engineering, pp. 1026–1033 (2016). https://doi.org/10.1109/COASE.2016.7743516

Soft Robotics, Sensing and Mobile Robots

In-silico Design and Computational Modelling of Electroactive Polymer Based Soft Robotics

Antonio J. Gil[1]([✉]) [iD], Rogelio Ortigosa[2] [iD], Jesus Martínez-Frutos[2] [iD],
and Nathan Ellmer[1] [iD]

[1] Zienkiewicz Centre for Computational Engineering, Bay Campus,
Swansea University, Swansea, UK
{A.J.Gil,n.s.ellmer}@swansea.ac.uk
[2] Technical University of Cartagena, Murcia, Spain
{rogelio.ortigosa,jesus.martinez}@upct.es

Abstract. The use of Electro-Active Polymers (EAPs) for the fabrication of evermore sophisticated miniaturised soft robotic actuators has seen an impressive development in recent years. This paper unveils the latest computational developments of the group related to three significant challenges presented in the *in-silico* modelling of EAPs, that are being explored with our in-house computational platform. These challenges, unique to the simulation of EAPs, include (i) robustly resolving the onset of potentially massive strains as a result of the significant flexibility of EAP components for soft robotics; (ii) accurately capturing the properties of multi-phased composites at a micro-scale within the macroscopic fields used in well-established computational modelling approaches (i.e. Finite Element Method); and (iii) optimising the electrode meso-architecture to enable device customisation for specific application required deformations. This paper also aims to demonstrate the in-silico design tools capability, robustness and flexibility, provided through a comprehensive set of numerical examples, including some novel results in electrode and EAP multi-material optimisation. With the upcoming addition of a 3D Direct-Ink-Writer (DIW) printer, the authors aim to close the loop allowing for in-house device design and optimisation, simulation and analysis as well as fabrication and testing.

Keywords: Electroactive Polymers · In-silico design · Topology optimisation · Rank-one laminates · Soft robotics

1   Introduction

Electroactive Polymers (EAPs) have emerged as a subclass of soft smart materials which are activated through the application of an electric stimulus. In recent

---

The first and fourth authors acknowledge the financial support received from the UK Defence Science and Technology Laboratory.

S. Pacheco-Gutierrez et al. (Eds.): TAROS 2022, LNAI 13546, pp. 81–91, 2022.
https://doi.org/10.1007/978-3-031-15908-4_7

years, research in these materials has significantly increased due to their incredible potential capabilities. Their low stiffness enables unprecedented strains, with extreme values of 1980%, as demonstrated experimentally [8]. The capabilities of EAP actuators have been demonstrated experimentally and research also shows that EAPs can be used as sensors and flexible energy harvesters [18]. Whilst applying an electric field triggers deformation as a result of electrostriction, physically deforming an EAP can produce an electric signal, due to the piezoelectric effect, which when received can be used for sensing capabilities or stored for energy harvesting purposes.

EAPs have often been referred to as artificial muscles given their actuation capabilities, fast response and high energy efficiencies [2]. This makes them perfect candidates for a wide range of soft robotic applications. In the field of humanoid robotics, EAPs can be used in stacks to form artificial muscles enabling human-like smooth control as opposed to traditional hard robotic mechanisms. This has been demonstrated by Duduta et al. [2] where EAP stacks were used to replicate a bicep, and extended by Guo et al. [4] to demonstrate muscles in the jaw and muscles enabling eye rotation. This ability to decrease robotic nature has the potential to vastly improve the development of prosthesis since the prosthetic could more closely mimic human limbs. An advantage of EAPs over other materials is that they have the ability to act as sensors as well as actuators, resulting in a self sensing capability. Once again this could accelerate the rate of improvement of prosthetics enabling functionality such as thermal and pressure sensing. Beyond the field of humanoid robotics, EAPs have multiple other applications in soft robotics. Figure 1 provides examples of crawling, swimming and flying robots which utilise EAP actuators. Other uses include grippers, tunable lenses and adaptive Braille displays.

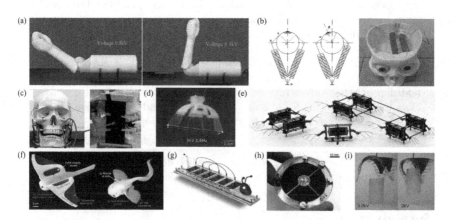

Fig. 1. Demonstration of the vast range of applications for EAPs in the field of soft robotics [4]. (a) EAP biomimetic bicep muscle; (b) Stacked DE configuration to rotate eyeball; (c) Stacked DE configuration to drive jaw; (d) Soft robotic jellyfish; (e) Flying robot; (f) Deep-sea soft robot; (g) Crawling caterpillar inspired robot; (h) EAP driven tunable lens; (i) Tulip inspired EAP gripper.

Amongst others, there are three significant challenges associated with modelling EAPs which are currently being addressed by the authors. The first one relates to modelling soft materials producing large strains (potentially massive), not previously an issue in hard robotics due to the use of mechanisms. Soft materials produce a highly non-linear and complex response which often requires an iterative solution approach, as implemented in the in-house in-silico computational tool, to solving for electric potential and displacement within the Finite Element Method (FEM). The next challenge relates to modelling a composite comprised of two or more materials. At a micro-scale, each Finite Element could be comprised of multiple materials. This creates a challenge when selecting or developing a constitutive model to use, since the properties of that material combination may not be accurately represented. The final challenge relates to designing a device that can produce the output required for a specific application. A large factor effecting the final deformation mode is the arrangement of electrodes and thus topology optimisation can be used to compute the optimal electrode meso-architecture.

Whilst the in-house in-silico design tool is continually being developed, the authors are about to explore the fabrication and testing of EAPs. 3D printing is a key progressive method of fabrication and with a Direct-Ink-Writing (DIW) 3D printer, the authors will have the ability to design and optimise EAPs using the developed framework, fabricate the configurations and test them, thus validating the simulation results. Having this capability closes the loop and potentially leads to real change in the way these materials are currently being designed. However, this goes beyond the scope of the current contribution.

This paper is organised as follows; Sect. 2 addresses all presented problems with the following subsection breakdown. Section 2.1 introduces a typical EAP and the problem definition before proceeding to address the challenges of solving highly non-linear problems using the concept of multi-variable convexity. Section 2.2 presents rank-one laminates and the challenges surrounding obtaining material properties for a combination of material phases represented by a single energy function. Section 2.3 details the use of topology optimisation to optimise the arrangement and design of electrodes to conform to a set of design criteria. Section 3.3 provides a comprehensive set of numerical examples to demonstrate the need to address the discussed challenges whilst showcasing the capability, robustness and flexibility of the in-house in-silico design and simulation tool. Finally, some concluding remarks are presented in Sect. 4.

2   In-silico Design Modelling Approach

2.1   Nonlinear Solid Electromechanics: A New Modelling Paradigm

The set of equations governing the physics of EAPs, namely the conservation of linear momentum and Gauss's law [9], can be mathematically stated as,

$$\text{DIV}\boldsymbol{P} + \boldsymbol{f}_0 = \boldsymbol{0}; \qquad \text{DIV}\boldsymbol{D}_0 - \rho_0 = 0, \tag{1}$$

where P is the first Piola-Kirchhoff stress tensor, f_0 denotes a Lagrangian body force, D_0 is the Lagrangian electric displacement field and ρ_0 represents the electric charge per unit volume. Rotational equilibrium dictates that $F^T P = P F^T$, where F represents the deformation gradient tensor. Faraday's law can be written as $E_0 = -\nabla_0 \phi$, with E_0 the Lagrangian electric field and ϕ the electric potential. The internal energy density e that encapsulates the necessary constitutive information to close the system of governing equations in (1) is introduced as $e = e(F, D_0)$.

The actuation (and strain) capability of EAPs is massive and this poses real challenges when modelling the materials electromechanical response, since the simulation must remain robust and reliable beyond the potential limited experimental information for moderate actuation. Fundamentally, the constitutive model must be sufficiently robust such that when simulations go beyond that of the laboratory experiments from which the constitutive model was developed, the reliability and accuracy of the model does not breakdown [3]. Figure 2(a) demonstrates a common prototypical example where an isotropic EAP film is undergoing material characterisation through classical experimentation [15]. Figure 2(b) presents the response of the constitutive model and careful analysis (i.e. computation of acoustic wave speeds) has shown that the constitutive model becomes ill-posed for any combination of E_0 and stretch λ within the red region, hence either limiting the simulation capability to smaller strains or providing unphysical results, the latter demonstrated by Fig. 2(c) with the appearance of a zero thickness shear band.

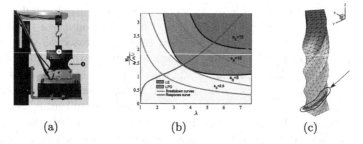

(a)   (b)   (c)

Fig. 2. (a) Material characterisation of EAP VHB4910; (b) Response curve (in blue) and stability analysis of widely used constitutive model for the standard experimental set up described here; (c) Development of localised deformations in unrealistic zero thickness shear bands in the simulation of a piezoelectric EAP. (Color figure online)

Recently, the concept of multi-variable convexity has been introduced by the authors [3,6,12,13] allowing for the internal energy function to be given as,

$$e\left(\nabla_0 x, D_0\right) = W\left(F, H, J, D_0, d\right); \quad d = F D_0, \tag{2}$$

where W represents a convex multi-variable functional in terms of its extended set of arguments $\mathcal{V} = \{F, H, J, D_0, d\}$, with $\{H, J\}$ the co-factor and the Jacobian of F, respectively. The concept of multi-variable convexity is paramount in ensuring a well-posed computer model, such that the problem guarantees the existence of real wave speeds and hence continues to produce physical results for the constitutive model regardless of the level of actuation, opening the possibility to explore unthinkable actuation possibilities.

2.2 Electroactive Polymer Design: Microstructure

Material properties are fundamental with respect to EAP performance. It is desirable to select a material with high electric permittivity in order to maximise the actuation range. However, materials with higher electric permittivity also exhibit higher stiffness which in itself can hinder the final actuation response [5]. This in turn counteracts the advantage gained. Since using one single material has its limitations in gains through material properties, focus has turned towards the design of tailor-made composite arrangements of multiple materials with varying properties to complement one another.

This brings with it significant challenges with regards to the constitutive model. When using a single material phase, the corresponding material constitutive model can be obtained through classical experiments in conjunction with a phenomenological based model [7]. Likewise, when using multiple material phases at a macro-scale, multiple constitutive models can be implemented and interchanged as the material definition changes. However, a significant challenge arises when modelling an EAP device, with multiple material phases at a micro-scale, requiring thus the development of multi-scale constitutive models. The authors presented in [9] a novel computational framework for the accurate simulation of rank-one EAP laminates and applied the principles of a rank-n homogenisation of convex multi variable phases in the context of highly deformable EAPs for soft robotics applications. The structure for a biphasic DE device can be seen below in Fig. 3.

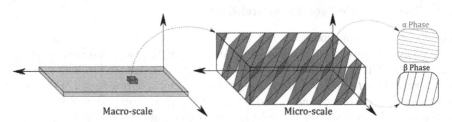

Fig. 3. Schematics of EAP device fabricated such that it is laminated with multiple material phases (α and β in this case) at a micro-scale level. The micro-scale image demonstrates that the lamination of a rank-one laminate does not need to be in an orthogonal direction. On the far right, the Figure presents the possibility of a rank-two laminate such that the various phases can also be formed of a laminate. This details a further challenge; can such a material be printed?

Section 2.1 presented the definition of the problem through the governing equations (1). This identified two quantities which are vital for the constitutive model, namely the deformation gradient tensor, $\boldsymbol{F}$, and the electric displacement field, $\boldsymbol{D}_0$. Since Fig. 3 presents two phases used at a micro-scale, the macro-scale quantities F and D_0 need to be obtained such that they represent both material phases. Under the assumption of a homogeneous response in each phase, these quantities are defined as the weighted sum of those in each phase, namely

$$F = c^a F^a + (1 - c^a) F^b; \qquad D_0 = c^a D_0^a + (1 - c^a) D_0^b, \qquad (3)$$

where c^a is the volume fraction of phase a $(1 - c^a$ for phase $b)$. Whilst F and D_0 can be decomposed to combine multiple materials, the internal energy functional also needs to represent the combination of material phases. This can be done through the introduction of an effective internal energy functional, $\hat{e}(F, D_0, \alpha, \beta)$, which similarly can be decomposed such that

$$\begin{aligned} \hat{e}(F, D_0, \alpha, \beta) &= c^a e^a \left(F^a \left(F, \alpha \right), D_0^a \left(D_0, \beta \right) \right) \\ &+ (1 - c^a) e^b \left(F^b \left(F, \alpha \right), D_0^b \left(D_0, \beta \right) \right) \end{aligned} \qquad (4)$$

where e^a and e^b are the respective materials internal energy functionals written in terms of the micro-scale fluctuations α and β. As a result of these decompositions, the various macroscopic quantities can be expressed as weighted averages of multiple materials, enabling the use of the same computational framework with the fields and models described by (3) and (4).

Another solution currently explored by the authors is that of developing a single internal energy functional which can closely model the response of a rank-one laminate without attempting to represent the different materials individually, with the potential to drastically simplify the modelling of multiple materials. It is also worth noting that in the future this raises the potential for a new design challenge, the optimisation of the volume fractions of materials to maximise the deformation.

2.3 Electrode Design: Meso-architecture

The design and arrangement of electrodes is another important factor when optimising EAP performance. Stacked configurations enable the designer to strategically place different designs of electrodes in specific locations to produce complex and novel deformations. Designing the electrode to form only a region of the layer results in the elastomer sandwiched within this region to experience an electric stimulus resulting in actuation whilst the remaining material does not experience an electric stimulus thus remaining passive and thereby enabling complex actuation. Figure 4 demonstrates the customisability of the design and placement of electrodes to produce a novel and complex mode of deformation.

When considering the use of EAPs for applications such as soft robotics, it is clear that the designer will have an end goal in the form of a desired actuation. It is therefore necessary that there be an approach in place to optimise the design for a given set of criteria. There is a wide spectrum of robust approaches available for topology optimisation of the meso-architecture, ranging from density-based methods, with the Solid Isotropic Material with Penalisation (SIMP) method as their maximum representative, level-set methods, phase-field methods, topological derivative methods and evolutionary methods [1,11,16,17].

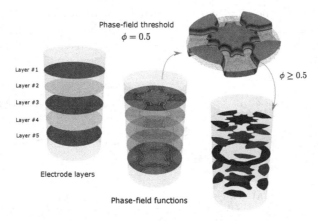

Fig. 4. Layer-by-layer extruded layout clearly displaying the intercalated electrodes. **Left:** DE device comprising of six elastomer layers and five intercalated surface regions. **Centre:** final distribution of the phase-field functions with the electrode regions in red and the voids in blue. **Right:** representation of the five electrodes by selecting the phase-field threshold equal to 0.5 [10]. (Color figure online)

The authors have explored the use of the phase-field method [10], where a continuous phase-field is used to describe the presence of an electrode region within the interface layer, being $\Psi_\varepsilon = \{\Psi_{\varepsilon^1} \ldots \Psi_{\varepsilon^N}\}$ the set of N phase field functions. This electrode phase field functions are extended to the volume via a suitable Laplacian extension, where the overall volume phase field function in the range [0, 1], where 0 represents a purely EAP region and 1 represents an electrode region. Intermediate values represent electrode boundaries. As a final ingredient of the phase field method, it remains to define a spatially varying free (enthalpy-type) energy density $\Psi(\Psi_\varepsilon, \boldsymbol{F}, \boldsymbol{E}_0)$ comprised of purely mechanical and electro-mechanical contributions.

To summarise the optimisation process, first consider the elastomeric configuration described in Fig. 5. The underlying objective of this particular layout is not to perfectly fit the electrically deformed EAP to a given target shape, but to ensure that its deformed configuration is endowed with certain desired morphological features. This can be achieved by focusing on the displacement, $\boldsymbol{u} = \boldsymbol{\phi}(\boldsymbol{X}) - \boldsymbol{X}$ (where $\boldsymbol{X}$ is the initial material coordinate and $\boldsymbol{\phi}(\boldsymbol{X})$ represents the mapping of $\boldsymbol{X}$ to its current spatial position), of specific critical points which can ultimately induce the desired morphological peculiarities. Considering the displacement of critical points allows for the formulation of an objective function which the topology optimisation process aims to minimise, subject to the satisfaction of a series constraints defined by the set of governing equations defining the problem (see Sect. 2.1). An initial electrode arrangement seed can then be used as an input and a Newton-Raphson nonlinear iterative algorithm is exploited until convergence. This topology optimisation technique has recently been extended to the possibility of considering a multi-material EAP, providing thus the capacity to optimise the design of both the electrode and the EAP polymer itself.

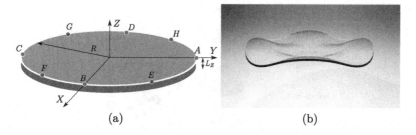

(a)   (b)

Fig. 5. (a) Points selected for optimisation. (b) Topology optimisation aided electrode design: the Z displacement of the red and green target points must be maximised along the positive and negative Z direction, respectively [10] (Color figure online).

3   Examples

3.1   Example 1: Demonstration of In-silico Design Tool Capability

The objective of this first example is to demonstrate the large strain and complex deformation capability of the in-silico design tool. The configuration is displayed in Fig. 6 and it presents a DE device which clearly provides a blueprint which could be used as a concept for a soft robotics gripper. Bending is obtained by positioning electrodes across the full span of each 'finger' and fixing it to a central square of material which remains passive hence providing a fixed plane enabling span-wise actuation.

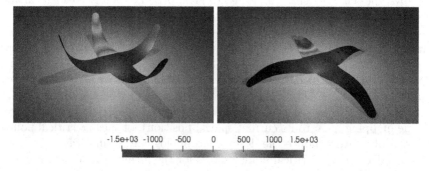

Fig. 6. Presents the rendering of a deformed configuration, demonstrating a large strain, and contour plot of the distribution of hydrostatic pressure p. These results have been obtained with the in-house in-silico design tool [14].

3.2   Example 2: Effects of Fibre Orientation

The objective of this example is to demonstrate the influence of microstructure fibre orientation on the deformation produced. A basic rectangular EAP device was used in this example which similarly to Example 3.1 has two full aerial electrodes, arranged at half thickness and at the bottom of the device. As the elastomer bends due to the applied electric field, the fibre orientation induces an additional torsional mode. Figure 7 clearly displays that with the fibres orientated at 0°, or parallel to the length, does not induce torsion but does reduce bending capability. With the fibres orientated at 45°, torsion and bending are induced and can thus be customised.

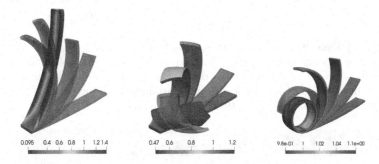

Fig. 7. Presents the deformations of an EAP with different fibre alignment, from left to right corresponding to orientations of 0°, 45° and 90°. The various snapshots corresponds to the actuation increments and the contour plots represent the deformation gradient tensors F_{22} component [6].

3.3   Example 3: Effects of Electrode Design Meso-architecture

This final example is being presented to demonstrate the use of topology optimisation as discussed in Sect. 2.3. The objective for this specific configuration is to maximise the displacement at locations $\{A, B, C, D\}$ and minimise at locations $\{E, F, G, H\}$. The success of the optimisation is calculated through the objective function given by

$$\mathcal{J}(\phi) = -(u_A + u_B + u_C + u_D) + (u_E + u_F + u_G + u_H) \qquad (5)$$

where u_Y is the vertical displacement of the specified point Y. The outcome of the optimisation process for the actuation mode is presented in Fig. 9. To summarise, Fig. 8 shows the five electrode layer extrusions demonstrating the optimised design of electrodes to obtain the deformation presented in Fig. 9. It is worth noting that even a slight change in objective can result in a significantly altered optimised configuration. This also demonstrates the usefulness of topology optimisation given that the optimised solution may not be trivial or easily conceived by an inexperienced designer.

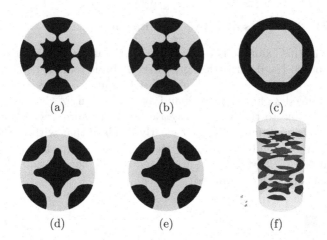

Fig. 8. (a)–(e) Final distribution of the phase-field functions at final TO iteration. Black colour is associated with electrodes and grey colour, with voids. (f) Displays a layer-by-layer layout with intercalated optimal electrode distribution (a phase-field threshold value of 0.5 has been used) where the Z dimension of the DE device has been enlarged for visualisation purposes [10] (Color figure online).

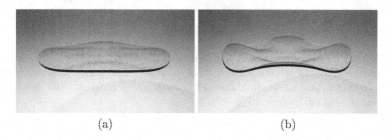

Fig. 9. Presents the evolution of the deformed configuration of the optimised layer-by-layer DE device for increasing values of the voltage gradient, $\Delta\varphi$, between alternating electrodes [10].

4   Concluding Remarks

This paper has presented some recent computational results regarding the in-silico design and analysis of Electro-Active Polymers (EAPs) subjected to potentially extreme actuation. First, the use of polyconvex strain energy functions is shown as a very beneficial mathematical requirement in order to ensure robust and accurate simulations. Subsequently, the consideration of rank-laminates for the EAP micro-architecture is shown as a useful tool in order to attain a variety of actuation modes. Finally, the use of topology optimisation in the design of the electrode meso-architecture demonstrates the unparalleled design opportunities offered by EAPs. Having a computational framework coupled with the ability to fabricate and test EAPs will enable future in-house experimental validation, further offering physical proof of concept alongside simulation results.

References

1. Aage, N., Andreassen, E., Lazarov, B., Sigmund, O.: Giga-voxel computational morphogenesis for structural design. Nature **550**, 84–86 (2017)
2. Duduta, M., Hajiesmaili, E., Zhao, H., Wood, R., Clarke, D.: Realizing the potential of dielectric elastomer artificial muscles. PNAS **116**, 2476–2481 (2019)
3. Gil, A.J., Ortigosa, R.: A new framework for large strain electromechanics based on convex multi-variable strain energies: variational formulation and material characterisation. CMAME **302**, 293–328 (2016)
4. Guo, Y., Liu, L., Liu, Y., Leng, J.: Review of dielectric elastomer actuators and their applications in soft robots. Adv. Intell. Syst. **3**, 2000282 (2021)
5. Hajiesmaili, E., Clarke, D.: Reconfigurable shape-morphing dielectric elastomers using spatially varying electric fields. Nature Communicationes **10**(183), 1–7 (2019)
6. Horák, M., Gil, A., Ortigosa, R., Kruzik, M.: A polyconvex transversely-isotropic invariant-based formulation for electro-mechanics: stability, minimisers and computational implementation. Under review (2022)
7. Hossain, M., Navaratne, R., Peric, D.: 3D printed elastomeric polyurethane: viscoelastic experimental characterizations and constitutive modelling with nonlinear viscosity functions. IJNLM **126**, 293–328 (2020)
8. Li, T., Keplinger, C., Baumgartner, R., Bauer, S., Yang, W., Suo, Z.: Giant voltage-induced deformation in dielectric elastomers near the verge of snap-through instability. JMPS **61**(2), 611–628 (2013)
9. Marín, F., Martínez-Frutos, J., Ortigosa, R., Gil, A.: A convex multi-variable based computational framework for multilayered electro-active polymers. CMAME **374**, 113567 (2021)
10. Martínez-Frutos, J., Ortigosa, R., Gil, A.J.: In-silico design of electrode meso-architecture for shape morphing dielectric elastomers. JMPS **157** (2021). https://doi.org/10.1016/j.jmps.2021.104594
11. Munk, D.J., Vio, G.A., Steven, G.P.: Topology and shape optimization methods using evolutionary algorithms: a review. Struct. Multidiscip. Optim. **52**(3), 613–631 (2015). https://doi.org/10.1007/s00158-015-1261-9
12. Ortigosa, R., Gil, A.J.: A new framework for large strain electromechanics based on convex multi-variable strain energies: conservation laws, hyperbolicity and extension to electro-magneto-mechanics. CMAME **309**, 202–242 (2016)
13. Ortigosa, R., Gil, A.J.: A new framework for large strain electromechanics based on convex multi-variable strain energies: finite element discretisation and computational implementation. CMAME **302**, 329–360 (2016)
14. Ortigosa, R., Gil, A.J., Martínez-Frutos, J., Franke, M., Bonet, J.: A new energy-momentum time integration scheme for non-linear thermo-mechanics. CMAME **372**, 113395 (2020)
15. Siboni, M.H., Castañeda, P.P.: Fiber-constrained, dielectric-elastomer composites: finite-strain response and stability analysis. J. Mech. Phys. Solids **68**, 211–238 (2014)
16. Takezawa, A., Nishiwaki, S., Kitamura, M.: Shape and topology optimization based on the phase field method and sensitivity analysis. J. Comput. Phys. **229**(7), 2697–2718 (2010)
17. Wang, M., Wang, X., Guo, D.: A level-set method for structural topology optimization. CMAME **192**, 227–246 (2003)
18. Zhao, Y., Yin, L.J., Zhong, S.L., Zha, J.W., Dang, Z.M.: Review of dielectric elastomers for actuators, generators and sensors. IET Nanodielectr. **3**, 99–106 (2020)

Exploration of Underwater Storage Facilities with Swarm of Micro-surface Robots

Yifeng He[1]([✉]), Barry Lennox[1], and Farshad Arvin[2]

[1] Department of Electrical and Electronic Engineering, University of Manchester, Manchester, UK
{yifeng.he,barry.lennox}@manchester.ac.uk
[2] Department of Computer Science, Durham University, Durham, UK

Abstract. Swarm robotics is a decentralised mechanism used to coordinate a large group of simple robots. An exploration task means fully scanning an unknown area using a large number of robotic swarms. It has great potential for use in many real-world applications, such as monitoring extreme environments. Although there are many research studies on swarm exploration, the real-world scenarios of the swarm algorithm have not been fully investigated. This paper proposes a new application scenario for swarm exploration to monitor nuclear waste storage facilities. To coordinate the robotic swarm, the active elastic sheet model was utilised, which is a bio-inspired collective motion mechanism. We implemented the exploration scenario in a wet storage facility using a swarm of low-cost autonomous micro-surface robots, *Bubbles*. We developed a realistic kinematic model of the Bubble platform and implemented the exploration scenario using large swarm sizes. This paper showed the feasibility of using a low-cost robotic platform for this new application, although the accuracy of the path planning was not very high.

Keywords: Swarm robotics · Exploration · Collective motion · Extreme environments

1 Introduction

In a nuclear power station, the wastes are stored in a pool of water called the spent fuel pond. The waste is packed in special rods and placed inside the spent fuel ponds (shown at the bottom of the pond in Fig. 1). Special underwater camera systems are used to check the nuclear waste's storage condition, position, and quantity. Every year International Atomic Energy Agency (IAEA) spends huge costs (over £25 million [1]) and efforts to inspect fuel waste storage using the manual IAEA DCM-14 camera [2]. The underwater camera, which is called the

This work was supported in part by EPSRC RAIN and RNE projects [EP/R026084/1 and EP/P01366X/1].

S. Pacheco-Gutierrez et al. (Eds.): TAROS 2022, LNAI 13546, pp. 92–104, 2022.
https://doi.org/10.1007/978-3-031-15908-4_8

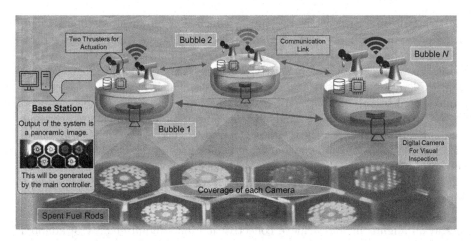

Fig. 1. "Big vision" of the proposed exploration system. A swarm of micro-surface robots, *Bubbles*, are visually inspecting an underwater storage facility to generate a panoramic image by stitching 100 images received from a swarm of bubbles at the various position of the pond.

Underwater Television (UWTV) system, checks the condition of waste fuel. It is a time-consuming and repetitive task to check the condition of the spent fuel pond regularly. Therefore, robotising the inspection task is a more economical choice. In this case, robots with special sensory systems are needed to carry out the inspection task. There are several robotic platforms developed for the inspection of nuclear storage facilities. As an example, for dry storage facilities, Cheah et al. [3] proposed a re-configurable robotic platform that crosses a small access point and inspects an extreme environment. Another example of robotic solutions for the extreme environment was proposed in [4], where a robotic solution was utilised to clean up decommissioning sites. In the case of underwater storage facilities, several robotic solutions were developed [5–8]. For example, MallARD [8] is a unique autonomous surface vehicle (ASV) developed for IAEA inspection tasks. Although the aforementioned systems were developed for robotising inspection tasks, they use a single robot. In the case of a large and unknown environment, the reliability of a single robot is a problem. Therefore, multiple robots need to be deployed.

Swarm robotics [9] is a bio-inspired mechanism that controls a large number of robots working at the same time. It is based on the collective behaviours of social animals like honeybees or birds [10]. Each of these animals does not have high intelligence, but working as a group could solve complex tasks like foraging and aggregation. When this technology is used in the robotic area, it could be simulated as each robot have some simple logic like following the robot in front. When a large number of robots work together, they can do more, better and faster than a single one of them. To control and coordinate a large number of robots, the related swarm algorithm is needed. Schmickl et al. [11] developed the BEECLUST aggregation mechanism which is a bio-inspired robotic algorithm based on the honeybees' thermotaxis. The robots can achieve an aggregation without prior knowledge with a little computational effort in the individual robot. There are various bio-inspired swarm behaviours, i.e. flocking, aggregation, exploration, collective transportation, etc., which have been successfully implemented by robots.

We need to have a low-cost and efficient coordination mechanism to overcome the exploration task in a nuclear storage facility. Collective Motion (CM) is one of the most common swarm behaviours that can be used in real-world applications. Ferrante et al. [12] introduced a new CM model based on the Active Elastic Sheet (AES) model. The idea of this algorithm is to place virtual springs between adjacent robots. The distance and angular difference between robots will apply repulsive and attractive force to each agent. This model allows a group of robots to stay in alignment and achieve collective motion. Raoufi et al. [13] adapted the AES model and optimised the model parameters, which are one step ahead toward the real-world application of the AES model. To implement linear and angular motions, a hundred robots were lined up on a 10×10 square. The result showed that the modification and the optimisation of the model improve the performance of the AES model.

There are many real-world studies on the application of multi-agent unmanned surface vehicles (USVs) [14–16]. Those studies proposed decentralised multi-agent control systems in complex ocean environments. However, they are not suitable for inspection of nuclear storage facilities due to their limited size and surrounding walls. Also, the robots must be able to understand their positions and orientations with high bandwidth communications, which are not available for large swarms of low-cost robots.

This paper proposed a novel method for inspecting underwater storage facilities using a swarm of the low-cost autonomous micro-surface robot (AMSR) (shown in Fig. 1). We first developed a new model of the AMSR, including drag force and shear stress. In terms of collective motion, the AES model was adapted to achieve the configuration of a large number of robots, up to 900. The results showed that the inverse rotational damping coefficient value, population of configuration and shape of configuration significantly affect the system's behaviour.

The proposed concept of swarm inspection can be deployed in real-world storage facilities to decrease the cost of inspection and generate a full pond image with a high frequency (1 image per 10 min) which is currently impossible to have due to the manual inspection method.

2   Collective Motion Mechanism

The CM mechanism used in this study is based on AES model [12]. The model is applied to multiple robots moving in a two-dimensional environment, the surface of the water. The linear velocity $\vec{x}_i$ and angular velocity $\dot{\theta}_i$ of each robot i are calculated by the following equations:

$$\dot{\overrightarrow{x}}_i = v_0\hat{n}_i + \alpha[(\overrightarrow{F}_i + D_r\hat{\xi}_r) \cdot \hat{n}_i]\hat{n}_i , \tag{1}$$

$$\dot{\theta}_i = \beta[(\overrightarrow{F}_i + D_r\hat{\xi}_r) \cdot \hat{n}_i^\perp] + D_\theta\xi_\theta , \tag{2}$$

where v_0 is the self-propulsion speed for each robot, α and β are tuning parameters for transition and rotation, Vector $\hat{n}_i$ is the heading direction of robot i, and the $\hat{n}_i^\perp$ is the perpendicular direction of it. The sum of the total spring-like force on each robot could be calculated by the following equations with initial distance l_{ij} and the spring constant k/l_{ij}. The connection between robot i with neighbourhood robots was set at $t=0$ and was not changed in the experiment. The sensing noise of force measurement in the equation is given by $D_r\hat{\xi}_r$. D_r is the noise strength coefficient, and $\hat{\xi}_r$ is a randomly oriented unit vector. The actuation noise is $D_\theta\xi_\theta$. D_θ is the noise strength coefficient, and ξ_θ is a random variable with a standard, zero-centred normal distribution of variance 1. In the ideal condition with no noise, D_r and D_θ equal to 0. In this case, all the robots are working in the ideal condition.

$$\overrightarrow{F}_i = \sum_{j \in S_i} -\frac{k}{l_{ij}}(|\overrightarrow{r}_{ij}| - l_{ij})\frac{\overrightarrow{r}_{ij}}{|\overrightarrow{r}_{ij}|}, \tag{3}$$

$$\overrightarrow{r}_{ij} = \overrightarrow{x}_j - \overrightarrow{x}_i, \tag{4}$$

where $\frac{k}{l_{ij}}$ is the spring constants, l_{ij} is the equilibrium distances, and r_{ij} is the distance between robots.

The elastic forces keep the distances between robots in a safe zone. A repulsive force will be applied if two robots become closer than the allowable safe distance, and if the two robots get far apart, an attractive force will be implemented to impose them to remain in a stable area.

3   Realisation of the Exploration

3.1   Robotic Platform

The robot platform that is used in this study is Bubble (shown in Fig. 1) which is an autonomous micro-surface robot (AMSR) with a 6.7 cm diameter. It is a unique swarm robotic system developed at the University of Manchester. The robot is a lightweight micro-robot that moves on the water surface for underwater inspection. It is driven by air from the two propellers on the top, reducing the chance of contamination to zero. Bubbles take images with their small camera facing toward the bottom of the robot. The image generated by the inspection system can be transferred back to the main station by wireless communication.

3.2   Simulated Platform

The simulation platform was developed in Matlab. In the simulations shown in Fig. 3 and Fig. 4, the circles are the robots, and the arrows on them are the heading directions. The movement of the robots was modelled based on force analysis shown in Fig. 2. The velocity of the robot was combined with the velocity given by the AES model and water surface resistance in both linear and angular movement. The velocity loss caused by the water surface resistance is calculated from the integration of drag force, F_D and shear stress, τ. Then the current position of each robot is calculated from the previous position and the integration of velocity. The drag equation, Taylor-Couette flow, v_θ, [17] and Newton's Law of Viscosity are presented below.

$$F_D = \frac{1}{2}\rho v^2 C_D A, \tag{5}$$

where F_D is the drag force which is the water surface resistance in linear movement, ρ is the density of the fluid, here is water, v is the velocity of the robot, C_D is the drag coefficient (the coefficient of a cylinder was chosen due to the shape of Bubble's chassis), and A is the cross-section area.

Bubble have a dome shape enclosure and cylinder shape chassis. In application, only the chassis cylinder stays in the water, so the drag coefficient of the cylinder was used in the calculation.

$$v_\theta = \Omega_1 \frac{\frac{\Omega_2}{\Omega_1} - (\frac{R_1}{R_2})^2}{1 - (\frac{R_1}{R_2})^2} r + \frac{\Omega_1 R_1^2 \frac{1 - \frac{\Omega_2}{\Omega_1}}{1 - (\frac{R_1}{R_2})^2}}{r}, \tag{6}$$

where Ω_1 is the angular velocity of a cylinder, Ω_2 is the angular velocity of fluid which is 0 here, R_1 is the radius of the cylinder, R_2 is the radius of the container of fluid, and v_θ is the fluid velocity at position radius, r.

$$\tau(\Omega_1) = \mu \frac{\partial v_\theta}{\partial \Omega_1}, \tag{7}$$

where $\tau(\Omega_1)$ is the shear stress at the height equal to Ω_1, and μ is the dynamic viscosity of the flow, which is water here.

By combining the water surface resistance and AES model, the dynamic model of the system is given by the following equation,

$$\begin{cases} \begin{bmatrix} V_i \\ \omega_i \end{bmatrix} = \begin{bmatrix} \overrightarrow{x}_i \\ \dot{\theta}_i \end{bmatrix} - \begin{bmatrix} V_i' \\ \omega_i' \end{bmatrix} \\ \begin{bmatrix} \dot{V}_i' \\ \dot{\omega}_i' \end{bmatrix} = \begin{bmatrix} \frac{1}{m}F_D \\ \frac{1}{m(\frac{l}{2})^2}\tau \end{bmatrix} \end{cases}, \tag{8}$$

where V_i' and ω_i are the induced linear and angular velocity respectively, V_i and is the linear velocity of the robot i, w_i' is the angular velocity of the robot i, $\overrightarrow{x}_i$ and $\dot{\theta}_i$ is the linear and angular velocity calculated by AES model, F_D is the drag force, dt is the sampling time of the system, m is the mass of the individual robot, τ is the shear stress, and l is the distance between the two propellers of the robot.

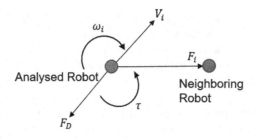

Fig. 2. Force diagram of an agent (robot). The orange circle indicates the target robot, and the blue circle is neighbouring. (Color figure online)

Table 1. Values of parameters and constants set in experiments

Parameters	Description	Value (units)
v_0	self-propulsion speed	0.002 (m/s)
Δt	iteration period	0.1 (s)
m	mass of single robot	0.05 (kg)
C_D	drag coefficient of cylinder	1.17
ρ	density of the fluid (water)	997 (kg/m^3)
A	cross-sectional area	0.0034 (m^2)
μ	viscosity of water at 25°C	0.89 (N·s/m^2)
l	distance between the centre of the two propellers	0.02 (m)
α	inverse translational damping coefficient	0.01
β	inverse rotational damping coefficient	0.12
k	spring constant	10 (N/m)

3.3 Experiments

The value of parameters in experiments was based on trial and error in the simulation environment. The application in real robots will be made in the future.

First, we investigate the effect of the simulated water environment on the developed model of Bubbles. In the first set of experiments, we used 25 robots and arranged them in a 5×5 square shape. The goal was to test the modelled force for the bubbles considering the drag force and shear stress, Eqs. (5 and 7). Hence, a circular path with a diameter of 0.2 m was chosen to test the model. A large deviation from the chosen path was expected; however, these sorts of errors in motion are normal for swarm systems shown in nature.

The second set of experiments focuses on the CM of the swarm, considering Eq. (8). Robots were assembled into two configurations, a hexagon and a square. The hexagon configuration contained 91 robots, with 6 robots on each side. The square configuration contained 10 robots on the side and 100 in total. All the robots were arranged with random initial orientations.

The third set of experiments investigated the effects of the swarm population on the system performance. Each configuration, hexagon and square, had 3 different populations. The hexagon configuration was tested with $N \in \{37, 61, 91\}$ robots and the square configuration was tested with $N \in \{100, 400, 900\}$ robots. Each set of experiments was repeated 20 times with random initial orientations for every run.

To investigate the proposed CM model, the fourth set of experiments investigated the effects of angular velocity β on the swarm performance. We tested a range of $\beta \in [0.1 \text{ to } 0.9]$ with $N = 100$ robots and $N = 91$ robots for square and hexagon configurations, respectively. Similar to the previous experiment, each experiment was repeated 20 times with random initial orientations. The setting of parameters and constants are listed in Table 1.

4   Results

This section presents the results of the performed experiments and brief discussions regarding the four different settings. All the experiments were performed in Matlab using the simulated model of the Bubbles.

4.1   Bubbles Movement

In the first experiment, we investigated the feasibility of the developed model for Bubbles' movement on the water surface. Figure 3 shows the circular movement of the robots in the simulated storage pond environment filled with water. The experiment was conducted for $t = 150$ s and the position of the team at $t = 50$ s, $t = 100$ s, and $t = 150$ s were marked. Compared to the specified circular path, the real trajectory of the robots contained a large error. This is because of the effect of the water surface resistance (both F_D and v_θ) added to the model, which made it harder for the robots to follow the path.

Figure 4 reveals the linear and angular errors between the expected and the real trajectories. The data was processed with root mean square and normalisation. The linear error curve was close to a parabola. The peak was in the middle which was about the top of the trace. In this position, robots had the maximum linear error. The angular error had a peak at about $t=2$ s. From $t=0$ s to $t=2$ s, the robots were dealing with the resistance of the water surface, and the error was increasing. After $t=2$ s, the driving force and water surface resistance reached a balance, and the error decreased slowly.

4.2   Collective Motion Model

In the second phase, we combined the Bubbles' movement model with the AES. Figure 5 shows screenshots from a randomly selected experiment with the hexagon configuration. The experiment took 120 s in total, and screenshots were taken every 60 s. In hexagon configuration, the robots that were not on the edge of the swarm had connections to the other 6 neighbouring robots with equal

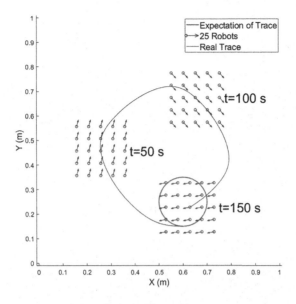

Fig. 3. Circular movement of $N = 25$ robots in a square configuration with the drag force, F_D, and shear stress, τ. The positions and orientations of the swarm at $t \in \{50, 100, 150\}$ s are marked on the trajectory. The red circle is the expected path, and the black curve is the real trajectory of the robots. (Color figure online)

length. Figure 6 shows screenshots from a randomly selected experiment with the square configuration. The experiment was conducted for 80 s in total, and screenshots were taken every 40 s. In the square configuration, the robots that were not on the edge of the swarm had connections to the other 8 neighbouring robots with two different lengths, which are horizontal & vertical and oblique directions. Compared to the hexagon configuration (shown in Fig. 5), the square configuration of the robots took less time to settle down. This was because of the more connections to the neighbouring robots, which made it easier for the square configuration to settle down.

4.3 Swarm Population

In this phase of experiments, we investigated the effects of swarm population sizes in both square and hexagon configurations. Figure 7 and Fig. 8 present the effect of population change on orientation, ω_i. The solid line indicates the median of all robots' orientations. The shaded area indicates the range between the first and third quartiles of robots' orientations.

In general, the median curves were very close to each other, and the shaded areas have a huge overlap. It means that the effect of the population size on the swarm was not significant. However, a large population size, $N = 91$, showed a slower collective motion than smaller populations. Also, as the population size increased, the settling curve was smoother. The smaller population had a sharper

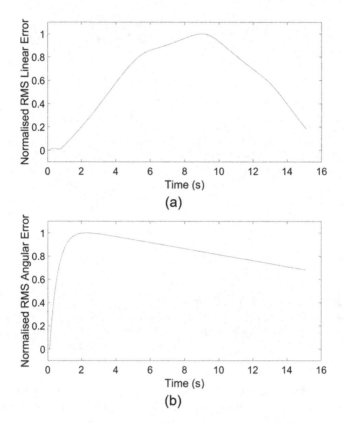

Fig. 4. (a) Linear and (b) angular errors of the circular movement of $N = 25$ robots tested in the first experiment with the drag force, F_D and shear stress, τ.

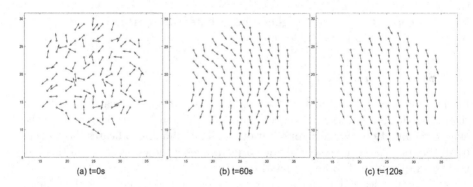

Fig. 5. Simulation result of $N = 91$ robots in a hexagon configuration with the drag force, F_D, and shear stress, τ. The positions and orientations of the swarm at $t \in \{0, 60, 120\}$ s are presented.

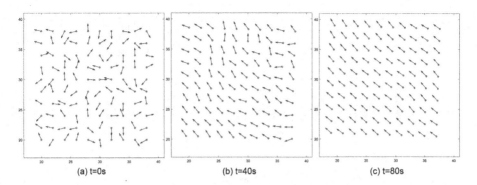

Fig. 6. Simulation result of $N = 100$ robots in a square configuration with the drag force, F_D, and shear stress, τ. The positions and orientations of the swarm at $t \in \{0, 40, 80\}$ s are presented.

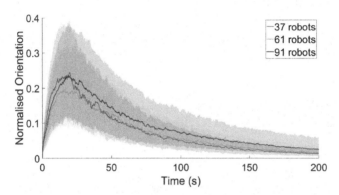

Fig. 7. Simulation result of $N \in \{37, 61, 91\}$ robots in a hexagon configuration with drag force, F_D, and shear stress, τ. The normalised orientations of the swarm between $t = 0$ s and $t = 200$ s are presented.

increase at the beginning of the experiment. This was because the orientation transmission that took a long time if there were a larger population resulted in an over-crowding phenomenon. The population did not have a significant effect on the peak of the curve, which was around $t= 20$ s.

4.4   Effects of Model Parameter

In the last phase of the experiments, we investigated the effects of the AES model parameter, β, on the performance of the swarm. Finding an optimal β will help us in the implementation of the real-world inspection scenarios to align robots faster and accurately. Figure 9 and Fig. 10 present the effects of β value on swarm orientation, ω_i. The results are presented with box plots where each box indicates the orientations of all the robots at all time steps in the specific β. In general, a larger β value leads to a smaller orientation value. A larger β

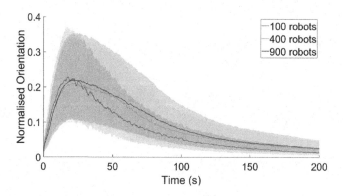

Fig. 8. Simulation result of $N \in \{100, 400, 900\}$ robots in a square configuration with drag force, F_D, and shear stress, τ. The normalised orientations of the swarm between $t = 0$ s and $t = 200$ s are presented.

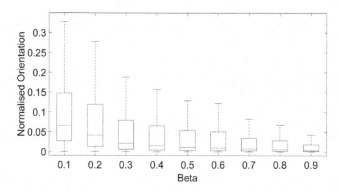

Fig. 9. Simulation result of $N = 91$ robots in a hexagon configuration with the drag force, F_D, and shear stress, τ. The normalised orientations of the swarm with inverse rotational damping coefficient, $\beta \in [0.1 \ldots 0.9]$ are presented.

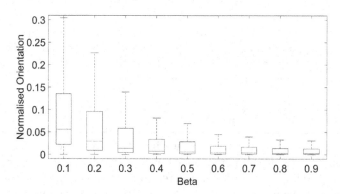

Fig. 10. Simulation result of $N = 100$ robots in a square configuration with the drag force, F_D, and shear stress, τ. The normalised orientations of the swarm with inverse rotational damping coefficient, $\beta \in [0.1 \ldots 0.9]$ are presented.

value represents a stronger force connection between robots. Compared to the hexagon configuration, the square configuration decreased faster as the β value increased. Square configuration had a larger impact due to more connections to the neighbouring robots.

5 Conclusion

The studied inspection scenario is based on a wet nuclear storage facility using micro-surface robots, *Bubbles*. We designed a motion model for the Bubbles considering water resistance. Compared to previous works, new applications were proposed for the AES model based on AMSR, and a new water surface model was developed. The observed results from the simulation experiments demonstrated the feasibility of using a swarm of micro-robots in such inspection scenarios. In future work, the algorithm will be applied to the real-world scenario using Bubble micro-robots. With the help of image analysis and image combination, this system will be able to inspect the nuclear waste storage facilities with minimum costs and effort.

References

1. Pepper, S., Farnitano, M., Carelli, J., Hazeltine, J., Bailey, D.: Lessons learned in testing of safeguards equipment. Brookhaven National Lab. Upton, NY (US), Technical report (2001)
2. Doyle, J.: Nuclear Safeguards, Security and Nonproliferation: Achieving Security with Technology and Policy. Elsevier (2011)
3. Cheah, W., Groves, K., Martin, H., Peel, H., Watson, S., Marjanovic, O., Lennox, B.: Mirrax: a reconfigurable robot for limited access environments arXiv preprint arXiv:2203.00337 (2022)
4. West, C., et al.: A debris clearance robot for extreme environments. In: Althoefer, K., Konstantinova, J., Zhang, K. (eds.) TAROS 2019. LNCS (LNAI), vol. 11649, pp. 148–159. Springer, Cham (2019). https://doi.org/10.1007/978-3-030-23807-0_13
5. Griffiths, A., Dikarev, A., Green, P.R., Lennox, B., Poteau, X., Watson, S.: AVEXIS-Aqua vehicle explorer for in-situ sensing. IEEE Robot. Autom. Lett. 1(1), 282–287 (2016)
6. Nancekievill, M., et al.: Development of a radiological characterization submersible ROV for use at fukushima daiichi. IEEE Trans. Nucl. Sci. 65(9), 2565–2572 (2018)
7. Lennox, C., Groves, K., Hondru, V., Arvin, F., Gornicki, K., Lennox, B.: Embodiment of an aquatic surface vehicle in an omnidirectional ground robot. In: 2019 IEEE International Conference on Mechatronics (ICM), vol. 1, pp. 182–186. IEEE (2019)
8. Groves, K., West, A., Gornicki, K., Watson, S., Carrasco, J., Lennox, B.: Mallard: an autonomous aquatic surface vehicle for inspection and monitoring of wet nuclear storage facilities. Robotics 8(2), 47 (2019)
9. Dorigo, M., Theraulaz, G., Trianni, V.: Reflections on the future of swarm robotics. Sci. Robot. 5(49), eabe4385 (2020)

10. Schranz, M., et al.: Swarm intelligence and cyber-physical systems: concepts, challenges and future trends. Swarm Evol. Comput. **60**, 100762 (2021)

11. Schmickl, T., et al.: Get in touch: cooperative decision making based on robot-to-robot collisions. Autonom. Agents Multi-Agent Syst. **18**(1), 133–155 (2009)

12. Ferrante, E., Turgut, A.E., Dorigo, M., Huepe, C.: Collective motion dynamics of active solids and active crystals. New J. Phys. **15**(9), 095011 (2013)

13. Raoufi, M., Turgut, A.E., Arvin, F.: Self-organized collective motion with a simulated real robot swarm. In: Althoefer, K., Konstantinova, J., Zhang, K. (eds.) TAROS 2019. LNCS (LNAI), vol. 11649, pp. 263–274. Springer, Cham (2019). https://doi.org/10.1007/978-3-030-23807-0_22

14. Liang, X., Qu, X., Hou, Y., Li, Y., Zhang, R.: Distributed coordinated tracking control of multiple unmanned surface vehicles under complex marine environments. Ocean Eng. **205**, 107328 (2020)

15. Huang, B., Song, S., Zhu, C., Li, J., Zhou, B.: Finite-time distributed formation control for multiple unmanned surface vehicles with input saturation. Ocean Eng. **233**, 109158 (2021)

16. Liu, Y., Song, R., Bucknall, R., Zhang, X.: Intelligent multi-task allocation and planning for multiple unmanned surface vehicles (USVS) using self-organising maps and fast marching method. Inf. Sci. **496**, 180–197 (2019)

17. Davey, A.: The growth of Taylor vortices in flow between rotating cylinders. J. Fluid Mech. **14**(3), 336–368 (1962)

Characterization of an Inflatable Soft Actuator and Tissue Interaction for In Vitro Mechanical Stimulation of Tissue

Frederick Forbes[1]($\boxtimes$), Abigail Smith[1], and Dana D. Damian[1,2]

[1] Sheffield Biomedical Robotics Lab, Automatic Control Systems Engineering Department, University of Sheffield, Sheffield S1 3JD, UK
{fforbes2,d.damian}@sheffield.ac.uk
[2] Insigneo Institute for in silico Medicine, University of Sheffield, Sheffield S1 3JD, UK

Abstract. Technology to improve tissue development is constantly being improved and refined. Soft robots have been utilized in medical settings due to their compliant nature, reducing the stiffness gradient at tissue-device interfaces. In this paper, we present a pneumatically actuated soft stimulating balloon capable of applying up to 70% strain to a phantom tissue construct at a pressure of 0.3 bar. Ecoflex^{TM}0050 is used as a biocompatible material for the membrane, and the interaction between the two was investigated by varying the scaffold stiffness and initial tension. Data from video tracking was used to compute the tensile strain applied to the scaffold. We present here, the first steps of characterizing the device for in vitro implementation and further integration into a custom bioreactor.

Keywords: Tissue engineering · Soft robotics · Mechanobiology

1 Introduction

In the field of tissue engineering, stimulation methods are used to mimic the body's native environment for healthy production of neotissue. Different stimulation methods and regimes have been implemented to stimulate targeted cell types and encourage cell proliferation and other cell functions, such as collagen deposition [1,2]. These methods can also increase the likelihood of achieving desired material properties, including tissue tensile strength [3]. Mechano-stimulation has been used to apply strain and induce cell action via shear [4], tensile [5] and compressive [6] stresses.

Bioreactors are commonly used to model the behaviour found in the cell's natural environment by providing a uni-directional stimulation, such as mechanical loading. Examples of rigid traditional bioreactors include Ebers [7], BioTense

This work was partially funded by The United Kingdom Engineering and Physical Sciences Research Council grant EP/S021035/1 and by a Department of Automatic Control and Systems Engineering, University of Sheffield, PhD scholarship.

S. Pacheco-Gutierrez et al. (Eds.): TAROS 2022, LNAI 13546, pp. 105–113, 2022.
https://doi.org/10.1007/978-3-031-15908-4_9

[8] and Cartigen [9]. However, stiffness gradients have been shown to affect cell activity and function [10], while soft interfaces better mimic the cell environment, therefore reducing the stiffness gradient at the boundary between the tissue construct and the actuator [11]. As a consequence, it is desirable to have a highly controllable interface where the strain intensity and direction can be regulated. Soft robots are suitable for such interfaces due to their intrinsically soft construction and the ability to control their deformation. This makes them a suitable candidate for the mechano-stimulation of tissue [12].

Research has been carried out on soft bioreactors capable of stretching and compressing cells to promote growth. Elastomeric poly-dimethylsiloxane (PDMS) membranes are widely used in combination with pneumatic or hydraulic actuation to apply strain or compress cells [13–15]. Liu et al. [16,17] also demonstrated a PDMS and hydrogel composite that combines stretch and compression, and integrates tissue stiffness measurements. Flexcell Inc have also developed commercially available bioreactors that exert strain by using a vacuum on rubber membrane microwells [18]. Finally, other methods of actuation of elastomeric membranes include work on pin-actuated flexible membranes for stretching by Kamotani et al. [19].

Most soft stimulation devices presented in the literature demonstrate the capability of stimulation from a single source. However, our aim is to add multidirectional stimuli using different sources. In [20], our group presented a robotic bioreactor equipped with stiffness-based control to stimulate tissue constructs. This is capable of providing a tensile strain by moving the clamps apart. This work presents a soft ballooning actuator that can be integrated into the previously developed bioreactor. It is able to apply a controllable strain to a tissue construct to increase the tensile stimulation modalities and directions. A concept illustration for this is shown in Fig. 1.

2   Methodology

The following section presents the design of the stimulating balloon, the manufacturing protocol for soft matter, the experimental set-up and procedure.

2.1   Stimulating Balloon Design and Integration into Bioreactor Chamber

The stimulating balloon required specific design parameters to ensure: 1) the materials exposed to cells are biocompatible, 2) controllable tensile strains can be applied to a tissue scaffold, 3) the actuator can be integrated with the current bioreactor for future combined stimulation regimes and 4) the chamber that houses the cells must be isolated from the external environment and able to be sterilized.

An exploded view diagram of the stimulating balloon is shown in Fig. 2. The assembly consists of a 1 mm thick membrane, secured using a cap with a

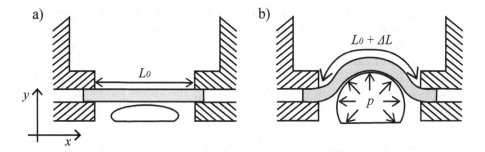

Fig. 1. Illustration of the presented stimulation method. The pink shaded area represents the tissue scaffold seeded with cells, the hatched area represents the clamps that hold the tissue scaffold in place and below is the ballooning membrane. a) When no stimulation is applied, L_0 is the length of the scaffold fixed between the two clamps, b) When the stimulating balloon is pressurized, p increases and causes the actuator to expand. The tissue scaffold is stretched, and the length increases by ΔL, representing a tensile strain. (Color figure online)

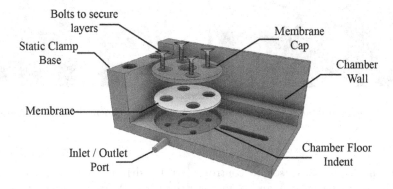

Fig. 2. Exploded-view diagram of the stimulating balloon assembly.

10 mm diameter central hole to allow the membrane to balloon out when pressurized. The membrane is made of Ecoflex^{TM}0050 (E50) (Smooth On Inc.), chosen for its biocompatibility [21], and is fabricated using the procedure described in the following section. The bioreactor floor and membrane cap are 3D printed (Formlabs Form 2) using clear resin.

Finally, the ballooning membrane is inflated and monitored via two 1 mm diameter channels connecting a syringe pump and pressure sensor to the pneumatic chamber.

2.2 Soft Matter Fabrication

To make the phantom scaffolds, Ecoflex^{TM}0030 (E30) (Smooth On Inc.), E50 and Moldstar^{TM}15 SLOW (MS15) (Smooth On Inc.) are combined in equal quantities with their respective A and B parts and mixed in an ARE-250 mixer (Thinky) for three minutes. Next, they were degassed and poured into durable resin moulds (Formlabs Form 3) and left to cure at room temperature. 10 mm × 20 mm × 1 mm scaffolds were moulded with a central row of small nodes (0.5 mm deep, 1 mm diameter) to allow tracking of different points during pressurization of the stimulating balloon. Three scaffolds for each material were made. Ballooning membranes were also made with E50, following the above procedure using a membrane mould.

2.3   Stimulating Balloon Experimental Set-Up and Procedure

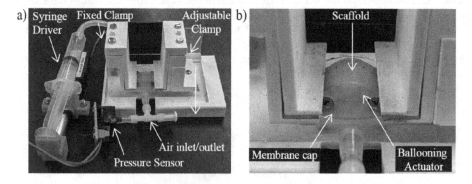

Fig. 3. a) Labelled images of the stimulating balloon experimental setup. b) Close-up labelled image of the scaffold and ballooning actuator.

An Arduino Nano was used to control a syringe driver which utilised a 12 V linear actuator (Amazon) and a motor driver (Sparkfun). A pressure sensor (Honeywell) was used to measure the pressure within the chamber. Close-up videos of the scaffold were captured using a microscope camera.

A scaffold was held in place above the membrane using one fixed and one adjustable 3D-printed clamp (Prusa i3 MK3), to accommodate different scaffold lengths and apply tension, as shown in Fig. 3. The pressure was then increased from 0 bar to 0.3 bar and decreased back to 0 bar in set increments. Each target pressure was held for two seconds and then updated. For each scaffold five cycles were captured.

The videos were imported to Tracker, a video tracking software. This was used to record the x and y coordinates of the nodes on the scaffold and the clamps in time, as shown in Fig. 4. Using the coordinates, the length between each node pair was calculated and summed to calculate a total scaffold length, L_t. The length of the scaffold at 0 bar was set as the original length, L_0. The change in length, was used to calculate the maximum percentage strain, ϵ, as shown in Eq. 1

$$\epsilon = (L_t - L_0)/(L_0 \times 100) \tag{1}$$

Finally, linear interpolation is used to determine the strain at the recorded pressures. The data from the five cycles for each scaffold were averaged. For the strain, the data is shown as the median and the error bars show the 95% confidence interval. For the pressure, the mean value is plotted and the error shown is the standard deviation.

Different elastomers were chosen for their varying stiffness; E30, E50 and MS15. The Young's modulus for the materials used in this experiment were derived using a uniaxial tensile test machine (IMADA MX2) and are shown in Table 1.

Fig. 4. Video stills of the stimulating balloon inflation at 0 bar, 0.2 bar and 0.3 bar. Yellow circles highlight the nodes that were recorded in Tracker. (Color figure online)

Table 1. Young's modulus for each phantom scaffold material

Material	Young's modulus (kPa)
Ecoflex^{TM}0030	40
Ecoflex^{TM}0050	120
Mold Star^{TM} 15 SLOW	410

Different pre-strains were applied to the scaffold and tested. The pretension of an E50 scaffold was varied by changing the distance between the clamps. For 0% strain, the scaffold was fixed and the clamp adjusted until the scaffold was just in tension. Using the initial length measured as the distance between the clamps, a new distance for each strain is calculated and the clamps adjusted. The distance between the clamps were measured and changed to apply 0, 5, 10 and 20% strains.

3   Results and Discussion

The results for how the strain is affected by 1) changing the stiffness of the phantom scaffold and 2) the pre-tension of the scaffold are presented here.

Figure 5 shows that by increasing the stiffness of the phantom scaffold material, this decreases the strain that the stimulating balloon applies for given pressure. E30 and E50 scaffolds demonstrate hyperelastic behaviour, shown by the

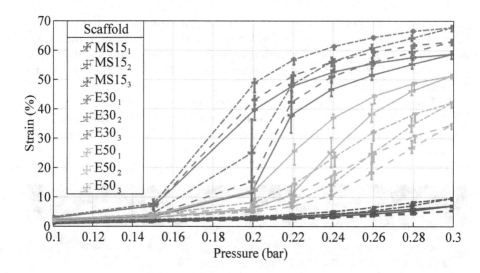

Fig. 5. The relationship between strain and pressure for different scaffold materials. This shows how the stiffness of the material changes the strain applied by the balloon. The materials used are MS15, E30 and E50.

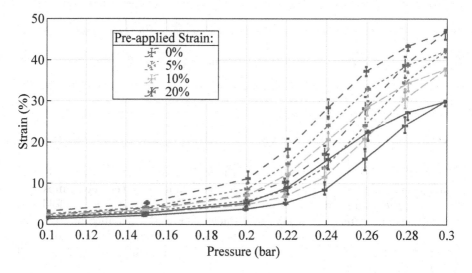

Fig. 6. The relationship between strain and pressure for various pre-tension values (0, 5, 10 and 20%) of an E50 scaffold. This shows how the initial tension applied to the phantom scaffold affects the strain produced by the balloon.

characteristic hysteresis curves. At 0.3 bar, the average maximum strain achieved for the E30, E50 and MS15 scaffolds were approximately 63, 43 and 7%, respectively. The results show hysteresis; within each hysteretic loop, inflation describes the lower half of the cycle and deflation is the top half. There is a large variation within samples of the same material, although they all follow the same trend. This could be due to how the scaffold was positioned, whether the tension was equal or due to manufacture variability e.g. slight differences in thickness. The error in strain is small for most target pressures, however, large error can be seen in the third scaffold for E30 at 0.2 bar. This is due to the ballooning phenomenon at higher pressures. More target pressures could be added in the ballooning range to allow more time for the membrane to react to the change in pressure and decrease dynamic affects. A dynamic study should also be carried out in future and compared to the results presented as this could allow faster frequency regimes to be implemented for more varied stimulation methods.

Figure 6 shows the results for varying pre-applied strain to an E50 scaffold. As the pre-applied strain is increased, the strain induced by the stimulating balloon reduces. This can be used to inform more advanced stimulation regimes by combining the modalities of both the stimulating balloon and current robotic bioreactor. The maximum strain achieved with the pre-applied 0, 5, 10 and 20% strains were 47, 42, 37 and 30% respectively. The sum of the maximum strain and the pre-applied strain are similar for each trial. This highlights the region where the actuator is no longer able to apply significant additional strain with increasing pressure.

4   Conclusion

This work presents the design and characterization of a stimulating balloon to increase the modalities of a robotic bioreactor presented in previous works [20]. These preliminary results show that the balloon is capable of providing a large range of tensile strains for scaffolds with varying stiffness. This information could be used for strain-based pressure control during in vitro experiments to follow stimulation regimes. The strain has been considered to act in one direction. By tracking more nodes to the scaffold, the local strain distribution could be better understood. This work could be further used as a building block to explore different configurations of balloons, for example, using an array and comparing how this affects the strain distribution of a tissue construct. Future in vitro experiments will be carried out to further develop this tissue engineering tool and combine the stimulation modalities of the bioreactor. As the stiffness of the tissue changes in real time, tensile testing of the scaffold can be carried out to adapt the pressure control of the stimulating balloon to apply the desired strain. Combined stimulation regimes could be investigated by using the relationship for pressure and strain at different initial strains discussed in this study.

Acknowledgements. The authors would like to thank Marco Pontin and Joanna Jones for their input into this work.

References

1. Lohberger, B., Kaltenegger, H., Stuendl, N., Rinner, B., Leithner, A., Sadoghi, P.: Impact of cyclic mechanical stimulation on the expression of extracellular matrix proteins in human primary rotator cuff fibroblasts. Knee Surg. Sports Traumatol. Arthrosc. **24**(12), 3884–3891 (2016)
2. Thanarak, J., Mohammed, H., Pashneh-Tala, S., Claeyssens, F., Green, N.: Enhanced collagen production from human dermal fibroblasts on poly (glycerol sebacate)-methacrylate scaffolds. In: 2018 11th Biomedical Engineering International Conference (BMEiCON), pp. 1–4. IEEE (2018)
3. Lee, J.K., et al.: Tension stimulation drives tissue formation in scaffold-free systems. Nat. Mater. **16**(8), 864–873 (2017)
4. Dewey, C.F., Jr., Bussolari, S.R., Gimbrone, M.A., Jr., Davies, P.F.: The dynamic response of vascular endothelial cells to fluid shear stress. J. Biomech. Eng. **103**(3), 177–185 (1981). https://doi.org/10.1115/1.3138276
5. Xu, J., Liu, M., Liu, J., Caniggia, I., Post, M.: Mechanical strain induces constitutive and regulated secretion of glycosaminoglycans and proteoglycans in fetal lung cells. J. Cell Sci. **109**(6), 1605–1613 (1996). https://doi.org/10.1242/jcs.109.6.1605
6. Shachar, M., Benishti, N., Cohen, S.: Effects of mechanical stimulation induced by compression and medium perfusion on cardiac tissue engineering. Biotechnol. Progr. **28**(6), 1551–1559 (2012). https://doi.org/10.1002/btpr.1633
7. TC-3 bioreactor. https://ebersmedical.com/tissue-engineering/bioreactors/load-culture/tc-3
8. Biotense bioreactor. https://www.admet.com/products/micro-testers/biotense-bioreactor/
9. Cartigen: Mechanical compression bioreactor systems. https://www.tissuegrowth.com/prod_cartilage.cfm
10. Discher, D.E., Janmey, P., Wang, Y.L.: Tissue cells feel and respond to the stiffness of their substrate. Science **310**(5751), 1139–1143 (2005)
11. Ghosh, K., et al.: Cell adaptation to a physiologically relevant ECM mimic with different viscoelastic properties. Biomaterials **28**(4), 671–679 (2007)
12. Perez Guagnelli, E., Nejus, S., Yu, J., Miyashita, S., Liu, Y., Damian, D.: Axially and radially expandable modular helical soft actuator for robotic implantables (2018)
13. Todros, S., Spadoni, S., Maghin, E., Piccoli, M., Pavan, P.G.: A novel bioreactor for the mechanical stimulation of clinically relevant scaffolds for muscle tissue engineering purposes. Processes **9**, 474 (2021)
14. Paek, J., et al.: Soft robotic constrictor for in vitro modeling of dynamic tissue compression. Sci. Rep. **11**, 1–11 (2021)
15. Carreira, S.C., Taghavi, M., Loriè, E.P., Rossiter, J.: FleXert: a soft, actuatable multiwell plate insert for cell culture under stretch. ACS Biomater. Sci. Eng. **7**, 2225–2245 (2021)
16. Liu, H., et al.: Microdevice arrays with strain sensors for 3D mechanical stimulation and monitoring of engineered tissues. Biomaterials **172**, 30–40 (2018). https://www.sciencedirect.com/science/article/pii/S0142961218303041
17. Liu, H., Usprech, J.F., Parameshwar, P.K., Sun, Y., Simmons, C.A.: Combinatorial screen of dynamic mechanical stimuli for predictive control of MSC mechano-responsiveness. Sci. Adv. **7**(19), eabe7204 (2021). https://www.science.org/doi/abs/10.1126/sciadv.abe7204

18. Tension cell stretching bioreactor system. https://www.flexcellint.com/category/tension
19. Kamotani, Y., et al.: Individually programmable cell stretching microwell arrays actuated by a braille display. Biomaterials **29**, 2646–2655 (2008)
20. Smith, A.F., Thanarak, J., Pontin, M., Green, N.H., Damian, D.D.: Design and development of a robotic bioreactor for in vitro tissue engineering. In: 2021 IEEE International Conference on Robotics and Automation (ICRA), pp. 12 428–12 434 (2021)
21. Luis, E., Pan, H.M., Sing, S.L., Bajpai, R., Song, J., Yeong, W.Y.: 3D direct printing of silicone meniscus implant using a novel heat-cured extrusion-based printer. Polymers **12**(5) (2020). https://www.mdpi.com/2073-4360/12/5/1031

EMap: Real-Time Terrain Estimation

Jacobus C. Lock, Fanta Camara, and Charles Fox[✉]

School of Computer Science, University of Lincoln, Lincoln, UK
chfox@lincoln.ac.uk

Abstract. Terrain mapping has a many use cases in both land surveyance and autonomous vehicles. Popular methods generate occupancy
maps over 3D space, which are sub-optimal in outdoor scenarios with
large, clear spaces where gaps in LiDAR readings are common. A terrain can instead be modelled as a height map over 2D space which can
iteratively be updated with incoming LiDAR data, which simplifies computation and allows missing points to be estimated based on the current
terrain estimate. The latter point is of particular interest, since it can
reduce the data collection effort required (and its associated costs) and
current options are not suitable to real-time operation. In this work,
we introduce a new method that is capable of performing such terrain
mapping and inferencing tasks in real-time. We evaluate it with a set of
mapping scenarios and show it is capable of generating maps with higher
accuracy than an OctoMap-based method.

1 Introduction

3D terrain mapping is a core problem in mobile robotics and efficient solutions
are crucial to enable robots to explore and perform tasks on various terrains.
Terrain data also has offline uses in site surveyance, such as to plan new construction projects, environmental monitoring to improve early interventions for
flooding, and determining agricultural subsidy payments dependant on terrain
quality. Many terrain mapping solutions currently employed use visual methods
that rely on many distinct, clear features and are therefore well-suited for indoor
or urban outdoor environments where these features are plentiful. However, such
features are much rarer in outdoor off-road environments which are largely flat
and bereft of many distinct static features, making the popular vision-based
methods less robust in these settings.

A popular approach to the terrain mapping problem uses point clouds captured from a LiDAR sensor and merges them together over time using methods
such as OctoMap [1] and UFOMap [2] to form a complete map of the environment. However, these methods become less robust the further away data captured by the LiDAR are from the actual sensor – significant gaps in the terrain
estimate are introduced as the gaps between LiDAR hits become larger. This is
not a particularly serious issue in populated urban or indoor areas, where large,
empty areas at further distances (25 m+) are fairly uncommon, but becomes
acute in off-road outdoor areas, where large, flat expanses with uneven surfaces

S. Pacheco-Gutierrez et al. (Eds.): TAROS 2022, LNAI 13546, pp. 114–127, 2022.
https://doi.org/10.1007/978-3-031-15908-4_10

Fig. 1. An example of a surface (left) reconstructed using EMap (right).

are the norm. Currently, this problem is addressed by having the sensor pass over the data-sparse areas multiple times to generate additional data with which to fill in the cloud map and increase the terrain estimate's fidelity. Such approaches are appropriate for, and incur little additional cost from, small autonomous robots and vehicles that can make many passes with minimal input from a human operator. However, where large industrial or agricultural robots and vehicles are involved, such a multi-pass approach can become very costly, particularly when human labour is required to monitor the work.

As an example, suppose a LiDAR sensor can detect points up to R meters away. The number of LiDAR hits decays as a function of the distance to the sensor (see Fig. 2 for the sampling density over R for the OS1-64 LiDAR used in this work). If one sets a minimum sampling density requirement for a terrain map, there will exist some range r_m from the sensor that demarcates the maximum distance from the sensor where the sampling density becomes too low and which will require additional passes to sufficiently map. A survey site of width $3r_m$, for example, will then require at least 2 back and forth passes to map with a sufficient number of point data. However, if r_m could be extended, the entire site could be mapped with fewer passes. In many applications, the savings could become substantial when considering the operational costs involved in land surveyance. For example, helicopter and drone-based LiDAR surveyance operations are common and the costs include equipment rent, pilot wage, and fuel, so any reductions in total travel time and distance could lead to a real and substantial economic and environmental impact.

A simple way to increase the effective scanning range r_m is to use a higher-cost LiDAR with an increased sampling density. Alternatively, approximating point positions in and around the gaps in the terrain estimate, based on actual LiDAR inputs surrounding the area, will effectively increase the sampling density and extend r_m. The widely used OctoMap [1] package can be used to create an occupancy map and perform interpolation between the occupied nodes to fill in the unknown nodes, thereby accomplishing the aforementioned approximation task. However, in this paper we show that this OctoMap-based interpolation approach is not robust enough to have a meaningful impact on reducing the surface estimation errors and increase a sensor's effective scanning range, r_m. We therefore introduce a new alternative method, EMap, based on energy minimisation techniques to reduce these errors, thereby increasing r_m and reducing the

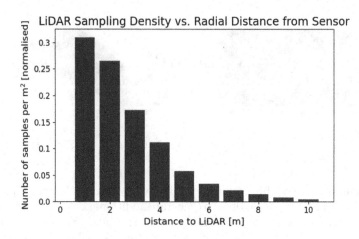

Fig. 2. Number of samples captured by the Ouster OS1 LiDAR used in this work as a function of distance distance to the sensor.

number of passes needed to generate an accurate terrain map. Figure 1 shows a sample surface reconstructed using the EMap method.

Many studies regard only online autonomous navigation as the use-case for real-time mapping. However, the parameters and requirements of land surveyance tasks differ significantly and are often not considered. In contrast, we devise a set of utility functions that represent both types of tasks and evaluate our method according to its performance in these simulated tasks. The contributions of this work are therefore as follows: First, a novel approach to terrain mapping, specialised for off-road settings that extends the effective LiDAR mapping range beyond that of OctoMap without significant additional computational cost. Second, a set of utility functions that resemble the priorities and constraints of terrain mapping scenarios.

2   Related Work

Computer vision techniques have successfully been used for surface reconstruction for many years and are quite mature at this point. Indeed, stereo vision systems are extensively used in the Mars rovers [3]. However, in the last decade researchers have become increasingly interested in using LiDARs to capture 3D environmental data [4–6]. These sensors offer several advantages over camera-based systems, such as being more robust to different lighting conditions and offering a wider field of view without distortion. Many modern Geographic Information Systems (GIS), which provide a map of a geographic area [7], rely on data captured by some form of LiDAR. Such maps are very useful for environmental and urban planners to predict floods, observe floral patterns over time, or to create relief maps, for example, and form so-called Digital Elevation Models (DEM). DEMs are often created by merging multiple point cloud observations over a large area together using supplemental localisation data from a GPS, for example. However, these models often break down when different terrain features are captured and are not properly classified [8,9]. For example, floral canopies may distort the terrain map's height estimate if these are not properly accounted for in the DEM. A smaller scale DEM, restricted to a single terrain type, would not be affected by these issues.

OctoMap [1] and a recent variant, UFOMap [2], offer such a LiDAR-based mapping approach suitable for use by mobile robots and their immediate surroundings. As LiDAR data are received, these systems organise them into an octree [10] structure, which is a highly scalable and optimised data structure for 3D geometric modelling and is very well-suited for high resolution mapping. Octree nodes and leaves are marked as free or occupied according to whether or not a LiDAR observation falls within a given node's range, indicating that the ray reflected off of an obstacle or has reached its maximum distance. The nodes are iteratively updated with each incoming LiDAR datum and eventually forms a complete high-resolution map of the robot's surroundings. Given these frameworks' octree-based structure, their fast update speed and low barrier to entry, they have become a popular choice for many roboticists' real-time mapping tasks. However, while beneficial for cluttered indoor and urban environments, OctoMap can leave significant areas in its terrain estimate unfilled, particularly at longer distances where hit densities are lower. This makes OctoMap and its derivative systems unreliable for the task of surface reconstruction in an outdoor, off-road context.

Machine learning models, such as SVMs, have been used to infer surface points at unobserved locations with reasonable success [11]. However, the actual terrain reconstruction and estimation process takes place offline. The GPMap [12] and GPOctoMap [13] frameworks are both terrain mapping and surface estimation approaches that use input data from the LiDAR to train a set of Gaussian Process (GP) regressors which fill in any gaps in the surface estimate. Both also use octree-based maps to discretise the environment and make the terrain data more amenable to additional processing. However, GPs are well known to be computationally expensive and, despite optimisations introduced by various authors to improve their scalability [14,15], they remain as such, making GPMap and GPOctomap unsuitable for real-time mapping and surface reconstruction tasks for reasonably-sized environments.

Other methods have been proposed for efficiently reconstructing the complete surface of an arbitrary 3D object [16]. One approach is to model the surface using an energy function and optimise it according to some structural parameters [17,18]. Such functions are relatively straightforward to minimise and present an efficient surface reconstruction pipeline. However these techniques have only been applied to 3D objects' surfaces and have not been used for environmental mapping. Indeed, given the flexibility of these methods, their proven computational efficiency and the problem at hand, we believe that an energy model-based approach could prove useful for terrain reconstruction tasks in an outdoor off-road setting.

3   Method

At their cores, mapping an outdoor off-road terrain and an urban one are functionally similar processes. OctoMap [1] and UFOMap [2] are popular, robust and freely available tools that can produce occupancy maps of various environments. However, they do not have the capability of inferring whether a node in an unknown occupancy state between other occupied nodes is occupied or free. This is an important factor for producing complete and accurate surveyance maps, as well as robots that require complete knowledge of the surrounding terrain to plan their movement and accomplish their tasks more effectively. The fact that rural outdoor environments are often continuous, albeit uneven, surfaces can be exploited to fill in these gaps and estimate a node's state if it is located on the same contour as its occupied neighbours.

Our approach, called EMap (Energy Minimisation Mapping), uses the aforementioned assumption of a continuous surface contour to find the surface estimate that best fits the input LiDAR reference data. As the name alludes to, EMap is based on the concept of energy minimisation (EM, sometimes called 'geometry optimisation'), which is a process to determine the optimal geo-spatial arrangement of objects according to an energy-based model. This approach is often used in computational chemistry to find the expected geometric arrangement of atoms in a molecule based on their inter-atomic energy bonds (a spring-like force that attracts or repels a pair of atoms based on the distance between them). The atoms' final resting positions will be located where their inter-atomic forces settle at a new equilibrium state and the net energy in the system is zero.

Applying this approach to a LiDAR-based terrain mapper is fairly straightforward. Suppose that at time t we have a set of surface nodes to approximate the terrain surface. Like the atoms discussed earlier, these nodes are connected to one another according to an energy model that is a function of the relative distance between neighbouring nodes (i.e. the spring-like forces described earlier). Incoming LiDAR point data at time $t + 1$ are then modelled as new nodes with additional spring forces between a new node and its nearest neighbour from the surface nodes from time t. This approximates additional energy being introduced to an enclosed system, resembling work done on the surface node system. The surface nodes are forced absorb the incoming energy and reach a new equilibrium by adjusting their relative positions. Since we are only interested in the map's surface topology, we can simplify the problem by fixing the surface nodes' x and y coordinates in the LiDAR's local frame, limiting all the nodes' displacements to the z dimension only. Refer to Fig. 3 for an example spring-node system exposed to an incoming LiDAR point.

Let us now mathematically formalise our EMap approach. The terrain surface estimate consists of a set of nodes with constant (x, y) coordinates and variable heights, z, measured relative to the LiDAR sensor's local frame. These are attached to one another in a grid pattern with springs with a spring constant k. A node s will therefore have between 2 and 4 neighbouring nodes influencing s's position, depending on its position in the grid (e.g. a corner node will only

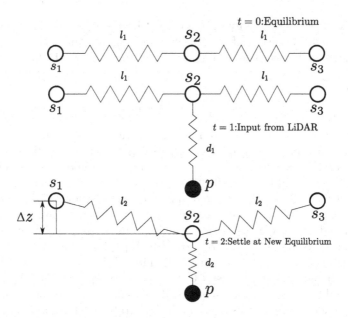

Fig. 3. Interactions between nodes, neighbours and LiDAR points.

have 2 connected neighbours). The total energy at a single node s at equilibrium at timestep $t = 0$ is then given by

$$E_s^{t=0} = \sum_{i=0}^{n} \frac{1}{2} k \Delta z_{si}^2, \qquad (1)$$

where n is the number of connected neighbours s has and Δz_{si} is the vertical-only difference in height between nodes s and i (since x and y are fixed, their deltas are eliminated from the spring displacement vector).

Incoming data from the LiDAR are modelled as work done on the surface estimate nodes, perturbing them from their equilibrium states. The work done by each incoming LiDAR point is modelled as another spring connecting each input point with its nearest surface node. In its equilibrium state at $t = 0$ and $\Delta z = 0$, the total net energy in the surface estimate's spring network is zero. However, when new LiDAR points are introduced at timestep $t = 1$, the system's net energy is no longer zero and the resultant energy at each node is calculated as

$$E_s^{t=1} = \sum_{i=0}^{n} \frac{1}{2} k_i \Delta z_{si}^2 + \sum_{j=0}^{m} \frac{1}{2} k_j d_{sj}^2, \qquad (2)$$

where m are the number of input LiDAR points attached to node s and d_{si} is the Euclidean distance between point j and node s. This perturbation results in a non-zero energy state for the surface estimate and Δz must be adjusted to compensate for the new energy introduced to the system. We ignore the springs' transient behavior in favour of the steady-state response and solve the system as a set of linear equations to determine Δz. Rewriting Eq. 2 in the form $Ax + b = c$ gives,

$$e = \frac{1}{2} K_s \Delta z + \frac{1}{2} K_d d, \tag{3}$$

where e is an $a \times 1$ vector containing the energy E_s at each node, a is the number of nodes in the surface estimate and K_s is an $a \times a$ diagonal matrix containing each node's effective spring constant (e.g. a node with 4 neighbours and $k = 10 \, \mathrm{N \, m^{-1}}$ will have an effective $k_{eff} = 40 \, \mathrm{N \, m^{-1}}$). Δz is an $a \times 1$ vector made up of the sum of the squared spring displacements, Δz_{si}^2, between the surface node and its neighbours and d is an $a \times 1$ vector containing the sum of the squared displacements between node s and its nearest m input points, d_{sj}^2 (see Eq. 2). Note that the term $\frac{1}{2} K_d d$ in Eq. 3 represents a fixed quantity of work that is done on the system by the input LiDAR points, and therefore remains unchanged. By setting $e = 0$, we can solve Eq. 3 analytically solved at the new equilibrium state. The required displacement that must be applied to each surface node to reach this new equilibrium state is determined by taking an element-wise square root of Δz. This process of performing work on the surface nodes and finding their new equilibrium positions is iterative and takes place for each LiDAR scan, refining the overall terrain estimate over time.

To find each node s's nearest input LiDAR points, we use a kD-tree search method, which is $\mathcal{O}(\log a)$ in complexity. However, the overall complexity is dominated by the matrix inversion process to solve Eq. 3. With our current constract of fixing the nodes' (x, y) coordinates, K_s is diagonal and can be inverted in linear time. However, we might relax this constraint in future work and we therefore cannot rely on the aforementioned diagonality to remain true indefinitely. Were therefore opt to use a conjugate gradient descent method to remain flexible and determine K_s^{-1} (K_s will always be semi-positive definite). This results in a complexity of $\mathcal{O}(a\sqrt{\kappa})$, where κ is K_s's condition number which is expected to be small. We can therefore anticipate a time complexity that grows linearly with the number of nodes in EMap's surface estimate.

4   Experiments

4.1   Setup

A Gazebo simulation was created to allow a LiDAR-mounted vehicle to drive over a surface at $1 \, \mathrm{ms^{-1}}$ and collect point data. The simulation environment geometry, shown in Fig. 1, is such that the angular pose and position of the LiDAR remained unchanged, despite variations in the surface shape the vehicle was driving over. This mimics the behaviour of a real large agricultural vehicle or UAV, neither of which are significantly affected by variations of their work surfaces (UAVs can keep their altitude quite stable in favourable weather conditions). Furthermore, the robot was limited to driving only forward along the x-axis and no steering or planning was implemented. The LiDAR sensor simulated is an Ouster OS1-64 with 512×64 beams in a 360° view around the sensor and 22.5° above and below its horizontal. Sensor noise was added and is simulated as (± 0.05 m) Gaussian noise. Only points within a 10 m radius from the sensor are considered. The terrain surface was generated with $z_s(x_s, y_s) = h(x_s, y_s) = \sin \frac{x_s}{\pi} \sin \frac{y_s}{\pi}$. The surface's sinusoidal pattern of peaks and troughs introduce periodic occlusions, thereby guaranteeing gaps in the sensor data and providing a challenging mapping task. In order to determine a realistic surface estimation error, we repeated the experiment 10 times, setting the robot's initial position along the y-axis at a new value for each run, 1 m apart. This provides sufficient resolution across the entire surface profile. The collected LiDAR data were processed by both the EMap and OctoMap systems.

EMap. Our EM-based method begins by transforming the incoming LiDAR data to the vehicle's local frame and filtering all points that fall outside the 10 m range. A kD-tree nearest neighbour search is then used to find the Euclidian distances between the incoming LiDAR points and their nearest surface nodes, followed by the EM process that determines the surface nodes' required displacements, which are then added to their z coordinates. To cover the 10 m work surface, the surface estimate was set to contain 40 nodes in the vehicle's x and y directions, giving 1600 surface nodes in total.

OctoMap. As a baseline, we implemented a simple interpolation layer on top of OctoMap to produce surface estimates. OctoMap was used rather than UFOMap, as it is mature and widely-used, and the authors of UFOMap did not report any significant increases in accuracy over OctoMap. OctoMap was used to build up a volumetric occupancy map with the incoming LiDAR data as it normally does. However, since the work surface is flat and continuous, we know that the topmost occupation nodes will form the surface estimate. Another 40×40-node surface estimate is then set to assume the position of these topmost octree nodes and model the underlying surface. The additional computation takes the form of a kD-tree search to find the surface's top layer and transform the surface nodes to that location.

4.2 Experiment Scenarios

We devised a number of example terrain mapping scenarios to evaluate the terrain mapping methods with. Each of these scenarios have their own set of constraints and priorities, reflected by a set of utility functions, which, for example, prioritise nearby points over those further away for obstacle detection purposes. These are two basic scenarios with minimal filtering, as well as two drivability ones. The utility functions, F, are applied to the surface estimates like a filter and range with $F(x, y) \in [0, 1]$. The mean square error (MSE) is,

$$\text{MSE} = \sum_t \frac{1}{a} \sum_a ((g(x, y)_t - h(x, y)_t) F(x, y))^2, \tag{4}$$

where g and h are the surface estimates given by EMap or OctoMap, and the ground truth, and a the total number of nodes in the surface estimate.

Baseline - Raw Points. This scenario is a naive scan including all input points equally, with a utility function $F_r(x, y) = 1$, and acts as the baseline scenario.

Mapping - Nearest Points. A nearest point scan simulates cases where only the points closest to the sensor are considered reliable. This gives the utility function

$$F_n(x, y) = \begin{cases} 1, & \sqrt{x^2 + y^2} < 0.25\,\mathrm{m} \\ 0, & \text{otherwise.} \end{cases} \tag{5}$$

Drive Planning - Gaussian. The first drivability scenario emphasises points at a middle distance, r_g, from the vehicle, while progressively ignoring points further away from r_g, mimicking the needs of a planner for autonomous vehicles:

$$F_g(x, y) = \exp\left(-\frac{1}{2}(\sqrt{x^2 + y^2} + r_g)^2\right). \tag{6}$$

Obstacle Detection - Cumulative Distribution Function. This second drivability scenario prioritises all data points closest to the sensor, which decays with the points' distance to the sensor and allows for effective obstacle detection nearby a vehicle. This utility function can be modelled by an un-normalised cumulative distribution function (CDF) centred around a threshold scanner range, r_s,

$$F_c(x, y) = 1 - \frac{1}{2}\left(1 + \frac{\mathrm{erf}(\sqrt{y^2 + x^2} - r_s)}{\sqrt{2}}\right). \tag{7}$$

The values for r_s and r_g were heuristically set to 4 m and 6 m.

5   Results

5.1   Reconstruction Accuracy

The MSE results for all of the scenarios across the 10 experiment runs are given in Table 1. These show EMap consistently generating more accurate terrain estimates for all of the experiment scenarios, improving upon the OctoMap baseline between approximately 29% and 44%. The standard deviations for the MSE's are also significantly reduced for the EMap system, indicating that the estimates are more precise in addition to being more accurate. Overall reductions in MSE in each scenario show that the effective scanning range, r_m, is extended when using EMap for terrain mapping. For example, the scanning range for the *CDF* scenario can be increased by 36.7%, to 5.47 m, over the baseline's 4 m without suffering a decrease in accuracy compared with OctoMap. This conclusion is further supported by the surface estimates' error spreads from the *raw* scenario shown in Fig. 6. These heatmaps show OctoMap's MSE significantly spiking around the edges furthest away from the sensor along the x-axis. The opposite is observed from EMap's result – the MSE is lowest furthest way from the sensor on the x-axis. The error scales for these two sets of results are quite different, so we consider the normalised MSEs. These further reinforce EMap's error values being smaller in general and also more consistent compared to OctoMap's results.

Table 1. Each scenario's terrain reconstruction accuracy for OctoMap and EMap.

Scenario	OctoMap	EMap	% Difference
Raw	74.6 ± 18.2	45.8 ± 6.3	38.6%
Nearest points	88.8 ± 51.4	50.0 ± 25.6	43.7%
Gaussian	1.21 ± 1.19	0.86 ± 0.67	28.9%
CDF	0.93 ± 0.58	0.59 ± 0.32	36.6%

The absolute MSE values in isolation are quite large, e.g. 45 cm for EMap's *raw* scenario. However, this can be explained by the cyclical, sinusoidal terrain that was used for the experiment, where the error fluctuates periodically with the vehicle's forward movement as the terrain transitions from a peak to a trough (see Fig. 5). This is because a peak occludes a portion of the terrain from the LiDAR's view, with its view only fully restored when the vehicle crests the peak and sees behind it.

5.2   Processing Time per Loop

Figure 6 shows a plot of EMap's processing time per loop as a function of a, the number of nodes in the surface estimate. The time was taken as the mean time per loop across a 30 s period for multiple values of a. Considering its formulation, EMap's computational complexity is expected to be linear and dependant on a only (see Sec. 4.1). Indeed, this expectation is confirmed by Fig. 6, where the processing time per loop grows linearly with the number of surface nodes and indicates that EMap can be scales reasonably well – doubling the surface resolution increases the computation time by a relatively low 25%. In the experiments, 1600 nodes were used, giving 16 nodes per m^2 and taking approximately 0.05 s to process, giving a 20 Hz update rate, achieving our goal of real-time terrain reconstruction.

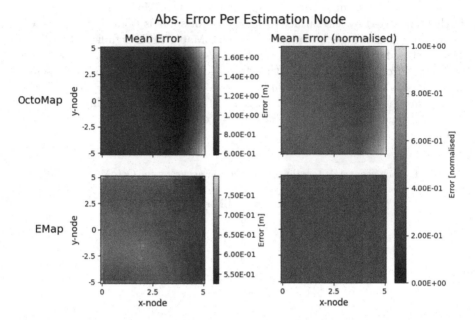

Fig. 4. Histogram of the MSEs recorded for both EMap and OctoMap during the raw scneario at each node on the estimation surface.

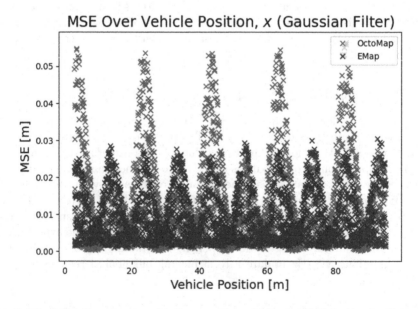

Fig. 5. The MSE from for over the distance the vehicle travelled during the Gaussian scenario as determined by EMap.

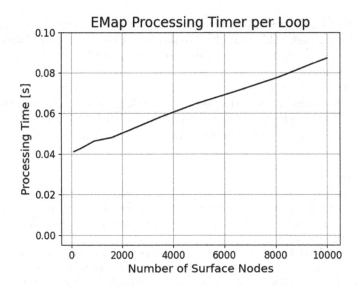

Fig. 6. The mean time taken by EMap to fit a surface to a new input cloud per LiDAR update loop.

6 Discussion

EMap showed a consistent reduction in MSE compared to the OctoMap baseline with a reasonable computational cost, allowing the terrain reconstruction process to be run in real-time. Beyond the improved accuracy over the baseline, the extension to r_m facilitated by EMap will lead to a direct reduction in the number of scans needed to build an accurate map. When this reduction is applied to an industrial-scale terrain mapping operation, e.g. large autonomous agricultural machinery, it could be very beneficial in reducing the overall operational cost and environmental impact.

The simulation experiments carried out in this work are sufficient for proving the viability of EMap as a concept. However, there are numerous limitations from using a sinusoidal terrain and simulations and additional work within more complex simulated and real environments are needed to properly test EMap's viability as a terrain mapping solution. Nevertheless, the results from this proof-of-concept work is promising and indicates that EMap is an avenue worth investigating more.

7 Conclusion

Based on results generated from simulation experiments, EMap reduces the MSE by up to 43.7% over Octomap, and extends the effective scanning range by 25% for one of the mapping scenarios, compared to that of the baseline. This added benefit comes at little additional computational cost and is accomplished in real time – though higher-resolution terrain maps can also be generated offline. For robotic mapping tasks, this could lead to significant cost savings and allow operators to generate more reliable long-distance traversal plans, further improving operational efficiency.

Future work should look into applying the EMap approach to a real-world scenario to determine its effectiveness therein. Furthermore, relaxing the strict condition of locking the nodes' (x, y) coordinates can be investigated to determine whether it can further improve EMap's surface estimation capabilities.

References

1. Hornung, A., Wurm, K.M., Bennewitz, M., Stachniss, C., Burgard, W.: OctoMap: an efficient probabilistic 3D mapping framework based on octrees. Auton. Robot. **34**(3), 189–206 (2013)
2. Duberg, D., Jensfelt, P.: UFOMap: an efficient probabilistic 3D mapping framework that embraces the unknown. arXiv preprint arXiv:2003.04749 (2020)
3. Gingras, D., Lamarche, T., Bedwani, J.-L., Dupuis, É.: Rough terrain reconstruction for rover motion planning. In: 2010 Canadian Conference on Computer and Robot Vision, pp. 191–198. IEEE (2010)
4. Malartre, F., Feraud, T., Debain, C., Chapuis, R.: Digital elevation map estimation by vision-lidar fusion. In: 2009 IEEE International Conference on Robotics and Biomimetics (ROBIO), pp. 523–528. IEEE (2009)
5. Sock, J., Kim, J., Min, J., Kwak, K.: Probabilistic traversability map generation using 3D-lidar and camera. In: 2016 IEEE International Conference on Robotics and Automation (ICRA), pp. 5631–5637. IEEE (2016)
6. Chiang, K.-W., Tsai, G.-J., Li, Y.-H., El-Sheimy, N.: Development of LiDAR-based UAV system for environment reconstruction. IEEE Geosci. Remote Sens. Lett. **14**(10), 1790–1794 (2017)
7. Survey, U.G.: The national map—new data delivery homepage, advanced viewer, lidar visualization. US Geological Survey, Technical report (2019)
8. Hladik, C., Alber, M.: Accuracy assessment and correction. Remote Sens. Environ. **121**, 224–235 (2012)
9. Werbrouck, I., et al.: Digital elevation model generation for historical landscape analysis based on LiDAR data, a case study in Flanders (Belgium). Expert Syst. Appl. **38**(7), 8178–8185 (2011)
10. Meagher, D.: Geometric modeling using octree encoding. Comput. Graph. Image Process. **19**(2), 129–147 (1982)
11. Yeu, C.-W., Lim, M.-H., Huang, G.-B., Agarwal, A., Ong, Y.-S.: A new machine learning paradigm for terrain reconstruction. IEEE Geosci. Remote Sens. Lett. **3**(3), 382–386 (2006)
12. Kim, S., Kim, J.: GPmap: a unified framework for robotic mapping based on sparse Gaussian processes. In: Mejias, L., Corke, P., Roberts, J. (eds.) Field and Service Robotics. STAR, vol. 105, pp. 319–332. Springer, Cham (2015). https://doi.org/10.1007/978-3-319-07488-7_22
13. Wang, J., Englot, B.: Fast, accurate gaussian process occupancy maps via test-data octrees and nested Bayesian fusion. In: 2016 IEEE International Conference on Robotics and Automation (ICRA), pp. 1003–1010. IEEE (2016)

14. Eriksson, D., Dong, K., Lee, E., Bindel, D., Wilson, A.G.: Scaling gaussian process regression with derivatives. In: Advances in Neural Information Processing Systems, pp. 6867–6877 (2018)
15. Tresp, V.: A Bayesian committee machine. Neural Comput. **12**(11), 2719–2741 (2000)
16. Berger, M., et al.: State of the art in surface reconstruction from point clouds. In: Eurographics 2014 - State of the Art Reports (2014)
17. Leung, C., Appleton, B., Lovell, B.C., Sun, C.: An energy minimisation approach to stereo-temporal dense reconstruction. In: Proceedings of ICPR (2004)
18. Labatut, P., Pons, J.-P., Keriven, R.: Robust and efficient surface reconstruction from range data. Comput. Graph. Forum **28**(8), 2275–2290 (2009)

Design and Preliminary In-Classroom Evaluation of a Low-Cost Educational Mobile Robot

Maximilian Stone[1,2], Pavel Orlov[1], and Ildar Farkhatdinov[2]([✉])

[1] London School of Mathematics and Programming, London, UK
[2] School of Electronic Engineering and Computer Science,
Queen Mary University of London, London, UK
i.farkhatdinov@qmul.ac.uk

Abstract. The design and evaluation of a low-cost educational mobile robot are presented in this paper. The robot is composed of a two-wheeled actuated platform, equipped with distance, position and inertial sensors and a programmable micro-controller. Several prototypes of the robot were built and tested in a specially organised learning session with children to explore the feasibility of the robot as an educational tool to teach robotics and programming. Collected user feedback demonstrated that the proposed system is comparable to commercially available educational robots in terms of functionality and performance.

Keywords: Educational robotics · Mobile robotics · STEM education

1 Introduction

Robotics education is an actively developing field of business and research [1]. The use of robots to teach children STEM subjects has been found efficient [2–6]. Various robotics solutions have been proposed by the industry and they are actively deployed in schools for conventional and extracurricular learning activities [7]. However, the application of robots in children's education is still limited in developing countries due to limited expertise and resources [8].

In this paper we describe a low-cost robotics solution that can be used to teach robotics and programming to children. We present the technical description of the designed two-wheeled mobile robot and demonstrate preliminary evaluation results of the robot. The material presented in this paper is based on the final year project of the first author.

2 Proposed Prototype

2.1 Functionality and Design Requirements

There exist multiple mobile robots for education. In collaboration with the London School of Mathematics and Programming (LSMP) we identified the required functionality for a low-cost educational mobile robot for children and compared it to an existing system that is used at LSMP (ROBBO, https://www.robbo. world).

The problem prompting a search for a new robot at LSMP was the cost of purchasing and maintaining the current robots in use. This applies not only to LSMP, but to other schools in general. Most robots in classrooms cost at least 100 GBP and some cost up to 500 GBP or more depending on their abilities. The lasting impact on the economy that the Covid-19 pandemic caused, even for well-funded institutions, meant that cutting costs whilst retaining education quality has been of utmost importance. A robot solution to this problem must be able to perform similarly to robots already on the market. The ROBBO robot was chosen as a comparison for the solution, as it is the most often used robot at LSMP. The solution must meet several design attributes that wheeled robots have in general, as well as cost and safety.

Features that the ROBBO robot has that the solution must include are:

1. a two-wheeled differential drive kinematics;
2. the motors/wheels should be equipped with encoders;
3. sensing to detect obstacles around the robot;
4. a widely available power source (9 V battery).

Additionally, a new robot should be:

- safe to use: prevention of electric shocks, sharp edges, etc.;
- easy of use: how easy it is to interface with the robot;
- low-cost;
- suitable to typical learning tasks: obstacle avoidance, line and wall following; navigation and parking;
- aesthetic and tidy design;
- resilient and sustainable allowing easy maintenance;
- long battery life.

2.2   Robot Design

Following the design requirements identified above we have built a two-wheeled mobile robot shown in Fig. 1. The components and materials required to build the prototype robot are (including their costs):

- Arduino Nano (14.40 GBP): the controller for the system, which uses an ATmega328 MCU. It has 32 KB of flash memory, 2 KB of which is used by the boot-loader, the rest of which is program space. It operates at 5 V, with an input voltage of 7–12 V, suitable for use with a 9V battery. Importantly, it offers 6 PWM pins, which two of are used by the motors for speed control. It has 22 digital GPIO pins, providing room for expansion. The Arduino platform was chosen over others (such as esp32) due to its hobbyist user friendly approach (open source and significant online community of users).

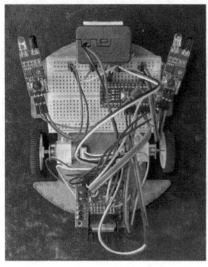 

Fig. 1. The two-wheeled mobile robot prototype: top and side views.

- The baseplate (0.84 GBP) is laser cut from a minimum 140 × 110 mm sheet of 2 mm medium-density fibreboard (MDF). It is lightweight and inexpensive. It is strong but quicker and easier to machine (manually if needed) than acrylic.
- An L298N PWM motor driver (0.81 GBP) to supply a higher voltage to the motors. It provides output for 2 DC motors and offers PWM speed control.
- Two motors (16.14 GBP) used are brushed DC motors, with two hall effect sensors used as encoders that support direction or doubling resolution. They use a gear ration to achieve a maximum speed of 1050 rpm, at 6 V input.
- The proximity sensors (3.76 GBP) use IR beams and a comparator circuit to detect objects in their presence. A beam is transmitted, and if the reflection is within a certain threshold, they change output from low to high, using an LED to indicate this. The support angle of obstacle detection is 35°.
- A wiring breadboard (0.24 GBP) is used to make connections between all devices and the microcontroller.
- Two 'D-hole' plastic and rubber wheels (0.30 GBP).
- The battery pack (0.19 GBP) to house a 9 V battery that must be purchased separately and offers a toggle switch to turn the robot on and off.
- A 0.95 cm (3/8 in.) ball caster (1.51 GBP) is used to support the battery's weight at the front of the robot.
- Jump wires (1 GBP) are used to connect all devices.
- Plastic 2 mm standoffs (0.02 GBP) and screws are used to secure the proximity sensors to the front of the robot.

A single kit yields a production cost of 39.06 GBP, without including a battery.

The robot drew a peak current of 330 mA at 9 V input, using a DC power supply to emulate a battery. Therefore, the robot consumes 2.97 W with motors at full speed. In contrast, the robot drew 230 mA at idle. This means an idle power consumption of 2.07 W. Taking the mean, 2.52 W can be assumed the average power consumption of the robot. If an end user will use a generic 9 V alkaline battery such as the Energizer Max 9 V Battery, which has a capacity of 610 mAh or 5.49 W-hours, at a power consumption of 2.52 W, the robot may be used for around 2 h and 11 min. At max speed, this would be 1 h and 50 min.

3 Experimental Evaluation

With the help of LSMP, we tested our robot's performance and functionality in a classroom and compared its usability with the ROBBO platform. A blended research approach was taken as part of an experiment in a real-world environment, using robotics lessons at LSMP as an opportunity to compare the two robots. The task chosen was the same wall following behaviour. Quantitative data were obtained by testing pupils' comprehension of the task after they attempt to program the algorithm through a short quiz, checking how many answers were correct. Qualitative data was obtained with ordinal scale questions about the attributes of the robots. This experiment provided an opportunity to simulate what using the prototype would be like in a classroom.

The aims of the experiments were:

- To compare the prototype and another robot in their abilities to teach a lesson.
- To evaluate the prototype in a real-world environment, where points of failure can be discovered and used for refinement.
- To understand children's impressions of the robot through their interactions with it.

3.1 Participants

Grouping participants. In total 11 pupils (ages 8–14) took part in the evaluation sessions. The pupils were divided into to groups based on their experience and skills with educational robots. This was done by interviewing the pupils' usual LSMP teacher about their subjective thoughts on each of the pupils' progress and understanding levels. Furthermore, the number of lessons pupils have attended at LSMP was factored in. An important control variable was ensuring that no pupil had attempted this task before. From this, two groups were made from pupils across five one-hour lesson groups used for the experiment:

- 'Experienced' (set A): pupils who meet one or more of the following: ¿1 than one term spent at LSMP, having prior experience with electronics or robots, good aptitude in the subject area already, strong willingness to solve problems, or older age (secondary school).
- 'Inexperienced', (set B): pupils who meet one or more of the following: pupils new to LSMP from January 2022, have programmed at least in Scratch with fair aptitude, or younger age (primary school).

Table 1 shows how pupils were split across the five sessions. There were an equal number of pupils both in set A and set B.

Table 1. Distribution (number of students) of experience across five sessions.

Session	1	2	3	4	5
Experienced pupils (set A)	2	1	1	2	0
Inexperienced pupils (set B)	0	2	0	0	3
Age range (years)	11–14	8–10	10–12	9–11	9–11
Robot used	Proposed Robot	ROBBO	Proposed Robot	ROBBO	Proposed Robot

3.2 Learning Session Structure

Each one-hour session was structured as follows:

- **15 mins.** An explanation of the wall following algorithm. This was to make the robot follow a wall using a loop polling a proximity sensor on one side of the robot. To mitigate time wasted setting up the robots, they were connected already to computers and an explanation of the interfaces (Arduino IDE, RobboScratch 3) was given. The setup was explained.
- **30 mins.** Pupils were given 30 min to complete the task, in which the teacher could provide help not related directly to the task if necessary. Pupils worked in groups and once they felt confident that their program would work, they deployed the code and placed the robot on the ground next to a wall. Trial and error were the expected method of solving the task. This involved changing variables such as the detection threshold, motor speeds, and duration of movement each loop.
- **15 mins.** Lastly pupils were given a handout that asked questions testing comprehension of the task, and ordinal scale questions that help to quantify the attributes of the robots. Furthermore, informal conversations were conducted to get pupils' opinions of both robots and debrief them on the research.

3.3 Evaluating Comprehension

Each pupil was asked to complete a quiz after a session. The comprehension questions were:

- **Q1.** How do you know if an obstacle is detected by one of the sensors? (There may be more than one answer depending on the robot you have been given)
- **Q2.** What is a condition that the robot must check is true in order to make a turn? (i.e., what does the robot 'see' electronically?)
- **Q3.** When the robot detects something on its left, which way should the robot turn?
- **Q4.** When the robot is turning, how many of its wheels should it turn to make a good turn?

The results of the quiz were used to understand if the pupils were able to efficiently learn the required materials.

Table 2. The proportion of correct answers for comprehension test for each robot and question

Platform	Q1, %	Q2, %	Q3, %	Q4, %	Mean ± st.dev. %
ROBBO	75	50	75	25	56.25 ± 20.73
Prototype	100	83	100	83	91.5 ± 8.5

3.4 Subjective Evaluation of the Robot

Following a quiz, each student was asked to complete a questionnaire to characterise design and usability aspects of the robot they used in the class. The students were asked whether they prefer to agree with one or the other statements about the robots. Ordinal scale with numeric levels 1 to 5 was used for each question, where selecting 1 corresponded to a participant to strongly agree with the first statement and selecting 5 corresponded to strongly agree with the second statement.

The ordinal scale questions were:

- Q1. Is the robot more of an inanimate (meaning, not alive) object to you (1) or more like a pet (5)?
- Q2. Do you think that the robot reacting to your code was able to help you more (1) in figuring out how to solve the problem, or the help provided by my explanation at the start (5)?.
- Q3. Do you think that the robot is cheap (1) or expensive (5) to make?
- Q4. Do you think the robot is more of a toy (1) or an electronic device (5)?

The above questions were designed to evaluate the efficacy of the robot as an educational tool as proposed in the educational robotics applications framework [9].

4 Results

4.1 Comprehension

The comprehension responses provided quantitative insight into pupils' understanding of the algorithm, based on how many correct answers were submitted.

Table 2 and Fig. 2 show the percentage of correct answers across both platforms. The ROBBO pupils provided 16 answers, 9 correct, from four participants. The prototype pupils provided 24 answers, 22 correct, from six participants.

The comprehension of the algorithm is noticeably higher in the prototype group, compared to the ROBBO group. This can be seen from a mean of 91.5% correct answers from their group. In comparison, the ROBBO group had a mean of 56.25%, which is a significant difference of 35.25%. This disparity is reinforced by the large standard deviation found in the ROBBO group, which is 20.73% in comparison to only 8.5% for the prototype group. A possible cause is that the data population size in the ROBBO group was only four pupils compared to six

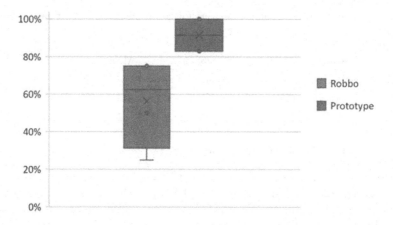

Fig. 2. Comprehension quiz evaluation results (box plots) for the ROBBO robot and the proposed prototype across all participants.

pupils in the other group, and one pupil having little to no understanding would bring the overall scores much lower than if the same happened in the prototype group.

It is also possible that the prototype is better at teaching concepts due to its less hidden approach to how it operates. In the ROBBO interface, a lot of configuration is already done automatically, such as COM port selection and pin values. On the prototype robot, the breadboard must first be inspected to see where the microcontroller's (Arduino Nano) pins lead to, aiding pupils' understanding of how the connection to a sensor, for example, is linked with a number (defining constant with a label) to the values shown on the serial monitor. In contrast, the ROBBO robot only requires toggling the sensors on or off. Although it is not the most significant difference, it may well contribute to the engagement levels of pupils depending on the robot used. The more that pupils must investigate by themselves, the more they will understand. Furthermore, as some older pupils were chosen for the prototype, the understanding level of the task could be inherently something easier for them based on progress in school. Lastly, analysis of individual responses showed that the variance in score was quite large compared to high scores with the prototype group. Therefore, evaluation of the robots in with a larger group of pupils is required in future work.

4.2   Subjective Evaluation

The subjective evaluations based on the ordinal scale were used to measure how well each robot adheres to the educational robotics principles [9], which would indicate how suitable the robot is in an educational setting. The results are presented in Table 3 and Fig. 3. In average the ROBBO robot and our prototype led to the same results.

Table 3. Ordinal scale responses

	Prototype			ROBBO		
Question	mean	median	st.dev	mMean	median	st.dev
Q1	2.5	3	0.76	2.5	2.5	1.12
Q2	3	3	1	3	2.5	1.22
Q3	3	3	0.57	3.5	2.5	1.12
Q4	3.33	4	0.94	3.5	2.5	1.12

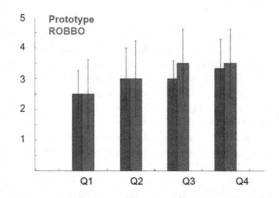

Fig. 3. Results for subjective responses (ordinal scale) across all participants for the ROBBO robot and the proposed prototype (mean and standard deviation).

We observed that the teacher played a larger part in helping pupils understand the task than the robots itself. This complements the efficiency of the robot being an educational tool in addition to a teachers' guidance, and also implies that the proposed prototype robot may be harder to understand by itself. Another factor that may have influenced this scoring by pupils is that the prototype robot looks more complicated than the ROBBO robot, due to its open design.

5 Conclusion

We proposed the design of a low-cost educational mobile robot and evaluated it in the real-world learning environment with the pupils. The performance and functionality of the proposed prototype proved similar to current robots in use, as it effectively taught pupils about a control theory algorithm in comparison to other robots used in schools. What was achieved was the successful implementation of a new, low-cost Arduino based wheeled robot that could compete with the ROBBO Robot Kit, used at LSMP. The robot was evaluated in two experiments comparing it to the Robot Kit, one which compared the accuracy of wall following, and one that took a blended approach to get both qualitative and quantitative data from pupils who interacted with both robots in a real-world classroom. Due to the project restrictions the prototype robot had a budget of 40 GBP or less and with that came a limit on what functionality the robot could have. Part of this was a choice of motor that was not suited for the application, as well as a lack of encoder resolution making it hard to track wheel positions. Line following, light sensors and better encoding motors are all future refinements to the robot that may be added at a premium, as well as Bluetooth capabilities which were initially part of the plan. The limitation of the study is low number of participants in the evaluation stage of the project.

References

1. Tsoy, T., Sabirova, L., Magid, E.: Towards effective interactive teaching and learning strategies in robotics education. In: 2017 10th International Conference on Developments in eSystems Engineering (DeSE), 14 Jun 14, pp. 267–272. IEEE (2017)
2. Benitti, F.B.V., Spolaôr, N.: How have robots supported STEM teaching? In: Khine, M.S. (ed.) Robotics in STEM Education, pp. 103–129. Springer, Cham (2017). https://doi.org/10.1007/978-3-319-57786-9_5
3. Cetin, M., Demircan, H.Ö.: Empowering technology and engineering for STEM education through programming robots: a systematic literature review. Early Child Dev. Care **190**(9), 1323–1335 (2020)
4. Stone, A., Farkhatdinov, I.: Robotics education for children at secondary school level and above. In: Gao, Y., Fallah, S., Jin, Y., Lekakou, C. (eds.) TAROS 2017. LNCS (LNAI), vol. 10454, pp. 576–585. Springer, Cham (2017). https://doi.org/10.1007/978-3-319-64107-2_47
5. Reich-Stiebert, N., Eyssel, F.: Robots in the Classroom: What Teachers Think About Teaching and Learning with Education Robots. In: Agah, A., Cabibihan, J.-J., Howard, A.M., Salichs, M.A., He, H. (eds.) ICSR 2016. LNCS (LNAI), vol. 9979, pp. 671–680. Springer, Cham (2016). https://doi.org/10.1007/978-3-319-47437-3_66
6. Luchin, R.M., Shirokolobov, I.Y., Sokolov, D.V., Kirilenko, I.A., Terekhov, A.N., Stone, A.: Improving control engineering education with TRIK cybernetic system. IFAC-PapersOnLine **50**(1), 15716–21 (2017)
7. Mubin, O., Stevens, C.J., Shahid, S., Al Mahmud, A., Dong, J.J.: A review of the applicability of robots in education. J. Technol. Educ. Learn. **1**(209–0015), 13 (2013)
8. Alimisis, D.: Educational robotics: open questions and new challenges. Themes Sci. Technol. Educ. **6**(1), 63–71 (2013)
9. Catlin, D., Blamires, M.: The principles of Educational Robotic Applications (ERA): a framework for understanding and developing educational robots and their activities. In: The 12th EuroLogo Conference (2010)

Internal State-Based Risk Assessment for Robots in Hazardous Environment

Jennifer David[1(✉)] ⬩, Thomas Bridgwater[1], Andrew West[2] ⬩,
Barry Lennox[2] ⬩, and Manuel Giuliani[1] ⬩

[1] Bristol Robotics Lab, University of the West of England, Bristol, UK
{jennifer.david,thomas.bridgwater,manuel.giuliani}@brl.ac.uk
[2] Robotics for Extreme Environments Lab at the School of Electrical
and Electronic Engineering, The University of Manchester, Manchester, UK
{andrew.west,barry.lennox}@uom.ac.uk

Abstract. Robots operating in a hazardous environment should be able to assess the risks involved before executing any given task. Though several risks can be considered in such a scenario, the risks based on environmental conditions are rarely explored. In this paper, we present a novel, risk-based navigation approach for robots in hazardous environments. We specifically investigate the environmental risks which can be measured and whose maximum state can be defined. These risks are integrated into the costmap of the robot to alter its traversability cost based on the robot's current state. In doing so, the robot can adjust its path to account for hazards it has encountered on the fly. We term this approach as the Internal State-based Risk Assessment framework. We validate this framework using simulations where a robot must navigate through a nuclear environment whilst optimizing its path to avoid high radiation and high-temperature zones. We show that the robot can alter its path to account for the encountered hazards that have been mapped onto its internal state.

Keywords: Risk assessment · Mobile robot · Nuclear environment · Costmaps

1 Introduction

As autonomous robotics moves towards ubiquity, the need for robots to safely assess risk becomes increasingly important; both to allow their autonomous capabilities to be fully utilized and to ensure their safe operation. We use a nuclear environment as an example of a real-world application that has multiple hazards that need to be accounted for during mobile robot navigation. These include: the robot's radioactive dose and the robot's internal temperature. If any of these states become critical, the robot can be rendered inert or, in the case of radiation, may cause the robot to become additional nuclear waste. Therefore, a risk-based navigation framework is required for robots that could keep these risks measured below the critical level.

© The Author(s), under exclusive license to Springer Nature Switzerland AG 2022
S. Pacheco-Gutierrez et al. (Eds.): TAROS 2022, LNAI 13546, pp. 137–152, 2022.
https://doi.org/10.1007/978-3-031-15908-4_12

Though risk is an important consideration in the real-world application of mobile robotics, risk has been defined and handled differently by various researchers. In general terms, risk is defined as the product of probability (the likelihood of an event occurring) and severity (the resulting magnitude of harm). Sometimes, the exposure, (i.e., the amount of time, number of cycles, etc.) of the event involved is also considered [4,6]. In this paper, we define risks from the aspect of risk perception and term it as an "internal state-based" property that depends on its present state. The state-based risks are those which can have a maximum state-defined and where this state can be measured, which are mostly environmental risks. As an example, consider temperature; when a robot travels via many heat sources, the internal temperature of the robot may rise to a critical level. This value can be defined and its internal state can also be measured at every instance. During autonomous navigation of the robot and depending on the robot's present temperature, the robot can take cautious decisions based on this internal state. The idea behind this approach is that risk is perceived differently by people based personal factors like psychological state, sociological background, and (inter-)disciplinary expertise. However, when it comes to risk perception by robots, it can be simplified to its contextual aspect, i.e., its information sources. For example, the robot can take or avoid taking a risk depending on its current state. Any risk that can be a.) measured and b.) a maximum state defined, can then be easily perceived by robots. This fits in with the ALARA ("as low as reasonably achievable") principle, which means all exposures should be kept as minimum as possible, though not necesarily.

In this paper, we focus on the navigation of a mobile robot that avoids environmental risks reaching user-defined critical levels. We present the Internal State-Based Risk Assessment (ISRA) framework as a general solution to this problem. The basis of this approach is the use of layered costmaps [7] which allows the preservation of data from different sources, as they do not lose information through concatenation into a single map. This is an important feature in our framework, as we store each risk value (not the sensor cost value) in a separate costmap layer. Also, a robot may experience a number of these environmental risks simultaneously, giving rise to the question: how may a robot optimize for the avoidance of many such environmental risks at the same time, whilst maintaining its mission objective? The second important feature of our framework addresses this question. During navigation, we alter the cost of traversing the map, based on the current state of each risk. For example, if the temperature is at 42% of its maximum state and radiation is at 55%, then the radiation will be afforded a higher cost (priority) and avoided more. As the state of the robot is subject to change based on the robot's experience in the environment, it provides an on-the-fly risk prioritization strategy. As will be seen later, this causes the path of the robot to change over time.

Our work has two major contributions. Firstly, it presents a novel method for robot navigation considering state-based risks into account. This is because environmental risks like radiation and temperature have not been explored widely in the literature. Secondly, it allows for on-the-fly risk prioritization based on the current internal state of the robot. By doing so, any number of state-based risks can be easily integrated into the system. By this approach, we hope to generalize the risk assessment framework to account for any environmental risks outside of those we use as examples in this paper. The use case for our study is a mobile robot navigating a nuclear environment that is exposed to temperature and radiation risks. Our simulation results show that the path of the robot changes on subsequent runs through the same environment due to the cumulative dose of radiation and temperature that the robot receives during operation. The robot then starts to avoid areas that are higher in radiation to a greater degree as time goes on, due to user-defined critical levels of the state-based risks.

The remainder of the paper is organized as follows: in the Sect. 2, we detail the related work on risk-based navigation using cost maps. The general principles behind the ISRA framework is outlined in Sect. 3. A brief description of our implementation and the experimental procedure to investigate the efficacy of the framework is shown in Sect. 4. We present the results of ISRA framework in Sect. 5 followed by a discussion and conclusions in Sect. 6.

2   Related Work

Due to the rapid increase in the use of robots in real-world hazardous environments, research in the area of risk-aware navigation has recently become more important. Though there are many ways of considering risk in robot navigation, they are mostly explored at the path-planning level. With the inception of costmaps, the cost function has been expanded to include more than simply the risk of collision. For self-driving cars, costmaps have been used to define traversable but undesirable regions, such as lanes with oncoming traffic, or pedestrian walkways [1]. In human-robot interaction (HRI), costmaps have been used to aid human comfort by increasing the cost of areas that encroach on a user's personal space [9]. The Mars rover employs vision to identify dangerous terrains such as loose ground or large rocks, this information is then fed into a costmap that is used to plan a collision-free path [16]. All these listed works have focused on static terrains. However, costmaps have also been used to identify and avoid dynamic obstacles [17], [18]. From these examples, it can be seen that costmaps are capable of encoding different constraints of the environment to produce paths that optimize for a variety of criteria. For this reason, we believe that costmaps make a logical basis for a risk-avoidance strategy.

Risk has received a multitude of definitions in the area of robot navigation. Voos and Ertle define risk based on the extended situation operator model, which models processes as a sequence of operators [20]. Kruusma and Svensson associated risk with the average speed of a robot, coupled with the number of turns it must make along its path [5]. Frequently, risk has been associated with the dangers of passing different types of terrain or collision with obstacles [16,19]. Proximity to human users has also been used as a metric to define risk [9]. To generalize risk for use in our framework, we define risk to be state-based environmental risks, these are risks to the robot due to the environment that are quantifiable by some state, as mentioned earlier. By approaching risk in this way we seek to generalize the definition so that our framework can encompass many risks, including those discussed above. It should be noted however that some risks do not directly fall into this definition, for example, the risk of following a sub-optimal path is not considered [13,14]. Other risks may be re-formulated to fit the definition such as terrain traversability; to do this one could break terrain into constituent components (e.g., maximum gap width or obstacle height) and measure the state of the robot about these. To track multiple risks in the manner we envisage, it is not possible to use a single monolithic costmap. Instead, we employ layered costmaps. Such costmaps have a significant advantage over monolithic costmaps: they can retain information in separate layers from different sources; they allow for transparency when it comes to the combination of risks (i.e. rules for combining layers); finally, they allow for rules to be defined for the combination of different data types stored in different layers. In previous work, layered costmaps have largely been used to enable safe HRI [8,10,12]. This usually involves a layer that corresponds to the static map, one that encodes costs for being too close to an operator and some that handle dynamic obstacles. These costs are then combined to generate an optimum path that takes into account human comfort. However, layered costmaps are not limited to utility in HRI and have been shown to be useful for vehicle path planning [11]; determination of gradient for traversal of unstructured environments [21]; and sensor fusion between ultrasound and LIDAR distance measurements [2].

Layered costmaps have been developed to represent risks associated with ionizing radiation, limiting total exposure by disincentivizing traversing through regions of increased dose rate [22], therefore prolonging robot lifetime in harsh environments. This has been combined with other information such as terrain height to give avoidance based on multiple risk vectors [3]. The approach developed in [22] can be exploited in this instance.

Though layered costmaps appear to present an efficient method for analyzing and quantifying environmental risk from different sensor data, there seems to be a paucity of material surrounding their use for costs outside of distance concerns and terrain traversability. Additionally, there currently exists in the literature no method of altering the priority of risks whilst a robot is operational. This is posed as an open research question by [7]. To this end, we propose the ISRA framework as a method for handling a multitude of discrete environmental risks using the examples of radiation and temperature. Furthermore, we present the ISRA framework's capability to rearrange the priority of risks, depending on the criticality of a given state.

3   Methodology

The main goal of ISRA is to provide a risk-sensitive navigational framework, where the risks considered are discrete risks caused by the environment that has some measurable state. These state-based risks are integrated into the global costmap as different layers which are used by the robot for navigation. This is

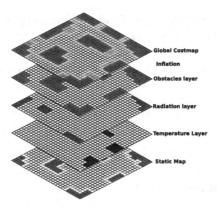

Fig. 1. The monolithic layered global costmap consists of one static layer followed by radiation, temperature and obstacle layers. The obstacle layer is then inflated (layer not shown in the map) to give the global costmap.

achieved using layered costmaps, where each layer constitutes a separate risk. Each layer in the costmap shares the same size and resolution, i.e., for every cell in an individual costmap layer, there is a corresponding cell at the same spatial location in all other layers. The costs in these layers are individually adjusted based on the robot's current state so that it can capture the "radiation risk" and "thermal risk" rather than the actual radiation or thermal cost values. These layers are then combined with other default layers like inflation and static map layers to form a global monolithic costmap on which path planning can be done, as shown in Fig. 1. There are many possible ways for combining these layers like the maximum value preservation policy, or taking the average/sum cost values across the different layers. So, as the robot navigates the environment, it builds the layered costmap with risks.

Furthermore, state-based risks can be cumulative or dissipative/diminishing with time. So, as long as the risk can be measured and an upper threshold defined, the interaction dynamics of that risk can be ignored. In our case, the temperature is dissipative; if the robot's temperature increases, that temperature may later be lost to the environment. If the robot is irradiated during a mission then that dose will keep increasing throughout the operation. Both these risks could be accounted for and prioritized using the proposed framework. Hence, this framework provides on-the-fly risk prioritization for path planning. Moreover, the framework is independent of the implementation of the costmap or the measurement units used, as long as the thresholds and the state observations have the same units. Therefore, this method for risk assessment, in general, works for any state-based environmental risks.

To better understand how ISRA works take a single layer, the temperature layer, as an example. The inputs for this layer are the robot's state observations and the user-defined thresholds for that state; in case of temperature, the robot may measure its internal temperature to be say, 35°C, while the user may have defined a maximum threshold of 50°C and a minimum threshold of 0°C. The *Robot State Updater* then calculates the robot's current state; for this case, it would be 60% of the robot's maximum allowable temperature. The state calculator then outputs the costs for the cost maps by scaling the values in the costmap to reflect the robot's state and the corresponding threshold values. If the temperature had increased, then the costs in the costmap would scale to reflect this new risk.

In the following section, we explain the ISRA framework components in detail.

3.1 Observation Sources

An observation from a radiation or temperature sensor contains the sensor readings and the metadata like the time and pose of the sensor value. The global pose of the observation can then be estimated using SLAM and the corresponding transformation which is then used to update the corresponding cell in the costmap layer. The radiation dose or the temperature from the sensor needs to be converted to a corresponding integer value with respect to the robot's present state (radiation and temperature).

Radiation. The final radiation dose is obtained by simply adding the dose value to the present radiation value at regular time intervals. This is because radiation doses are cumulative.

$$R_f = R_c + dose \tag{1}$$

where R_c is the current radiation dose of the robot and R_f is the final radiation dose of the robot. To begin with, it is believed that the robot is not exposed to any radiation at all. So, R_c is set to zero.

Temperature. Updating the temperature of the robot is different from radiation because the temperature varies due to heat losses. To address this we use the specific heat equation which gives the final temperature of the robot as,

$$T_f = \frac{(M_c * C_c * T_c) + (M_h * C_h * T_h)}{(M_c * C_c) + (M_h * C_h)} \tag{2}$$

where T_f is the final temperature of the robot; M_c is the mass of the robot, taken to be 120 kg; C_c is the specific heat capacity of the robot, taken to be 0.9 J kg^{-1} °C^{-1}; T_c is the robot's current temperature; M_h is the mass of the air surrounding the robot, taken to be 2 kg; C_h is the specific heat capacity of air, taken to be 0.718 J kg^{-1} °C^{-1}; and T_h is the temperature of the air around the robot, which can be found using the simulated or real temperature sensor.

3.2   User-Defined Thresholds

At the start of the mission, the upper and lower thresholds are user-defined which can be estimated as follows. The average dose rate for a robot during nuclear-decommissioning tasks is 1.4 mGy s^{-1} [15]. The typical maximum dose a semi-conductor can withstand is 1 kGy. With the assumption that in a year, a robot could be expected to carry out around 1000 small inspection missions within a nuclear environment, which is approximately three missions per day. Therefore, the upper threshold value (U) is adjusted so that the robot does not exceed a dose of 1000 mGy, by giving the robot a threshold on a single mission basis, considering cumulative dose. For temperature, the upper threshold of a robot depends on the type of robot deployed. For example, in the case of a Neobotix MPO-700 robot, the internal temperature of 35 °C, with an ambient air temperature of 50 °C, so we consider this temperature as the maximum threshold in our case.

The upper threshold values will decrease as the accumulated dose or temperature increases over time. The lower thresholds (L) are set to the minimum value of zero for radiation and temperature. And we assume the temperature and radiation does not drop significantly below the lower threshold.

3.3   Robot State Updater

In our implementation, the *Robot State Updater* is the method for altering the values of the costmaps to reflect the robot's current state and the change in risk that this brings. As described earlier, this involves taking the robot's state observations and user defined thresholds as inputs and outputting an updated costmap. To update the costs in each costmap layer, the upper threshold value is modified using a ROS dynamic reconfigure server to alter what sensor value is considered the maximum cost, thereby scaling all values in the costmap to this new upper threshold value.

3.4   Costmaps

It should be noted that for the utility of layered dynamic costmaps, we use the `costmap2d` package of the ROS `navigation` stack. This package functionality also directly integrates into the path planning module of the navigation stack called `move base`. This path planning and execution utility accepts costmaps for environmental awareness, current robot position and a goal position, computing a minimized global path and managing robot trajectory during the maneuver.

Since, the sensor values are point-source, this value is inflated by a user-defined radius (the robot radius size) in the costmap and all the cell values in this region are updated. Costmap cells hold 8-bit integer values, where 0 corresponds to free space (no obstacles or additional cost) and 254 represents lethal obstacle or the certainty that the center of the robot will be in collision. The maximum value of 255 is reserved for unknown cells where data is not available. By setting a cell value between 0–253, it is possible to express the additional cost of traversing that cell in that given layer with varying degrees of severity. The radiation and temperature layers each hold cell values based on their respective sensor observations, the severity of which is adjusted by the thresholds. The rounded integer values for the final costmap are truncated between 0 and 255 in the event they are smaller than the lower threshold value or exceed the upper threshold value respectively.

So, the state observation value (S) is converted into a risk integer value for the cost C in the costmap using Eq. 3.

$$C = 253 * \frac{(S - L)}{(U - L)} \quad \text{where } U > L \tag{3}$$

where, L is the lower threshold of the state value and U is the upper threshold of the state value and U is always greater than L. For example, in the case of temperature it is given by,

$$U = 253 - 253 * \left(\frac{T_f}{50}\right) \tag{4}$$

where $50\,°C$ is the maximum temperature of the robot. In the case of radiation, to begin with, the costmap values were scaled based on the maximum dose of $1000\,mGy$ and the maximum costmap value of 253. Later, the costmap values are scaled and updated based on the newly calculated upper threshold values depending upon the current state.

3.5   Combining Layers

The global monolithic costmap used for robot navigation is obtained by combining all the costmap layers. The radiation and temperature layers are combined with the other layers by the maximum preservation policy, i.e., accepting the maximum value of all the layers. For a given number of layers, n, and cell index, i, the final cost in the monolithic costmap, F_c, is given by Eq. 5.

$$F_c[i] = \max\left(C_1[i], C_2[i], ..., C_n[i]\right) \tag{5}$$

This type of layer combination is important for many reasons. Firstly, it preserves the cost of lethal obstacles that is important for navigation; secondly, it ensures the cost does not undergo integer overflow that can be caused by adding all the costs and thirdly, it automatically introduces preference for avoiding a particular risk among the many risk layers. Other methods such as taking average of all values in the layers or prioritizing one layer will not yield such results.

3.6   Risk Prioritization

During navigation, all the cells in a costmap layer are recalculated using Eq. 3 to reflect the modified thresholds, resulting in higher or lower costs depending upon the change in values of the threshold respectively. This is independently managed by the *Robot State Updater*. By adjusting the upper threshold values, risks can be exaggerated or depreciated based on the existing robot state. This provides on-the-fly prioritization of risks.

3.7   Path Planning and Execution

It is assumed that we have a priori map of the environment available for the robot. Any path search algorithm such as A* or Dijkstra could be used for planning the global path. As the robot navigates (either teleoperated or autonomously), the costmap is updated. After a certain number of runs, the robot adapts the path based on the updated new cost with radiation and temperature risks.

4   Experiments

4.1   Implementation

We use the layered costmap implementation developed by Lu et al. [7] in the ROS `navigation` stack. Our layered global costmap consists of four layers: a static layer received from SLAM (Simultaneous Localization And Mapping) or the `map_server` package, an inflation layer for the static obstacles, the radiation risk layer, and the temperature risk layer. An additional custom plugin layer has been developed for temperature and radiation risks in the `costmap2d` package[1] written in C++ and python based on [22]. The nuclear environment world, radiation, and temperature sources are simulated in the Gazebo 3D simulator. The setup was run on ROS Kinetic on a Ubuntu 16.04 machine with an Intel Core i7 CPU with an octa-core processor. We conducted our simulations on the Neobotix MPO-700 robot (Gazebo model) which is an omnidirectional robot with four independent omni-drives.

4.2   Simulated Environment

The simulated Gazebo world was designed to include multiple cylindrical blocks to represent barrels that may be present within a nuclear environment, along with rectangular blocks to represent walls, skips, or other hazards.

Sources. The temperature and radiation sources are created by modifying the ground plane of the simulation environment, shown in Fig. 2. As can be seen in Fig. 3, there are multiple colored areas rendered on the ground plane, which radially decrease in intensity; these represent higher risk areas. Red areas represent higher temperature regions, whilst green areas represent higher radiation zones. The yellow area represents a section that is both high in radiation and temperature. The ground plane image is adjusted to fit with the dimensions and resolution of the costmaps (20×20 m with resolution of 0.05 m/pixel).

---

[1] https://github.com/jenniferdavid/ISRA.

Sensors. To mimic the radiation/temperature sensing capability, we use a downward-facing color sensor (single-pixel camera) that measures the intensity of red, green, and blue (R, G, B) channels of the ground plane image. These are then reported as a single value depending on the channel - red for temperature and green for radiation. The use of black as a background color ensures the default reading for radiation or temperature is 0. The maximum value possible for each channel is 255, based on the 8-bit integer value encoding of the camera model in Gazebo.

This method allowed for spatial resolution of radiation and temperature intensity in an easily scalable and co-existing manner. For example, if the robot were to observe a measurement of value (200, 0, 0), it would be passing through a high-temperature area, whereas (200, 30, 0) corresponds to a combination of high temperature and weak radiation values at the same location.

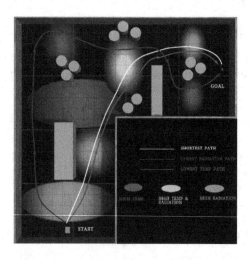

Fig. 2. The shortest path is shown in white color which is the default path that the robot takes during navigation. The shortest radiation path is denoted by blue color and the shortest temperature path is denoted by pink color. (Color figure online)

4.3   Costmap Updates

The environment was simulated, with sensors being approximated by the one-pixel camera measuring the intensity of the RGB feed. The pixel intensities were then converted to corresponding values for radiation/temperature. For radiation, the pixels values were divided by 100 so that a maximum pixel value of 255 corresponds to 2.55 mGy dose. In the case of temperature, the pixel values were divided by 2 so that a maximum pixel value of 255 corresponds to 172°C. The upper threshold values are modified using the ROS dynamic `reconfigure` server. It alters the sensor value which is considered the maximum cost, thereby scaling all values in the costmap to this new upper threshold value.

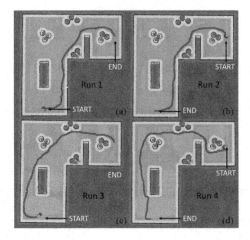

Fig. 3. In (a), the robot initially takes the shortest path (white color in Fig. 2), after a couple of runs in (b) and (c), the robot takes the shortest radiation path in (d) as the radiation risk prioritized more than the temperature risk in this case. (Color figure online)

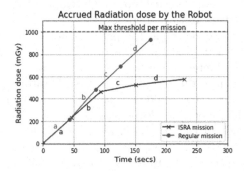

Fig. 4. The radiation dose accrued by the robot while navigating between start and end goals - with ISRA and without ISRA (regular or normal mission) is demonstrated here.

4.4 Navigation

For mapping and navigation, the `gmapping` and `move_base` ROS packages are used. For global path planning, the default Neobotix tuning parameters are used with the `navfn` global path planner, which uses Dijkstra's algorithm. We used the `NeoLocalPlanner`, developed by Neobotix as the local path planner with its default tuning parameters.

4.5 Tests

We conducted experiments to evaluate the performance of the implemented ISRA framework for doing a monitoring task in a simulated nuclear environ-

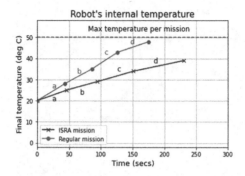

Fig. 5. The final temperature of the robot calculated using Eq. 2 is shown here when it navigates between the given start and end goals - with ISRA and without ISRA (regular or normal mission) framework.

ment. The placement of the colored areas in the Gazebo map was conceived so that there was a clear lowest temperature and lowest radiation path, shown in Fig. 2. Furthermore, it was designed so that it would be impossible to reach the end goal without passing through both high temperature and high radiation regions. This was so that during operation the robot's state would be forced to evolve, and this would reflect in the path the robot would choose - as the radiation increased we expected the robot to favor the lower temperature path and vice versa. Many different scenarios with varied radiation and temperature values were tested to just the robustness of the algorithm. In this paper, we explain one such scenario that could explain ISRA framework easily.

To begin with, the robot was teleoperated to create a static map of the simulated environment which could be used by the robot for navigating with the ISRA framework. On this static map, the robot was required to autonomously plan the optimal (shortest) path from a given start position to a goal position while avoiding obstacles. The robot then maneuvers and starts navigating from the goal position considering it as the start position in the second run. During navigation, the layered costmap is updated with temperature and radiation risks. After a certain number of repeated runs, when the global costmap is fully updated, it is expected that the robot can modify its path to the shortest path which has minimum radiation and temperature levels. Since we considered the radiation as cumulative, and temperature as dissipative, the robot would start to avoid the higher radiation zones as it accrued dose. The number of repeated runs required depends on the size and resolution of the map, the radiation and temperature sources, etc.

5   Results

Figure 3 shows how the planned path evolved using the framework. The resulting path in the global costmap from the nuclear monitoring task is shown after each half run (i.e., from start to end, end to start). The evolution of the path from

3(a)-(d) highlights well how the ISRA framework accounts for environmental risks and alters the robot's path during navigation. As the radiation dose of the robot only increases during operation, the cost of traversing radiation zones will only increase as time moves forward. Contrary to this, the robot's temperature may increase or decrease with time. Due to this, the cost of traversing high-temperature regions remains fairly constant during operation as heat is lost to the surroundings whilst the robot passes through cooler areas. These changing costs are accounted for in the path of the robot, as was the aim of ISRA. A video of one of the experiment runs can be seen at https://youtu.be/iUFOOIbQk7k.

In 3(a), the initial costmap and path can be seen, at this point, the robot follows the highest radiation route, which is also the optimal (shortest) path to the goal. On the return trip in 3(b), the costmap has been updated as is illustrated by the increase in the size of pink areas. However, the path remains the same as the robot's assessment of the radiation and temperature risk remains the same. In 3(c) the robot's path has changed, whilst the pink areas of the costmap that denote high radiation zones have grown significantly. The robot now avoids the initial patch of radiation near its start point, but later still passes through the radiation region in the top right of the map. Finally, on the return trip in 3(d) the robot's path follows the lowest radiation, highest temperature path as the costs for radiation have increased dramatically.

The radiation doses and the final temperature of the robot (considering heat dissipation) during this scenario are shown in Figs. 4 and 5. In the regular mission, the robot aims to find the optimal path for navigation and ignores the radiation and temperature values. As a result, the robot builds up radiation and temperature on the go and so can fail prematurely. But when the robot navigates with ISRA framework, the robot considers radiation and temperature values of the environment and modifies its path based on this value to keep the robot safe. This is also seen in Fig. 3 that there is a steady rise in radiation during 3(a) and 3(b) because the robot is not aware of the environment and takes time to update the costmap. So, the robot plans the shortest path which is also the high radiation path. During 3(c) and 3(d), the robot gets aware of the environmental risks and modifies the path accordingly. This causes a very small rise in radiation dose accrued by the robot and its temperature which is seen from the graph. It is also seen that without the ISRA framework, the robot is unaware and it always takes the shortest path to its goal leading to high radiation and temperature. The robot easily crosses its allowable maximum threshold per mission limit.

The shortest path length and the time taken for each of the consecutive runs are shown in Table 1. As it can be seen that the robot gets cautious more and more during navigation. It trades off both the path length and the time taken to complete the mission for safe navigation of the robot with reduced radiation and temperature exposures.

Overall, the goal of risk-sensitive path planning using layered costmaps has been achieved; the robot was able to move through the environment and alter its path based on its internal present state, with respect to temperature and radiation. Though we have demonstrated the method using only two risks, the ISRA framework may be generalized to any risk that is measurable and may have a maximum state defined. Future work will involve deploying the ISRA framework on real-world setup with radiation and thermal sensor and sources. Also, it is possible to implement a local costmap variant of the ISRA framework to allow for more reactive risk prioritization. This would allow the robot to avoid risks reactively when they are encountered. However, due to the limited look-ahead, the cost update needs to be remodeled to allow for smooth path transition.

Table 1. The shortest path and time taken for the given scenario using ISRA. Without the ISRA framework, the robot takes the same optimal path (as the Fig. 3(a)) in all the consecutive runs with path length - 142 units and time taken −46 s.

Test runs	Path length (units)	Total time (secs)
Start-Goal - a	142	46
Start-Goal - b	145	48
Start-Goal - c	165	57
Start-Goal - d	180	79

6   Conclusion

In this paper, we presented the Internal State-based Risk Assessment (ISRA) framework. The goal of this framework is to provide online risk-sensitive path planning for a robot, through the use of layered costmaps. These costmaps are adjusted to reflect the robot's current state in each of the risks and merged to form a global costmap that can be used for path planning. The ISRA framework is designed to be utilized for any state-based environmental risk and for any number of risks that need to be accounted for; with each risk occupying a separate layer in the costmap structure. To test the efficacy of this framework, we simulated a nuclear monitoring task using the Gazebo simulator and a simulated Neobotix MPO-700 robot. This robot was tasked with moving from a start point to an endpoint and back again, whilst avoiding its exposure to radioactive dose and its increase in internal temperature. The results from experimentation show that the robot was able to adapt its path to account for its internal state. On successive runs, the cumulative dose of radiation caused the cost of traversing high radiation regions to increase, compelling the robot to favor higher temperature areas and avoid higher radiation areas. Future work will involve testing the framework with real-world robots with temperature and radiation sources and sensors.

Acknowledgement. The authors wish to thank Dr. Thomas Wright of the University of Manchester for the concept of a single-pixel detector for monitoring radiation and temperature. This work was supported by UK Engineering and Physical Sciences Research Council (EPSRC) for the Robotics for Nuclear Environments Programme Grant (grant no. EP/P01366X/1), the TORONE consortium (EP/P018505/1), RAIN Hub (EP/R026084/1) and the Royal Academy of Engineering (CiET181913).

References

1. Ferguson, D., Likhachev, M.: Efficiently using cost maps for planning complex maneuvers. Lab Papers (GRASP), p. 20 (2008)
2. Forouher, D., Besselmann, M.G., Maehle, E.: Sensor fusion of depth camera and ultrasound data for obstacle detection and robot navigation. In: 2016 14th International Conference on Control, Automation, Robotics and Vision (ICARCV), pp. 1–6. IEEE (2016)
3. Groves, K., Hernandez, E., West, A., Wright, T., Lennox, B.: Robotic exploration of an unknown nuclear environment using radiation informed autonomous navigation. Robotics 10(2), 78 (2021). https://doi.org/10.3390/robotics10020078
4. Jannadi, O.A., Almishari, S.: Risk assessment in construction. J. Constr. Eng. Manag. 129(5), 492–500 (2003)
5. Kruusmaa, M., Svensson, B.: A low-risk approach to mobile robot path planning. In: Pasqual del Pobil, A., Mira, J., Ali, M. (eds.) IEA/AIE 1998. LNCS, vol. 1416, pp. 132–141. Springer, Heidelberg (1998). https://doi.org/10.1007/3-540-64574-8_399
6. Kweon, Y.J., Kockelman, K.M.: Overall injury risk to different drivers: combining exposure, frequency, and severity models. Accid. Anal. Prev. 35(4), 441–450 (2003)
7. Lu, D.V., Hershberger, D., Smart, W.D.: Layered Costmaps for context-sensitive navigation. In: 2014 IEEE/RSJ International Conference on Intelligent Robots and Systems, pp. 709–715. IEEE (2014)
8. Luo, R.C., Huang, C.: Human-aware motion planning based on search and sampling approach. In: 2016 IEEE Workshop on Advanced Robotics and its Social Impacts (ARSO), pp. 226–231. IEEE (2016)
9. Mainprice, J., Sisbot, E.A., Jaillet, L., Cortés, J., Alami, R., Siméon, T.: Planning human-aware motions using a sampling-based costmap planner. In: 2011 IEEE International Conference on Robotics and Automation, pp. 5012–5017. IEEE (2011)
10. Marques, F., Gonçalves, D., Barata, J., Santana, P.: Human-aware navigation for autonomous mobile robots for intra-factory logistics. In: Ham, J., Spagnolli, A., Blankertz, B., Gamberini, L., Jacucci, G. (eds.) Symbiotic 2017. LNCS, vol. 10727, pp. 79–85. Springer, Cham (2018). https://doi.org/10.1007/978-3-319-91593-7_9
11. Morales, N., Arnay, R., Toledo, J., Morell, A., Acosta, L.: Safe and reliable navigation in crowded unstructured pedestrian areas. Eng. Appl. Artif. Intell. 49, 74–87 (2016)
12. Morales, Y., et al.: Including human factors for planning comfortable paths. In: 2015 IEEE International Conference on Robotics and Automation (ICRA), pp. 6153–6159. IEEE (2015)
13. Murphy, L., Newman, P.: Risky planning: path planning over costmaps with a probabilistically bounded speed-accuracy tradeoff. In: 2011 IEEE International Conference on Robotics and Automation, pp. 3727–3732. IEEE (2011)
14. Murphy, L., Newman, P.: Risky planning on probabilistic costmaps for path planning in outdoor environments. IEEE Trans. Rob. 29(2), 445–457 (2012)
15. Nancekievill, M.J.: The radiation tolerance and development of robotic platforms for nuclear decommissioning. The University of Manchester (United Kingdom) (2018)
16. Ono, M., Fuchs, T.J., Steffy, A., Maimone, M., Yen, J.: Risk-aware planetary rover operation: autonomous terrain classification and path planning. In: 2015 IEEE Aerospace Conference, pp. 1–10. IEEE (2015)

17. Pendleton, S., Shen, X., Ang, M.: Moving obstacle avoidance via time-varying cost map. In: Proceedings of the 2013 IFTOMM International Symposium Robot Mechatronics, pp. 978–981 (2013)
18. Philippsen, R., Kolski, S., Macek, K., Jensen, B.: Mobile robot planning in dynamic environments and on growable costmaps. In: Workshop on Planning with Cost Maps at the IEEE International Conference on Robotics and Automation (2008)
19. Schroder, J., Gindele, T., Jagszent, D., Dillmann, R.: Path planning for cognitive vehicles using risk maps. In: 2008 IEEE Intelligent Vehicles Symposium, pp. 1119–1124. IEEE (2008)
20. Voos, H., Ertle, P.: Online risk assessment for safe autonomous mobile robots-a perspective. In: 7th Workshop on Advanced Control and Diagnosis ACD 2009, Zielona Gora, Poland (2009)
21. Wang, C., et al.: Autonomous mobile robot navigation in uneven and unstructured indoor environments. In: 2017 IEEE/RSJ International Conference on Intelligent Robots and Systems (IROS), pp. 109–116. IEEE (2017)
22. West, A., Wright, T., Tsitsimpelis, I., Groves, K., Joyce, M.J., Lennox, B.: Real-time avoidance of Ionising radiation using layered costmaps for mobile robots. Frontiers in Robotics and AI (2022). https://doi.org/10.3389/frobt.2022.862067

Robotic Learning, Mapping and Planning

Investigating Scene Visibility Estimation Within ORB-SLAM3

Dominic Rugg-Gunn and Jonathan M. Aitken[✉]

Department of Automatic Control and Systems Engineering,
University of Sheffield, Sheffield, UK
{drugg-gunn1,jonathan.aitken}@sheffield.ac.uk

Abstract. Scene Visibility Estimation offers a collection of metrics that give a good indication of the quality of images that are being supplied to a Visual or Visual-Inertial Simultaneous Location and Mapping algorithm. This paper will investigate the application of these metrics during switching between camera and IMU-based localisation within the popular visual-inertial ORB-SLAM3 algorithm. Application of the metrics provides more flexibility compared to a static threshold and incorporating the metrics within the switch provides a reduction in the error in positioning.

Keywords: Simultaneous Localisation and Mapping · Visibility

1 Introduction

1.1 Background

Simultaneous Localisation And Mapping (SLAM) is a method used by mobile robots to construct a map of the surrounding environment and to estimate it's position within that map. It is now used in an increasing number of practical fields due to improvements with computation and sensing.

Many environments pose challenges to existing pose estimation strategies SLAM in conjunction with appropriate sensors, provides a strong alternative [1]. Cameras commonly used as sensors as they provide a large amount of information at a relatively low cost [14]. For this, algorithms which perform Visual-Inertial-SLAM (VI-SLAM), harness the localisation capabilities of Visual Odometry (VO) in conjunction with inertial measurements in order to estimate the robot's pose. VI-SLAM also performs a mapping process that tracks observed features relative to the agent, enabling a computational understanding of an unknown environment [4].

Cameras suffer from visual artefacts such as lens flares and occlusion, often reducing the reliability of the localisation and mapping. These artefacts are detected as features, and propagate into the algorithm as incorrect associations, significantly impairing performance [2].

Supported by the Department of Automatic Control and Systems Engineering at the University of Sheffield. Also this work is supported by the UK's Engineering and Physical Sciences Research Council (EPSRC) Programme Grant EP/S016813/1.

S. Pacheco-Gutierrez et al. (Eds.): TAROS 2022, LNAI 13546, pp. 155–165, 2022.
https://doi.org/10.1007/978-3-031-15908-4_13

Previous work [7] developed Scene Visibility Estimation (SVE) metrics, that use a camera feed to assess the quality of the visual data and the visibility of the scene captured. This paper will implement SVE in a state-of-the-art VI-SLAM algorithm and use the metrics to evaluate performance with the aim of generating a more accurate and reliable pose estimation.

2   Related Work

2.1   Visual Simultaneous Localisation and Mapping

Visual Simultaneous Localisation and Mapping (V-SLAM) is a subsection of SLAM focused on using cameras as the sensor input to the algorithm. This incorporates functionality from Visual Odometry (VO) and combines it with the map generation capabilities inherent in SLAM algorithms [12]. VO works by isolating features in each frame and tracking the movement of these through multiple frames to infer the motion the agent must have taken.

V-SLAM is an advancement upon VO, introducing capabilities such as loop-closure which reduces the drift suffered in pose estimation, by referencing features to past features in the map and adjusting accordingly [1].

ORB-SLAM2 is a prominent V-SLAM algorithm, but is indirect as it includes an additional feature identification step. Built upon ORB-SLAM, it uses an ORB feature detector to incorporate clusters of pixels into a feature description before selecting features to use in the algorithm [11]. This is often faster and more data efficient than direct (individual pixel) methods, though some solutions such as LDSO use feature extraction methods to aid pixel selection and can produce results comparable to indirect methods [9].

2.2   Visual-Inertial Simultaneous Localisation and Mapping

VI-SLAM incorporates an IMU sensor to the V-SLAM pipeline. This adds precise measurements of movements and rotations but is prone to drift over extended periods of time, it therefore complements the V-SLAM algorithm well to increase system precision and robustness [5]. Two of the most significant VI-SLAM algorithms are VINS-Mono and ORB-SLAM3 [6].

VINS-Mono (monocular Visual Inertial Navigation System) is a tightly coupled mono VI-SLAM algorithm. Using a single camera and IMU, it considers the coupling of all sensors before pose estimation is performed. To optimise performance VINS-Mono pre-integrates the IMU data between frames, which reduces computation of superfluous pose estimation nodes [10]. The algorithm was primarily designed for use on-board UAS for pose estimation, but has proven capable in many other fields such as the automotive and agricultural research areas [8,15].

ORB-SLAM3 is built upon ORB-SLAM2 with the integration of an IMU sensor. It supports a variety of camera types and configurations, as well as incorporating a multi-map strategy to increase robustness to poor quality visual data (either from sensor errors or from a feature-sparse environment) [4]. ORB-SLAM3's superior performance is well noted [4,6,13] and motivates its use within this paper.

2.3   Scene Visibility Estimation

Scene Visibility Estimation [7] is a novel method to improve robustness by estimating the visibility of detected features. This was achieved on top of the ORB-SLAM2 algorithm by extracting and analysing tracked visual features. The results showed it responded reliably in difficult conditions such as fog, direct sunlight, and dirt on the lens.

To track the scene visibility, three metrics (S_{a-c}) were proposed, where each tracked a different aspect of the presented scene. The metric S_a represents a general ratio of the features N_F to the desired number of features $N_{F,\ max}$ such that: $S_a = \frac{N_F}{N_{F,\ max}}$. With a low S_a implying poor visibility, this would also be effective in low contrast operation or for handling feature sparse environments.

Component S_c broadly operates in the same way but using tracked features N_T. It does, however, incorporate an estimation step to determine the number of features that should be visible based on the local map N_{Lv}, and is defined as $S_c = \frac{N_T}{N_{Lv}}$. This should be effective in dynamic environments where tracked features a quickly and frequently lost between keyframes, however results for this didn't show a strong correlation.

The final metric (S_b) is the most complex. It aims to capture the distribution of features, the frame is divided into equal bins and a Chi-Square test is performed to quantify the homogeneity of the extracted features (χ^2). This result is then scaled to a 'worst case' scenario (χ_w^2) where all features appear in one eighth of the bins. When a part of the view is obscured any features in that section cannot be identified, however, estimating which previously tracked features should be identified can be used to identify feature absence. This presents as a skew in feature homogeneity, and propagates such that $S_b \to 0$ as $\chi^2 \to 0$ [7].

2.4   Adaptation of Scene Visibility Estimation in ORB-SLAM3

A modification was required to component A. The concept of this is that with decreased visibility the number of features extracted would decrease and lower the value of SVE_a. As ORB-SLAM3 almost always extracts the requested number of features, making this value uninformative. This metric was altered to express the ratio of tracked features (N_{F_T}) to the number required for high quality localisation expressed as a fraction of the desired number of features $(N_{F_{\max}})$.

3   Disturbance Generation

This section will discuss Blur, Downsampling and Occlusion disturbances, and how they can be applied to the data sequence to be used. These disturbances can then be used to corrupt elements of the EuRoC dataset [3] commonly used with ORB-SLAM3 [4], allowing an insight to the response of ORB-SLAM3 to varying intensities of different visual disturbances.

3.1 Blur

Bluring of the image feed is an attempt to replicate fog and rain, which are both very common-place in the real world applications of SLAM for example in smoke, dust, and generally decreased visibility in underwater situations.

The blur was implemented via OpenCV's Gaussian Blur, which generates a Gaussian kernel with dimensions $n \times n$ and convolves the input image with this. To vary the strength of the blur, the kernel dimensions are varied leading to increased blurring of the image with higher n. In preliminary testing, all localisation attempts by ORB-SLAM3 failed before the blur kernel size reached 50 pixels. To best explore the range before this point, a step-size of 5 was selected, giving a testing set of 11 intensities with dimensions $n \times n$ for $n \in [0, 5...45, 50]$. Examples of these kernel sizes can be seen in Fig. 1, with a weak blur shown in Fig. 1a and a strong shown in Fig. 1b.

(a) Kernel Size $n = 5$ (b) Kernel Size $n = 50$

Fig. 1. Example frames with different blur kernel sizes

3.2 Downsampling

The second augmentation performed was resolution downsampling. This was chosen partially to present an alternative implementation to blur for low visibility scenarios. In addition, image resolution is important to consider in it's own right as it is closely linked to hardware costs, with higher resolution cameras costing significantly more. This augmentation helps to investigate the extent to which a lower resolution, low cost, cameras impact the performance of the localisation in ORB-SLAM3.

The resolution downsampling was implemented via OpenCV's Resize, which is used to resamples the image array according to a provided downsampling factor (applied to both x and y dimensions). Preliminary tests were conducted that identified a downsampling factor of 1/0.1 was the point at which the initialisation failed, which is a resolution of just 75 × 48 px. Ten sample points were selected from the range [1,0.1] in order to cover it with a reasonable level of granularity. This resulted in the final downsampling factors to be tested of 1/[1.0, 0.9...0.2, 0.1].

Examples of the frames at these resolutions can be seen in Fig. 2 where Fig. 2a shows the smallest downsampling factor, taking the image to a resolution of 676 × 432 px. Figure 2b depicts the largest amount of downsampling (enlarged for visibility), and is the point at which the resolution is too low for the system to initialise.

(a) Downsampling Factor $DF = 1/0.9$ (b) Downsampling Factor $DF = 1/0.1$

Fig. 2. Example frames with different downsampling factors

3.3   Occlusion

The third disturbance selected was Occlusion. The ORB-SLAM3 system incorporates a place recognition module from ORBSLAM2, which is designed to resume tracking after temporal occlusions. In this test set the occlusion is static and persistent throughout the sequence, in order to investigate the systems robustness to scenarios with dirt or rain on the camera lens. To achieve this, a black square is generated in the center of the image as though an object was stuck to the lens of the camera. This appear in the centre of the image and different intensities are generated by adjusting the region's dimensions to produce a $n \times n$ absence of data. The smallest dimension of the image was 480 px, so the upper bound for n was chosen to be 450 px as this could be easily divided into ten steps to produce the final range of $n \in [50, 100...400, 450]$. Examples of the extremes of the occlusion disturbance can be seen in Fig. 3 with the smallest and largest occlusion sizes are shown in Fig. 3a and Fig. 3b respectively.

(a) Occlusion Size $n = 50$ (b) Occlusion Size $n = 450$

Fig. 3. Example frames with different occlusion sizes

3.4 Data Aggregation

In summary, three simple disturbances are applied to a baseline sequence from the EuRoC dataset. These each have 9–10 different levels, on which ORB-SLAM3 was be tested 100 times in order to aggregate the results and reject anomalies in the system's performance.

4 Improving SVE and Adapting ORB-SLAM3

The original ORB-SLAM3 pipeline incorporates a switching-behaviour for using visual or inertial data which is based on the number of features extracted from the image, typically set to 15 with the IMU initialised, or 50 when not. This is used as a primitive equivalent of the SVE, used to dictate to the system whether the image localisation should be used or the IMU odometry.

To test the current state of behaviours these evaluations were replaced with comparisons to the SVE using thresholds of 0.1 and 0.3 respectively. With little to no disturbances applied, the majority of the SVE ($\mu \pm \sigma$) lies above 0.3 so this was chosen to be a reasonable upper threshold. The lower threshold of 0.1 was chosen from manually inspecting how the SVE responds to the visually challenging portions of the sequence.

Combining the insights learnt so far, the components of the SVE metric appear to work well to indicate the visibility. However the process of combining them does not focus on the most important aspects for ORB-SLAM3's switching-behaviour. The equation currently used to do this is outlined in Eq. (1), where it can be seen that the number of extracted features (represented in SVE_a) only constitutes 20% of the overall metric. In order to improve the performance of the ORB-SLAM3 pipeline when the SVE metric is used to govern the switching-behaviour, two improvements are proposed to weight SVE_a more heavily.

$$\text{SVE} = 0.2 \times \text{SVE}_a + 0.4 \times \text{SVE}_b + 0.4 \times \text{SVE}_c \qquad (1)$$

The first of improvement proposal is outlined in Eq. (2), and alters the weightings such that component A bears twice the weighting of either components B or

C, which are equally weighted. This keeps to the same structure in [7], but seeks to redistribute the influence such that the switching-behaviour is more accurate and robust.

$$\text{SVE} = 0.5 \times \text{SVE}_a + 0.25 \times \text{SVE}_b + 0.25 \times \text{SVE}_c \qquad (2)$$

The alternate improvement deviates from the original structure as shown in Eq. (3), making the number of tracked features of paramount importance to dictate the scene's visibility. This structure uses the SVE_a metric as a scaling factor for the remaining metrics, and returns this result to a linear response by taking the square-root which results in a behaviour similar to a geometric mean.

The thresholds for this method were determined by scaling the original thresholds of 15 and 50, with best visibility ($\text{SVE} = 1$) set to occur with 250 tracked features, the original thresholds were divided by this to produce values of 0.04 for 15 features and 0.2 for 50.

$$\text{SVE} = \sqrt{\text{SVE}_a \times (0.5 \times \text{SVE}_b + 0.5 \times \text{SVE}_c)} \qquad (3)$$

5 Results

To analyse the performance of the two options for improving the SVE metrics, each was built into separate ORB-SLAM3 instances with the thresholds described in the previous section. These two ORB-SLAM3 builds were then run with each of the 31 sequences 100 times.

5.1 SVE Improvements

The plots of the SVE metrics are shown in Fig. 4, Fig. 5, and Fig. 6, showing the responses to each of the different disturbances.

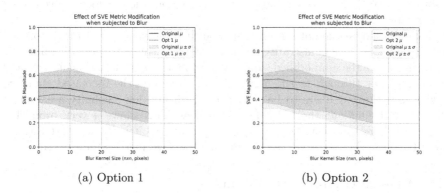

(a) Option 1   (b) Option 2

Fig. 4. Comparison of modified SVE metrics subjected to blur

The modified metrics showed the least difference from the original metric when subjected to the Blur disturbances, the results of which can be seen in Fig. 4. These mean values for both metric options are almost completely parallel to the original for all intensities. Which indicates they generally agree on the relative visibilities of the different blur intensities. The larger standard deviation illustrates a greater variation of the metric throughout each test run, so it is likely that the modified metrics provide a more varied and accurate indication of the true visibility throughout the sequence.

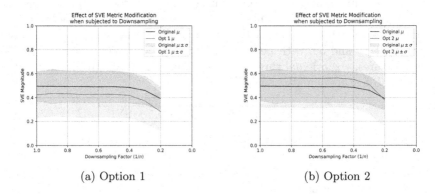

(a) Option 1   (b) Option 2

Fig. 5. Comparison of modified SVE metrics subjected to downsampling

The responses to downsampling shown in Fig. 5 also exhibit the increased standard deviation of the modified metrics, with this being continually demonstrated throughout the sequence. As was seen in responses to the Blur, the mean value of both metrics stay parallel up to a downsampling factor of 1/0.5. A this point Option 2 drops first, but it shortly followed by Option 1 and the Original at 1/0.4, however both the modified versions do so with a steeper gradient. This shows an increased sensitivity to poor visibility conditions which is even more exaggerated in Option 2.

Figure 6 shows some of the most significant improvement with the modified metrics. Option 1 demonstrates an increased sensitivity to poor visibility by diverging from the unmodified equivalent from the lowest occlusion size and continuing this through to the highest. It also exhibits the increased standard deviation making it likely to be identifying high and low visibility areas more effectively throughout the individual sequences. This shows a very promising step towards representing the true scene visibility, as it is known that there is disturbance at this point yet neither of the other two metrics indicate this.

5.2   Adapted ORB-SLAM3 Results

With the original ORB-SLAM3 switching algorithm as the baseline, Fig. 7a, Fig. 7b, and 7c show comparisons between this baseline and to two pipelines with the SVE-based switching-behaviour implemented.

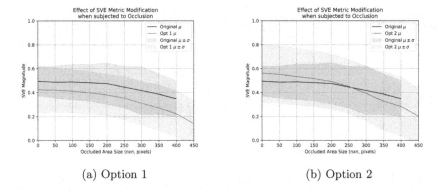

(a) Option 1   (b) Option 2

Fig. 6. Comparison of modified SVE metrics subjected to occlusion

Figure 7a shows the relative performance of the localisation as the Blur kernel size increases. It can be seen that all algorithms completely fail beyond a kernel size of 35, indicating the first steps in successfully stopping visual localisation when scene visibility is severely affected. Throughout the lower ranges Option 1 displays poor performance, multiple points deviate significantly from the baseline and almost always have greater RMS error. By contrast, Option 2 exhibits very good performance with little deviation from the performance of ORB-SLAM3's Original switching-behaviour, and strongly reflects the expected general trend.

With Downsampling applied to the visual data, Fig. 7b shows a generally similar performance between all three systems, this is most evident when DF $= 1/0.8 \rightarrow 1/0.4$. Both the Original and Option 1 switching-behaviours show spikes at DF $= 1/0.9$, this is due to a couple of smaller outliers not being rejected which appear to be the same reason for the peak in Option 1. Interestingly, Option 2 seems to be more robust to this with no unexpected spikes observed due to outliers in either the blur or downsampling tests.

The final filter applied was occlusion, the results of which can be seen in Fig. 7c. In this it can be seen that Option 1 is again showing relatively poor rejection of bad tracking data, with the SVE metric failing to trigger adequate switching in order to prevent failures within the localisation process. The performance of this remained in line with the other two systems until an occluded area of 150 × 150 px, at which point the error began to increase before sharply failing beyond 250 × 250 px. Option 2's performance remained much closer to the Original results, with a slight peak likely due to outliers at 300 × 300 px. Notably, neither Option 1 or Option 2 were successful in preventing tracking at 450 × 450. The Original failing to reach this point indicates that the number of tracked features was very low which would make localisation estimates poor.

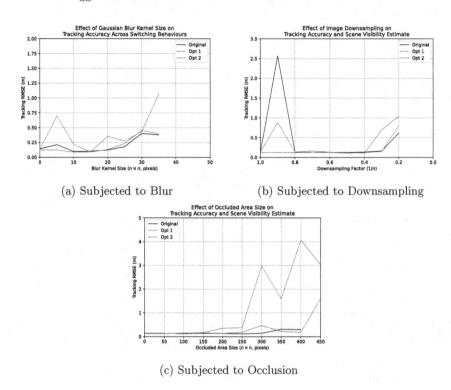

(a) Subjected to Blur   (b) Subjected to Downsampling

(c) Subjected to Occlusion

Fig. 7. Comparison of original ORB-SLAM3 switching behaviour and proposed SVE-based switches

6   Conclusions and Future Work

This paper has investigated the application of Scene Visibility Estimation within ORB-SLAM3. The EuRoC dataset has been corrupted using a collection of techniques that produce effects analogous to blur, occlusion and downsampling. The SVE metrics have been implemented within ORB-SLAM3, and used to provide an adaptive threshold for switching between localisation using either the camera or IMU feeds. SVE provides a more complete set of measurements of the quality of the image feed, and this allows the switching process to be more efficient resulting in a more accurate localisation when compared to the standard ORB-SLAM3 baseline. Option 2 performed very well, being consistently similar to the original pipeline and in some cases out performing it. Future work will focus on the optimisation of the mix of the SVE metrics to minimise position error.

References

1. Aitken, J.M., et al.: Simultaneous localization and mapping for inspection robots in water and sewer pipe networks: a review. IEEE Access **9**, 140173–140198 (2021)

2. Bailey, T., Durrant-Whyte, H.: Simultaneous localization and mapping (SLAM): part II. IEEE Rob. Autom. Mag. **13**(3), 108–117 (2006)
3. Burri, M., et al.: The EuRoC micro aerial vehicle datasets. Int. J. Rob. Res. **35**(10), 1157–1163 (2016)
4. Campos, C., Elvira, R., Rodríguez, J.J.G., Montiel, J.M., Tardós, J.D.: ORB-SLAM3: an accurate open-source library for visual, visual-inertial, and multimap slam. IEEE Trans. Rob. **37**, 1–17 (2021)
5. Chen, Y., Zhou, Y., Lv, Q., Deveerasetty, K.K.: A review of V-SLAM*. In: 2018 IEEE International Conference on Information and Automation (ICIA), pp. 603–608 (2018)
6. Cheng, J., Zhang, L., Chen, Q., Zhou, K., Long, R.: A fast and accurate binocular visual-inertial slam approach for micro unmanned system. In: 2021 IEEE 4th International Conference on Electronics Technology (ICET), pp. 971–976 (2021)
7. Haggart, R., Aitken, J.M.: Online scene visibility estimation as a complement to SLAM in UAVs. In: Fox, C., Gao, J., Ghalamzan Esfahani, A., Saaj, M., Hanheide, M., Parsons, S. (eds.) TAROS 2021. LNCS (LNAI), vol. 13054, pp. 365–369. Springer, Cham (2021). https://doi.org/10.1007/978-3-030-89177-0_38
8. He, Y., Chai, Z., Liu, X., Li, Z., Luo, H., Zhao, F.: Tightly-coupled vision-gyro-wheel odometry for ground vehicle with online extrinsic calibration. In: 2020 3rd International Conference on Intelligent Autonomous Systems (ICoIAS), pp. 99–106 (2020)
9. Mur-Artal, R., Tardós, J.D.: ORB-SLAM2: an open-source slam system for monocular, stereo, and RGB-D cameras. IEEE Trans. Rob. **33**(5), 1255–1262 (2017)
10. Qin, T., Li, P., Shen, S.: VINS-mono: a robust and versatile monocular visual-inertial state estimator. IEEE Trans. Rob. **34**(4), 1004–1020 (2018)
11. Rublee, E., Rabaud, V., Konolige, K., Bradski, G.: ORB: an efficient alternative to SIFT or SURF. In: 2011 International Conference on Computer Vision, pp. 2564–2571 (2011)
12. Savaria, D.T., Balasubramanian, R.: V-SLAM: vision-based simultaneous localization and map building for an autonomous mobile robot. In: 2010 IEEE Conference on Multisensor Fusion and Integration, pp. 1–6 (2010)
13. Sharafutdinov, D., et al.: Comparison of modern open-source visual SLAM approaches (2021)
14. Zaffar, M., Ehsan, S., Stolkin, R., Maier, K.M.: Sensors, SLAM and long-term autonomy: a review. In: 2018 NASA/ESA Conference on Adaptive Hardware and Systems (AHS), pp. 285–290 (2018)
15. Zhou, S., Zhao, H., Chen, W., Liu, Z., Wang, H., Liu, Y.H.: Dynamic state estimation and control of a heavy tractor-trailers vehicle. IEEE/ASME Trans. Mechatron. **26**(3), 1467–1478 (2021)

Tactile and Proprioceptive Online Learning in Robotic Contour Following

Pablo J. Salazar$^{(\boxtimes)}$ and Tony J. Prescott

Department of Computer Science, University of Sheffield, Sheffield S1 4DP, UK
{pjsalazarvillacis1,t.j.prescott}@sheffield.ac.uk

Abstract. Purposive and systematic movements are required for the exploration of tactile properties. Obtaining precise spatial details of the shape of an object with tactile data requires a dynamic edge following exploratory procedure. The contour following task relies on the perception of the angle and position of the sensor relative to the edge of the object. The perceived angle determines the direction of exploratory actions, and the position indicates the location relative to the edge for placing the sensor where the angle tends to be perceived more accurately. Differences in the consistency of the acquired tactile data during the execution of the task might induce inaccuracies in the predictions of the sensor model, and therefore impact on the enactment of active and exploratory movements. This work examines the influence of integrating information from robot proprioception to assess the accuracy of a Bayesian model and update its parameters to enhance the perception of angle and position of the sensor. The incorporation of proprioceptive information achieves an increased number of task completions relative to performing the task with a model trained with tactile data collected offline. Studies in biological touch suggest that tactile and proprioceptive information contribute synergistically to the perception of geometric properties and control of the sensory apparatus; this work proposes a method for the improvement of perception of the magnitudes required to actively follow the contour of an object under the presence of variability in the acquired tactile data.

Keywords: Active touch · Online learning · Contour following · Exploratory procedure

1 Introduction

Tactile sensing provides the capability of interacting with the world by establishing direct contact with objects and surfaces to extract relevant properties for achieving a task. The required interaction implies that specific movements need to be performed to elicit the tactile properties associated to the executed motion [11]. The relevance of the tactile information needed to achieve a desired outcome is translated into the active nature of touch. Active touch involves the execution of an action-perception loop in which dedicated actions are intended to guide the spatially constrained sensory apparatus [6]. The execution of these

© The Author(s), under exclusive license to Springer Nature Switzerland AG 2022
S. Pacheco-Gutierrez et al. (Eds.): TAROS 2022, LNAI 13546, pp. 166–178, 2022.
https://doi.org/10.1007/978-3-031-15908-4_14

actions is conducted by taking into account the tactile and proprioceptive sensory information, its prior understanding, as well as knowledge about the task that is being executed [21].

The human hand has evolved to serve as a skillful tool for perception of tactile properties. The hand consists of glabrous and non glabrous skin; being the former, present in the palmar skin, the most receptive part to mechanosensation due to its high density innervation that is correlated with psychophysical spatial acuity [2]. This highly innervated area contains four types of receptors that respond to low thresholds of skin deformation, contact events, and sensitivity to high frequency stimuli. When these receptors receive a stimulus related to the sensitive-related physical property, the information is conveyed to the somatosensory cortex to be processed and encoded [22]. Studies in non-human primates have identified four areas in the primary somatosensory cortex, i.e. Broadmann areas 3a, 3b, 1 and 2, these areas have been described as being hierarchical and interconnected [5,7,8]. In that sense, higher-in-hierarchy areas, with the function of processing more complex information, receive information from their lower-in-hierarchy counterparts, as well as information from areas dedicated to sensing and execution of motor behaviour. According to these studies, at the base of the hierarchy, 3a area receives proprioceptive spatial information form muscle spindles; 3b area retrieves information from receptors located closer to the skin surface; area 1 obtains information from rapidly adapting fibers; and area 2 receiving proprioceptive signals, as well as information from the previously mentioned areas to process complex touch. The processed information in the primary somatosensory cortex is conveyed to the secondary somatosensory cortex which processes information that is conveyed to cortical areas in charge of the execution of motor commands and recognition of physical properties [4].

Apart from apprehending semantic representations from mechanoreception, tactile and proprioceptive information contribute to the processing of complex touch as well as active touch by means of the intentional exploration of surfaces and objects. The exploratory essence of touch has been characterised under the term of 'Exploratory Procedures'. EPs are described as stereotypical movements that subjects execute when prompted to learn about a certain tactile property [12]. Material properties of an object can be retrieved by performing characteristic actions such as lateral motion for texture, pressure for compliance and static contact for temperature. Geometric properties such as global shape and volume can be obtained with the enclosure exploratory procedure; the exact shape and volume can be retrieved through following the contour of the object [13]. These characteristics of human touch are inspiring the development of technologies and tactile systems to result in remarkable sensing capabilities [15].

Providing robotic systems with the capacity to sense and draw conclusions about tactile data can be essential for the achievement of tasks that require feedback from physical interaction with the environment; such tasks include grasping, in-hand manipulation, and object exploration [10]. The execution of these tasks can be benefited by possessing knowledge about the shape of the object. Retrieval of geometric object information through touch is generally attained by mapping from data related to sensor deformation to the pose of the sensing device relative to the object [17]. This process contributes with information for the control and guidance of movement of the sensory apparatus to extract the global or exact shape according to the objectives of the perceiver.

Tactile perceptual systems are restricted to the size of the sensor, thus acquiring geometric information through touch has been a compelling object of study in examining methods to effectively place the sensor where information relevant to the task can be obtained [23]. Retrieval of tridimensional surfaces have been achieved through the registering of coordinates where the event of touching the object has occurred. These coordinates are used as an input in a function approximator that provides an estimate of the object shape in three dimensions [24]. The implicit hurdle in using these models is determining the next sampling position to attain a fast and accurate shape estimation [3,9,20]. Inspired from psychophysical studies in touch, the obtention of the exact shape of an object has been investigated by means of the replication of contour following exploratory procedures in robotic platforms [19]. Tactile information related to sensor deformation has been related to allocentric sensor localisation to follow the contour of objects. These methods rely on Bayesian inference in which the hypotheses for perceptual classes given the tactile data are updated with the acquisition and accumulation evidence to make a decision regarding a perceptual outcome [16,18].

Although the implementation of contour following exploratory procedure using Bayesian methods using only tactile data in robotic platforms has demonstrated the feasibility of successfully obtaining the exact shape of the contour of an object, the effect of taking into account the proprioceptive information from the robotic platform for assessing and updating a probabilistic model remains to be studied.

Obtaining the exact shape of an object through tactile information requires perception models that can accurately infer a position of the sensor with respect to an object using tactile data. However, tactile data acquisition can be effected by sensor noise, hysteresis-induced errors, and the wear and tear off of the sensor [10]. These possible issues can lead to deficiencies in the repeatability of tactile measurements, and consequently a reduction in accuracy of perceptual outcomes. In that sense, the mapping of tactile data into sensor position can be supported by the millimetric, precise and accurate information that robot proprioception can provide.

The present work evaluates the effects of implementing a Bayesian probabilistic model for sensor localisation with respect to the edges of an object to execute a contour following exploratory procedure with tactile data. Additionally, we examine the integration of proprioceptive information in the assessment and updating of the model, in which, perception accuracy is enhanced leading to improvements in task completion and reduction of exploratory steps to follow the contour of the object.

2   Methods

2.1   Robotic Setting

The robotic system used for the acquisition of the tactile information and movement of the sensor to perform a contour following exploratory procedure consists
of a TacTip biomimetic tactile sensor [1] mounted on a robotic platform able to
perform movements in the Cartesian space. This setting is used in an action-
perception closed loop to execute the exploratory procedure with information
obtained from the tactile sensor.

Robotic Platform. The robotic platform is composed of a Yamaha "XYX"
robot and an Actuonix P-16 linear actuator, providing horizontal and vertical
movements respectively, as can be seen in Fig. 1a. The Yamaha robot has been
used in previous studies on active touch with fingertips and artificial whiskers [14]
offering an accuracy of about $20\mu m$ in the positioning of the sensor in the $x - y$
plane. The linear actuator spans a stroke of 50mm allowing a vertical motion
of the sensor. The robotic platform allows the execution of precise movements
in the x and y axes for the positioning of the sensor to establish a relationship
between the acquired tactile data and the location of the sensor relative to the
object.

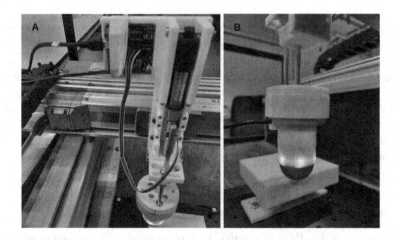

Fig. 1. Robotic setting. A) The Robotic platform consists of a Yamaha "XYX" robot
and an Actuonix P-16 linear actuator for displacements in the Z axis. B) TacTip
sensor [1] and object for contour following

Tactile Fingertip Sensor. The TacTip Sensor (Fig. 1b) is a biomimetic soft
optical tactile sensor. Inspired in the shallow layers of glabrous skin, the sensor contains a 20mm-radius hemispheric compliant pad with 127 pins acting as

markers whose shear displacement is related to the deformation of the compliant component. The behaviour of the markers is captured by a webcam with a resolution of 640×480 pixels, sampled at approximately 20 fps. The software for marker detection and tracking, implemented in [16], provides data of the displacement of each marker in the x and y axes. The information obtained from the sensor is used to train a Bayesian probabilistic classifier for the localisation of the sensor with respect to an allocentric origin of coordinates located at the edge of the object and identification of angular classes for exploration. The object used for the contour following task is a rectangular surface with a length of 110 mm on each side (Fig. 1b). However, the method can be extended performing the task on right-angled objects.

Sensorimotor Integration. The control of the robotic platform is achieved through serial communication between the computer and the robotic devices. The Yamaha robot and the linear actuator provide position feedback and position control. Both are integrated in a python script. Similarly, the data obtained from the TacTip data processor are included as an input to a probabilistic classifier that relate tactile information to sensor position. The action-perception loop obtains information from the sensor, and executes the movements for the completion of the task, i.e. contour following of an object, taking into account the predictions of the probabilistic classifier.

Acquisition of Tactile Data. Tactile data acquisition follows a tapping procedure against the surface close to the edges to elicit a displacement of the internal markers of the TacTip Sensor. Discrete taps along a range between -9mm and 9mm in an interval of 1mm with respect to each of the edges comprise the data for each angular class. In that sense, an angular class contains 19 taps, and position classes as can be observed in Fig. 2. Each position class consists of two streams of data corresponding to the tracking of 127 marker positions (Fig. 2c) for the horizontal (Fig. 2a), and vertical (Fig. 2b) axes respectively. The data collection process is replicated for perceptual angles of $[0, 90, 180, 270]°$ giving a total of 76 perceptual classes to train a probabilistic Bayesian classifier.

2.2 Bayesian Probabilistic Classifier

A Multinomial Naive Bayes Classifier is implemented as a sensor model for the mapping from tactile data to angle and position of the sensor. In which, the probability of a class given a measurement is proportional to the likelihood of the measurement given the class multiplied by the prior probability of the class:

$$P(c|z) \, \alpha \, P(c) \prod_{1 \leq k \leq n_b} P(z_k|c), \tag{1}$$

where $P(z_k|c)$ is interpreted as a quantification of the contribution of the evidence z_k to the correctness of class c. Tactile data is spatiotemporally encoded

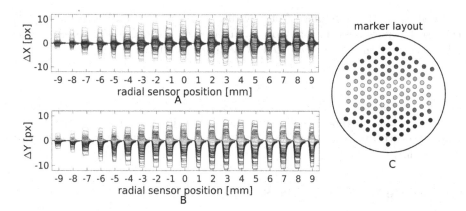

Fig. 2. Tactile data (taps) for 19 position classes corresponding to angle perceptual class: 0°. A) Tracking of horizontal marker displacement (ΔX). B) Tracking of vertical marker displacement (ΔY). C) Layout of 127 internal markers of the TacTip sensor, colours on each plot correspond to the respective marker position

in histograms. Each stream of data corresponding to a single tap is distributed into a histogram composed of 100 bins. Specifically, each bin of the histogram contains the number of times that a marker displacement in the x and y axes occur within a certain pixel variation range. $[z_1, z_2, ..., z_n]$ corresponds to each marker displacement belonging to a bin in the histogram, being n_z the number of samples from the stream of sensory data.

The best class for each tap from the Bayesian model corresponds to the most likely or *maximum a posteriori* (MAP) class c_{map}:

$$c_{map} = \arg\max_{c \in C} \hat{P}(c|z) = \arg\max_{c \in C} \hat{P}(c) \prod_{1 \le k \le n_z} \hat{P}(z_k|c). \qquad (2)$$

The values of the parameters $\hat{P}(c)$ and $\hat{P}(z_k|c)$ are estimated from the training data. The prior probability is estimated with the assumption that all classes are equally likely to occur, thus flat priors are set for each class, being N_c the number of classes:

$$\hat{P}(c) = \frac{1}{N_c} \qquad (3)$$

The conditional probability $\hat{P}(z|c)$ is calculated as the relative frequency of marker displacements corresponding to a certain pixel range that belongs to class c:

$$\hat{P}(z|c) = \frac{Z_{cz}}{\sum_{z' \in V} Z_{cz'}}, \qquad (4)$$

where Z_{cz} is the number of occurrences of a marker displacement in a pixel variation range for a tap stream data from class c. An independence assumption has been made between samples for each tracked marker in the x and y axes for model simplification. Even though this assumption might not be fulfilled in the real world, the outcomes from the model tend to be still reasonable [25]. Due to the sparseness that may occur within the encoding of the sensory data, a Laplace smoother is implemented by adding a one to each count:

$$\hat{P}(z|c) = \frac{Z_{cz} + 1}{\sum_{z' \in B}(Z_{cz'} + 1)}. \tag{5}$$

This smoothing method can be interpreted as a uniform prior for the occurrence of a certain displacement in a pixel variation range stated by the encoding histogram.

2.3   Active Bayesian Tactile Sensing

Tactile sensing for contour following requires an active approach for perception and selection of action. Active sensing implies modifying the state parameters of the sensor in order to acquire information relevant to the completion of the task. In this work, the perception of the angle of the sensor relative to the edge of an object is pertinent for the execution of exploratory tactile data acquisition to follow the contour of an object. An accurate perception of the angular perceptual class relies on modifying the radial position of the sensor. The repositioning of the sensor requires the localisation of the sensor with respect to the edge of the object. Sensor localisation is performed by the implementation of a probabilistic Bayesian classifier. The Bayesian model outputs the most likely perceptual class regarding to angle and position of the sensor. Given that some position classes will provide a more accurate angular perception, the sensor needs to be radially moved to the place where accuracy tends to be higher. This procedure leads to a correct perception of angular class for the execution of further tangential exploratory movements.

Active Contour Following. The process for contour following takes place when a taping procedure against the object elicits the deformation of the compliant component of the sensor. The data from the tracking of maker displacement is then spatiotemporally encoded, and incorporated as evidence for the perceptual classes. The most likely class is selected by obtaining the *maximumaposteriori* of all classes. A fixation range in which the data acquisition can provide an accurate angular class is selected offline. The selection of the range takes into account the accuracy of the classifier on test data. Being the case that the perceptual outcome from the classifier states that the sensor is localised outside of the fixation range, the sensor will be radially moved to be located within that range. When the sensor is placed in the fixation range, and the outcome of the classifier determines that the sensor is within that range, a exploratory tangential motion relative to the perceived angle is executed. A scheme of the process can be observed in Fig. 3a.

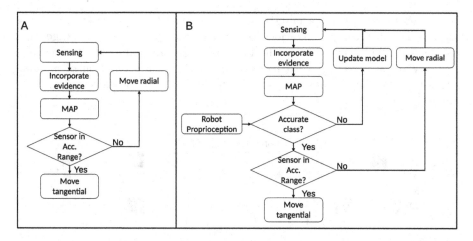

Fig. 3. Active Bayesian tactile sensing. A) Active sensing process B) Active sensing with online learning

Online Learning. Robot proprioception provides accurate information about the location of the robot in the workspace. This information can be used for supporting the mapping from tactile data to angle and position of the sensor with respect to an edge of the object. This information can be transformed to act as an automatic label provider given that the position of the object is previously known. Therefore, proprioceptive data is included in the process to assess the accuracy of the probabilistic classifier. In that sense, the angle and position outcomes from the classifier are compared with the labels from proprioception. Given the case in which the model does not provide an accurate perceptual class, the encoded tactile information becomes a training data point with the label given by the actual perceptual class followed by the updating of the model parameters. Conceding that the angle and position classes provided by the model are accurate, the process follows similar steps as in the active contour following process as seen in Fig. 3b.

3   Results

3.1   Angle and Position Perception

The Bayesian probabilistic classifier is tested offline with a set of data obtained with the same procedure as for the acquisition of training data. The classification absolute error for the angular classes (Fig. 4a) provides us with understanding of the position classes in which the angle is correctly classified, thus the fixation range can be determined. Furthermore, the absolute classification error for the position classes contributes to the identification of a fixation point. The fixation point is the location where the perception of angle and position tends to be accurate. Results in Fig. 4b suggest that the fixation point should be set as the −1 mm position perceptual class given the accurate response for angle and position classification. The fixation point is extended into a fixation range, this position span will eventually be the location where angular perceptual classes are likely to be perceived with more accuracy. Correct perception of angular classes leads to the execution of proper exploratory movements to achieve the completion of the task.

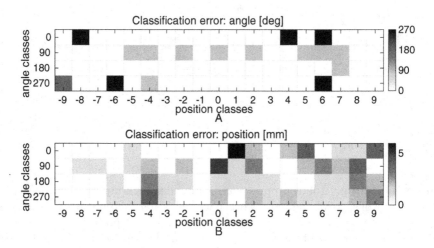

Fig. 4. Angle and position discrimination from the probabilistic Bayesian classifier. A) Absolute error for angle classification. B) Absolute error for position classification

3.2 Online Learning

Proprioceptive information from the robot is used to generate the ground truth of each perceptual class. Knowledge of the actual angle and position classes is employed to assess the accuracy of the sensor model. Figure 5 presents the ground truth as a solid line; each point illustrates the place where the robot executed a tap for data acquisition. The assessment and learning procedure is executed for each tap. When the model provides an inaccurate prediction, the ground truth serves as a label to update the conditional probability of the data belonging to the actual class. The learning process is carried on until the model produces an accurate prediction. As the figure displays, the distribution of the data points that require one or two times of model updating are concentrated outside of the corners. This effect can be attributed to the variation in consistency of the behaviour of the linear actuator when executing vertical movements. Additionally, as presented in the figure, the data points that require more than three times to update the model parameters are located on the corners of the object. This increase in the number of times the model is updated might happen given that the training data was not acquired by directly tapping on the corners. The

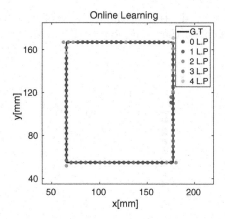

Fig. 5. Online learning in a contour following setting. Black solid line represents the ground truth of figure contour. Each point represents a tap on the edge of the object. Blue, red, green, magenta, cyan points correspond to the number of taps used for learning and updating the model (Color figure online)

initial model might provide correct predictions of perceptual classes. However, the prediction of angle and position with data streams subject to variability in the execution of vertical movements demands the update of the parameters to improve the accuracy of the predictions of the model.

3.3   Active Contour Following

The initial and updated models are tested under the same conditions as previously presented in Fig. 3a where the movement policy relies on executing radial motions to place the sensor within a fixation range, and perform tangential exploratory movements with respect to the predicted angle to follow the contour of the object. In that sense, three trials were executed for both models. The execution of the task with the initial model represented in Fig. 6a reveals that the contour following procedure was completed only in one out of three trials. It has to be highlighted that the initial model was not trained with data where the sensor is placed on the corners; thus, the inaccuracy of the probabilistic classifier had incidence in predicting the required angular class to perform tangential exploratory movements for the completion of the task. Testing the updated model for contour following results in the completion of the task on three out of three trials, as presented in Fig. 6b. This result shows that an accurate perception of angular classes leads to the execution of the necessary exploratory taps to completely follow the contour of the object. The updated model outperforms the outcome of the initial model not only in the completion of the task, but in the number of taps required to follow the contour of the object. While 208 taps were needed to complete the task with the initial model, contour following of the object using the updated model was achieved with 131, 144, and 152 number of taps for each trial. This reduction of the number of taps to complete the task presents an improvement in the time required for its achievement.

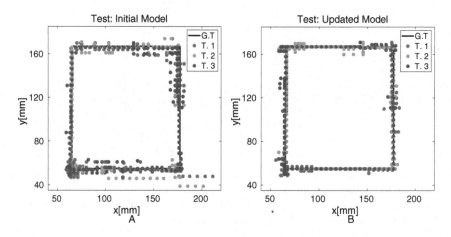

Fig. 6. Active contour following test. Where black solid line represents the ground truth of the figure contour. Each point depicts the position of an executed tap. Red points: first trial; green points: second trial; blue points: third trial. A) Trials on contour following: Initial model. B) Tests on contour following: Model after parameter updating. (Color figure online)

4   Discussion

In this work, a sensorimotor action-perception loop was implemented for following the contour of an object. A Bayesian probabilistic classifier was trained as a sensor model to map from tactile data to angle and position classes of the sensory device relative to the edges of the object. The predictions of the classifier were used for the localisation of the sensor and the identification of angular perceptual classes to perform exploratory movements. However, the variability present in the acquired tactile data, due to the response of the linear actuator, was translated into inaccuracies in the predictions of the classifier. The integration of tactile and proprioceptive information for guidance and control of the sensory apparatus in the hierarchical structure of the somatosensory system inspired the inclusion of robot proprioception for the improvement of accuracy in tactile perception. Specifically, the information from robot proprioception was taken into account for the assessment of the model and performing online learning when required. The initial and updated models were tested under the same circumstances on three trials for each classifier. As showed in the results section, taking into account the ground truth for assessing the predictions of the classifier, and updating the parameters of the model had an incidence in the completion of the task resulting in three out of three completed trials; as opposite to one out of three completions of the task for the initial model. Additionally, the number of taps required to follow the contour of the object were reduced using the updated model. Therefore, the assessment and updating of the model with proprioceptive information can result convenient in situations where there is variability in the execution of vertical movements involved in the tapping procedure for the acquisition of tactile data. This variation in the consistency of tactile data might be present in real world applications, thus the improvement of the sensor model for prediction of angle and position displays the potential to attain robust perception of the magnitudes required to perform the contour following task.

Acknowledgments. This work is supported by European Union's Horizon 2020 MSCA Programme under Grant Agreement No. 813713 NeuTouch.

References

1. Chorley, C., Melhuish, C., Pipe, T., Rossiter, J.: Development of a tactile sensor based on biologically inspired edge encoding. In: 2009 International Conference on Advanced Robotics, pp. 1–6 (2009). https://ieeexplore.ieee.org/document/5174720
2. Corniani, G., Saal, H.P.: Tactile innervation densities across the whole body. J. Neurophysiol. **124**(4), 1229–1240 (2020). https://doi.org/10.1152/jn.00313.2020
3. Driess, D., Hennes, D., Toussaint, M.: Active multi-contact continuous tactile exploration with Gaussian process differential entropy. In: 2019 International Conference on Robotics and Automation (ICRA), vol. 2019-May, pp. 7844–7850. IEEE (2019). https://doi.org/10.1109/ICRA.2019.8793773
4. Felleman, D.J., Van Essen, D.C.: Distributed hierarchical processing in the primate cerebral cortex. Cereb. Cortex **1**(1), 1–47 (1991). https://doi.org/10.1093/cercor/1.1.1
5. Gardner, E.P.: Somatosensory cortical mechanisms of feature detection in tactile and kinesthetic discrimination. Can. J. Physiol. Pharmacol. **66**(4), 439–454 (1988). https://doi.org/10.1139/y88-074
6. Gibson, J.J.: Observations on active touch. Psychol. Rev. **69**(6), 477–491 (1962). https://doi.org/10.1037/h0046962
7. Iwamura, Y., Iriki, A., Tanaka, M.: Bilateral hand representation in the postcentral somatosensory cortex. Nature **369**(6481), 554–556 (1994). https://doi.org/10.1038/369554a0
8. Iwamura, Y., Tanaka, M., Sakamoto, M., Hikosaka, O.: Rostrocaudal gradients in the neuronal receptive field complexity in the finger region of the alert monkey's postcentral gyrus. Exp. Brain Res. **92**(3), 360–368 (1993). https://doi.org/10.1007/BF00229023
9. Jamali, N., Ciliberto, C., Rosasco, L., Natale, L.: Active perception: building objects' models using tactile exploration. In: 2016 IEEE-RAS 16th International Conference on Humanoid Robots (Humanoids), pp. 179–185. IEEE (2016). https://doi.org/10.1109/HUMANOIDS.2016.7803275
10. Kappassov, Z., Corrales, J.A., Perdereau, V.: Tactile sensing in dexterous robot hands - review. Robot. Auton. Syst. **74**, 195–220 (2015). https://doi.org/10.1016/j.robot.2015.07.015
11. Lederman, S.J., Klatzky, R.L.: Haptic perception: a tutorial. Attent. Percept. Psychophys. **71**(7), 1439–1459 (2009). https://doi.org/10.3758/APP.71.7.1439

12. Lederman, S.J., Klatzky, R.L.: Hand movements: a window into haptic object recognition. Cogn. Psychol. **19**(3), 342–368 (1987). https://doi.org/10.1016/0010-0285(87)90008-9
13. Lederman, S.J., Klatzky, R.L.: Extracting object properties through haptic exploration. Acta Psychol. **84**(1), 29–40 (1993). https://doi.org/10.1016/0001-6918(93)90070-8
14. Lepora, N.F.: Biomimetic active touch with fingertips and whiskers. IEEE Trans. Haptics **9**(2), 170–183 (2016). https://doi.org/10.1109/TOH.2016.2558180
15. Lepora, N.F.: Touch, vol. 1. Oxford University Press, Oxford (2018). https://doi.org/10.1093/oso/9780199674923.003.0016
16. Lepora, N.F., Aquilina, K., Cramphorn, L.: Exploratory tactile servoing with active touch. IEEE Robot. Autom. Lett. **2**(2), 1156–1163 (2017). https://doi.org/10.1109/LRA.2017.2662071
17. Li, Q., Kroemer, O., Su, Z., Veiga, F.F., Kaboli, M., Ritter, H.J.: A review of tactile information: perception and action through touch. IEEE Trans. Robot. **36**(6), 1619–1634 (2020). https://doi.org/10.1109/TRO.2020.3003230
18. Martinez-Hernandez, U., Dodd, T., Prescott, T.J., Lepora, N.F.: Active Bayesian perception for angle and position discrimination with a biomimetic fingertip. In: 2013 IEEE/RSJ International Conference on Intelligent Robots and Systems, pp. 5968–5973. IEEE (2013). https://doi.org/10.1109/IROS.2013.6697222
19. Martinez-Hernandez, U., Dodd, T.J., Natale, L., Metta, G., Prescott, T.J., Lepora, N.F.: Active contour following to explore object shape with robot touch. In: 2013 World Haptics Conference (WHC), pp. 341–346. IEEE (2013). https://doi.org/10.1109/WHC.2013.6548432
20. Matsubara, T., Shibata, K.: Active tactile exploration with uncertainty and travel cost for fast shape estimation of unknown objects. Robot. Auton. Syst. **91**, 314–326 (2017). https://doi.org/10.1016/j.robot.2017.01.014
21. Prescott, T.J., Diamond, M.E., Wing, A.M.: Active touch sensing. Philos. Trans. R. Soc. B: Biol. Sci. **366**(1581), 2989–2995 (2011). https://doi.org/10.1098/rstb.2011.0167
22. Saal, H.P., Bensmaia, S.J.: Touch is a team effort: interplay of submodalities in cutaneous sensibility. Trends Neurosci. **37**(12), 689–697 (2014). https://doi.org/10.1016/j.tins.2014.08.012
23. Seminara, L., Gastaldo, P., Watt, S.J., Valyear, K.F., Zuher, F., Mastrogiovanni, F.: Active haptic perception in robots: a review. Front. Neurorobot. **13**, 53 (2019). https://doi.org/10.3389/fnbot.2019.00053
24. Yi, Z., et al.: Active tactile object exploration with Gaussian processes. In: 2016 IEEE/RSJ International Conference on Intelligent Robots and Systems (IROS), vol. 2016-Novem, pp. 4925–4930. IEEE (10 2016). https://doi.org/10.1109/IROS.2016.7759723
25. Zhang, H.: The optimality of Naive Bayes. In: Barr, V., Markov, Z. (eds.) Proceedings of the Seventeenth International Florida Artificial Intelligence Research Society Conference, FLAIRS 2004, Florida, vol. 2, pp. 562–567 (2004). https://aaai.org/Library/FLAIRS/2004/flairs04-097.php

Learning Cooperative Behaviours in Adversarial Multi-agent Systems

Ni Wang[1]([✉])[iD], Gautham P. Das[2][iD], and Alan G. Millard[3][iD]

[1] Paris-Saclay University, Gif-sur-Yvette, France
`niwang.fr@gmail.com`
[2] Lincoln Agri-Robotics, University of Lincoln, Lincoln, UK
`gdas@lincoln.ac.uk`
[3] Department of Computer Science, University of York, York, UK
`alan.millard@york.ac.uk`

Abstract. This work extends an existing virtual multi-agent platform called RoboSumo to create TripleSumo—a platform for investigating multi-agent cooperative behaviors in continuous action spaces, with physical contact in an adversarial environment. In this paper we investigate a scenario in which two agents, namely 'Bug' and 'Ant', must team up and push another agent 'Spider' out of the arena. To tackle this goal, the newly added agent 'Bug' is trained during an ongoing match between 'Ant' and 'Spider'. 'Bug' must develop awareness of the other agents' actions, infer the strategy of both sides, and eventually learn an action policy to cooperate. The reinforcement learning algorithm Deep Deterministic Policy Gradient (DDPG) is implemented with a hybrid reward structure combining dense and sparse rewards. The cooperative behavior is quantitatively evaluated by the mean probability of winning the match and mean number of steps needed to win.

Keywords: Multi-agent cooperation · Reinforcement learning

1 Introduction

With the success of AlphaGo, AI in games has been gaining increasing attention from researchers around the world [1]. In the physical world, agents exhibit intelligent behaviours at multiple spatial and temporal scales [2]. In [3], a multi-agent platform RoboSumo[1] was designed to investigate the potential of continuous adaptation in non-stationary and competitive multi-agent environments through meta-learning. In that platform, two agents, either homogeneous or heterogeneous, learn to play a 'sumo' game against each other. The one that successfully pushes its opponent off the square arena wins the match.

This work benefited from the advice of Assistant Professor Shinkyu Park at King Abdullah University of Science and Technology (KAUST).

[1] https://github.com/openai/robosumo.

S. Pacheco-Gutierrez et al. (Eds.): TAROS 2022, LNAI 13546, pp. 179–189, 2022.
https://doi.org/10.1007/978-3-031-15908-4_15

While RoboSumo allows multi-agent physical interaction to be investigated in adversarial scenarios, the platform does not offer support for exploring cooperative behaviors among agents. In this paper, we extend RoboSumo such that a new agent is added and can team up with one of the existing agents. This new agent must learn a policy to cooperate with its pre-defined partner, and play against their opponent. We train the system with Deep Deterministic Policy Gradient (DDPG), a reinforcement learning algorithm which learns a Q-function with off-policy data and the Bellman equation, and concurrently learns a policy using the Q-function [4]. The training result is evaluated through both qualitative observations of the agents' behaviors in simulation, and two quantitative parameters – 'mean winning rate' and 'steps needed to win'. The code developed for training, testing, and evaluation is open for public access[2]. The major contributions of this work are: to establish a virtual platform that allows both cooperative and competitive interactions to be explored in physical contact-rich scenarios, and to report baseline results for the two evaluation metrics after training the system with DDPG.

The next section of this paper reviews related work on multi-agent games based on virtual platforms; Sect. 3 describes our extension of RoboSumo and establishes TripleSumo; Sect. 4 details our methodology for training the agent with the DDPG algorithm, followed by an evaluation of training results. The final section summarises our findings and outlines plans for future work.

2   Related Work

Games provide challenging environments to quickly test new algorithms and ideas of reinforcement learning (RL) in a safe and reproducible manner [5]. Therefore, recent years have witnessed the development of a series of novel virtual game platforms that have fuelled reinforcement learning research. While some research focuses on a single agent tackling a task, many cases are based on adversarial models, where agents compete against each other to improve the overall outcome of a system.

In 2020, 'Google Research Football' [5] was designed as an open-source platform where agents are trained to play football in simulated physics-based 3D scene. Three scenarios were provided with varying levels of difficulties. Three RL algorithms, namely Importance Weighted Actor-Learner Architecture (IMPALA), Proximal Policy Optimization Algorithms (PPO), and Ape-X DQN, were implemented by the authors to report baselines. This popular platform was demonstrated to be useful in developing AI methods, for example, 'TiKick' [6]. However, 'Google Research Football' assumes the actions are synchronously executed in multi-agent settings, limiting its utility. In response to this, 'Fever Basketball' [7] was developed—an asynchronous sports game environment for multi-agent reinforcement learning.

Similarly based on virtual football games, [2] studied integrated decision-making at multiple scales in a physically embodied multi-agent system by developing a method that combines imitation learning, single- and multi-agent rein-

---

[2] https://github.com/niart/triplesumo.

forcement learning, and population-based training, making use of transferable representations of behaviour. This research evaluated agent behaviours using several analysis techniques, including statistics from real-world sports analytics.

[8] introduced a 'hide-and-seek' game to investigate agents learning tool use. Through training in this environment, agents build a series of six distinct strategies and counter strategies. This work suggested a promising future of multi-agent co-adaptation, which could produce complex and intelligent behaviors.

When it comes to RL-based methods for multi-agent cooperation, [9] tackled the limitation of Q-learning in a non-stationary environment, resulting in variance of the policy gradient as the number of agents grows. They presented an adaptation of actor-critic methods that consider action policies of other agents, and a training regimen utilising an ensemble of policies for each agent that leads to more robust multi-agent policies.

CollaQ [10] decomposes the Q-function of each agent into a 'self term' and an 'interactive term', with a Multi-Agent Reward Attribution (MARA) loss that regularises the training. This method was validated in the 'StarCraft multi-agent challenge' and was demonstrated to outperform existing state-of-the-art techniques.

In a multi-agent pursuit-evasion problem, [11] used shared experience to train a policy with curriculum learning for a given number of pursuers, to be executed independently by each agent at run-time. They designed a reward structure combining individual and group rewards to encourage good formation.

Similarly in the pursuit-evasion problem, [12] presented a new geometric approach of learning cooperative behaviours in a 2-pursuer single evader scenario to reduce the capture time of the evader. This method was shown to be scalable thanks to categorisation and removal of redundant pursuers.

These virtual games offer useful experimental platforms and learning methods for multi-agent teamwork in adversarial environments. However, physical contact between interactive agents in continuous domain is rarely investigated. Our work meets this need by developing a platform that facilitates research into multi-agent cooperation in physical contact-rich environments. This paper introduces TripleSumo, which extends the RoboSumo platform, and presents reinforcement-learning of cooperative behaviours in an adversarial multi-agent setting.

3   TripleSumo

Based on the RoboSumo framework built with the software toolkit OpenAI/Gym [13] and the MuJoCo [14] physics engine, TripleSumo adds one more agent to the system (see Fig. 1). In this scenario, 'Ant' (red) and 'Bug' (blue) team up and play against their opponent 'Spider' (green) on a square arena ('Tatami') (see Fig. 2). Agent behaviors are trained and observed in designated continuous action spaces. To simplify the interfaces, this preliminary work sets up all agents to be four-legged and the same size. However, the three agents differ from one another in contact force (see Table 1). Morphological and physical features of the agents are subject to free choices according to future research demands. Once the

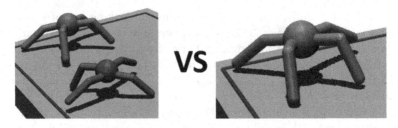

Fig. 1. Competitive relation between agent 'Spider' (green, right) and the pair of 'Bug' (blue, middle) and 'Ant' (red, left) (Color figure online)

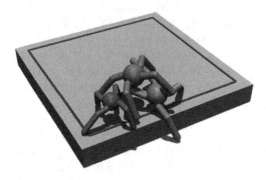

Fig. 2. The simulated virtual platform 'TripleSumo', where two agents (red and blue) play against the green agent on a Tatami. (Color figure online)

game starts, the three agents interact through physical contact and the match lasts until the centre of mass of any of the three agents falls outside the edge of the arena. The two agents 'Ant' and 'Spider' have been pre-trained through DDPG to create an ongoing game (see supplementary video 1). 'Spider' will win the game if it manages to push either 'Ant' or 'Bug' off the arena. Alternatively, the team of 'Ant' and 'Bug' will win the game if they manage to push off 'Spider'.

4 Experimental Results

This section implements a commonly used reinforcement learning algorithm DDPG to train the new agent. In order to infer the strategies of both its opponent and partner, the agent 'Bug' is trained to learn an action policy during an

Table 1. Control range of contact force of heterogeneous agents

	Control range of contact force (in Newtons)
'Spider' (green)	$[-0.22, 0.22]$
'Ant' (red)	$[-0.20, 0.20]$
'Bug' (blue)	$[-0.18, 0.18]$

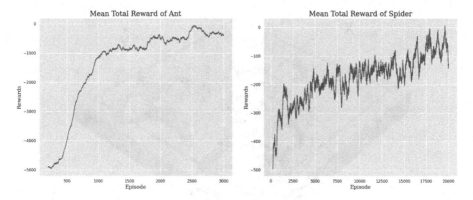

Fig. 3. Mean total rewards received by 'Ant' over 3,000 epochs of training (left); Mean total rewards received by 'Spider' over 20,000 epochs of training (right); a rolling mean filter of 200 applied to each graph.

ongoing match[3], where 'Ant' and 'Spider' are playing against each other. The ongoing game is created by training 'Ant' for 3,000 epochs with DDPG first, and afterwards training 'Bug' for 20,000 epochs (Fig. 3), with reward structures similar to Eqs. (1), (2), but in different directions.

4.1 Reward Shaping

The reward function used in this experiment consists of two parts:

$$Reward \ = \ Dense \ Reward \ + \ Sparse \ Reward \tag{1}$$

In the 'Dense' part, each single step of the agent's movement is associated with a value which adds up to the total reward of the current epoch. This 'Dense Reward' is decomposed into four terms—'opponent velocity reward', 'partner velocity reward', 'self velocity reward', and a constant punishment (Eq. 2), where C_1, C_2 and C_3 are constant coefficients inserted to each term of dense reward function.

$$
\begin{aligned}
Dense \ reward = \ & C_1 \ * \ opponent \ velocity \ reward \\
& + \ C_2 \ * \ self \ velocity \ reward \\
& + \ C_3 \ * \ partner \ velocity \ reward \\
& + \ still \ punishment
\end{aligned}
\tag{2}
$$

In each step, the agent receives an 'opponent velocity reward' which is decomposed to an X component and a Y component. Its X component has an absolute value proportional to the opponent's speed along the X-direction, and is assigned to be positive if the opponent is moving backwards from the agent, and negative if the opponent moves towards the agent. The Y component of 'opponent

---

[3] supplementary video 1: https://www.youtube.com/watch?v=nxzi7Pha2GU.

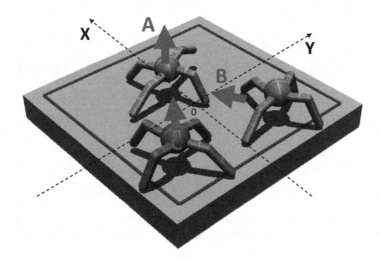

Fig. 4. Direction of allocating positive dense reward: A. opponent velocity reward; B. partner velocity reward; C. self velocity reward.

velocity reward' is defined in a similar way in the Y direction. 'Self velocity reward' and 'partner velocity reward' have absolute values proportional to the agent's and its partner's speeds respectively, assigned to be positive if the agent or its partner moves towards its opponent, while assigned to be negative if they move away from their opponent. That is, the agent will be rewarded if itself or its partner moves towards their opponent, or if the opponent moves backwards from the agent, and will be punished on the contrary. The 'still punishment' is a negative constant to ensure the agent will be punished if it remains stationary. Figure 4 shows the direction of allocating positive dense reward to the agent. On the other hand, the 'Sparse' part of the reward function is associated with the result of game. A score of +500 or −400 will be allocated if the team wins or loses the game respectively (see Algorithm 1). The sparse reward will be 0 by default if the epoch exceeds the maximum number of steps without a side winning.

Algorithm 1. Sparse part of reward function

> **while** An epoch is ongoing **do**
>   **if** The opponent falls off Tatami **then**
>   reward += 500
>   **else if** 'Bug' or 'Ant' falls off Tatami **then**
>   reward −= 400
>   **end if**
> **end while**

Table 2. Hyper-parameters in DDPG implementations

Hyper-parameter	Value
Optimiser	Adam
Actor learning rate	$1e-4$
Critic learning rate	$1e-3$
Discount factor (γ)	0.99
Target update factor (τ)	0.01
Steps per epoch	500
Batch size	64
Maximum epochs	20,000
Replay buffer size	1,000,000
Update stride	30

Table 3. Definition of local winning rate at a certain epoch

Result of an epoch	Local winning rate
Team wins	$+1$
Team loses	-1
Time expires without result	0

Important hyper-parameters are summarised in Table 2. Over the course of training for 20,000 epochs, the agent demonstrates increasing mean values of both dense and sparse rewards, as shown in Fig. 5.

4.2   Performance Evaluation

The action policy of 'Bug' resulting from this training is observed in a test across 20,000 epochs[4], where the agents demonstrate cooperative behavior and stable values of both dense and sparse rewards (see Fig. 6). Additionally, in order to evaluate the efficiency of agents' cooperation, we used the two metrics: MWR and 'steps needed to win' to analyse the training result.

A metric 'winning rate' (WR) is defined as the probability of winning the game at a certain phase during training or testing. During training, the local WR at a certain epoch is assigned to be '+1' if the team wins the game; assigned to be '−1' if the team loses the game; and assigned to be '0' if the epoch reaches maximum number of steps without winning or losing. The definition of local WR is described in Table 3. A 'mean WR' is calculated as the rolling mean value of local winning rate when the training or testing reaches a certain epoch. Intuitively, a positive WR indicates the team is stronger than opponent, while a negative WR indicates the team is weaker than its opponent, and a zero WR

---

[4] supplementary video 2: https://www.youtube.com/watch?v=C4xGuIyeY5A.

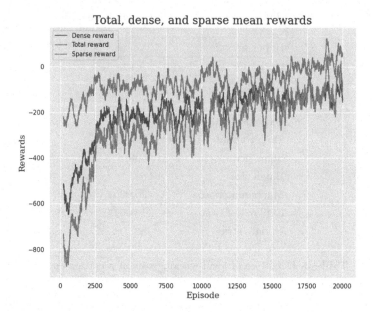

Fig. 5. Mean of total rewards (orange), Dense reward (blue), and Sparse reward (green) received by 'Bug' in each epoch during training. A rolling mean filter of 200 is applied. The final dense and total rewards stay below zero due to a constant 'still punishment' term in reward function. (Color figure online)

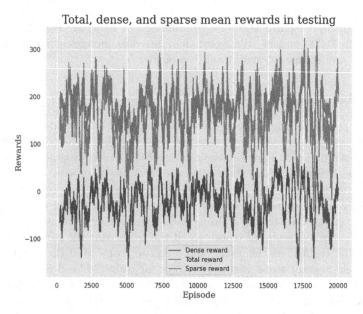

Fig. 6. Mean of total rewards (orange), Dense reward (blue), and Sparse reward (green) received by 'Bug' in a test of 20,000 epochs. A rolling mean filter of 200 is applied. (Color figure online)

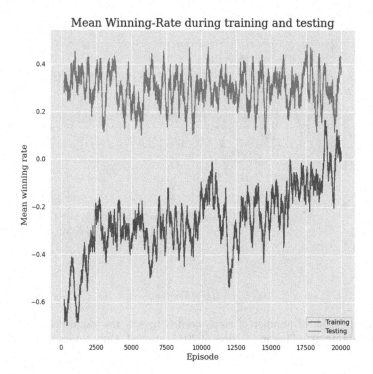

Fig. 7. MWR of the team increases as training progresses (blue). The MWR rising from negative to positive indicates the team ends up with stronger competency than its opponent. MWR of the team remains positive (between 0.15 and 0.47) in testing of 20,000 epochs (orange). A rolling mean filter of 200 was applied to each graph. (Color figure online)

indicates the two sides have similar levels of competency. With a rolling mean filter of λ, the mean WR (denoted as MWR) at epoch α (denoted as E_α) is:

$$MWR_\alpha = \frac{sum\ of\ all\ WRs\ in\ recent\ \lambda\ epochs\ until\ E_\alpha}{\lambda} \qquad (3)$$

The variations of MWR during training and testing are plotted in Fig. 7, which indicate that the team's competency improves as the training progresses, and remains stable in the resulting policy. In other words, the agent 'Bug' has learned to cooperate with 'Ant' and contribute to the teamwork.

Another metric 'number of steps needed to win a game' is defined to reflect the cost of time for a successful teamwork. Its rolling mean (computed in a way similar to Eq. 3) reflects the variation of teamwork efficiency during the training process. In Fig. 8, the plot indicates that the team reaches higher levels of efficiency in teamwork as they are trained, resulting in reducing the amount of steps or time needed to win the game.

Fig. 8. Mean value of number of steps needed to win the game decreases over the course of training. A rolling mean filter of 200 is applied. Only games won by the team are counted.

5   Discussion and Future Work

This preliminary work extended an existing virtual multi-agent platform Robo-Sumo into TripleSumo, which contains three players in a sumo game. Two agents are predefined to team up and play against the other agent. As a baseline, cooperative behaviors were investigated by training the newly added agent with the reinforcement learning algorithm DDPG, using a hybrid reward structure during an ongoing match. Both the sparse and dense parts of mean rewards are demonstrated to increase and eventually converge as the training process progresses. The teamwork increases in competency and efficiency, as reflected by an increasing mean winning rate and a decreasing mean number of steps needed to win a game, which indicates successful cooperation between the agents in this adversarial environment. While this work has focussed exclusively on DDPG, our future research will investigate the peformance of other RL algorithms with respect to learning cooperative strategies in multi-agent systems.

The scenario presented in this paper is similar to learning cooperative behaviours in a 2-pursuer single evader scenario to reduce the capture time of the evader, with direct applications in swarm robotic systems. A natural extension is to increase the complexity of the environment, to include more pursuing agents making it a M-Pursuer single-evader scenario and incorporating probabilistic observations about the prey positions. It would then be possible to evolve different categorical behaviours such as 'interceptor', 'escort', and 'redundant' for the pursuer agents.

The next step of this research is to investigate a more complex scenario of non-predefined pairing for cooperation in TripleSumo. With three or more agents playing against one another, the game will continue until only one agent remains on the arena. All agents will learn to freely choose to team up with a non-predefined partner in order to remain as long as possible in the game.

References

1. Yin, Q., Yang, J., Ni, W., Liang, B., Huang, K.: AI in games: techniques, challenges and opportunities. ArXiv, vol. abs/2111.07631 (2021)
2. Liu, S., et al.: From motor control to team play in simulated humanoid football. ArXiv, vol. abs/2105.12196 (2021)
3. Al-Shedivat, M., Bansal, T., Burda, Y., Sutskever, I., Mordatch, I., Abbeel, P.: Continuous adaptation via meta-learning in nonstationary and competitive environments. ArXiv, vol. abs/1710.03641 (2018)
4. Lillicrap, T.P., et al.: Continuous control with deep reinforcement learning. CoRR, vol. abs/1509.02971 (2016)
5. Kurach, K., et al.: Google research football: a novel reinforcement learning environment. In: AAAI (2020)
6. Huang, S., et al.: TiKick: towards playing multi-agent football full games from single-agent demonstrations. ArXiv, vol. abs/2110.04507 (2021)
7. Jia, H., et al.: Fever basketball: a complex, flexible, and asynchronized sports game environment for multi-agent reinforcement learning. ArXiv, vol. abs/2012.03204 (2020)
8. Baker, B., et al.: Emergent tool use from multi-agent autocurricula. ArXiv, vol. abs/1909.07528 (2020)
9. Lowe, R., Wu, Y., Tamar, A., Harb, J., Abbeel, P., Mordatch, I.: Multi-agent actor-critic for mixed cooperative-competitive environments. ArXiv, vol. abs/1706.02275 (2017)
10. Zhang, T., et al.: Multi-agent collaboration via reward attribution decomposition. ArXiv, vol. abs/2010.08531 (2020)
11. de Souza, C., Newbury, R., Cosgun, A., Castillo, P., Vidolov, B., Kulić, D.: Decentralized multi-agent pursuit using deep reinforcement learning. IEEE Rob. Autom. Lett. **6**, 4552–4559 (2021)
12. Von Moll, A., Casbeer, D.W., Garcia, E., Milutinović, D.: Pursuit-evasion of an evader by multiple pursuers. In: 2018 International Conference on Unmanned Aircraft Systems (ICUAS), pp. 133–142 (2018)
13. Brockman, G., et al.: OpenAI gym. ArXiv, vol. abs/1606.01540 (2016)
14. Todorov, E., Erez, T., Tassa, Y.: MuJoCo: a physics engine for model-based control. In: 2012 IEEE/RSJ International Conference on Intelligent Robots and Systems, pp. 5026–5033 (2012)

Task Independent Safety Assessment for Reinforcement Learning

Mark Jocas[1]([✉]), Firas Zoghlami[1], Philip Kurrek[1], Mario Gianni[1], and Vahid Salehi[2]

[1] Faculty of Science and Engineering, University of Plymouth, Plymouth, UK
{mark.jocas,firas.zoghlami,philip.kurrek,mario.gianni}@plymouth.ac.uk
[2] Department of Mechatronics, University of Applied Sciences Munich, Munich, Germany
vahid.salehi_douzloo@hm.edu

Abstract. Given the black-box characteristics of a robotic system using reinforcement learning, validating its behaviour is an extensive process. Especially if the main focus lies on efficient task execution and at the same time predefined requirements or safety standards must be met for real-world applications. Once a particular system is verified to behave according to safety requirements, this may no longer be the case if the underlying conditions are modified.

As research yields more efficient and performant algorithms rather than safer and controllable algorithms, their safe use should be ensured. Our approach enables the use of an algorithm for the execution of the main task while leaving the assessment of the cause-effect relationship in terms of safety to another instance. This way, the presented approach preserves efficiency at the main task level with as little interference as possible. The tasks of safety assessment and task execution are separated to the extent possible, allowing the initially learned safety assessment to be applied to varying tasks and scenarios with minimal effort. The main challenges hereby are the provision of sufficient information for a reliable safety assessment and the precise allocation of the sparse rewards in terms of safety requirements. Finally, we evaluate Task Independent Safety Assessment on three different picking, placing and moving tasks. We show that the main task is guided to safe behaviour by safety instance and even converges against safe behaviour with additional learning phase of the main task.

Keywords: Safe reinforcement learning · Robotics

1 Introduction

An increasingly widespread discipline of machine learning is reinforcement learning, in which an agent interacts with the environment and observes the results of that interaction in order to achieve the maximum cumulative reward for the specified objective. This method imitates the trial-and-error method used by

S. Pacheco-Gutierrez et al. (Eds.): TAROS 2022, LNAI 13546, pp. 190–204, 2022.
https://doi.org/10.1007/978-3-031-15908-4_16

humans to learn, which is also based on taking actions and receiving positive or negative feedback. Furthermore, deep learning is enabling reinforcement learning to scale to problems that were previously intractable. Latest scientific research in computer science and advanced computing capacities are now allowing robots to learn policies directly from inputs in the real world [1, 14, 26, 28]. The resulting application of Deep Neural Networks (DNN) can find compact low-dimensional representations of high-dimensional data. Model-based reinforcement learning, on the other hand, is able to learn a transition model, that allows the modelling of the environment without interacting with it directly [13, 15, 18, 23].

The number of existing approaches with specific characteristics for implementation, however, hinders real world adoption, especially when certain safety regulations have to be met. Although research on safe reinforcement learning is increasing [8], there is a lack of methods for the safe implementation of algorithms that are not explicitly safety oriented. Even if the application is implemented in consideration of the safety aspects, a small change of the inputs or of the underlying neural network may lead to unforeseen events and even unsafe behaviour. This is because the mode of operation based on probabilistic modelling and distributions without concrete validation of safe behaviour can disrupt its balance.

Therefore, our approach aims to define a generalized procedure to implement different algorithms safely while considering their characteristics. After a discussion of possible pitfalls in the target definition and overall specification of the system, we illustrate the approach on a pick, place, and move example. Instead of a specific algorithm, which might allow a well-balanced safety consideration and task performance, we elaborate a general neural network structure that may include different mathematical approaches for optimization. In this manner, the here discussed related work and future approaches can be nested within this framework. At the same time, we provide a framework, in which an agent can explore and learn in a constrained action-space without harming itself or its environment. Furthermore, the learned safety evaluation in the suggested neural network structure is being preserved independent of the task, on which the main task agent is being trained. Based on this, we show that the main task can be exchanged without compromising the safety instance, indicating task independent safety assessment.

2   Background

To define whether an agent is compliant with safety restrictions, it first needs to be established what is considered safe or unsafe behaviour. After a classification of different approaches for safe reinforcement learning, the trade-off between performance and safety is discussed. Subsequently, the problem of sparse rewards and dense reward signals is outlined, which is a major concern in reinforcement learning even without the consideration of safety. Finally, the problem of the necessity for correct environment interpretation needs to be addressed.

2.1   Safe Reinforcement Learning

The dynamics of complex applications are often uncertain or only partially known. Additional uncertainties can arise from several sources. Sensor input may be noisy, the dynamics of the robot may not be accurately modelled, the deployment environment may not be well described or include other actors with unknown dynamics and planning. A critical, domain-specific challenge in robot control learning is the need to implement and formally guarantee the safety of robot behaviour, not only for the optimized policy, but also during the learning phase to avoid costly hardware failures and improve convergence. Ultimately, these safety guarantees can only be derived from the assumptions and the characteristics captured in the problem formalization.

In this work, we adopt following definition of a safety property:

> "A safety property expresses that, under certain conditions, something never occurs." [6]

By that safety means, that under given conditions an undesirable event will never occur. These undesirable events in our consideration are actions leading to damaging of itself or the environment of the agent. These can also be enfolded as domain-specific undesirable events or behaviours. For real-world use, however, it must at least be guaranteed that the applications are controllable and do not endanger their environment or themselves. Due to this problem research extends reinforcement learning to include the safety aspect to safe reinforcement learning [11]. With given knowledge of operating conditions, the model-driven approach provides guarantees on the dynamic model [22]. The data-driven approach of reinforcement learning allows high adaptability to new contexts at the expense of providing formal guarantees [29]. These data-driven approaches can be categorized into Objective Manipulation, Knowledge Incorporation or External Interference or as a combination of several methods.

With Objective Manipulation the primary task is adjusted to prevent the agent from entering safety-critical states based on the defined objective or task interpretation [2,7,12,16,30]. However, restricting learning behaviour by withholding bad data does not allow the agent to understand why an action taken is appropriate [9]. Therefore, containment techniques are not a long-term solution for AI safety, but an instrument that enables the testing and development of methods [5]. With Knowledge Incorporation external knowledge is added in order to guide the agent towards the safe state space [1,4,20]. With these approaches, however, it must be determined in advance which knowledge must be provided to the agent to achieve safe behaviour both in the learning and in the later operational phases. With External Interference agent' actions can be overridden at constraint violation in order to improve safety [3,24,27]. However, for these approaches, either an approximate model or a safety controller is needed in advance to determine which states should be considered as unsafe. Current approaches therefore use either human "in the loop" [27] or prescribed safety algorithms [10].

2.2 Balance of Performance and Safety

The limitation of agents by safety restrictions has, certainly, great effects on their behaviour. A balance must be found between safety and performance so that the restrictions are not too restrictive, and the agent can continue to perform its primary tasks efficiently while avoiding dangerous situations. An algorithm can therefore guarantee safe, but potentially suboptimal exploration caused by restriction of the attention to a subset of guaranteed safe policies [21]. This is the case if an agent is trained only on "good" data, it has no way to understand why the taken action is appropriate. It would prefer these actions, but not necessarily reject other alternative actions that would have diminished the objective given heterogeneous data [9].

The balance is additionally affected when an agent is to be transferred from simulation to real world, where training and execution environments differ. The so-called blind spots [25] resulting from incomplete representation of the actual states of the world, prevent a reliable differentiation between the numerous states. These lead to unexpected mistakes of an agent due to inconsistencies between the training environment and the real world, which can lead to unexpectedly unsafe behaviour. The degraded performance and unexpected errors of the agent in the blind spots also lead to changed inputs of the safety functionality.

As the process of learning policies aims to maximize the expectation of the return in problems, it is also important to ensure reasonable system performance and/or respect safety constraints during the learning and/or deployment process. At this point, there is therefore no consensus on how a certain level of safety can be guaranteed without impairing the performance of the primary task.

2.3 Environment Interpretation

The safety properties must be derived from the available information on the operational environment. This requires an interpretation of the data to determine the relations, for which different approaches from reinforcement learning can be used.

Model-free approaches without specific consideration of safety, cannot guarantee safety during the learning phase and safety can be only approximately achieved after sufficient learning time. The basic problem is that without a model, safety must be learned through environmental interactions and not interpreted by the modelled consequences of environment behaviour. That means that safety can be violated during early learning interactions, if not ensured by constraints otherwise. On the other hand, model-based approaches can only guarantee safe behaviour if the model that serves as the basis for the safety assessment very accurately reflects the real world and its characteristics. The example of learning an environment model directly from raw pixel images [13] shows that such a dynamic model is vulnerable to exploitation by the agent. A policy that exploits the incompleteness of such a model during the optimization process may fail completely in the real environment. How to make use of both model-based and model-free learning is a central problem in reinforcement learning [23].

Where the intended environment of the application is already known to a large extent, the provided inputs can be pre-processed and provided efficiently. For instance, with the focus on artificial intelligence [19], it is possible to examine systems, processes and data for relevant contexts. This information can be verified for correctness [31], to present a reliable overview for the agent, which provides the basis for determining safe handling procedures.

3   Design and Implementation

Compared to existing implementations of shielding approaches that are known to us, we follow the data-driven approach for high adaptability to new contexts of task independent safety assessment. Unlike existing shielding approaches, our safety controller is learned from the reward function and not prescribed. Our approach is introduced using the example of a pick and place environment for the robotic system. Following the consideration of the basic approach design, the problem formalization with reference to safety is described. The essential role of data selection based on the respective task scopes is highlighted in combination with the corresponding data pre-processing.

3.1   Approach Design

The structure of the classical loop between the agent and its environment for reinforcing learning is divided into two parts, which is inspired on the Post-Posed Shielding [3] framework as shown in Fig. 1. In addition to the first agent (Task Agent), that focuses on the execution of the task, there is a second agent (Safety Agent), which assesses the safety of the actions intended by the first agent. In addition to the actions to be evaluated, the safety agent receives pre-processed visual inputs and sensor readings of the environment to efficiently interpret relevant information. In addition, the safety condition of the environment is provided

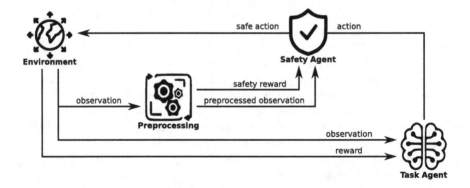

Fig. 1. Agent relations to each other and the environment.

to the safety agent based on the safety definition in combination with the thresholds of the sensors. This yields the reward that the safety agent obtains from the evaluation of the intended action based on compliance with the safety definition.

The agents are separated from each other as far as possible to minimize interference and keep the safety assessment independent of the task agent's policy. The task agent therefore receives the initial definition of the tasks to be performed, which can vary during the process execution. Analogously, the safety agent is assigned an initial safety definition through the reward function and only evaluates the actions of the task agent on it, regardless of what the action is intended to accomplish for the main task. As a result, the knowledge about the task execution is only available to the task agent and, in contrast, the knowledge regarding the safety definition is only available to the safety agent.

3.2   Agent Inputs

When defining the required inputs, sufficient information must be provided to ensure that the tasks can be solved with the knowledge provided. However, an excessively large base of data makes efficient functionality difficult, as a distinction must be made between highly and less relevant information. For example, information for determining position is necessary for a navigation task, but not necessarily for an area not being considered at the moment of decision.

In our pick and place environment, we formulate the safety definition to avoid collisions of the tool with the environment and the objects in it. Under consideration of this, the two agents require differing inputs only relevant for the specific task solving, as shown for our example in Table 1. However, it is not necessary, that the task and safety agents obtain separate inputs, as these can be combined and interpreted differently according to the main objective. For the task agent the inputs are limited to the most necessary ones regarding the task execution. The task agent only receives the current position of the tool, the position to be reached and visual input, as its task in this case is to move an obstacle to a target position. This allows the task execution to be learned efficiently with state-of-the-art algorithms. The safety agent, on the other hand, does not need the information about the position to be reached, but the action the task agent intends to take in addition to the current position of the tool. An essential prerequisite is that the safety assessment must be able to perceive

Table 1. Provided inputs to Task Agent and Safety Agent.

Inputs	Task execution	Safety assessment
Tool position	✓	✓
Target position	✓	–
Visual input	✓	✓
Intended action	↺	✓
Collision sensor	–	✓

the conditions defined to be safe. Otherwise, no statement can be drawn about the safety of actions or even, in the worst case, a false sense of safety can be feigned. Therefore, in this case the safety agent is provided with pre-processed visual input from an RGBD sensor and information on collisions.

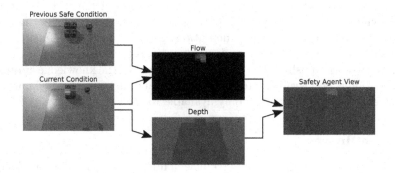

Fig. 2. Pre-processed visual inputs.

As shown in Fig. 2, the RGB image of the previous safe condition is compared with the current condition. This results in a flow image, which highlights the intensity of the changed parts of the image in colour and makes other areas appear black. The resulting image is combined with the depth channel of the RGBD sensor and then presented to the safety agent. This assumes, that the camera is static, but eliminates the need for the safety agent to learn how to detect movement in a scene using the raw image values.

4   Experiments

The design of a task independent safety assessment for reinforcing learning is tested in a simulated environment (Unity3D) in order to prevent any unforeseen consequences for allowing unwanted and desired dangerous scenarios. These scenarios are integrated into the Unity Machine Learning Agents Toolkit [17] to train intelligent agents using reinforcement learning.

The experimental setup consists of several scenarios. First, a task agent is trained without explicit consideration of any safety criteria. The attempts with their successes and failures serve the safety agent. It learns the relationship between intended actions of the task agent and the possible resulting violations of the safety criteria provided by the safety reward function. Subsequently, the initial task agent continues its training and the previously developed behaviour is refined, considering the newly acquired knowledge of the safety agent. Once trained for a given domain, the safety agent is reused to train differing task agents in other scenarios with the same safety definition. Finally, the learned behaviour for different tasks is compared without and with safety interference.

4.1   Setup

Agents structure differs according to the nature of an agents' task. The movement of an object between way-points in the main tasks requires different inputs than those required to assess the safety of an intended action, as described in Sect. 3.2. At the same time, the scenarios differ depending on the task to be performed, but not on the safety assessment, which is intended to be task independent.

Main Tasks. The three scenarios of placing on the stack, removing from the stack, and moving an object while avoiding collisions with obstacles have a similar structure. These only differ in the randomly generated start and target positions as well as the random arrangement of the scene. This means that the target for placing the object on the stack is always a reasonable position on already stacked pieces or directly on the table. On the other hand, when removing an object from the stack, the start position is a reasonable position on the stacked pieces. For collision-free moving of the object, the positions used are the same as for placing on the stack, with the difference that additional obstacles are arranged in the direct path between the start and target position. Initially, the task agent only learns a behaviour that is considered optimal based on the information available. Since there is no knowledge of the existing safety agent or its interference in particular actions, only the fastest way to reach the target position by the shortest path is learned.

The episode continues until the ItemPosition matches the TargetPosition or the episode is brought to an end by EndEpisode, e.g. when the maximum number of steps within an episode is reached. In each step of the episode of each

---

Algorithm 1. Reward function for Main Task

1: **inputs:** $ItemPos(x, y, z), TargetPos(x, y, z)$
2: **while** $CurrentStep < MaxStep$ **do**
3:     **if** $ItemPos == TargetPos$ **then**
4:         SetReward($+5$)
5:         EndEpisode()
6:     **else**
7:         AddReward($-1/MaxSteps$)
8:     **end if**
9: **end while**

---

main task, where a step is a time frame between agents decisions, the current item position in space is compared with the target position to be reached. If the item hasn't yet reached the target position, a small negative reward is assigned. Otherwise, a positive reward is given, and the episode is brought to an end. The policy learned in this way can be indirectly influenced by the safety assessment agent by classifying the actions of the task agent to be performed as undesirable and suppressing those. However, the agent has no knowledge of this and only considers these actions as not contributing to success, as they do not to the cumulative reward maximization, which is the main objective. In our experiment, we suppress the action by not allowing the movement to be performed and letting the agent choose a different action in the next step. This is a simplification of logic, since in this case the agent can get into an endless loop by choosing unsafe actions over and over again. A more complex logic can also be used here with a backup strategy that, for example, directs the agent back towards a condition that is considered to be safe. However, this is not the main focus here, since safe backup strategies must also be validated for safe behaviour.

Safety Assessment Task. The task of safety assessment is always the same regardless of how the main task has changed. The aim is always to prevent the task agent from causing a collision of the object to be moved with the environment by validating the intended action. During the learning phase, the association between certain actions and the resulting collisions is learned through observation. The learned safety assessment is then used directly to modify task agents or to further training their behaviour. In the latter case, the task agent has the possibility to adapt the behaviour according to the safety constraints known only to the safety agent. These therefore have to be deduced from the interception of the unsafe behaviour without knowing the precisely defined safety criteria.

The episode of a safety agent continues until it is terminated by a falsely evaluated action as supposedly safe, which subsequently leads to a collision. For

---

Algorithm 2. Reward function for Safety Assessment Task

1: **inputs:** $ItemPosition(x, y, z)$, $IntendedAction(x, y, z)$,
   $VisualInput(RGBD)$, $CollisionOccurred(bool)$
2: **while** $True$ **do**
3:    **if** $CollisionOccurred == False$ **then**
4:       AddReward($SafetyAssessment_{t-1}/MaxSteps$)
5:    **else**
6:       **if** $SafetyAssessment_{t-1} < 0$ **then**
7:          AddReward($SafetyAssessment_{t-1}/MaxSteps$)
8:       **else if** $SafetyAssessment_{t-1} > 0$ **then**
9:          SetReward(-1)
10:         EndEpisode()
11:      **end if**
12:   **end if**
13: **end while**

---

this purpose, the measurement of a collision is continuously used to decide. If no collision has occurred, the agent receives a small reward. If no collision occurs, the agent receives a small reward according to its safety evaluation. When an action is classified as unsafe without a subsequent collision, the reward is therefore negative. It should be emphasized that the agent in the learning phase only observes, but does not intervene. If an action classified as unsafe were to be prevented, then it would be impossible to subsequently determine whether the action had actually led to a collision.

If a collision has occurred, it is checked whether the agent has predicted it correctly. In case the action causing a collision was assessed to be unsafe, the agent receives a small positive reward. However, if the assessment was incorrect, a negative reward is assigned and the episode ends. On the one hand, it motivates the safety assessment agent not to classify a dangerous action as falsely safe, since in this case no further rewards can be obtained, which intuitively corresponds to most real-world use cases. On the other hand, unsafe actions are assigned higher negative values, which allows for a greater overall divergence of the safety assessment.

4.2   Results

Initially the task agent is trained on the Place On Stack task and in parallel the safety agent learns to identify an impending collision. In Fig. 3, the cumulative rewards of the two agents are shown in the area highlighted in green as Initial Task Training and Safety Assessment Training. The safety agent first achieves positive rewards until the task agent adapts its behaviour and comes closer to the target position. This results in more frequent collisions with the stacked objects, which are still unknown to the safety agent. Due to the higher number of chances to classify a collision as falsely safe, the length of the episodes is also reduced. For the task agent, the length of the episodes decreases, once it completes the task faster. Then both agents achieve a constant cumulative reward.

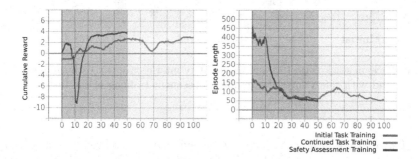

Fig. 3. Cumulative Reward and Episode Length in the different training phases. (Color figure online)

Subsequently, task agent is trained further, but now with the interference of safety agent. Training progress on the example of placing on the stack is shown in Fig. 3 in the yellow highlighted area as Continue Task Training. The reward drops at first, as the previous actions that lead to the successful completion of the task, but cause collisions, are now interrupted. In addition, the interruption delays the achievement of the goal, which is visible in the episode length. Finally, task agent adapts to interference and an equally high level of reward is achieved. The other task agents for the two remaining scenarios are trained similarly. But the safety agent that has already been trained is reused to apply the safety assessment that has been learned for the domain.

Place on Stack. In Fig. 4 the behaviours of the task agent are compared and visualized as trajectories for the same Place On Stack task. The initially learned behaviour (a) without any knowledge about possible collisions with objects results in the shortest trajectory between the start and target position. Thereby the stack is tipped over while approaching the position. With the interfered initial learned behaviour (b) by safety agent the trajectory is being modified. First the distance to the table is increased, as this reduces the chance of a collision and thus increases the value of the safety assessment. Finally, the target position is reached, but an object is moved, because the task agent persists on its learned behaviour, unless this is restricted. The interfered adapted behaviour (c) results in a stronger curved trajectory, since the task agent had the possibility to adapt the behaviour and therefore takes detours to be less constrained and still reach the target efficiently. Due to these detours, the target position is approached in a wider curve and thus the neighbouring object is not moved.

(a) Initial   (b) Interfered   (c) Adapted

Fig. 4. Place on stack trajectories without safety interference (a), with safety interference (b) and with safety interference after subsequent training of the task agent (c).

Pick from Stack. Figure 5 shows the behaviour for Pick From Stack, which is reverse to the previous task. The initial behaviour (a) is again only the shortest connection of the start to target positions and therefore does not prevent collisions. However, the interfered initial behaviour (b) does not cause collisions, because safety agent prevents the task agent from lowering the item too early, and the task agent can still reach the target with a slightly modified trajectory. The interfered adapted behaviour (c) also shows the adjustment of the trajectory with larger curves, as these increase the distance to the stack as well as to the table and thus reduce the risk of collision of future actions.

(a) Initial   (b) Interfered   (c) Adapted

Fig. 5. Pick from stack trajectories without safety interference (a), with safety interference (b) and with safety interference after subsequent training of the task agent
(c).

Avoid Objects. In conclusion, the trajectories for task of Avoiding Objects are
shown in Fig. 6, which demonstrates moving to the target position on the stack
and obstacles placed on the shortest path. The initial behaviour (a) again has no
possibility to perceive and avoid a collision. The interfered initial behaviour (b),
on the other hand, is so strongly manipulated by safety agents that the trajectory
leads around the placed obstacles but cannot prevent the neighbouring object
from being pushed. The interfered adapted behaviour (c), however, appears like
the interfered initial behaviour. This also leads around the placed obstacles but
approaches the target position minimally further from the side and thus prevents
a collision with the neighbouring object. Since the task agent has no way of
perceiving the obstacles, collision avoidance in (b) and (c) results only from the
interference of the safety agent. In the adapted behaviour (c), however, the task
agent has additionally learned to deal with the safety agents' interference and
to solve the task accordingly.

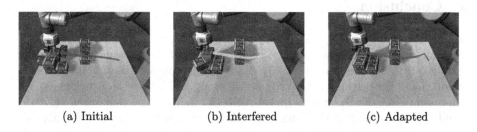

(a) Initial   (b) Interfered   (c) Adapted

Fig. 6. Avoid objects trajectories without safety interference (a), with safety interference (b) and with safety interference after subsequent training of the task agent (c).

4.3 Safety Interference

Without subsequent adaptation of the behaviour by the task agent to take safety
constraints into account, the agent constantly tries to perform the same action
or very similar action again. If the task agent gets the possibility to adapt the
behaviour, it can expect that an unsafe action will be blocked repeatedly. The

task agent therefore learns to choose an action that is still suitable for solving its task, but differs more from the previous action, as it is less likely to be considered a violation by safety agent and is therefore permitted. Although the upward arc of the curve then lengthens the path for the task execution, the probability of meeting safety criteria unknown to the task agent is considerably reduced. This results in the stronger deviation of the trajectory achieved with safety assessment and the increasing distance to potential collisions from the trajectory achieved without safety assessment.

Knowledge on safety compliance is provided to the safety agent in a concise form and then indirectly passed on to a task agent as needed. The inclusion of the knowledge from different AI algorithms enables a more complete assessment of the prevailing situation with which an agent must cope properly. For example, an algorithm for the semantic interpretation of a scene can also provide information relevant for safety assessment, even if it is designed with a different focus. This information then feeds into a non-safety-oriented algorithm designed for efficient task execution. The balance between performance and safety is also shifted from the task agent to the safety agent, which does not have to be developed from scratch for new tasks, but instead is reusable for unchanged safety constraints. However, the learned safety controller does not provide formal guarantees of safety compliance. It rather provides a way to introduce non-safety-oriented algorithms with safety restraints. Due to a continuous evaluation of safety by the safety agent, the reward signal of the task agent also does not have to be modified which in some cases could lead to a strong performance drop. Nevertheless, it is important to ensure that the algorithm used for task agent can deal robustly with interfered intended actions, either by stopping the agent or by using a backup policy to restore a safe state.

5   Conclusion

In this paper, we present task independent safety assessment for reinforcement learning by separating the main task from the safety assessment of actions intended to serve the main task. By directing the focus of both agents to different goals, they achieve their respective goals and guide the other agent to comply by adjusting their own target realizations. We show that the main task could be learned and at the same time the safety constraints could be adopted by an agent, without direct specification of these in the reward function of the main task. This relies on the safety assessment agent having all the information it needs to determine whether the safety objectives have been achieved and that a correct conclusion is drawn from this information. Our results also indicate that even algorithms that are not explicitly safety-oriented are able to adapt to the safety restrictions. Moreover, this is even possible without explicit definition of the safety requirements, but indirectly implication by a different instance through interference on intended unsafe actions. We also show that safety assessment performs in a task independent manner, if the actions to be observed are already familiar. This allows once-learned safety assessment to be reused across different tasks. How to ensure that to be reused safety assessment is applicable for a specific task is yet to be researched.

The three tasks to be executed in our experiment could initially be performed by the task agent without compliance with the safety criteria. By observing the learning phase of a single task, the safety agent was able to derive the compliance with the safety constraints. This was subsequently used for interference in the event of not meeting the safety restrictions. This served as a basis for successfully learning all three defined tasks in compliance with the safety criteria.

References

1. Abbeel, P., Coates, A., Ng, A.Y.: Autonomous helicopter aerobatics through apprenticeship learning. Int. J. Robot. Res. **29**(13), 1608–1639 (2010)
2. Achiam, J., Held, D., Tamar, A., Abbeel, P.: Constrained policy optimization. arXiv preprint arXiv:1705.10528 (2017)
3. Alshiekh, M., Bloem, R., Ehlers, R., Könighofer, B., Niekum, S., Topcu, U.: Safe reinforcement learning via shielding. arXiv preprint arXiv:1708.08611 (2017)
4. Arulkumaran, K., Deisenroth, M.P., Brundage, M., Bharath, A.A.: A brief survey of deep reinforcement learning. arXiv preprint arXiv:1708.05866 (2017)
5. Babcock, J., Kramar, J., Yampolskiy, R.V.: Guidelines for artificial intelligence containment. arXiv preprint arXiv:1707.08476 (2017)
6. Bérard, B., Bidoit, M., Finkel, A., Laroussinie, F., Petit, A., Petrucci, L., Schnoebelen, P.: Systems and Software Verification: Model-Checking Techniques and Tools. Springer, Heidelberg (2013)
7. Berkenkamp, F., Turchetta, M., Schoellig, A.P., Krause, A.: Safe model-based reinforcement learning with stability guarantees. arXiv preprint arXiv:1705.08551 (2017)
8. Brunke, L., et al.: Safe learning in robotics: from learning-based control to safe reinforcement learning. Ann. Rev. Control Robot. Auton. Syst. **5**, 411–444 (2021)
9. Gao, Y., Lin, J., Yu, F., Levine, S., Darrell, T., et al.: Reinforcement learning from imperfect demonstrations. arXiv preprint arXiv:1802.05313 (2018)
10. Garcia, J., Fernandez, F.: Safe exploration of state and action spaces in reinforcement learning. CoRR abs/1402.0560 (2014). http://arxiv.org/abs/1402.0560
11. Garcia, J., Fernández, F.: A comprehensive survey on safe reinforcement learning. J. Mach. Learn. Res. **16**(1), 1437–1480 (2015)
12. Geibel, P., Wysotzki, F.: Risk-sensitive reinforcement learning applied to control under constraints. J. Artif. Intell. Res. **24**, 81–108 (2005)
13. Ha, D., Schmidhuber, J.: World models. arXiv preprint arXiv:1803.10122 (2018)
14. Ha, S., Xu, P., Tan, Z., Levine, S., Tan, J.: Learning to walk in the real world with minimal human effort. arXiv preprint arXiv:2002.08550 (2020)
15. Hafner, D., et al.: Learning latent dynamics for planning from pixels. In: Chaudhuri, K., Salakhutdinov, R. (eds.) Proceedings of the 36th International Conference on Machine Learning. Proceedings of Machine Learning Research, vol. 97, pp. 2555–2565. PMLR, 09–15 June 2019. http://proceedings.mlr.press/v97/hafner19a.html
16. Hans, A., Schneegaß, D., Schäfer, A.M., Udluft, S.: Safe exploration for reinforcement learning. In: ESANN, pp. 143–148 (2008)
17. Juliani, A., et al.: Unity: a general platform for intelligent agents. arXiv preprint arXiv:1809.02627 (2018)

18. Kaiser, L., et al.: Model-based reinforcement learning for Atari. arXiv preprint arXiv:1903.00374 (2019)
19. Kurrek, P., Jocas, M., Zoghlami, F., Stoelen, M., Salehi, V.: AI motion control - a generic approach to develop control policies for robotic manipulation tasks. In: Proceedings of the Design Society: International Conference on Engineering Design, vol. 1, no. 1, pp. 3561–3570 (2019). https://doi.org/10.1017/dsi.2019.363
20. Menda, K., Driggs-Campbell, K., Kochenderfer, M.J.: DropoutDAgger: a Bayesian approach to safe imitation learning. arXiv preprint arXiv:1709.06166 (2017)
21. Moldovan, T.M., Abbeel, P.: Safe exploration in Markov decision processes. arXiv preprint arXiv:1205.4810 (2012)
22. Osborne, M., Shin, H.S., Tsourdos, A.: A review of safe online learning for nonlinear control systems** this work has been jointly funded by the EPSRC and BAE systems under an industrial case studentship. In: 2021 International Conference on Unmanned Aircraft Systems (ICUAS), pp. 794–803. IEEE (2021). The authors would also like to thank the following researchers for their kind assistance. Sumeet Singh, Ian Manchester and Johan Löfberg
23. Pan, F., et al.: Policy optimization with model-based explorations. In: Proceedings of the AAAI Conference on Artificial Intelligence, vol. 33, pp. 4675–4682 (2019)
24. Phan, D.T., Grosu, R., Jansen, N., Paoletti, N., Smolka, S.A., Stoller, S.D.: Neural simplex architecture. In: Lee, R., Jha, S., Mavridou, A., Giannakopoulou, D. (eds.) NFM 2020. LNCS, vol. 12229, pp. 97–114. Springer, Cham (2020). https://doi.org/10.1007/978-3-030-55754-6_6
25. Ramakrishnan, R., Kamar, E., Dey, D., Horvitz, E., Shah, J.: Blind spot detection for safe sim-to-real transfer. J. Artif. Intell. Res. **67**, 191–234 (2020)
26. Rosenstein, M.T., Barto, A.G., Si, J., Barto, A., Powell, W.: Supervised actor-critic reinforcement learning. In: Learning and Approximate Dynamic Programming: Scaling Up to the Real World, pp. 359–380 (2004)
27. Saunders, W., Sastry, G., Stuhlmueller, A., Evans, O.: Trial without error: towards safe reinforcement learning via human intervention. arXiv preprint arXiv:1707.05173 (2017)
28. Stooke, A., Lee, K., Abbeel, P., Laskin, M.: Decoupling representation learning from reinforcement learning. In: International Conference on Machine Learning, pp. 9870–9879. PMLR (2021)
29. Tambon, F., et al.: How to certify machine learning based safety-critical systems? A systematic literature review. arXiv preprint arXiv:2107.12045 (2021)
30. Thomas, P., Theocharous, G., Ghavamzadeh, M.: High confidence policy improvement. In: Proceedings of the 32nd International Conference on Machine Learning (ICML 2015), pp. 2380–2388 (2015)
31. Zoghlami, F., Kurrek, P., Jocas, M., Masala, G., Salehi, V.: Usage identification of anomaly detection in an industrial context. In: Proceedings of the Design Society: International Conference on Engineering Design, vol. 1, no. 1, pp. 3761–3770 (2019). https://doi.org/10.1017/dsi.2019.383

Sensing Anomalies as Potential Hazards: Datasets and Benchmarks

Dario Mantegazza[1]([⊠])[iD], Carlos Redondo[2], Fran Espada[2],
Luca M. Gambardella[1], Alessandro Giusti[1][iD], and Jérôme Guzzi[1][iD]

[1] Dalle Molle Institute for Artificial Intelligence (IDSIA), USI-SUPSI,
Lugano, Switzerland
`dario.mantegazza@idsia.ch`
[2] Hovering Solutions Ltd., Madrid, Spain

Abstract. We consider the problem of detecting, in the visual sensing data stream of an autonomous mobile robot, semantic patterns that are unusual (i.e., anomalous) with respect to the robot's previous experience in similar environments. These anomalies might indicate unforeseen hazards and, in scenarios where failure is costly, can be used to trigger an avoidance behavior. We contribute three novel image-based datasets acquired in robot exploration scenarios, comprising a total of more than 200k labeled frames, spanning various types of anomalies. On these datasets, we study the performance of an anomaly detection approach based on autoencoders operating at different scales.

Keywords: Visual anomaly detection · Dataset for robotic vision · Deep learning for visual perception · Robotic perception

Supplementary Material

Code, video, and data available at https://github.com/idsia-robotics/hazard-detection.

1 Introduction

Many emerging applications involve a robot operating autonomously in an unknown environment; the environment may include hazards, i.e., locations that might disrupt the robot's operation, possibly causing it to crash, get stuck, and more generally fail its mission. Robots are usually capable to perceive hazards

This work was supported as a part of NCCR Robotics, a National Centre of Competence in Research, funded by the Swiss National Science Foundation (grant number 51NF40_185543) and by the European Commission through the Horizon 2020 project 1-SWARM, grant ID 871743.

S. Pacheco-Gutierrez et al. (Eds.): TAROS 2022, LNAI 13546, pp. 205–219, 2022.
https://doi.org/10.1007/978-3-031-15908-4_17

that are expected during system development and therefore can be explicitly accounted for when designing the perception subsystem. For example, ground robots can typically perceive and avoid obstacles or uneven ground.

In this paper, we study how to provide robots with a different capability: detecting *unexpected* hazards, potentially very rare, that were not explicitly considered during system design. Because we don't have any model of how these hazards appear, we consider anything that is novel or unusual as a potential hazard to be avoided.

Animals and humans exhibit this exact behavior [32], known as *neophobia* [22]: "the avoidance of an object or other aspect of the environment solely because it has never been experienced and is dissimilar from what has been experienced in the individual's past" [33]. We argue that autonomous robots could benefit from implementing neophobia, in particular whenever the potential failure bears a much higher cost than the avoidance behavior. Thus, for example, for a ground robot it makes sense to avoid unusual-looking ground [35] when a slightly longer path on familiar ground is available; or a planetary rover might immediately stop a planned trajectory if something looks odd, waiting for further instructions from the ground control.

Our experiments are motivated by a similar real-world use case in which a quadrotor equipped with sophisticated sensing and control traverses underground tunnels for inspection of aqueduct systems. During the flights, that might span several kilometers, the robot is fully autonomous since it has no connectivity to the operators; they wait for the robot to either reach the predetermined exit point or—in case the robot decides to abort the mission—backtrack to the entry. In this context, a crash bears the cost of the lost hardware and human effort, but most importantly the lost information concerning the hazard that determined the failure, that remains unknown. It then makes sense to react to unexpected sensing data by aborting the mission early and returning to the entry point;[1] operators can then analyze the reported anomaly: in case it is not a genuine hazard, the system can be instructed to ignore it in the current and future missions, and restart the exploration.

After reviewing related work (Sect. 2), we introduce in Sect. 3 our **main contribution**: three image-based datasets (one simulated, two real-world) from indoor environment exploration tasks using ground or flying robots; each dataset is split into training (only normal frames) and testing sets; testing frames are labeled as normal or anomalous, representing hazards that are meaningful in the considered scenarios, including sensing issues and localized or global environmental hazards. In Sect. 4, we describe an anomaly detection approach based on autoencoders, and in Sect. 5 we report and discuss extensive experimental results on these datasets, specifically exploring the impact of image sampling and preprocessing strategies on the ability to detect hazards at different scales (Fig. 1).

---

[1] Similarly, retention of information following encounters with novel predators is one of the recognized evolutionary advantages of neophobic animals [21].

Fig. 1. A Robomaster detects an anomaly in the camera frame: cautiousness is required.

2 Related Work

2.1 Anomaly Detection Methods

Anomaly Detection (AD) is a widely researched topic in Machine Learning; general definitions of anomalies are necessarily vague: e.g., "an observation that deviates considerably from some concept of normality" [26], or "patterns in data that do not conform to expected behavior" [3]. When operating on high-dimensional inputs, such as images, the problem often consists in finding *high-level* anomalies [26] that pertain to the data semantics, and therefore imply some level of understanding of the inputs. Methods based on deep learning have been successful in high-level anomaly detection, in various fields, including medical imaging [30], industrial manufacturing [10,31], surveillance [2], robot navigation [35], fault detection [13], intrusion detection [1] and agriculture [5].

A widespread class of approaches for anomaly detection on images, which we adopt in this paper as a benchmark, is based on undercomplete autoencoders [4,18]: neural reconstruction models that take the image as input and are trained to reproduce it as their output (e.g., using a Mean Absolute Error loss), while constraining the number of nodes in one of the hidden layers (the *bottleneck*); this limits the amount of information that can flow through the network, and prevents the autoencoder from learning to simply copy the input to the output. To minimize the loss on a large dataset of normal (i.e., non-anomalous) samples, the model has to learn to compress the inputs to a low-dimensional representation that captures their high-level information content. When tasked to encode and decode an anomalous sample, i.e., a sample from a different distribution than the training set, one expects that the model will be unable to reconstruct it correctly. Measuring the reconstruction error for a sample, therefore, yields an indication of the sample's anomaly. Variational Autoencoders [16] and Generative Adversarial Networks (GAN) [9] can also be used for Anomaly Detection tasks, by training them to map vectors sampled from a predefined distribution (i.e., Gaussian or uniform) to the distribution of normal training samples. Flow-based generative models [7] explicitly learn the probability density function of the input data using Normalizing Flows [17].

One-Class Classifiers, such as Deep SVDD [25] and deep OC-SVM [8], can also be used as anomaly detectors; these methods define a decision boundary around the training instances in their respective latent spaces.

2.2   Anomaly Detection on Images

In recent work, Sabokrou et al. [27] propose a new adversarial approach using an autoencoder as a reconstructor, feeding a standard CNN classifier as a discriminator, trained adversarially. During inference, the reconstructor is expected to enhance the inlier samples while distorting the outliers; the discriminator's output is used to indicate anomalies.

Sarafijanovic introduces [29] an Inception-like autoencoder for the task of anomaly detection on images. The proposed method uses different convolution layers with different filter sizes all at the same level, mimicking the Inception approach [34]. The proposed model works in two phases; first, it trains the autoencoder only on normal images, then, instead of the autoencoder reproduction error, it measures the distance over the pooled bottleneck's output, which keeps the memory and computation needs at a minimum. The authors test their solution over some classical computer vision datasets: MNIST [6], Fashion MNIST [36], CIFAR10, and CIFAR100 [19].

2.3   Application to Robotics

Using Low-Dimensional Data. Historically, anomaly detection in robotics has focused on using low-dimensional data streams from exteroceptive or proprioceptive sensors. The data, potentially high-frequency, is used in combination with hand-crafted feature selection, Machine Learning, and, recently, Deep Learning models. Khalastchi et al. [13,14] use simple metrics such as Mahalanobis Distance to solve the task of online anomaly detection for unmanned vehicles; Sakurada et al. [28] compare autoencoders to PCA and kPCA using spacecraft telemetry data. Birnbaum [1], builds a nominal behavior profile of Unmanned Aerial Vehicle (UAV) sensor readings, flight plans, and state and uses it to detect anomalies in flight data coming from real UAVs. The anomalies vary from cyberattacks and sensor faults to structural failures. Park et al. tackle the problem of detecting anomalies in robot-assisted feeding, in an early work the authors use Hidden Markov Models on hand-crafted features [23]; in a second paper, they solve the same task using a combination of Variational Autoencoders and LSTM networks [24].

Using High-Dimensional Data. An early approach [2] to anomaly detection on high-dimensional data relies on image matching algorithms for autonomous patrolling to identify unexpected situations; in this research, the image matching is done between the observed data and large databases of normal images. Recent

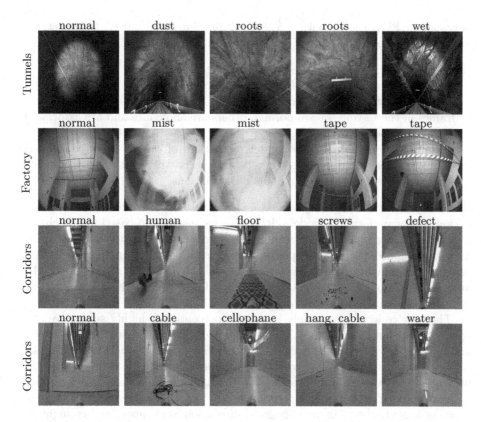

Fig. 2. The testing datasets are composed of normal images and by images of different anomaly classes.

works use Deep Learning models on images. Christiansen et al. [5] propose Deep-Anomaly, a custom CNN derived from AlexNet [20]; the model is used to detect and highlight obstacles or anomalies on an autonomous agricultural robot via high-level features of the CNN layers. Wellhausen et el. [35] verify the ground traversability for a legged ANYmal [11] robot in unknown environments. The paper compares three models - Deep SVDD [25], Real-NVP [7], and a standard autoencoder - on detecting terrain patches whose appearance is anomalous with respect to the robot's previous experience. All the models are trained on patches of footholds images coming from the robot's previous sorties; the most performing model is the combination of Real-NVP and an encoding network, followed closely by the autoencoder.

3   Datasets

We contribute three datasets representing different operating scenarios for indoor robots (flying or ground). Each dataset is composed of a large number of grayscale or RGB frames with a 512 × 512 px resolution. For each dataset, we define four subsets:

- a training set, composed of only normal frames;
- a validation set, composed of only normal frames;
- a labeled testing set, composed of frames with an associated label; some frames in the testing set are normal, others are anomalies and are associated with the respective anomaly class;
- an unlabeled qualitative testing set, consisting of one or more continuous data sequences acquired at 30 Hz, depicting the traversal of environments with alternating normal and anomalous situations.

The training set is used for training anomaly detection models, and the validation set for performing model-selection of reconstruction-based approaches – e.g., determining when to stop training an autoencoder. The testing set can be used to compute quantitative performance metrics for the anomaly detection problem. The qualitative testing set can be used to analyze how the model, the autoencoder in our case, outputs react to a video stream as the robot traverses normal and anomalous environments.

The very concept of anomaly in robotic perception is highly subjective and application-dependent [1,5,35]. Whether a given situation should be considered an anomaly depends on the features of the robot and on its task; for example, consider a robot patrolling corridors with floors normally clear of objects; the presence of screws and bolts littering the ground could be hazardous for a robot with inflated tires that could get punctured, but completely irrelevant for a drone or legged robot. On an orthogonal dimension, some applications might be interested in determining anomalies regardless of whether they pose a hazard to the robot: in a scenario in which a robot is patrolling normally-empty tunnels, finding anything different in the environment could be a sign of an intrusion and should be detected. The appearance of anomalies in forward-looking camera streams is also dependent on the distance from the robot; wires or other thin objects that might pose a danger to a robot could be simply invisible if they are not very close to the camera. Our labeled testing sets are manually curated, and we used our best judgment to determine whether to consider a frame anomalous or not: frames with anomalies that are not clearly visible in the 512 × 512 full-resolution images are excluded from the quantitative testing set, but they are preserved in the qualitative testing sequences.

3.1 *Tunnels* Dataset

The dataset, provided by Hovering Solutions Ltd, is composed of grayscale frames from simulated drone flights along procedurally-generated underground tunnels presenting features typically found in aqueduct systems, namely: random dimensions; random curvature radius; different structures on the floor; tubing, wiring, and other facilities attached to the tunnel walls at random positions; uneven textured walls; various ceiling-mounted features at regular intervals (lighting fixtures, signage). The drone flies approximately along the centerline of the tunnel and illuminates the tunnel walls with a spotlight approximately coaxial with the camera. Both the camera and the spotlight are slightly tilted upwards.

This dataset is composed of 143070 frames: 72854 in the training set; 8934 in the validation set; 57081 in the quantitative labeled testing set (40% anomalous); 4201 in the qualitative testing sequences.

Three anomalies are represented: *dust*, *wet* ceilings, and thin plant *roots* hanging from the ceilings (see Fig. 2). These all correspond to hazards for quadrotors flying real-world missions in aqueduct systems: excessive amounts of dust raised by rotor downwash hinder visual state estimation; wet ceilings, caused by condensation on cold walls in humid environments, indicate the risk of drops of water falling on the robot; thin hanging roots, which find their way through small cracks in the ceiling, directly cause crashes.

3.2 *Factory* Dataset

This dataset contains grayscale frames recorded by a real drone, with a similar setup to the one simulated in the Tunnels dataset, flown in a testing facility (a factory environment) at Hovering Solutions Ltd. During acquisition, the environment is almost exclusively lit by the onboard spotlight.

This dataset is composed of 12040 frames: 4816 in the training set; 670 in the validation set; 6001 in the quantitative testing set (53% anomalous); 553 in the qualitative testing sequences.

Two anomalies are represented: *mist* in the environment, generated with a fog machine; and a signaling *tape* stretched between two opposing walls (Fig. 2). These anomalies represent large-scale and small-scale anomalies, respectively.

3.3 *Corridors* Dataset

This dataset contains RGB frames recorded by a real teleoperated omni-directional ground robot (DJI Robomaster S1), equipped with a forward-looking camera mounted at 22.5 cm from the ground, as it explores corridors of the underground service floor of a large university building. The corridors have a mostly uniform, partially reflective floor with few features; various side openings of different size (doors, lifts, other connecting corridors); variable features on the ceiling, including service ducts, wiring, and various configurations of lighting. The robot is remotely teleoperated during data collection, traveling approximately along the center of the corridor.

This dataset is composed of 52607 frames: 25844 in the training set; 2040 in the validation set; 17971 in the testing set (45% anomalous); 6752 in qualitative testing sequences.

8 anomalies are represented, ranging from subtle characteristics of the environment affecting a minimal part of the input to large-scale changes in the whole image acquired by the robot: *water* puddles, *cables* on the floor; *hanging cables*

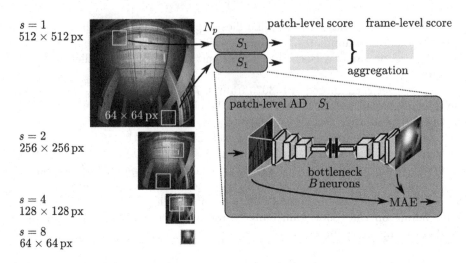

Fig. 3. Anomaly detection model: using an autoencoder to compute the patch-level anomaly scores, which are aggregated in a frame-level score.

from the ceiling; different mats on the *floor*, *human* presence, *screws* and bolts on the ground; camera *defects* (extreme tilting, dirty lens) and *cellophane* foil stretched between the walls. Examples of these anomalies are in Fig. 2.

4   Experimental Setup

4.1   Anomaly Detection on Frames

We define an anomaly detector as a function mapping a frame (512×512) to an anomaly score, which should be high for anomalous frames and low for normal ones. The frame-level anomaly detector relies on a patch-level anomaly detector (see Fig. 3), which instead operates on low-resolution inputs (64×64), which is a typical input size for anomaly detection methods operating on images [12,35].

First, the frame is downsampled (using local averaging) by a factor $s \in \{1, 2, 4, 8\}$; we will refer to the respective models as S_1, S_2, S_4 and S_8. The resulting downsampled image, with resolution $512/s \times 512/s$, is standardized to zero mean and unit variance, independently for each channel; we then extract N_p 64×64 patches, at random coordinates, such that they are fully contained in the downsampled image. The patch-level anomaly detector is applied to each patch, producing N_p anomaly scores; these are aggregated together (e.g., computing their average) to yield the frame-level anomaly score.

Note that in the case of S_8, $N_p \equiv 1$ since a unique patch can be defined on a 64×64 downsampled image. This corresponds to the special case in which the whole frame (after downsampling) is directly used as input to the patch-based detector. This approach is simple and attractive but is unsuitable to detect small-scale anomalies since it can not leverage the full resolution of the frame.

Table 1. AUC values for models at all scales

scale	**Avg**	Tunnels				Factory			Corridors								
	all	all	dust	root	wet	all	mist	tape	all	water	cellophane	cable	defect	hang. cable	floor	human	screws
S_8	**0.82**	**0.82**	0.54	0.76	0.87	**0.90**	0.95	0.48	**0.74**	0.63	0.66	0.70	1.00	0.44	0.85	0.67	0.48
S_4	**0.62**	**0.89**	0.62	0.79	0.94	**0.24**	0.25	0.17	**0.73**	0.81	0.70	0.81	1.00	0.41	0.38	0.73	0.30
S_2	**0.60**	**0.88**	0.63	0.80	0.93	**0.21**	0.20	0.30	**0.71**	0.78	0.70	0.75	0.99	0.50	0.51	0.56	0.40
S_1	**0.55**	**0.85**	0.61	0.80	0.88	**0.12**	0.10	0.25	**0.69**	0.72	0.73	0.68	0.90	0.60	0.59	0.51	0.55

4.2 Patch-Level Anomaly Detector

Patch-level anomalies are detected with a standard approach based on the reconstruction error of an autoencoder. The encoder part operates on a 64×64 input and is composed of four convolutional layers with a LeakyReLU activation function; each layer has a number of filters that is double the number of filters of the previous layer; we start with F 3×3 filters for the first layer. Each Convolution has stride 2 thus halving the resolution of the input. The neurons of the last layer of the encoder are flattened and used as input to a fully connected layer with B neurons (bottleneck); the decoder is built in a specular manner to the encoder, and its output has the same shape as the encoder's input; the output layer has a linear activation function, which enables the model to reconstruct the same range as the input. During inference, the patch-based anomaly detector accepts a patch as input and outputs the Mean Absolute Error between the input patch and its reconstruction, which we interpret as the patch anomaly score.

4.3 Training

For a given scale s, the autoencoder is trained as follows: first, we downsample each frame in the training set by a factor s; then, as an online data generation step, we sample random patches completely contained in the downsampled frames.

We use the Adam [15] optimizer to minimize the mean squared reconstruction error, with an initial learning rate of 0.001, which is reduced by a factor of 10 in case the validation loss plateaus for more than 8 epochs. Because the size of the training set of different datasets is widely variable, we set the total number of epochs in such a way that during the whole training, the model sees a total of 2 million samples; this allows us to better compare results on different datasets.

The approach is implemented in PyTorch and Python 3.8, using a deep learning workstation equipped with 4 NVIDIA 2080 Ti GPUs; training each model takes about 1 h on a single GPU.

4.4   Metrics

We evaluate the performance of the frame-level anomaly detector on the testing set of each dataset. In particular, we quantify the anomaly detection performance as if it was a binary classification problem (normal vs anomalous), where the probability assigned to the anomalous class corresponds to the anomaly score returned by the detector. This allows us to define the Area Under the ROC Curve metric (AUC); an ideal anomaly detector returns anomaly scores such that there exists a threshold t for which all anomalous frames have scores higher than t, whereas all normal frames have scores lower than t: this corresponds to an AUC of 1. An anomaly detector returning a random score for each instance, or the same score for all instances, yields an AUC of 0.5. The AUC value can be interpreted as the probability that a random anomalous frame is assigned an anomaly score larger than that of a random normal frame. The AUC value is a meaningful measure of a model's performance and does not depend on the choice of threshold.

For each model and dataset, we compute the AUC value conflating all anomalies, as well as the AUC individually for each anomaly (versus normal frames, ignoring all other anomalies).

5   Results

5.1 S_8 Model Hyperparameters

Figure 4a explores the choice of the bottleneck size B for model S_8. Increasing B reduces reconstruction error for both anomalous and normal data; the reconstruction error best discriminates the two classes (higher AUC, higher average gap between the two classes) for intermediate values of B (16 neurons): then, the autoencoder can reconstruct well normal data while lacking the capacity to properly reconstruct anomalous samples. These findings apply to all three datasets. Figure 4b investigates a similar capacity trade-off: autoencoders with a small number of filters for the first convolution layer (*first layer size*) are not powerful enough to reproduce well even normal samples, therefore have lower discriminating performance. For the rest of the Section, we only report results for bottleneck size $B = 16$ and first layer size $F = 128$.

5.2   Patch Aggregation

Figure 4c: top explores the impact of N_p on the anomaly detection performance of model S_2; we observe that, for the Tunnels and Corridors datasets, the performance increases as N_p increases. This is expected, as more patches are processed and aggregated to compute the frame-level score. Only for Tunnels, S_2 outperforms S_8 for 10 or more patches.

On the contrary, for the Factory dataset, the model S_2 performs worse than chance at detecting anomalies and assigns lower scores than normal data. This

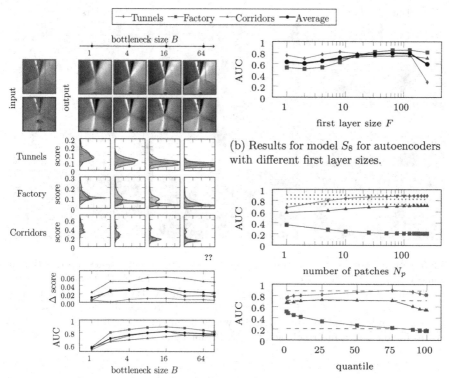

(b) Results for model S_8 for autoencoders with different first layer sizes.

(a) Results for different autoencoder's bottleneck sizes for model S_8. Top two rows: for the same two samples (normal in green, anomalous in red), autoencoder reconstructions. Center: score distributions over the testing set. Bottom: mean score difference between anomalous and normal samples and AUC of the anomaly detector.

(c) Results for model S_2 when aggregating the scores of multiple patches extracted from each frame. Top: AUC, when aggregating by averaging, for different numbers of patches, compared to S_8 (dotted). Bottom: AUC, when aggregating 250 patches by computing a quantile (solid) or by averaging (dashed).

Fig. 4. Experimental results

is due to the testing set being dominated by the mist anomaly, which is not detectable at low scales as discussed in Sect. 5.3.

Figure 4c: bottom reports how computing the 0.7–0.8 quantile offers a slightly better aggregation than averaging.

5.3 Scales and Anomalies

Table 1 summarizes the most important results on all model scales, datasets, and anomalies. We note that most anomalies are best detected by the full-frame approach S_8; this is especially true for large-scale anomalies that cover a significant portion of the frame, such as mist for Factory, or human and floor for Corridors.

Tunnels, dust   Factory, mist   Corridors, defect

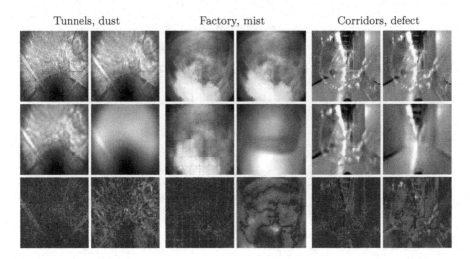

Fig. 5. Comparison between S_1 and S_8: pairs of identical input images representing an anomaly (top row); Autoencoder's outputs (central row) for S_1 (left) and S_8 (right); the absolute value of the difference between input and output (bottom row, using a colormap where yellow is high and blue is low). Only for this illustration, for S_1 we regularly sample 64 patches to cover the whole input image, and we use the output patches to compose a full-resolution image. (Color figure online)

In contrast, S_8 underperforms for small-scale anomalies, that cover few pixels of the downsampled image (e.g., dust and roots for Tunnels; cellophane, water, and hanging cable for Corridors); in this case, small-scale models sometimes have an advantage over S_8.

In contrast, we observe that small-scale models struggle with the large-scale mist anomaly, returning consistently lower anomaly scores than normal frames, which yields AUC values well below 0.5. Figure 5 compares how S_1 and S_8 reconstruct a mist frame: clearly, S_8 fails to capture the large-scale structure of mist, which yields high reconstruction error as expected in an anomalous frame; in contrast, since individual high-resolution patches of the mist frame are low-contrast and thus easy to reconstruct, the S_1 model yields very low reconstruction error and, thus, low AUC.

Some anomalies, such as defect for Corridors, are obvious enough that models at all scales can detect them almost perfectly.

5.4   Run-Time Evaluation

The accompanying video features several runs where a quadcopter uses the S_8 model to detect anomalies on-board to recognize and avoid unforeseen hazards. Figure 6 illustrates execution on a sequence that is part of the qualitative testing set for Factory; in the figure, we manually annotated the ground truth presence of hazards such as mist (first red interval) and tape (second red interval). In the experiment, the robot captures a camera frame, computes an anomaly score,

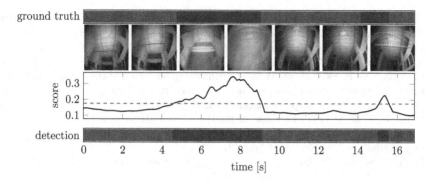

Fig. 6. Part of the qualitative testing dataset in the Factory scenario where the drone first passes through mist and then below a tape. Top: the manually added labels (green: normal, red: anomalous) and seven frames sampled from the timeline. Center: the score returned by the S_8 model (solid black) and anomaly threshold t (dashed red). Bottom: the anomaly detector output. (Color figure online)

and raises an alarm when the score passes a predefined threshold. The example shows how the drone is able to detect first a long area of mist and later a small signaling tape.

6   Conclusions

We introduced three datasets for validating approaches to detect anomalies in visual sensing data acquired by mobile robots exploring an environment; various anomalies are represented, spanning from camera malfunctions to environmental hazards: some affect the acquired image globally; others only impact a small portion of it. We used these datasets to benchmark an anomaly detection approach based on autoencoders operating at different scales on the input frames. Results show that the approach is successful at detecting most anomalies (detection performance with an average AUC metric of 0.82); detecting small anomalies is in general harder than detecting anomalies that affect the whole image.

References

1. Birnbaum, Z., et al.: Unmanned aerial vehicle security using behavioral profiling. In: 2015 International Conference on Unmanned Aircraft Systems (ICUAS), pp. 1310–1319 (2015). https://doi.org/10.1109/ICUAS.2015.7152425
2. Chakravarty, P., Zhang, A., Jarvis, R., Kleeman, L.: Anomaly detection and tracking for a patrolling robot. In: Proceedings of the Australasian Conference on Robotics and Automation, pp. 1–9 (2007)
3. Chandola, V., Banerjee, A., Kumar, V.: Anomaly detection: a survey. ACM Comput. Surv. **41**(3) (2009). https://doi.org/10.1145/1541880.1541882

4. Cho, K., et al.: Learning phrase representations using RNN encoder-decoder for statistical machine translation. In: Proceedings of the 2014 Conference on Empirical Methods in Natural Language Processing (EMNLP), pp. 1724–1734 (2014). https://doi.org/10.3115/v1/D14-1179

5. Christiansen, P., et al.: DeepAnomaly: combining background subtraction and deep learning for detecting obstacles and anomalies in an agricultural field. Sensors **16**(11), 1904 (2016). https://doi.org/10.3390/s16111904

6. Deng, L.: The MNIST database of handwritten digit images for machine learning research [best of the web]. IEEE Signal Process. Mag. **29**(6), 141–142 (2012). https://doi.org/10.1109/MSP.2012.2211477

7. Dinh, L., Sohl-Dickstein, J., Bengio, S.: Density estimation using real NVP (2016). https://doi.org/10.48550/ARXIV.1605.08803

8. Erfani, S.M., Sothers: High-dimensional and large-scale anomaly detection using a linear one-class SVM with deep learning. Pattern Recogn. **58**, 121–134 (2016). https://doi.org/10.1016/j.patcog.2016.03.028

9. Goodfellow, I.J., et al.: Generative adversarial networks (2014). https://doi.org/10.48550/ARXIV.1406.2661

10. Haselmann, M., Gruber, D.P., Tabatabai, P.: Anomaly detection using deep learning based image completion. In: 2018 17th IEEE International Conference on Machine Learning and Applications (ICMLA), pp. 1237–1242 (2018). https://doi.org/10.1109/ICMLA.2018.00201

11. Hutter, M., et al.: ANYmal - a highly mobile and dynamic quadrupedal robot. In: 2016 IEEE/RSJ International Conference on Intelligent Robots and Systems (IROS), pp. 38–44 (2016). https://doi.org/10.1109/IROS.2016.7758092

12. Kerner, H.R., et al.: Novelty detection for multispectral images with application to planetary exploration. In: Proceedings of the AAAI Conference on Artificial Intelligence, vol. 33, no. 01, pp. 9484–9491 (2019). https://doi.org/10.1609/aaai.v33i01.33019484

13. Khalastchi, E., Kalech, M., Kaminka, G.A., Lin, R.: Online data-driven anomaly detection in autonomous robots. Knowl. Inf. Syst. **43**(3), 657–688 (2014). https://doi.org/10.1007/s10115-014-0754-y

14. Khalastchi, E., et al.: Online anomaly detection in unmanned vehicles. In: The 10th International Conference on Autonomous Agents and Multiagent Systems, AAMAS 2011, Richland, SC, vol. 1, pp. 115–122 (2011)

15. Kingma, D.P., Ba, J.: Adam: a method for stochastic optimization (2014). https://doi.org/10.48550/ARXIV.1412.6980

16. Kingma, D.P., Welling, M.: Auto-encoding variational bayes (2013). https://doi.org/10.48550/ARXIV.1312.6114

17. Kobyzev, I., Prince, S.J., Brubaker, M.A.: Normalizing flows: an introduction and review of current methods. IEEE Trans. Pattern Anal. Mach. Intell. **43**(11), 3964–3979 (2021). https://doi.org/10.1109/TPAMI.2020.2992934

18. Kramer, M.: Autoassociative neural networks. Comput. Chem. Eng. **16**(4), 313–328 (1992). https://doi.org/10.1016/0098-1354(92)80051-A. Neutral network applications in chemical engineering

19. Krizhevsky, A.: Learning multiple layers of features from tiny images. Master's thesis, University of Toronto (2009)

20. Krizhevsky, A., Sutskever, I., Hinton, G.E.: ImageNet classification with deep convolutional neural networks, vol. 25 (2012)

21. Mitchell, M.D., et al.: Living on the edge: how does environmental risk affect the behavioural and cognitive ecology of prey? Anim. Behav. **115**, 185–192 (2016). https://doi.org/10.1016/j.anbehav.2016.03.018

22. Moretti, L., Hentrup, M., Kotrschal, K., Range, F.: The influence of relationships on neophobia and exploration in wolves and dogs. Anim. Behav. **107**, 159–173 (2015). https://doi.org/10.1016/j.anbehav.2015.06.008

23. Park, D., et al.: Multimodal execution monitoring for anomaly detection during robot manipulation. In: 2016 IEEE International Conference on Robotics and Automation (ICRA), pp. 407–414 (2016). https://doi.org/10.1109/ICRA.2016.7487160

24. Park, D., et al.: A multimodal anomaly detector for robot-assisted feeding using an LSTM-based variational autoencoder. IEEE Robot. Autom. Lett. **3**(3), 1544–1551 (2018). https://doi.org/10.1109/LRA.2018.2801475

25. Ruff, L., et al.: Deep one-class classification. In: Dy, J., Krause, A. (eds.) Proceedings of the 35th International Conference on Machine Learning. Proceedings of Machine Learning Research, vol. 80, pp. 4393–4402, 10–15 July 2018

26. Ruff, L., et al.: A unifying review of deep and shallow anomaly detection. Proc. IEEE **109**(5), 756–795 (2021). https://doi.org/10.1109/JPROC.2021.3052449

27. Sabokrou, M., Khalooei, M., Fathy, M., Adeli, E.: Adversarially learned one-class classifier for novelty detection. In: 2018 IEEE/CVF Conference on Computer Vision and Pattern Recognition, pp. 3379–3388 (2018). https://doi.org/10.1109/CVPR.2018.00356

28. Sakurada, M., Yairi, T.: Anomaly detection using autoencoders with nonlinear dimensionality reduction. In: Proceedings of the MLSDA 2014 2nd Workshop on Machine Learning for Sensory Data Analysis, MLSDA 2014, New York, NY, USA, pp. 4–11 (2014). https://doi.org/10.1145/2689746.2689747

29. Sarafijanovic-Djukic, N., Davis, J.: Fast distance-based anomaly detection in images using an inception-like autoencoder. In: Kralj Novak, P., Šmuc, T., Džeroski, S. (eds.) DS 2019. LNCS (LNAI), vol. 11828, pp. 493–508. Springer, Cham (2019). https://doi.org/10.1007/978-3-030-33778-0_37

30. Schlegl, T., Seeböck, P., Waldstein, S.M., Schmidt-Erfurth, U., Langs, G.: Unsupervised anomaly detection with generative adversarial networks to guide marker discovery. In: Niethammer, M., et al. (eds.) IPMI 2017. LNCS, vol. 10265, pp. 146–157. Springer, Cham (2017). https://doi.org/10.1007/978-3-319-59050-9_12

31. Scime, L., Beuth, J.: A multi-scale convolutional neural network for autonomous anomaly detection and classification in a laser powder bed fusion additive manufacturing process. Addit. Manuf. **24**, 273–286 (2018). https://doi.org/10.1016/j.addma.2018.09.034

32. Sloan Wilson, D., Clark, A.B., Coleman, K., Dearstyne, T.: Shyness and boldness in humans and other animals. Trends Ecol. Evol. **9**(11), 442–446 (1994). https://doi.org/10.1016/0169-5347(94)90134-1

33. Stöwe, M., Bugnyar, T., Heinrich, B., Kotrschal, K.: Effects of group size on approach to novel objects in ravens (corvus corax). Ethology **112**(11), 1079–1088 (2006). https://doi.org/10.1111/j.1439-0310.2006.01273.x

34. Szegedy, C., et al.: Going deeper with convolutions. In: 2015 IEEE Conference on Computer Vision and Pattern Recognition (CVPR), pp. 1–9 (2015). https://doi.org/10.1109/CVPR.2015.7298594

35. Wellhausen, L., Ranftl, R., Hutter, M.: Safe robot navigation via multi-modal anomaly detection. IEEE Robot. Autom. Lett. **5**(2), 1326–1333 (2020). https://doi.org/10.1109/LRA.2020.2967706

36. Xiao, H., Rasul, K., Vollgraf, R.: Fashion-MNIST: a novel image dataset for benchmarking machine learning algorithms (2017). https://doi.org/10.48550/ARXIV.1708.07747

Robotic Systems and Applications

Integration and Robustness Analysis of the Buzz Swarm Programming Language with the Pi-puck Robot Platform

Aiden Neale[✉] and Alan G. Millard

Department of Computer Science, University of York, York, UK
{arn519,alan.millard}@york.ac.uk

Abstract. In this paper, we present an open-source integration of the Buzz swarm programming language with the Pi-puck robot platform. We then analyse the effect of packet loss and sensor noise on neighbour sensing in Buzz using a simple aggregation algorithm as a case study. Through infrastructural testing on this physical robot platform, we evaluate how well swarm algorithms developed in Buzz can cope with perturbations. We find that aggregation is reasonably tolerant to packet loss, however struggles to tolerate inaccurate neighbour sensing. Finally, we suggest future work that could mitigate the effect of embedded platform imperfections when developing swarm algorithms in Buzz.

Keywords: Swarm robotics · Swarm programming · Buzz · Pi-puck

1 Introduction

Developing control algorithms for robot swarms is a difficult task requiring significant expertise, as individual behaviours must be specified such that the desired collective behaviour emerges from interactions between the robots and their environment. Throughout the evolution of swarm robotics, various approaches have been taken to programming collective swarm behaviours. Brambilla et al. [4] group these design methods into two distinct categories: automatic design and behaviour-based design.

Automatic design – casting the design problem as an optimisation problem [6] – demands a well-defined objective function to guide the optimisation process towards creating a successful swarm algorithm. Behaviour-based design is a more traditional approach to designing swarm algorithms that requires human developers to manually program the collective behaviours themselves. Francesca et al. [7] showed that domain experts programming swarms using constrained parametric modules were able to create swarm algorithms that outperformed those generated automatically. However, unconstrained experts performed worse than constrained automatic design. Therefore, if collective behaviours are to be programmed by hand, it is necessary for swarm programming languages to provide

© The Author(s), under exclusive license to Springer Nature Switzerland AG 2022
S. Pacheco-Gutierrez et al. (Eds.): TAROS 2022, LNAI 13546, pp. 223–237, 2022.
https://doi.org/10.1007/978-3-031-15908-4_18

frameworks and constructs that facilitate the development of performant swarm algorithms.

In this paper we present an open-source integration of the Buzz swarm programming language for the Pi-puck robot platform [2,18] (an extension of the e-puck [19]). We also present the results of robustness analysis of Buzz as a swarm programming language, specifically investigating the effect of packet loss and sensor noise on aggregation – a building block of many swarm behaviours. This paper reviews related works in Sect. 2, then details our open-source Buzz integration with the Pi-puck and experimental methodology in Sect. 3. In Sect. 4 we examine Buzz's performance under the influence of packet loss and sensor noise, summarising our findings in Sect. 5.

2   Related Work

Behaviour-based design can be approached in broadly two ways: macroscopic (designing the swarm as a collective to produce swarm-like behaviour) and microscopic (designing behaviours through low-level programming at an individual robot scale), however each approach has its drawbacks. Traditionally, programming a robot swarm is a complex and tedious task, involving a trial-and-error bottom-up process of iterative refinement. In recent years, efforts have been made to create swarm programming languages to ease the process of designing collective behaviours. These provide a top-down approach, programming the swarm as a single entity, abstracting away the complications of a bottom-up approach.

Koord [10] is an event-driven domain specific language for programming robot swarms that utilises a series of abstractions that ease the difficulty of programming collective behaviours. Low-level drivers that control sensors and actuators are abstracted from the developer, wrapped into functionality that is the same regardless of the robot platform. Koord also implements distributed shared variables that are abstractly accessible by all robots using the keyword **allread**. The language further provides control over concurrency using mutual exclusions. Koord has been tested on heterogeneous swarms in both simulation and hardware [10], however only by the original developers to date.

Buzz [24] is a domain specific language created with the intent of blending the design of swarm behaviours with a top-down and bottom-up approach to improve programmability. Buzz's main aim is to "provide a set of primitives which accelerates the implementation of swarm-specific behaviors" [30]. Buzz is open-source and extensible, so it can easily be ported to enhance existing infrastructure [24]. It provides users with both single-robot primitives (in the form of robot-specific and neighbour manipulation) and swarm based primitives, such as swarm management and communication through 'virtual stigmergy' [24]. Implementing new Buzz primitives is straightforward, providing support for heterogeneous robot swarms, which makes Buzz scalable. This means that it can work with existing robotics frameworks such as ROS, OROCOS, and YARP [24].

Buzz assumes that the target robot platform has a device for handling situated communication [31], to enable its neighbour management and virtual stigmergy features. However, the robot platforms that Buzz is currently implemented

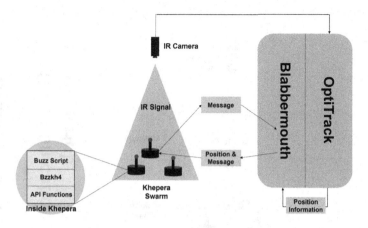

Fig. 1. Overview of Khepera IV integration with Buzz (reproduced from [14])

on do not have range-and-bearing sensor hardware, nor any other method of on-board situated communication. Buzz has been integrated with a range of platforms, namely the Kilobot [28], Khepera IV [29], and Cognifly drone [3], as well as the ARGoS [25] swarm robotics simulator.

Due to the memory capacity of the Kilobot's micro-controller, and because it does not run embedded Linux, the Buzz Virtual Machine (see Sect. 3.2) cannot be executed on it. The Kilobot instead runs a minimal version of Buzz called BittyBuzz [5], which utilises circular buffers to implement dynamic memory management.

Buzz runs on the Khepera IV through integration with OptiTrack cameras (for robot tracking) and Blabbermouth (to handle communication between the robots and send position updates), as shown in Fig. 1. Blabbermouth is a C-based software hub created for intercommunication between robots [26]. A Buzz interpreter called BzzKh4 [27] handles the processing of information passed to the Khepera robot during run-time. This also connects to the API functions that control the Khepera robot's functionality.

Buzz integration for the Cognifly drone is based on that of the Khepera IV. The program BuzzCognifly [13] features similar functionality to BzzKh4, integrating with their flight controller APIs, and provides a more user-friendly cross-compilation and installation process. It also use a 'communication hub' called commhub_udp [12] developed in Python that improves upon Blabbermouth.

In this paper, we investigate Buzz integration with the Pi-puck as an alternative differential drive robot platform to the Khepera IV. We have integrated Buzz with the Pi-puck using the same approach as that used for the Cognifly drone (see Fig. 2). To analyse the robustness of swarm behaviours written in Buzz, we have evaluated its performance with increasing levels of packet loss. Although range-and-bearing hardware exists for the e-puck robot [11], Garattoni et al. [8] demonstrate that the distance estimation is unreliable even at short ranges. We have therefore also analysed Buzz's performance with the inclusion

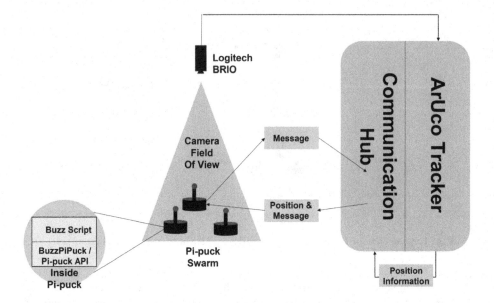

Fig. 2. Overview of our Pi-puck integration with Buzz (adapted from [14])

of virtual sensor noise, to assess the feasibility of running Buzz algorithms on fully embedded systems with on-board range-and-bearing hardware.

3 Methodology

To evaluate the robustness of Buzz algorithms, a series of experiments were carried out in order to stress test the infrastructure used to implement its language constructs. This section details the experimental setup, our Buzz integration with the Pi-puck, and the experimental methodology.

3.1 Experimental Environment

The experimental environment integrated eight Pi-puck robots in a (1.8 m × 0.9 m) arena with an overhead camera (Logitech BRIO) and a server, which processed 1080p video from the camera to track the robots' positions and orientations in real time. For the purpose of this setup, the server was a 4-core Intel i3-2328M Lenovo ThinkPad Edge Laptop with 4 GB RAM, running Ubuntu 20.04.3 LTS. The server also hosted our Robot Communication Hub software (explained in Sect. 3.2). For simplicity, communication between the camera's location data and the robots was handled dynamically during runtime, by monitoring ports that were statically assigned to each robot based on their unique IDs. All communication was routed through a local network.

3.2   Software

Buzz's run-time platform is a stack-based virtual machine written in C called the Buzz Virtual Machine (BVM) [24]. Buzz is an extension language, meaning it requires an underlying system to exist before it can function on a robot platform. It needs infrastructure that handles communication between, and localisation of, robots, which then directly modifies values within the Buzz Virtual Machine/other Buzz structures. It also requires software infrastructure to manipulate the robot platform's sensors/motors, as these are handled through register hooks and not directly through Buzz. Low-level hardware drivers for the motors and sensors were developed such that they could be operated through Buzz scripts. We have developed `BuzzPiPuck` [20] – a piece of software that acts as an intermediary between the Pi-puck robot's low-level drivers and Buzz code, which is based on the Cognifly drone integration with Buzz [13].

BuzzPiPuck. In order to run a compiled Buzz script on the Pi-puck, it needs to be interpreted by a language that is native to the robots. Buzz was written in C to encourage compatibility across a variety of robot platforms. `BuzzPiPuck` is primarily developed in C, and creates a compiled executable called `BzzPuck` that can be executed on Pi-puck robots in order to run compiled Buzz scripts. It also provides control over communication type, communication length, and assignment of IDs internally for each robot.

`BuzzPiPuck` as an underlying architecture serves three key purposes. Its first purpose is to setup networking infrastructure on the Pi-pucks enabling inter-robot communication. It does this by initialising UDP (User Datagram Protocol) sockets, which it uses to broadcast and receive messages from the server. These control how a robot perceives its location in the real world at any given moment. With the ability to receive messages across the network, it allows the Pi-pucks to receive information regarding their absolute location, as well as messages passed through Buzz-handled operations, such as swarm management and virtual stigmergy.

Its second purpose is to control the Pi-pucks' movement and sensors through low-level drivers programmed in C. Drivers that are external to Buzz are integrated into the language as C closures. The Buzz Virtual Machine takes a string as an ID and registers each function to a relative string, which can be referenced in the Buzz script. For example: control mechanisms of the Pi-puck are written in C and the functionality is referenced to a string `set_wheels` in Buzz scripts. This enables a blended approach for programming swarm behaviours, with the ability to program complex controllers at a lower level but approach general behaviour at a higher level.

Similarly, Buzz functionality can be accessed from within the C executable, allowing it to control how and when Buzz functions are called, and forms the constructs of how the Buzz script is iterated through. As such, `BuzzPiPuck`'s final purpose is to handle the interpretation of the Buzz script, as well as manage the supply of information to the Buzz Virtual Machine. During run-time,

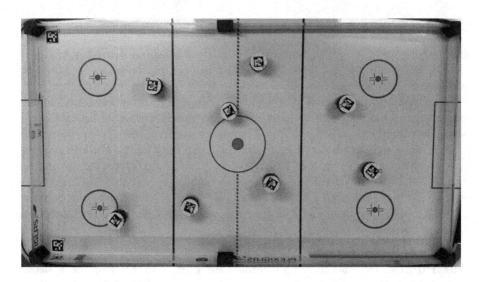

Fig. 3. ArUco Tracker software view – tracking the locations of 8 Pi-pucks and positional scaling markers from overhead

the BVM requires updates to Buzz's neighbour stack in order for it to determine which robots are within neighbour range. Additionally the Buzz Virtual Machine controls the processing of all incoming and outgoing messages from the communication server.

Robot Communication Hub. We have developed software called the Robot Communication Hub [21] to handle all communication between a visible-light camera tracking system and robots, handling messages such as those used for inter-robot communication, as well as Buzz's virtual stigmergy functionality. The code for the Robot Communication Hub is based on that used for the Cognifly project [12], which integrated with infra-red OptiTrack cameras to perform a similar task. The code was stripped of OptiTrack references and reimplemented to integrate a simple webcam with OpenCV for image processing. The Robot Communication Hub is broken down into two parts: it handles ArUco tag [9] detection, identification, and coordinate retrieval; and packetisation and network-forwarding for communication between robots and the tracking server.

In order to monitor the position/orientation of the Pi-pucks, they must be observed in real-time with an overhead camera (see Fig. 3). The ArUco tracker uses the OpenCV-Python library [22] to initialise the camera and detect the ArUco tags. As OpenCV operates on pixel coordinates rather than in metric units, transformations must be performed before the distance between pairs of robots can be calculated. As such, two ArUco tags were placed in the environment separated by a known distance to determine the scaling between pixel coordinates and metric units. The ArUco tag on top of each robot can then be used to calculate its metric coordinates, as well as the robot's bearing based on the orientation of the tag.

The Communication Hub controls all communication between server and robot for updating `BuzzPiPuck` with up-to-date information regarding positioning, and also controls communication between robots for the purpose of virtual stigmergy and inter-robot communication. It does this by sending constructed byte objects across a UDP server that it creates and hosts at a frequency 500 Hz. UDP was preferred over other networking protocols such as TCP as the robots must react in real-time, so low latency and transmission speed are more important than reliable transmission. To accommodate this, the frequency of the communication hub is high enough that dropped messages are negligible under normal conditions. The communication hub runs two dedicated threads in order to stop blocking: a 'receiving' thread, and an 'auto-forward' thread.

3.3 Experimental Methodology

We evaluated the robustness of Buzz by stress testing the supporting infrastructure that it relies upon. This was achieved by analysing a Pi-puck swarm's ability to perform a simple Buzz aggregation algorithm while measuring the total average distance between individual robots in the swarm. Aggregation was chosen as the case study, as it is the building block for more complex swarm behaviours [17]. Robust performance with this basic swarm behaviour should indicate Buzz's ability to perform with more complex behaviours [17]. Additionally, aggregation relies on Buzz's neighbour constructs, which require range-and-bearing sensing of some description. The creators of Buzz have provided a subset of basic behaviours as scripts [23], and the algorithm used in our experiments was a slightly altered version of the aggregation script, shown in Listing 1.

For each experiment, the results were compared to a set of 10 control runs of the software without stress testing being applied. Each set of experiments were run 10 times, with the robots' positions and orientations randomised between runs. The average inter-robot distance was used as a heuristic for aggregation quality, to determine how well Buzz performed when relying upon imperfect infrastructure. There were two forms of independent testing run on the infrastructure to test the performance of Buzz, as described below.

Incorporating packet loss into the underlying infrastructure, by emulating packets dropped in communication between the Robot Communication Hub and the Pi-pucks, allows the effectiveness in a real-world environment to be tested. In real-world applications of swarm robotics, wireless communication is not completely reliable, especially in situations such as tasks handled in dangerous environments, or in larger swarms where packet collision and data corruption is likely due to limited communication bandwidth. This means that packets may be dropped, which would disrupt the quantity of position updates that each individual in the swarm received. These tests were run at a 25%, 50%, 75% and 99% packet loss, where the aggregation of the swarm was measured through the average distance between individual robots. Packet loss, in this case, was implemented as a biased coin flip determining which packets were output to

```
 1  function aggregate() {
 2      neighbors.foreach(function(rid, data) {
 3          degrees = rtod(data.azimuth)
 4          if(degrees < 25  and degrees > (-25)) {
 5              set_wheels(50.0, 50.0)
 6          }
 7          else if(degrees > 25) {
 8              set_wheels(50.0, 20.0)
 9          }
10          else {
11              set_wheels(20.0, 50.0)
12          }
13      })
14  }
```

Listing 1. Aggregation case study: `rid` is an internal Buzz variable representing the ID of the robot; `data` is an internal Buzz construct containing the distance, azimuth and elevation to a neighbour; `rtod` is a function that converts radians to degrees.

other robots in the swarm by the Robot Communication Hub. The `BuzzPiPuck` process for stepping through a Buzz script involves clearing the Buzz Virtual Machine neighbour structure and supplying the BVM with information about neighbours and their locations. By purposefully omitting packets (simulating packet loss), the Buzz Virtual Machine is not supplied all the information it needs to appropriately assign neighbours, though each robot was always aware of its own location. Packet loss would not be an issue for neighbour sensing in a fully embedded implementation that uses on-board range-and-bearing sensors. However, it would still affect inter-robot communication and Buzz constructs such as virtual stigmergy.

As range-and-bearing hardware for the e-puck robot is prone to noise [8], we analysed the ability of a robot swarm to aggregate if Buzz received information from noisy sensors. In a fully embedded system, a robot platform's on-board sensors and actuators are typically their only method of communicating with other robots within a swarm, therefore sensor noise affects inter-robot coordination. As these experiments were conducted in a laboratory setting, and the Pi-puck robots used were not equipped with range-and-bearing hardware, an overhead camera was used to determine the positions of the robots in real-time. With this setup, a robot could be told its absolute position with minimal loss of accuracy, but noise was added to the true coordinates of the detected tags. The noise was generated randomly following a Gaussian distribution centred on the robot's true location, and used standard deviation as the independent variable. The standard deviation values tested were: 1 cm, 5 cm, 10 cm and 20 cm.

To further analyse Buzz's performance, experiments were carried out to investigate the interactions between different levels of packet loss and sensor noise, to determine the extremities Buzz could withstand. Buzz's performance is expected to be affected most when both packet loss and sensor noise are at their highest,

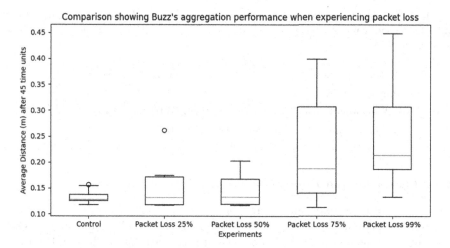

Fig. 4. Boxplot showing aggregation performance of the swarm with increasing levels of packet loss

though the magnitude of the effect is an important indicator of Buzz's robustness as a swarm programming language. These experiments were run 10 times per change in variable, with 250 runs conducted in total.

4   Results and Analysis

Results were obtained by running each set of experiments ten times per independent variable. For both the sensor noise and packet loss experiments, three statistical tests were run for each data point in comparison to the control run. Three statistical tests were chosen to review the performance: the Mann Whitney-U test [15], the Kolmogorov-Smirnov test [16], and the Vargha-Delaney 'A' Measure [32]. All of these tests are non-parametric, as the data cannot be assumed to follow a normal distribution. The Mann Whitney-U test determines the difference in medians between two distributions. The Kolmogorov-Smirnov test is used to test the probability of samples being drawn from the same distribution. The Vargha-Delaney 'A' Measure indicates scientific (rather than statistical) significance [1]. It returns the probability that a randomly selected sample from one population will be larger than a sample randomly drawn from another, which is then compared against thresholds set by its authors to determine the effect size: 0.5 - No effect; 0.56 - Small effect; 0.64 - Medium effect; 0.71 - Large effect.

For each experiment, a significance threshold α of 0.05 was used, such that the null hypothesis is rejected at a 95% confidence level. Each experiment was run for 45 time steps. It is important to note that a Pi-puck is approximately 7 cm in diameter, which means that the aggregation metric will never reach a value less than this.

Table 1. Statistical analysis of packet loss experiments, to 3 significant figures. Bold values are significant according to α threshold of 0.05. Asterisked values are classed as a large effect.

Packet loss amount	25%	50%	75%	99%
Mann-Whitney U test	0.970	1.00	**0.00312**	$\mathbf{4.40 \times 10^{-4}}$
Kolmogorov-Smirnov test	0.418	0.787	**0.0123**	$\mathbf{2.17 \times 10^{-4}}$
Vargha-Delaney 'A' Measure	0.508	0.500	0.719*	0.855*

4.1   Packet Loss in Robot Communication

The results of these experiments are shown in Fig. 4 and Table 1. The medians are quite similar across the control experiment and at 25% and 50% packet loss, meaning that the aggregation behaviour was relatively unaffected. However, despite the median result of each experiment remaining similar, the spread of the distributions increases with the amount of packet loss. It is evident that packet loss of 75% and above significantly affected the swarm's ability to aggregate, with the spread of the data roughly 5 times greater than the control run. As shown in Table 1, for both the 25% and 50% experiments, the null hypothesis could not be rejected for either the Mann Whitney-U test or the Kolmogrov-Smirnov test. At higher levels of packet loss, the results were statistically significant and the null hypothesis was rejected. Both 75% and 99% packet loss resulted in a large effect size according to the Vargha-Delaney 'A' Measure.

Due to the implementation of the simulated packet loss, individual robots in the Pi-puck swarm were unable to determine where their neighbours were for certain iterations of the Buzz script. At lower percentages of packet loss, this meant that the occasional robot would appear to be missing to another robot. However, due to the broadcast frequency of the Robot Communication Hub, this did not affect the quality of aggregation. This explains why the null hypothesis could not be rejected in either the Mann Whitney-U or the Kolmogorov-Smirnov test, as the robots still received adequate location updates to allow them to perform manoeuvres to aggregate. As packet loss increased to 75% and 99%, robots received fewer updates from the Robot Communication Hub about their location. This caused the Pi-pucks to continue on their current path rather than altering it, as they would have no neighbours to compare their location to. This meant that robots would vastly overshoot one another, or loop endlessly in circles (at the highest packet loss). If the Robot Communication Hub were run with a lower frequency of packet transmission, we expect that the performance would be degraded further. In a fully embedded implementation, robot hardware would therefore need to ensure continuity of neighbour sensing, to avoid this degradation of performance with Buzz algorithms that rely upon range-and-bearing data. It is anticipated that similar degradation in performance would be observed for Buzz algorithms that rely upon inter-robot communication, and those that utilise the virtual stigmergy functionality.

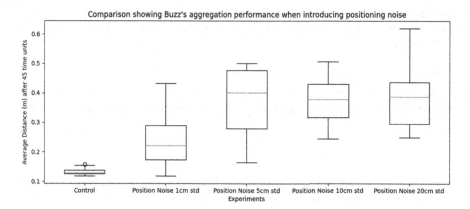

Fig. 5. Boxplot showing aggregation performance of the swarm with increasing levels of sensor noise

4.2   Artificial Sensor Noise in Robot Positioning

Artificial sensor noise had a greater impact on the performance of swarm aggregation. There are several notable discoveries from running the set of experiments relating to the addition of artificial sensor noise. Firstly, even slight inaccuracies in the locations (given through artificial sensor noise), produced aggregation that had a mean average distance twice that of the control run, as seen in Fig. 5. Results past 5 cm standard deviation have similar distributions and medians - this is likely due to the size of the arena limiting the possible spread of the robots, so would be expected to be greater in a larger arena. As shown in Table 2, all of the results were determined to be statistically significant, and were classed as a large effect by the Vargha-Delaney 'A' Measure.

The Buzz script (Listing 1 had a tolerance of 25° on either side of a Pi-puck's front heading, where it determined a neighbour to be directly in front of it. With the incorporation of noise, the location of the neighbour (in the robot's 'eyes') is erratic and likely jumps between its field of view and its blind spot. From visual observation, it is notable that as the standard deviation of sensor noise increased, the robots began to spiral indefinitely, as they were unable to pinpoint an accurate location on any of their neighbours. Inaccurate range-and-bearing sensing directly affects a swarm's ability to aggregate, so significantly higher average inter-robot distances are to be expected as sensor noise increases.

4.3   Joint Effect of Packet Loss and Artificial Sensor Noise

The 3D colour map shown in Fig. 6 depicts the relationship between packet loss and sensor noise with respect to the swarm's ability to aggregate. The points plotted represent the median value of each set of results. From the graph, it can be seen that the addition of artificial sensor noise has a much more immediate effect on the quality of the aggregation. With both variables at their maximum,

Table 2. Statistical analysis breakdown of the experiments run with sensor noise. Bold values are significant according to α threshold of 0.05. Asterisked values are classed as a large effect.

Sensor noise amount	1 cm std	5 cm std	10 cm std	20 cm std
Mann-Whitney U test	**0.00580**	**1.83×10^{-4}**	**1.83×10^{-4}**	**1.83×10^{-4}**
Kolmogorov-Smirnov test	**0.00206**	**1.08×10^{-5}**	**1.08×10^{-5}**	**1.08×10^{-5}**
Vargha-Delaney 'A' Measure	0.708*	0.878*	0.878*	0.878*

the aggregation performed the worst, with little to no aggregation occurring at a median value of approximately 0.5 m. In comparison to sensor noise, the effect of packet loss was unnoticeable at lowest levels, whereas the effect of sensor noise was extreme – doubling the spread of the aggregation from 0.12 m to 0.25 m. At its worst, the robots failed to aggregate, and averaged a distance of 0.53 m – an aggregation spread around 4 times that of the control run.

Buzz, as a swarm programming language, held up relatively well at lower thresholds of infrastructural testing, however struggled under extremities. When considering programmability – Buzz's main aim – it allows the development of aggregation algorithms with ease (once the background infrastructure is setup for the robot platform). However, due to Buzz's extensible nature, it only functions as well as its underlying infrastructure. As such, any infrastructural strain will harm the performance of swarm algorithms developed with the language. Infrastructural imperfections are to be expected, so any swarm programming language should be able to accommodate these imperfections. Buzz's top-down

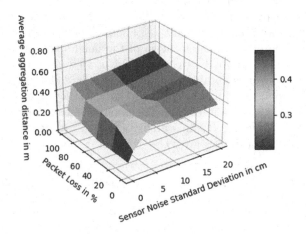

Fig. 6. 3D colour map showing the effect of packet loss and sensor noise on aggregation quality, where each point represents the average of 10 experiments.

focus enables simplistic programming of complex swarm behaviours (common amongst other swarm programming languages like Koord), freeing the developer of low-level concerns. However, it interfaces with low-level drivers that could be modified to accommodate real-world imperfections such as sensor noise, rather than introducing error checking into the high-level language itself.

5   Conclusion and Future Work

This paper has presented an open source integration of the Buzz swarm programming language with the Pi-puck robot platform and has analysed the effect of packet loss and position sensing noise on a simple aggregation algorithm as a case study. From the experimental results, it is evident that Buzz is quite tolerant to dropped packets, performing well at even 50% packet loss. However, Buzz struggles to tolerate inaccurate range-and-bearing sensing in its implementation. Buzz provides abstraction to the level that a programmer chooses, which puts the problems of packet loss and sensor noise back into the hands of the developer, allowing them to accommodate for infrastructural limitations in their embedded platforms. Buzz is currently a useful language for programming robotic swarm simulations and experiments in controlled lab conditions, however poorly implemented embedded infrastructure (controllers poorly adapted for sensor noise/external imperfections) hamper its ability in real-world performance, as expected with any application.

Although we only focus on the single case study of aggregation in this paper, we expect the results to generalise to other swarm behaviours that require range-and-bearing sensing and virtual stigmergy. In future work, we will extend our research to analyse a wider range of swarm behaviours in Buzz, notably that of foraging and task allocation due to its parallels with aggregation. For Buzz to become a widely adopted programming language for robot swarms, it requires robust hardware for it to be built upon. In order to function on a fully embedded robot, it can tolerate 50% packet loss and around 5–10 cm of inaccuracy in range-and-bearing sensor readings. Future development of Buzz could integrate a middleware layer between the BVM and the low-level API calls that drive the robot platform. This middleware layer could be used to fine-tune sensor readings in order to systematically ensure that noisy sensors do not hamper the quality of the developed swarm algorithms. This would enable simulator-like functionality despite the imperfections of the real world.

References

1. Alden, K., Read, M., Timmis, J., Andrews, P.S., Veiga-Fernandes, H., Coles, M.: Spartan: a comprehensive tool for understanding uncertainty in simulations of biological systems. PLoS Comput. Biol. **9**(2), e1002916 (2013)
2. Allen, J.M., Joyce, R., Millard, A.G., Gray, I.: The pi-puck ecosystem: hardware and software support for the e-puck and e-puck2. In: Dorigo, M., et al. (eds.) ANTS 2020. LNCS, vol. 12421, pp. 243–255. Springer, Cham (2020). https://doi.org/10.1007/978-3-030-60376-2_19
3. de Azambuja, R., Fouad, H., Beltrame, G.: When being soft makes you tough: a collision resilient quadcopter inspired by arthropod exoskeletons. CoRR abs/2103.04423 (2021)
4. Brambilla, M., Ferrante, E., Birattari, M., Dorigo, M.: Swarm robotics: a review from the swarm engineering perspective. Swarm Intell. **7**(1), 1–41 (2013)
5. Fouad, H., St-Onge, D., Beltrame, G.: BittyBuzz: a software stack for microcontroller-powered robot swarms. In: Affiche présentée lors de la conférence: Colloque annuel ReSMiQ (2019)
6. Francesca, G., Birattari, M.: Automatic design of robot swarms: achievements and challenges. Front. Robot. AI **3**, 29 (2016)
7. Francesca, G., et al.: An experiment in automatic design of robot swarms. In: Dorigo, M., et al. (eds.) ANTS 2014. LNCS, vol. 8667, pp. 25–37. Springer, Cham (2014). https://doi.org/10.1007/978-3-319-09952-1_3
8. Garattoni, L., Francesca, G., Brutschy, A., Pinciroli, C., Birattari, M.: Software infrastructure for e-puck (and TAM). Technical report, IRIDIA, Université Libre de Bruxelles (2016)
9. Garrido-Jurado, S., Muñoz-Salinas, R., Madrid-Cuevas, F.J., Marín-Jiménez, M.J.: Automatic generation and detection of highly reliable fiducial markers under occlusion. Pattern Recogn. **47**(6), 2280–2292 (2014)
10. Ghosh, R., Hsieh, C., Misailovic, S., Mitra, S.: Koord: a language for programming and verifying distributed robotics application. Proc. ACM Program. Lang. **4**(OOPSLA), 1–30 (2020)
11. Gutiérrez, Á., Campo, A., Dorigo, M., Donate, J., Monasterio-Huelin, F., Magdalena, L.: Open e-puck range & bearing miniaturized board for local communication in swarm robotics. In: 2009 IEEE International Conference on Robotics and Automation, pp. 3111–3116. IEEE (2009)
12. Hassan, H.A., Arseneault, S.: `commhub_udp` (2022). https://www.github.com/Hassan-Ali-Hassan/commhub_udp. Accessed 19 Apr 2022
13. Hassan, H.A., Beltrame, G.: `BuzzCognifly` (2022). https://www.github.com/Hassan-Ali-Hassan/BuzzCognifly. Accessed 19 Apr 2022
14. Li, G., St-Onge, D., Pinciroli, C., Gasparri, A., Garone, E., Beltrame, G.: Decentralized progressive shape formation with robot swarms. Auton. Robot. **43**(6), 1505–1521 (2018). https://doi.org/10.1007/s10514-018-9807-5
15. Mann, H.B., Whitney, D.R.: On a test of whether one of two random variables is stochastically larger than the other. Ann. Math. Stat. 50–60 (1947)
16. Massey, F.J., Jr.: The Kolmogorov-Smirnov test for goodness of fit. J. Am. Stat. Assoc. **46**(253), 68–78 (1951)
17. Mataric, M.J.: Designing and understanding adaptive group behavior. Adapt. Behav. **4**(1), 51–80 (1995)
18. Millard, A.G., et al.: The Pi-puck extension board: a Raspberry Pi interface for the e-puck robot platform. In: 2017 IEEE/RSJ International Conference on Intelligent Robots and Systems (IROS), pp. 741–748 (2017)

19. Mondada, F., et al.: The e-puck, a robot designed for education in engineering. In: Proceedings of the 9th Conference on Autonomous Robot Systems and Competitions, vol. 1, pp. 59–65. IPCB: Instituto Politécnico de Castelo Branco (2009)
20. Neale, A.: BuzzPiPuck (2022). https://www.github.com/AidenNeale/BuzzPiPuck. Accessed 19 Apr 2022
21. Neale, A.: Robot Communication Hub (2022). https://www.github.com/AidenNeale/Robot_Communication_Hub. Accessed 19 Apr 2022
22. OpenCV: OpenCV (2022). https://opencv.org/. Accessed 23 Apr 2022
23. Pinciroli, C.: Buzz Examples (2018). https://www.github.com/MISTLab/Buzz_Examples. Accessed 21 Apr 2022
24. Pinciroli, C., Beltrame, G.: Buzz: an extensible programming language for heterogeneous swarm robotics. In: 2016 IEEE/RSJ International Conference on Intelligent Robots and Systems (IROS), pp. 3794–3800 (2016)
25. Pinciroli, C., et al.: ARGoS: a modular, parallel, multi-engine simulator for multi-robot systems. Swarm Intell. **6**, 271–295 (2012)
26. Pinciroli, C., et al.: Blabbermouth (2016). https://github.com/ilpincy/blabbermouth. Accessed 27 Apr 2022
27. Pinciroli, C., et al.: BzzKh4 (2016). https://github.com/MISTLab/BuzzKH4. Accessed 27 Apr 2022
28. Rubenstein, M., Ahler, C., Nagpal, R.: Kilobot: a low cost scalable robot system for collective behaviors. In: 2012 IEEE International Conference on Robotics and Automation, pp. 3293–3298 (2012)
29. Soares, J.M., Navarro, I., Martinoli, A.: The Khepera IV mobile robot: performance evaluation, sensory data and software toolbox. In: Reis, L.P., Moreira, A.P., Lima, P.U., Montano, L., Muñoz-Martinez, V. (eds.) Robot 2015: Second Iberian Robotics Conference. AISC, vol. 417, pp. 767–781. Springer, Cham (2016). https://doi.org/10.1007/978-3-319-27146-0_59
30. St-Onge, D., Varadharajan, V.S., Li, G., Svogor, I., Beltrame, G.: ROS and Buzz: consensus-based behaviors for heterogeneous teams. arXiv:1710.08843v1, pp. 1–7 (2017)
31. Støy, K., et al.: Using situated communication in distributed autonomous mobile robotics. In: SCAI, vol. 1, pp. 44–52 (2001)
32. Vargha, A., Delaney, H.D.: A critique and improvement of the CL common language effect size statistics of McGraw and Wong. J. Educ. Behav. Stat. **25**(2), 101–132 (2000)

Implementing and Assessing a Remote Teleoperation Setup with a Digital Twin Using Cloud Networking

Erwin Jose Lopez Pulgarin[(⊠)]🔟, Hanlin Niu🔟, Guido Herrmann🔟, and Joaquin Carrasco🔟

Department of Electrical and Electronic Engineering (EEE),
University of Manchester, Manchester, UK
{erwin.lopezpulgarin,hanlin.niu,guido.herrmann,
joaquin.carrasco}@manchester.ac.uk

Abstract. Teleoperation of robotic devices such as robotic manipulators is an important functionality for operation when access to a location is restricted. Teleoperation requires to both display relevant information to an operator in the local side, and to send control commands to the remote side, which only becomes more challenging when no direct connection (i.e., wired connection) is available. New digital representations such as digital twins increase the complexity of any teleoperation system, as digital twins tend to rely on virtual reality (VR) representations, combining heterogeneous data sources coming from both local and remote sides at different data rates (e.g., camera feedback, robot positions and control signals). A remote teleoperation scheme for a robotic manipulator was implemented and assessed. The teleoperation system includes a user requesting new positions for the robot's end-effector from the remote side, and an inverse kinematics solver with the robot controller in the local side. A cloud-based networking solution to connect the robot (i.e., remote side) and the operator (i.e., local side) was implemented using a general internet connection available in Windows and Linux. Its functionality was tested and compared against a wired teleoperation scenario, showing that the average experience and performance of the cloud-based solution is the same as the wired scenario. All the configuration scripts for the cloud-based solution and the data analysis scripts are available at https://doi.org/10.5281/zenodo.6840823, to be used as a baseline for future developments.

Keywords: Teleoperation · Control · Digital twin · Cloud computing · Networking · Robotics

1 Introduction

Teleoperation has become the standard solution to operate a device located in a remote or restricted area. In robotics, teleoperation has seen large adoption

This project was funded by the EPSRC grants [EP/R026084/1] and [EP/S03286X/1].

in many applications, including robot surgery [1] and nuclear decommissioning [13]. However, many of its aspects are still open research challenges, as it involves areas such as Human Robot Interaction (HRI), robotics, user interface design, networking and control.

A teleoperation system involves a Human Machine interface (HMi) to present information to (e.g., video feed) and capture inputs (e.g., joystick inputs) from the human operator, which becomes a critical part of the system's performance [4]. The dynamic aspect of visualization and control interfaces has a considerable impact on performance and need special consideration when designing a teleoperation system. Although delays (i.e., time it takes for information to be sent and received) are an important dynamic aspect, jitter (i.e., time difference between delays) plays a significantly larger role in producing discomfort and instabilities in control. Considering that humans can adapt to delayed signals to an extent [1], it is then important to reduce delay but eliminate the differences in delay as much as possible.

Digital Twins have gained relevance in both academic and industrial fields [2,12], as it promises the possibility of creating a digital replica of a system connected to its real counterpart, which is aimed at improving its understanding and controllability. As such, a digital twin is more than a realistic simulation or a display for sensor data, as it is designed for a particular business or task-oriented applications [3,19]. The use of a Digital Twin for teleoperation would make the system more realistic, as it would include environmental data in a 3D environment, which would make controlling the Digital Twin as similar as controlling the Real Robot itself. These benefits come with an increase in the bandwidth necessary to accommodate more sensor and robot data, potentially making the system slow or unstable. Solutions to reduce data size exist in the form of compression and decompression schemes [14], but the requirement for lager bandwidth in comparison to traditional teleoperation remains.

Many modern robotic systems are built on top of standard general computing units, running Linux and the Robotic Operating System (ROS) [16], with access to consumer networking based on TCP/IP for addressing and communicating with other devices in a local network, either wired or wireless. Other data transmission stacks exist such as Fieldbus over RS-485, industrial Ethernet such as Modbus and industrial wireless such as HART [12], but recent trends have pushed to adopt IP-enabled solutions like Ethernet to facilitate intercommunication with high-level functionality such as the Internet. In fact, many remote teleoperation systems rely on the internet to connect remote and local sides, including commercial solutions [5,18] for remote teleoperation of robotic arms. However, reliable remote teleoperation using a general internet connection is still an open challenge of great technological complexity.

This work explores a remote teleoperation scheme designed to control a robotic arm equipped with a gripper. By creating a digital twin of the remote side [10,11], control commands can be delivered to the robot, whilst receiving both a video feed from the controlled scene and an updated state of the robot, both visualized as part of a digital twin. The local and remote sides were able to communicate with each other using a Virtual Network created on a cloud provider's virtual machine. This allowed for the ROS-based system to work over long distances, providing acceptable performance for realistic teleoperation applications. This scheme was tested against a wired connection and its performance compared. The remainder of this paper is divided as follows: Sect. 2 explains the teleoperation system used, the cloud-based networking solution, and the designed testing methodology. Section 3 shows the results of the implemented technology and its measured performance. Finally, Sect. 4 discusses conclusions and future work.

2 Methods

2.1 Teleoperation System

The remote teleoperation system was composed of a robotic system with a robot arm to be controlled remotely (i.e., remote side) and a digital twin in VR to control and visualize the robot on (i.e., local side). This setup is based on previous work for local (i.e., wired) teleoperation setups [10,11], with reported good performance and stability. Both sides had their functionalities implemented in software running on personal computers (PCs) connected to several devices, as seen in Fig. 1. Each side will be explained next.

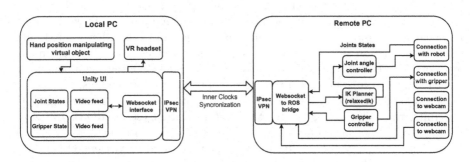

Fig. 1. Components of Teleoperation system for both Local and Remote sides.

Local Side. The local side was designed for seamless teleoperation, including aspects of intuitive teleoperation, intuitive hand gestures and immersive displays [7,9]. A digital twin was designed using Unity 2019, replicating the remote environment of a UR5 CB3 robot, a 3-Finger Adaptive Robot Gripper and two webcams placed on the top and the side of a table, as seen in Fig. 2; the robot and gripper joints move based on the information received from the remote side. An HTC Vive Pro headset is used to display and navigate the digital twin in a VR environment, and a Leapmotion device is used to capture hand pose and commands to interact with the digital twin. The system runs on a Dell Alienware 15 R4 Laptop (Intel i7-8750 2.20 GHz, 16 GB RAM) over Windows 10. The user can interact with a virtual marker in the VR scene, and any change to its position and orientation is sent to the remote side to be replicated by the real robot. The user can open or close the gripper by closing or opening their hand whilst manipulating the virtual marker. The system uses ROS# to take advantage of the ROS framework for message serialization, and its Websocket interface to communicate with the robotic system bidirectional.

Fig. 2. Digital Twin presented in the local side on VR.

Remote Side. The remote side runs a system based on ROS Melodic, connecting a UR5 CB3 robot equipped with a 3-Finger Adaptive Robot Gripper and two Logitech C920 webcams. The UR5 and gripper are interfaced via one Ethernet/IP cable each, with the cameras using USB2. The system runs on a Dell Alienware 15 R4 Laptop (Intel i7-8750 2.20 GHz, 16 GB RAM) over Linux Ubuntu 16. The Websocket rosbridge server is used to send and receive messages to non-native ROS clients such as the Digital Twin. The inverse kinematics planner relaxedik [17] is used to generate feasible joint angles from the position and orientation changes sent by the user. A joint position controller is used to move the robot with the angles generated by relaxedik. Gripper commands sent by the user (i.e., open or close) are replicated by the gripper controller.

Both remote and local sides can be seen in Fig. 3, with an operator attempting to grab an object in the remote side, aided by the digital twin with the video feeds of the remote workspace.

2.2   Cloud-Based Networking

For non-remote deployments (i.e., physically close to each other), the Local and Remote sides described in Sect. 2.1 communicate with each other by being

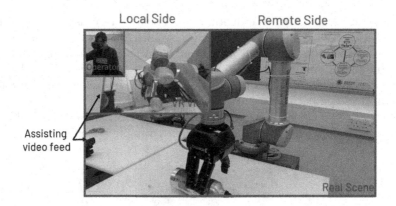

Fig. 3. Teleoperation setup. Local side with visualization (HTC Vive Pro for VR View) and control (Leapmotion) devices, and Remote side with the controlled robot (UR5) and additional sensor feedback (two webcams) from the Real Scene.

connected to the same local network in the form of a Wi-Fi (e.g., IEEE 802.11a/b/g/n/ac) or wired router, and both sides being addressable by an IP address in the same subnet, as described by the OSI model for layer 1 (i.e., Physical Layer) and 3 (i.e., Network Layer) respectively. As both sides were expected to have a stable connection to the internet, a solution that worked at the layer 3 of the OSI model was selected, to take advantage of the internet connection and to use the functionality of the ROS system using TCP messages (i.e., OSI layer 4, Transport Layer).

A virtual machine was used to generate a connection between the sides, allowing for messages to be sent in both directions. The virtual machine had a public IP address, which makes it addressable by both Local and Remote sides. Instead of forwarding messages using a custom implementation, a standard enterprise-ready group of protocols were selected to set up a secure connection between the sides. The group of protocols is referred to as IPSec [8] or "Internet Protocol Secure", providing additional functionality such as concealing the information exchanged (i.e., encryption) and validating the source where the packets come from (i.e., authentication), which are both fundamental in any modern internet connection. IPSec works on Linux and Windows Operating Systems (OSs) with good performance compared to newer standards such as WireGuard, which can outperform in Linux installations but are still being optimized for Windows OSs [15].

For the virtual machine, an Amazon AWS EC2 instance was used, configured as a m5.xlarge instance (2 vCPU at 3.0 GHz, 8 GB RAM, up to 10 Gbps Bandwidth) in the Europe (London) region (eu-west-2), running Ubuntu 20.04.1 LTS Linux and kernel GNU/Linux 5.4.0-1024. The software stack used for IPsec was Libreswan with xl2tpd as the L2TP provider. Authentication and encryption were done using username, passwords and a Pre-shared key with aes128-sha1-modp2048 for Phase1 and aes128-sha1 for the Phase2 algorithm.

It could be argued that using a virtual machine from a cloud provider such as Amazon (AWS) or Google (GCP) can bring loss of control over the application, as it is a complex infrastructure managed by a third party, with restrictions and configurations requiring a steep learning curve (e.g., custom network routing, throttling and bandwidth limitations). However, mature cloud providers give large control over the machine configuration and its networking limitations (e.g., the selected m5 instance provides up to 10 Gbps of throughput), which helps to select the appropriate configuration. This solution is to our knowledge the only way besides peer to peer (P2P) communication that allows to avoid the buffer and desynchronization effects induced by third-party routing services aimed at streaming general media or relaying assets in virtual networks (e.g., local server exposed to a public IP) without expensive traffic markup at the Internet Service Provider (ISP) level.

2.3   Testing and Validation

A set of experiments and metrics were used to validate the remote teleoperation scheme and its performance compared to a traditional wired setup. The digital twin was used in the local side to operate the robot on the remote side whilst data was being recorded on both ends, as seen in Fig. 4. Data in the remote side was recorded using the ROS tool rosbag, which saves any selected topic on disk

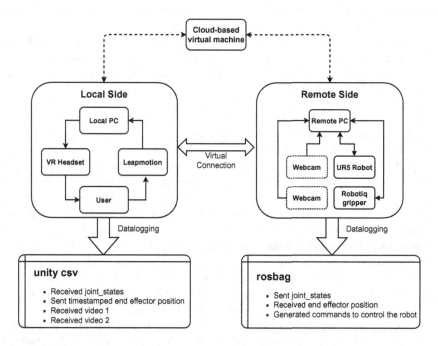

Fig. 4. Remote teleoperation components, with data being recorded during experimental validation.

and estimates the effective frequency rate of the topic. In the local side, data was recorded as a comma separated value file (csv) using a custom file written per topic of interest, recording a timestamp and the value of the topic just after it is sent or received. On the remote side, the joints position, the end effector positions requested by the local side and the generated commands to move the robot arm were recorded. In the local side, joints position, requested new position for the arm and the time of arrival for each video frame were recorded. These data were recorded to compare the impact of the setup in the data used for visualization (e.g., joint states and video feed) and to control the robot (e.g., end effector position and commands to control robot) in both sides.

The experiment consisted of a user reaching towards a position to grasp an object, using controlled movements of the robot's end effector in all directions (i.e., x, y and z axes) at a constant low speed. This action was performed for both wired and remote scenarios. The wired scenario involved using a RJ45 cable to connect the Remote PC directly to the Local PC assigning static IPs, reducing jitter to a minimum whilst achieving maximum throughput. The remote scenario had both sides connected to the internet with a general, non-managed network (i.e., Eduroam), sharing traffic with other users and having no control over the underlying networking infrastructure (e.g., this network does not allow for peers to share network packets between each other without special IT configuration); all traffic was routed to the virtual machine in London and back to our labs in Manchester. During both scenario, both local and remote sides were on the same room as a safety measure, but the remote setup has been used over larger distances such as from Edinburgh to Manchester.

Analysis and performance metrics were generated based on the network performance and its impact on the application (i.e., digital twin receiving data from the robotic system and controlling it simultaneously) during both scenarios. The following process was followed:

1. **Nominal Bandwidth and Latency measurements:** The nominal bandwidth and latency of each scenario was measured, to quantify the ideal performance in both scenarios. These measures serve only as an indicator of expected performance, as network performance concerning the internet is always an estimation that changes over time due to congestion. For the wired scenario, these measures were done point to point. For the remote scenario, the bandwidth and latency were first measured from each point to the virtual server, to then connect them and measure it point to point; this was done to understand the impact of the re-routing taking place in the virtual server.

2. **Differences in delay per topic:** The effective timing or differences in delay between the data received per channel were analysed. As a delay is the time between two consecutive messages, a difference in delay or jitter does not measure how fast messages are received but how consistent its speed is; large differences in delay should impact performance, as sudden burst of position commands should generate motion artefacts (i.e., jittery) in the robot motion.

3. **Torque variability on the robot:** The reported control effort (i.e., torque exerted by each joint during operation) was analysed to quantify motion

smoothness, as large sudden values would coincide with sudden position changes caused by delays or burst of data in the network.

Latency estimation was done using the ping and netperf tools to get complete knowledge about latency; ping uses the ICMP protocol, whilst netperf uses TCP under its TCP_RR profile. Both latency tools were tried with interval burst every 10 ms. For bandwidth estimation, netperf with the TCP_STREAM profile was used. The difference in delays was analysed using both the reported rosbag frequency rate and by calculating the delay as the time difference of subsequent messages based on their timestamp. Netperf version 2.7 was used, built on a Docker based on Linux Alpine 3.7 running on each side as clients and on the virtual machine as a server. Data analysis was performed using Python 3.7 with the pandas and numpy libraries. All network testing lasted for 120 s each.

3   Results

Experiments were performed, with two experimental trials per configuration and a duration of one minute each. The user reported a responsive and uninterrupted operation. No messages were lost during any of the experimental trials.

Bandwidth and latency were measured in each setup. The wired setup reported latencies around 1 ms, with ICMP traffic reporting 0.5 ms in average and 1.8 ms in average for TCP traffic. Estimated bandwidth was 111 MegaBytes per second (MBps) for TCP traffic. These performance metrics were expected, as both sides were using a Gigabit Ethernet connection. For the remote setup, the latency and bandwidth from each side to the virtual server was of 12 ms (11 ms ICMP, 15 ms TCP) and 9.82 MBps respectively, which is a drop relative to the reported average of 16 MBps for Eduroam. The latency and bandwidth reported after connecting the sides using the virtual machine were of 20 ms (19 ms ICMP, 22 ms TCP) and 7 MBps. As a point of reference, the estimated maximum necessary bandwidth to accommodate for the data being transferred during teleoperation was around 4.6 Mbps. This was calculated using the approximate size of the message, times its frequency rate per topic: two video topics of 75 Kb each 30 Hz require 4.5 Mbps, one joint state topic of 0.5 Kb 100 Hz requires 0.05 Mbps and one end-effector position change topic requiring 0.025 Mbps. Although the remote setup brings larger latency and smaller bandwidth, its estimated values are enough to connect the digital twin to the robotic system.

The difference in delay per channel was analysed between remote and local side. Table 1 shows the statistical descriptors of the calculated delay per topic for both setups and with different transmission loads (i.e., with and without the video topic) on the remote side. The wired setup reported the shortest mean delays with the lowest standard deviation, as expected from using a dedicated network with no additional traffic. In contrast, the remote setup showed larger standard deviation and maximum values, with messages taking longer to reach or be sent. These large values are due to burst of messages being queued and delivered at once, as proven by achieving lower minimum delays as transmission

Table 1. Delay measured in the remote side for all topics for both setups and under different transmission loads.

Data channel	Statistic	Remote setup		Wired setup	
		No video	Video	No video	Video
Joints position [ms]	mean	7.9	9.1	0.16	9.9
	std	2.1	4.8	0.05	0.05
	max	15.2	29.86	3.67	10.3
	min	6.7	0.002	0.002	9.6
End effector position request [ms]	mean	8.0	9.1	0.1	10.0
	std	2.1	7.1	0.05	0.04
	max	15.2	98.6	3.3	10.3
	min	6.6	0.002	0.001	9.72
Commands to Robot [ms]	mean	8.0	9.1	0.1	10.0
	std	2.11	8.67	0.05	0.05
	max	15.1	150.9	3.9	10.67
	min	6.7	0.003	0.002	9.29

load increases (i.e., minimum delay during video transmission is small). Similarly, the use of video increased delay for both setups, resulting in similar mean delays for both setups.

Delays in the local side were similar in average between setups, with large variability in some data channels, as seen in the remote side. Table 2 shows the statistical descriptors of the calculated delay per topic for both setups and with different transmission loads (i.e., with and without the video topic) on the local side. Similar to results in Table 1, average values were similar between setups, with larger variability in some data channels; the new requested position was the least affected as it is generated in the local side. Maximum delay for the video feed data channels suggest that the remote setup can induce up to 6 frames delay, in comparison to 1 frame in the wired setup. In addition, the received joints position can be delayed up to three times more in the remote setup. However, these artefacts were not perceived from the user perspective.

To complement the measured delay results, reported frequency rates from the recorded rosbags were analysed. No significant difference was reported between setups or during video transmission, with frequency drops from 6034 Hz to 5866 Hz under remote operation and from 6009 Hz to 5882 Hz under wired operation. It is worth nothing that this only reflects on the bandwidth used in the remote side and not on the overall performance of the system.

Assessing the reported control effort from the robot position controller would show how high control forces were during teleoperation. Considering that no sudden movements were performed by the operator, all reported values should be similar. Table 3 shows the absolute reported values, with a similar behaviour to the control and sensor measurements provided in Table 1 and 2. High variability

Table 2. Delay measurements in the local side for all topics for both setups and under different transmission loads.

Data channel	Statistic	Remote setup		Wired setup	
		No video	Video	No video	Video
Joints position [ms]	mean	8.7	8.7	8.7	8.7
	std	5.24	6.17	3.74	4.27
	max	123	156	30	53
	min	0.0	0.0	1.0	0.001
End effector position request [ms]	mean	10.13	10.10	10.12	10.12
	std	10.37	9.71	10.7	10.4
	max	641.0	588.0	677.0	708.0
	min	2.0	2.0	2.0	3.0
Video feed 1 [ms]	mean		36.4		36.34
	std		12.93		8.2
	max		163.0		68.0
	min		2.0		1.0
Video feed 2 [ms]	mean		36.4		36.46
	std		13.47		8.05
	max		185.0		66.00
	min		4.0		2.0

and maximum values in these measurements implies that slight vibrations and aggressive motion were present when using the remote setup. The user confirmed this behaviour and described it as sporadic, only occurring momentarily and not affecting the task itself. This behaviour is evident when observing Joint 1, 2 and 3, which were primarily used whilst positioning the end effector. However, overall average metrics point at the task not being negatively affected by the remote setup.

The results show similar average performance between wired and remote setups. However, the impact of network latency is seen to increase the standard deviation and maximum values reported in Tables 1 and 2, with the remote setup producing larger and more varied delays. These results are expected from a non-managed network sharing traffic with other users, as no timing guaranties can be given in such networks. The impact of these delays are reduced thanks to the controller in the remote side dealing with the robot's dynamics, and the digital twin providing enough feedback to the user in the form of visualization of the remote robot and video feed to reduce the likeliness of user-induced oscillations (i.e., aggressively corrective behaviour). These results should serve as a baseline of performance in remote teleoperation, understanding that external factors such as internet congestion can affect overall performance. However, achieving similar average performance to that of a wired setup with little reconfiguration is of great value for testing and development.

Table 3. Absolute value of the control effort per joint for both setups and under different transmission loads.

Data channel	Statistic	Remote setup		Wired setup	
		No video	Video	No video	Video
Joint 1 [Nm]	mean	1.61	1.58	1.52	1.68
	std	0.69	0.67	0.57	0.34
	max	5.58	12.47	4.14	3.67
	min	0.002	0.004	0.01	0.01
Joint 2 [Nm]	mean	1.06	1.19	1.4	1.14
	std	0.67	0.67	0.72	0.37
	max	5.84	6.71	5.14	5.96
	min	0.0	0.0	0.0	0.002
Joint 3 [Nm]	mean	0.7	0.69	0.71	0.26
	std	0.45	0.57	0.52	0.36
	max	4.38	12.38	3.4	6.2
	min	0.0	0.0	0.0	0.0
Joint 4 [Nm]	mean	0.3	0.26	0.24	0.19
	std	0.18	0.18	0.16	0.09
	max	1.14	1.30	0.91	0.96
	min	0.0	0.0	0.0	0.0
Joint 5 [Nm]	mean	0.17	0.19	0.20	0.09
	std	0.13	0.14	0.13	0.08
	max	0.72	0.67	0.70	0.68
	min	0.0	0.0	0.0	0.0
Joint 6 [Nm]	mean	0.15	0.18	0.19	0.11
	std	0.12	0.11	0.10	0.09
	max	0.64	1.48	0.61	0.71
	min	0.0	0.0	0.0	0.0

4   Conclusions

This work presented an implementation and assessment of a remote teleoperation setup that creates a reliable solution for remote teleoperation, by relaying network traffic via the internet. By using a custom virtual machine with a public IP address, local and remote sides were connected securely through the internet, allowing for similar performance as in a wired setup. A digital twin is used in the local side to visualize and interact with the remote side, aiding in the teleoperation. This approach relies on open technology (e.g., TCP, Websockets, ROS, Linux) and can be used with any modern computer with a stable internet connection. Measuring delays whilst using the Virtual Network connection shown it had a small impact on the robot controllability and smoothness of motion, not perceived in most cases.

Future work will focus on using peer to peer (P2P) and mesh communication in the cloud, based on technology that allows to solve Network Address Translation (NAT) such as WebRTC [6], exploring how dedicated data channels per type of data (i.e., video, control signals) with time-frame synchronization can be used for remote teleoperation.

References

1. Anvari, M.: Remote telepresence surgery: the Canadian experience (2007). https://doi.org/10.1007/s00464-006-9040-8
2. Barricelli, B.R., Casiraghi, E., Fogli, D.: A survey on digital twin: definitions, characteristics, applications, and design implications (2019). https://doi.org/10.1109/ACCESS.2019.2953499
3. Chang, C.T., Rosen, E., Groechel, T.R., Walker, M., Forde, J.Z.: Virtual, augmented, and mixed reality for HRI (VAM-HRI). In: Companion 2022 ACM/IEEE International Conference on Human-Robot Interaction (2022). https://doi.org/10.5555/3523760.3523991. https://vam-hri.github.io/
4. Chen, J.Y.C., Haas, E.C., Barnes, M.J.: Human performance issues and user interface design for teleoperated robots. IEEE Trans. Syst. Man Cybern. Part C (Appl. Rev.) **37**(6), 1231–1245 (2007). https://doi.org/10.1109/TSMCC.2007.905819. https://ieeexplore.ieee.org/document/4343985/
5. Extend Robotics: VR—Extend Robotics—England. https://www.extendrobotics.com/
6. Garcia, B., Gortazar, F., Lopez-Fernandez, L., Gallego, M., Paris, M.: WebRTC testing: challenges and practical solutions. IEEE Commun. Stand. Mag. **1**(2), 36–42 (2017). https://doi.org/10.1109/MCOMSTD.2017.1700005
7. Ghosh, A., Paredes Soto, D.A., Veres, S.M., Rossiter, A.: Human robot interaction for future remote manipulations in Industry 4.0. IFAC-PapersOnLine **53**(2), 10223–10228 (2020). https://doi.org/10.1016/j.ifacol.2020.12.2752
8. Goethals, T., Kerkhove, D., Volckaert, B., Turck, F.D.: Scalability evaluation of VPN technologies for secure container networking. In: 2019 15th International Conference on Network and Service Management, pp. 1–7 (2019). https://doi.org/10.23919/CNSM46954.2019.9012673
9. Hirschmanner, M., Tsiourti, C., Patten, T., Vincze, M.: Virtual reality teleoperation of a humanoid robot using markerless human upper body pose imitation. In: IEEE-RAS International Conference on Humanoid Robots, vol. 2019-Octob, pp. 259–265. IEEE Computer Society (2019). https://doi.org/10.1109/Humanoids43949.2019.9035064
10. Jang, I., Carrasco, J., Weightman, A., Lennox, B.: Intuitive bare-hand teleoperation of a robotic manipulator using virtual reality and leap motion. In: Althoefer, K., Konstantinova, J., Zhang, K. (eds.) TAROS 2019. LNCS (LNAI), vol. 11650, pp. 283–294. Springer, Cham (2019). https://doi.org/10.1007/978-3-030-25332-5_25
11. Jang, I., Niu, H., Collins, E.C., Weightman, A., Carrasco, J., Lennox, B.: Virtual kinesthetic teaching for bimanual telemanipulation. In: 2021 IEEE/SICE International Symposium on System Integration SII 2021, pp. 120–125. Institute of Electrical and Electronics Engineers Inc. (2021). https://doi.org/10.1109/IEEECONF49454.2021.9382763

12. Lu, Y., Liu, C., Wang, K.I.K., Huang, H., Xu, X.: Digital twin-driven smart manufacturing: connotation, reference model, applications and research issues. Robot. Comput.-Integr. Manuf. **61**, 101837 (2020). https://doi.org/10.1016/j.rcim.2019.101837. https://www.sciencedirect.com/science/article/pii/S0736584519302480
13. Marturi, N., et al.: Towards advanced robotic manipulation for nuclear decommissioning: a pilot study on tele-operation and autonomy. In: International Conference on Robotics and Automation for Humanitarian Applications, RAHA 2016 - Conference Proceedings. Institute of Electrical and Electronics Engineers Inc. (2017). https://doi.org/10.1109/RAHA.2016.7931866
14. Pacheco-Gutierrez, S., Niu, H., Caliskanelli, I., Skilton, R.: A multiple level-of-detail 3D data transmission approach for low-latency remote visualisation in teleoperation tasks. Robotics **10**(3), 89 (2021). https://doi.org/10.3390/ROBOTICS10030089. www.mdpi.com/2218-6581/10/3/89/htm
15. Pudelko, M., Emmerich, P., Gallenmüller, S., Carle, G.: Performance analysis of VPN gateways. In: 2020 IFIP Networking Conference, pp. 325–333 (2020)
16. Quigley, M., et al.: ROS: an open-source robot operating system. In: ICRA Workshop on Open Source Software, Kobe, Japan, vol. 3, p. 5 (2009)
17. Rakita, D., Mutlu, B., Gleicher, M.: RelaxedIK: real-time synthesis of accurate and feasible robot arm motion. In: Robotics: Science and Systems, Pittsburgh, PA, pp. 26–30 (2018)
18. Shadow Robot: Shadow Robot Company. http://www.shadowrobot.com/
19. Shibusawa, R., Nakashige, M., Oe, K.: DualityBoard: an asymmetric remote gaming platform with mobile robots and the digital twins. In: Proceedings of the 2022 ACM/IEEE International Conference on Human-Robot Interaction, HRI 2022, pp. 1035–1039. IEEE Press (2022)

Agent-Based Simulation of Multi-robot Soil Compaction Mapping

Laurence Roberts-Elliott[1]([✉]) [iD], Gautham P. Das[1] [iD], and Alan G. Millard[2] [iD]

[1] Lincoln Agri-Robotics, University of Lincoln, Lincoln, UK
{lrobertselliott,gdas}@lincoln.ac.uk
[2] Department of Computer Science, University of York, York, UK
alan.millard@york.ac.uk

Abstract. Soil compaction, an increase in soil density and decrease in porosity, has a negative effect on crop yields, and damaging environmental impacts. Mapping soil compaction at a high resolution is an important step in enabling precision agriculture practices to address these issues. Autonomous ground-based robotic approaches using proximal sensing have been proposed as alternatives to time-consuming and costly manual soil sampling. Soil compaction has high spatial variance, which can be challenging to capture in a limited time window. A multi-robot system can parallelise the sampling process and reduce the overall sampling time. Multi-robot soil sampling is critically underexplored in literature, and requires selection of methods to efficiently coordinate the sampling. This paper presents a simulation of multi-agent spatial sampling, extending the Mesa agent-based simulation framework, with general applicability, but demonstrated here as a testbed for different methodologies of multi-robot soil compaction mapping. To reduce the necessary number of samples for accurate mapping, while maximising information gained per sample, a dynamic sampling strategy, informed by kriging variance from kriging interpolation of sampled soil compaction values, has been implemented. This is enhanced by task clustering and insertion heuristics for task queuing. Results from the evaluation trials show the suitability of sequential single item auctions in this highly dynamic environment, and high interpolation accuracy resulting from our dynamic sampling, with avenues for improvements in this bespoke sampling methodology in future work.

Keywords: Multi-robot co-ordination · Mapping · Simulation · Agriculture · Soil science

1 Introduction

Agriculture 4.0: the digitisation and automation of sensing, decision making, and operations in agriculture, has the potential to reduce waste and environmental

This work was supported by the UKRI's E3 fund via Lincoln Agri-Robotics.

harms, while simultaneously increasing crop yields. Critical to crop health and yield is management of the soil in which these crops are grown [1]. Spatial mapping of soil properties, is an important practice in precision farming, enabling localised soil management to address spatially variable deficiencies [2].

One soil property that must be minimised to produce high yields and reduce negative environmental impacts is soil compaction. Soil compaction is an increase in soil density and decrease in porosity due to load, vibration, or pressure [3]. It often results from the pressure of heavy machinery operating on the soil. High soil compaction reduces the ability of a crop's roots to penetrate the soil, reducing crop yields [4], and also results in lower concentration of organic matter, reducing the soil's ability to sequester CO_2 [5]. Retrospective land management to reduce soil compaction often involves deep tillage, with the heavy machinery required for this consuming large amounts of fossil fuels [6].

Mapping soil compaction enables this operation to be localised to the areas where it is needed, reducing the time and fuel requirements of deep tillage. For the tillage to effectively alleviate the soil compaction, it is also important that compaction is measured at a various depths, so that the machinery can be set to operate at the depth where the compaction is highest. There can be significant variance across a field as to what depth the compaction is most pronounced at, making high resolution mapping useful for this purpose [7].

Soil compaction is traditionally measured manually with handheld instruments, but this a time-consuming process. Methods for automated mapping of soil properties have been developed, decreasing time requirements while mapping at higher resolutions. For higher resolution soil mapping, and measurement at depths below the soil surface, ground-based autonomous mobile robots have been used effectively, such as [8]'s use of the Thorvald agricultural robot platform [9] to map soil compaction in 3D. Unfortunately, ground-based robots take a longer time to map the same area as UAVs. An intuitive next step to improve time efficiency, as yet unexplored in the literature on automated soil mapping, is the development and testing of a multi-robot system for ground-based soil property mapping. The work presented in this paper aims to demonstrate the utility of an efficient multi-agent spatial sampling simulation, for identifying methods of task allocation and dynamic sampling that best enable performant multi-robot mapping of soil compaction.

Soil mapping is a coverage problem, but with due to large spatial variations in soil compaction, sampling should be optimised using dynamic sampling, identifying the locations which provide the greatest information gain to environment modelling. [8] uses kriging interpolation [10] to predict soil property values in unsampled locations, using the value and position of sampled data. They also identify informative sampling locations for a single robot using kriging variance. We extend this approach for simultaneous identification of multiple task locations for a multi-robot system.

A major challenge in multi-robot systems is ensuring efficient coordination among the robots. Multi-robot task allocation (MRTA) is one of the many strategies commonly used to address this challenge. Among the different MRTA strategies, auction based approaches have been effective for dynamic task environments, where tasks are created continuously during the operation of a multi-robot team [11]. Such auction-based task allocation approaches should be suited to multi-robot soil sampling with dynamic sampling.

The core contributions of this paper are:

1. Evaluation of the performance of different MRTA methods and sampling strategies for multi-robot soil compaction mapping in simulation.
2. Extension of dynamic informative sampling location identification to multi-robot systems; and
3. An extension of the Mesa agent-based modelling framework [12], to be released as free open-source software, for rapid testing of task allocation and sampling methods for multi-agent spatial sampling systems;

The remainder of this paper is structured as follows: A related work section gives an overview of research and topics which serve as background and influence on the work of this paper. This is followed by a methodology section, which introduces an agent-based simulation of multi-robot soil compaction mapping, extending the Mesa simulation framework, and the experimental design for trials conducted within this simulation comparing methods of multi-robot task allocation, and sampling strategies. Then the results of these trials are detailed and discussed in the results section, and lastly conclusions drawn from the findings of this work, and avenues for future work are discussed in Sect. 5.

2 Related Work

2.1 Outdoor Ground Robots

Outdoor ground-based mobile robots can measure soil property data at very high spatial resolutions, lacking the issue of distance from the soil surface reducing image resolution, and having the ability to sample at various depths, and any number of points using probe sensors [13]. [14] demonstrates this, creating a layered map compositing stereo RGB, Visible/Near Infrared (VIS-NIR), and thermal images to create a high resolution 3D map including surface readings of the soil temperature and Normalized Difference Vegetation Index (NDVI), a proxy for density of plant life.

A unique advantage of ground-based outdoor robots over other types of automated soil sensing systems is that they can measure soil properties more directly and at various depths beneath the surface of the soil using probe sensors. This enables the mapping of soil properties in 3D, as demonstrated by [8], using the Thorvald agricultural robot platform equipped with an automated penetrometer to create a 3D map of soil compaction at sampling locations informed by kriging variance.

2.2 Multi-Robot Systems (MRSs)

A high sampling resolution is required to capture spatially variable soil properties, and this can be difficult to achieve for a large area within a reasonable time budget using a single robot or traditional manual measurements. Multi-robot systems have been used to reduce the time required to complete different coverage problems by parallel execution of tasks [15]. However, multi-robot soil property mapping is not well explored yet, necessitating identification of transferable methods from application of MRSs in related areas such as coverage planning, environment sampling, and dynamic task creation and allocation.

In [16], the authors show the use of a swarm of UAVs to identify volunteer potatoes in a field of sugar beet crop, using RGB aerial imagery captured and processed by the UAVs using traditional computer vision methods, and positioned in a shared co-ordinate system using GPS and IMU. The field is partitioned such that UAVs each explore non-overlapping areas of approximately equal size, moving through these in a sweeping pattern, a method developed by [17]. Such partitioning algorithms are important for efficient task allocation, further highlighted by [18], who extend Voronoi based environment partitioning to account for the heterogeneous speed, battery life, and traversability of their multi-robot team. The authors also employ an informative sampling method to generate sampling goals where these will best improve the quality of a Gaussian Process model's prediction of a distribution that is only partially sampled. This informative sampling is based on the Gaussian Process Upper Confidence Bound (GP-UCB) strategy [19]. Other relevant works that could be extended for multi-robot soil mapping are existing single-robot systems such as the examples discussed in Sect. 2.1.

Of the numerous challenges faced by a prospective multi-robot soil mapping system, and outdoor MRSs in general, the work of this paper focuses on addressing the challenge of identifying performant methods of multi-robot coordination. We test the performance of a set of combinations of multi-robot task allocation and sampling methods for multi-robot spatial sampling in a multi-robot soil compaction mapping simulation described in Sect. 3.1 in trials detailed in Sect. 3.2. Often, agricultural robots are constrained to operate around obstacles in their environment, such as between rows of trees or crops in polytunnels, fields, and orchards. This can present a challenge, with deadlocking and collisions likely between robots sharing such limited space. Co-ordination of navigation and task allocation within a MRS is necessary to address this, such as in the work of [20], dynamically allocating the parking locations of robots to maximise their availability for collecting strawberries from pickers in narrow polytunnels, considering the locations of humans and other robots to reduce the incidence of deadlocking. [11] show that a key component of multi-robot coordination, the task allocation methodology, should be selected according to the nature of the problem being addressed by the MRS. Comparing a set of auction-based task allocation methods, its authors found that the Sequential Single-Item (SSI) auction method resulted in the lowest distance, and a close second lowest runtime for task environments with dynamic task creation and clustered or distributed starting positions for the robots. This suggests SSI is suitable for the dynamic task generation present in multi-robot soil mapping which utilises a dynamic sampling methodology, such as that of the single-robot soil compaction mapping

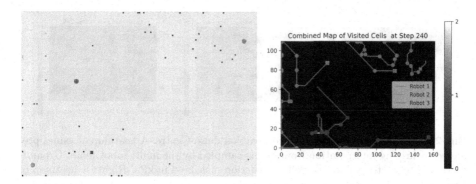

Fig. 1. Left: A screenshot from the Mesa based simulation of multi-robot spatial sampling. Robots are denoted by coloured circles. Sampled cells are denoted by grayscale squares with their intensity values corresponding to the value sampled there, in contrast to the off-white background. Right: A map of the number of times each cell has been visited, with robot trajectories and sampling points overlaid. The first sampling point is marked with a square, the last with a cross, and others with a circle.

informed by kriging variance in the work of [21]. A set of combinations of multi-robot task allocation and sampling methods are tested in a high-level abstracted simulation of a multi-robot soil mapping system detailed in Sect. 3.1.

3   Methodology

3.1   Agent-Based Simulation

A simulation of multi-robot spatial sampling has been developed in Python using the Mesa agent-based modelling framework. The Mesa framework was chosen because of its simplicity, with an intuitive API, and an abstract modelling of agents using simple 2D geometry within the cells of a 2D grid, which results in its low computational complexity. This low computational cost is also seen in the visualisation of this 2D grid with Mesa's built-in web-based user-interface which also provides live graphing of variables, and live adjustment of parameters. The Mesa-based simulation developed in this work abstracts robots as agents located within the cells of a 2D grid representing a top-down projection of an open arable field. In its present stage of development, there are no obstacles in the environment for the robots to avoid except for each other. Robots can move from their current cell to any other cell following a path calculated using A* path-finding. This allows for the likelihood of collisions to be reduced by having each robot calculate its paths using a costmap particular to each robot, wherein the cells occupied by or neighbouring robots are assigned higher costs penalising movement too close to other robots.

The robots in this simulation can be assigned sampling goal cells, which they will navigate to, and then sample the cell's corresponding value from an underlying distribution of data with the same dimensions and co-ordinate system

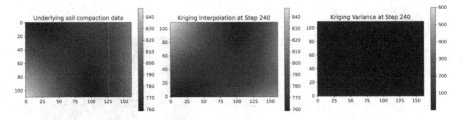

Fig. 2. Left: The ground-truth soil compaction data. Centre: A heatmap of values predicted by kriging interpolation from points sampled by the multi-robot team. Ground-truth and predicted values are soil compaction measured in kPa. Right: A heatmap of kriging variance. These figures are generated from the same simulated sampling mission pictured in Fig. 1.

as the 2D grid. Sampled values are represented on the 2D grid by changing the background colour of sampled cells to a shade of gray, with brighter shades indicative of higher values. This visualisation can be seen in a screenshot of the simulation pictured in Fig. 1.

The distribution sampled by robots in the simulation is comprised of soil compaction data recorded in a grid pattern in an arable field at 0 cm (surface) depth by a Thorvald robot with an automated penetrometer from a dataset created in [8]. Every point recorded in this ground-truth soil compaction data is interpolated to a grid wherein each cell comprises a $2\,m^2$ area, 162 cells long and 110 cells wide. The compaction measurements were recorded within an area approximately $324 \times 220\,m$. This interpolation is performed so that the grid environment of the simulation can be a higher resolution than that of the grid sampling, while still allowing robots to sample any cell of the environment. In this abstracted simulation, robots can move from their current cell to a neighbouring cell in 1 step of simulation time.

Kriging interpolation [10] is used to estimate the entire underlying distribution when only a subset of the cells have been sampled. This interpolation is calculated each time one of the robots samples a new value. In the first step of the simulation, robots sample at their randomised starting locations, as kriging interpolation requires at least 2 samples to interpolate from. Alongside a prediction of the ground-truth soil compaction, pictured in Fig. 2 (left), the kriging interpolation also outputs its variance: a matrix of values representing uncertainty in the prediction for each point. A multi-robot dynamic sampling strategy is enabled by this kriging variance, extending the kriging-based sampling of [8]. These goals can then be allocated to the robots using a multi-robot task allocation algorithm. Initially, x goals were created at the x highest variance cells, where x is the number of robots, with the aim of reducing the number of samples required to achieve accurate interpolation.

A limitation of this approach was observed in testing: the goals generated from each round of interpolation have a tendency to be located in very close proximity to each other, all selected from a small region where the highest vari-

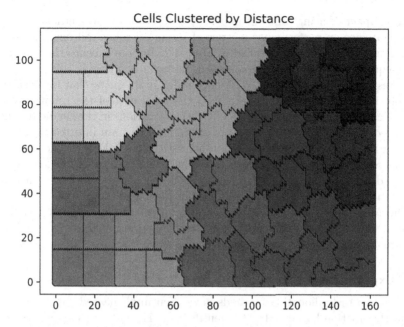

Fig. 3. Color-coded clusters of cells from the simulation's grid environment, produced by distance-based hierarchical clustering.

ance values are located. This results in sub-optimal sampling, as the variance in such a region is made lower, and the accuracy of interpolation adequately improved, by just one sample being measured there. Once one robot has sampled within this highest variance area, other robots would better improve the accuracy of the interpolation by sampling from other high variance regions of the environment. This is similar to an issue in single-robot spatial sampling noted in [22], where goals generated by dynamic sampling using the variance of Gaussian Process Regression for a single-robot sampling mission would be generated within a sub-optimally close proximity of each other. The authors addressed this by dynamically limiting the search space for high variance locations, selecting the size of the search area continuously using a reinforcement learning mode. Inspired by this solution of dynamic environment partitioning, we addressed this issue by partitioning the 2D grid environment using Euclidean distance based hierarchical clustering of all cell locations at the start of the simulation. This clustering is pictured in Fig. 3. Clusters are created using cophenetic distance, with the threshold value calculated as $\frac{\sqrt{A}}{4}$, where A is the area of the environment. The value of the denominator can be adjusted, with greater values resulting in a greater number of clusters. Goals are created from the highest variance cell within each cluster, reducing the incidence of redundant goals being generated too close to another goal. Once a sample has been taken within a cluster, goals are no longer generated within that cluster, encouraging wider exploration of the environment.

The impact of using different multi-robot task allocation methods and sampling strategies on performance metrics of the multi-robot soil mapping system are measured in the trials detailed in Sect. 3.2. Robots execute their allocated tasks sequentially from a task queue. An insertion heuristic is calculated when a new task is allocated to a robot for each index in its queue that the task could possibly be inserted at. This heuristic is the total cost of the robot travelling from its current position through all of the task locations in the candidate queue, calculated using A* path-finding. New sampling tasks are inserted in a robot's queue at the index where this insertion heuristic score is lowest. The simulation also has some visual outputs: heatmaps of the kriging interpolation, kriging variance, and the number of times a cell has been visited by the robots, with robot trajectories overlaying the latter, pictured in Figs. 1 and 2.

The Mesa-based simulation is used to run many simulated soil sampling missions with different combinations of parameters and methods of multi-robot co-ordination such as task allocation.

3.2   Experimental Design

To date, two task allocation methods have been implemented within the simulation: the auction-based SSI [23], identified in [11] as being particularly effective for dynamic task environments, and Round Robin (RR), a naive approach that distributes tasks evenly and indiscriminately between all of the robots. There are also currently two sampling strategies implemented: the kriging-based multi-robot Dynamic Sampling (DS) algorithm described in Sect. 3.1, and Random Sampling (RS), which after each round of kriging interpolation generates a number of sampling tasks equal to the number of robots, each located at a unique randomly selected unsampled cell that has not been allocated to a robot yet. In a 162×110 cell grid in the simulation, containing no obstacles, with each cell representing a 2×2 m area, 3 robots were initialised at random positions and tasked with sampling the interpolated surface soil compaction data described in Sect. 3.1. This multi-robot soil mapping mission was run for 240 steps of simulation time. The sampling mission can be executed for a longer time to allow the space to be sampled completely, but 240 steps was observed to be sufficient to allow all methods to produce a reasonably accurate interpolated map of soil compaction in initial test runs of each method.

10 of these trials were executed for each of the 4 conditions, with visual outputs and performance metrics recorded for each trial. These 4 conditions are derived from the possible combinations of the 2 task allocation methods, and 2 sampling strategies implemented in the simulation. Thus, the set of conditions is: {SSI-DS, SSI-RS, RR-DS, RR-RS}. The simulation's random number generation shares the same seed between trials across different conditions. The performance metrics recorded for each trial are as follows:

- Root Mean Squared Error (RMSE) of the kriging interpolation calculated by its difference from the ground truth soil compaction data.
- Mean of the kriging variance, with higher values representing greater overall uncertainty in the predictions of the kriging interpolation.

Table 1. Means and standard deviation (σ) of metrics across trials conducted in the agent-based simulation experiment described in Sect. 3.2.

Mean of Sim. Experiment Results	SSI DS	RR RS	SSI RS	RR DS
RMSE of kriging interpolation	5.61 σ 2.65	7.61 σ 4.29	3.84 σ 1.52	7.28 σ 1.09
Mean of kriging variance	90.14 σ 45.36	72.00 σ 41.36	38.78 σ 30.28	123.80 σ 52.59
Number of cells sampled	45.63 σ 5.32	13.89 σ 1.96	20.80 σ 5.07	31.90 σ 8.08
Mean time to complete a task (s)	16.47 σ 4.64	44.79 σ 6.92	28.67 σ 5.71	23.49 σ 6.68
Maximum visits to a cell	2 σ 0	2 σ 0	2 σ 0	2.6 σ 0.7
Total distance travelled (m)	671.5 σ 5.35	703.11 σ 1.96	640.50 σ 35.83	685.50 σ 8.13
Total idle time (s)	45.50 σ 5.35	13.89 σ 1.96	76.50 σ 35.83	31.50 σ 8.13

Table 2. One-tailed Welch's t-tests comparing the results of trials from the 1st and 2nd best performing conditions for each metric.

Significance testing results	Best method	2nd best method	p-value
RMSE of kriging interpolation	SSI RS	SSI DS	0.0520
Mean of kriging variance	SSI RS	RR RS	0.0286
Number of cells sampled	RR RS	SSI RS	0.0009
Mean time to complete a task (s)	SSI DS	RR DS	0.0074
Maximum visits to a cell	SSI DS, RR RS, SSI RS	RR DS	0.0119
Total distance travelled (m)	RR RS	RR DS	0.0230
Total idle time (s)	RR RS	RR DS	2.89E-05

- Number of cells sampled.
- Mean time to complete a task in seconds.
- Maximum visits to a cell, to serve as a proxy of soil compaction, an undesirable effect of excessive traffic on soil porosity.
- Total distance travelled in meters.
- Total idle time in seconds. The sum of the time each robot spent without a task to execute.

4   Results and Discussion

The results of the 10 simulated trials per condition described in Sect. 3.2 are summarised in Table 1 as the mean σ standard deviation of the metrics recorded for these 10 trials. Values in bold, with a light green cell fill color indicate the best performance for a metric. Cells with a yellow fill color denote that the method performed 2nd best by their corresponding metric. One-tailed Welch's t-tests [24] were performed comparing the results of trials from the 1st and 2nd best performing conditions for each metric, using a significance level of 0.05. These tests investigated the alternative hypothesis that the best performing condition's trials score significantly higher than those of the 2nd best scoring condition. These tests and their resulting p-values are documented in Table 2.

The results show that SSI-RS, the auction-based SSI, with robots each bidding on tasks based on their A* cost for travelling to the task location, combined

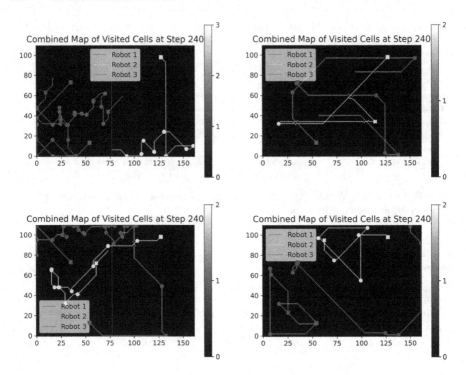

Fig. 4. Maps, from the last step of the 1st trial of each condition of the simulated experiment, of the number of times each cell has been visited, with robot trajectories and sampling points overlaid. Top left: RR-DS. Top right: RR-RS. Bottom left: SSI-DS. Bottom right: SSI-RS.

with random sampling of unsampled cells, achieves the best performance across 4 of the 7 metrics recorded. This is greater than the number of metrics any other tested method showed best performance in. These 4 metrics are: RMSE (Fig. 6), mean kriging variance (Fig. 5), maximum visits to a cell, and total distance travelled. It should be noted that SSI-RS does not perform significantly better than SSI-DS, the 2nd best method, in RMSE of kriging interpolation. It is also important to note that SSI-DS, SSI-RS, and RR-RS all achieve the same score for maximum visits to a cell, indicating identical performance across these methods in avoiding excessive soil compaction. RR-DS is the only method tested that performs worse than these other methods for maximum visits to a cell, and this performance difference was found to be statistically significant (Fig. 5).

RR-RS was found to perform best in 3 metrics, the 2nd highest after SSI-RS. These metrics are number of cells sampled, maximum visits to a cell, and total idle time. As previously discussed, RR-DS shares the low maximum visits to a cell with SSI-DS and SSI-RS. RR-RS sampled the fewest cells, but RR-RS scored the highest for RMSE of kriging interpolation, and for mean time to complete a task, so a low number of samples does not suggest strong performance in other

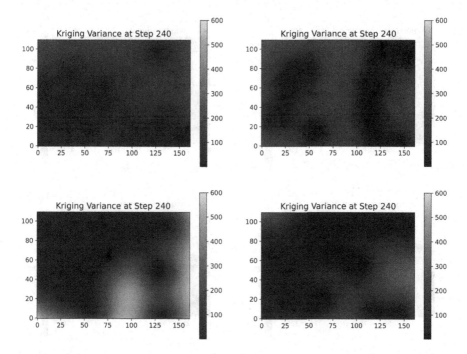

Fig. 5. Kriging variance, from kriging interpolation at the last step of the 1st trial of each condition of the simulated experiment. Top left: RR-DS. Top right: RR-RS. Bottom left: SSI-DS. Bottom right: SSI-RS.

metrics. It also saw the longest mean time to complete a sampling task, which explains the low number of samples and belies the naivety of round-robin task allocation, and random sampling. In stark contrast, SSI-DS, which sampled the highest number of cells, did not perform significantly worse than the best method when it came to the interpolation RMSE. SSI-DS also saw the lowest mean time to complete a task, due to the distance-based auctioning of tasks in SSI (Fig. 5).

One method of multi-robot soil compaction sampling, RR-DS, did not come 1st in any metric, and scored 2.6 for mean maximum visits to a cell, making it the only method to score above 2. This suggests that RR-DS is likely to cause greater soil compaction than the other methods tested. RR-DS did achieve the 2nd best performance in mean time to complete a task, and total idle time. The best 2 methods for time to complete a task, SSI-DS and RR-DS, both employ dynamic sampling, indicating that dynamic sampling is better than random sampling at reducing the time to complete a task. Meanwhile idle time is lowest for the two methods that used round robin task allocation. This is likely due to round robin distributing tasks evenly between the robots. In contrast, SSI, bidding with A* path-cost, occasionally leaves a robot without a task when there are no sampling goals generated at that time that the robot can reach quicker than another robot (Fig. 6).

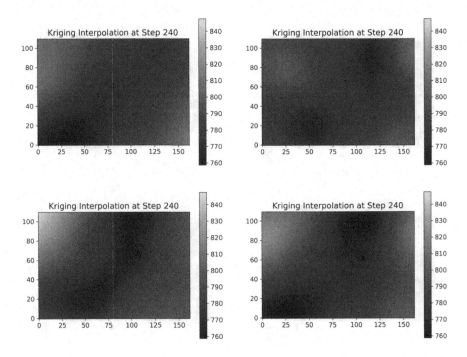

Fig. 6. Soil compaction (kPa) values predicted by kriging interpolation, from the last step of the 1st trial of each condition of the simulated experiment. Top left: RR-DS. Top right: RR-RS. Bottom left: SSI-DS. Bottom right: SSI-RS.

5   Conclusions and Future Work

At the time of writing, multi-robot soil mapping is a critically under-explored area of research, with the potential to provide high resolution mapping of soil properties measured directly and at varying depths on-the-ground demonstrated in single-robot soil mapping works [13,21], in much shorter time. As literature on multi-robot soil mapping is sparse, this work has developed a computationally efficient agent-based simulation to facilitate rapid comparative testing of methods of multi-robot co-ordination and sampling strategies for a multi-robot soil mapping system. The more performant methodologies for multi-robot soil mapping identified using this abstract simulation, will later be implemented as a physical multi-robot soil mapping system, saving vast amounts of time that would be required to adequately test a wide range of approaches using a real-world MRS.

The work of this paper only investigates the performance of the tested methods for 3 robots sampling the surface soil compaction data from [8]. Other spatially distributed datasets may see different results, and so spatial data on other soil properties, from fields of different shapes and sizes, will be sampled by varying numbers of robots in further testing of the performance of methods of MRTA and dynamic sampling. This will help to produce more generalisable comparisons between multi-robot soil mapping methods, while also testing their scalability.

Following improvements to its documentation, our simulation, based on the Mesa simulation framework, will be released as free open-source software on the first author's GitHub account: https://github.com/laurencejbelliott/ under a permissive MIT license. Due to the abstract design of the simulation, the code should require little modification to extend to simulation of multi-robot/multi-agent spatial sampling for other applications.

Future work may see additional criteria beyond A* path-finding cost included in the calculation of bids for auction-based task allocation methods such as SSI, e.g., multiplying the cost of traversing a cell by the number of visits the robot team has made to the cell, penalising excessive soil compaction and sub-optimally close operation of multiple robots. A limited number of simple task allocation algorithms have been implemented for initial testing, but more contemporary state-of-the-art methods of task allocation will be implemented and compared. Traditional methods of selecting locations for soil properties measurements, such as in a grid or W-shaped pattern, will be implemented and compared in addition to random and dynamic sampling methods tested here.

The bespoke dynamic sampling method developed in this work to extend the method of [8] to multiple robots, combined with SSI, was shown to be effective at minimising the RMSE of the interpolated soil compaction map, but not better or significantly worse than SSI with random sampling. To improve dynamic sampling's performance, different clustering and goal selection methodologies will be investigated, and other dynamic sampling methods will be tested, such as the Monte Carlo next best view approach described in [13] which addresses some of the issues of the greedy next best view approach our work extends from [8].

References

1. McGrath, J.M., Spargo, J., Penn, C.J.: Soil fertility and plant nutrition. In: Plant Health, pp. 166–184. Elsevier (2014). https://doi.org/10.1016/B978-0-444-52512-3.00249-7
2. Robert, P.: Characterization of soil conditions at the field level for soil specific management. Geoderma **60**(1), 57–72 (1993). https://doi.org/10.1016/0016-7061(93)90018-G. https://www.sciencedirect.com/science/article/pii/001670619390018G
3. Weiler, M., McDonnell, J.J.: Soil development and properties—water storage and movement. In: Burley, J. (ed.) Encyclopedia of Forest Sciences, pp. 1253–1260. Elsevier, Oxford (2004). https://doi.org/10.1016/B0-12-145160-7/00249-0. www.sciencedirect.com/science/article/pii/B0121451607002490
4. Jorajuria, D., Draghi, L., Aragon, A.: The effect of vehicle weight on the distribution of compaction with depth and the yield of Lolium/Trifolium grassland. Soil Tillage Res. **41**(1), 1–12 (1997). https://doi.org/10.1016/S0167-1987(96)01085-9. https://www.sciencedirect.com/science/article/pii/S0167198796010859
5. Brevik, E., Fenton, T., Moran, L.: Effect of soil compaction on organic carbon amounts and distribution, South-Central Iowa. Environ. Pollut. **116**, S137–S141 (2002). https://doi.org/10.1016/S0269-7491(01)00266-4. https://www.sciencedirect.com/science/article/pii/S0269749101002664

6. Chamen, W.C.T., Vermeulen, G.D., Campbell, D.J., Sommer, C.: Reduction of traffic-induced soil compaction: a synthesis. Soil Tillage Res. **24**(4), 303–318 (1992). https://doi.org/10.1016/0167-1987(92)90116-S. https://www.sciencedirect.com/science/article/pii/016719879290116S
7. Barik, K., Aksakal, E.L., Islam, K.R., Sari, S., Angin, I.: Spatial variability in soil compaction properties associated with field traffic operations. CATENA **120**, 122–133 (2014). https://doi.org/10.1016/j.catena.2014.04.013. https://www.sciencedirect.com/science/article/pii/S0341816214001118
8. Fentanes, J.P., Gould, I., Duckett, T., Pearson, S., Cielniak, G.: 3D soil compaction mapping through kriging-based exploration with a mobile robot. arXiv:1803.08069 [cs] (2018)
9. Grimstad, L., From, P.J.: Thorvald II - a modular and re-configurable agricultural robot. IFAC-PapersOnLine **50**(1), 4588–4593 (2017). https://doi.org/10.1016/j.ifacol.2017.08.1005. https://www.sciencedirect.com/science/article/pii/S2405896317314830
10. Oliver, M.A., Webster, R.: Kriging: a method of interpolation for geographical information systems. Int. J. Geogr. Inf. Syst. **4**(3), 313–332 (1990). https://doi.org/10.1080/02693799008941549
11. Schneider, E., Sklar, E.I., Parsons, S., Özgelen, A.T.: Auction-based task allocation for multi-robot teams in dynamic environments. In: Dixon, C., Tuyls, K. (eds.) TAROS 2015. LNCS (LNAI), vol. 9287, pp. 246–257. Springer, Cham (2015). https://doi.org/10.1007/978-3-319-22416-9_29
12. Masad, D., Kazil, J.: Mesa: an agent-based modeling framework, pp. 51–58 (2015). https://doi.org/10.25080/Majora-7b98e3ed-009
13. Fentanes, J.P., Badiee, A., Duckett, T., Evans, J., Pearson, S., Cielniak, G.: Kriging-based robotic exploration for soil moisture mapping using a cosmic-ray sensor. J. Field Robot. **37**(1), 122–136 (2020). https://doi.org/10.1002/rob.21914
14. Milella, A., Reina, G., Nielsen, M.: A multi-sensor robotic platform for ground mapping and estimation beyond the visible spectrum. Precis. Agric. **20**(2), 423–444 (2019). https://doi.org/10.1007/s11119-018-9605-2
15. Almadhoun, R., Taha, T., Seneviratne, L., Zweiri, Y.: A survey on multi-robot coverage path planning for model reconstruction and mapping. SN Appl. Sci. **1**(8), 847 (2019). https://doi.org/10.1007/s42452-019-0872-y
16. Albani, D., IJsselmuiden, J., Haken, R., Trianni, V.: Monitoring and mapping with robot swarms for agricultural applications. In: 2017 14th IEEE International Conference on Advanced Video and Signal Based Surveillance (AVSS), pp. 1–6 (2017). https://doi.org/10.1109/AVSS.2017.8078478
17. Maza, I., Ollero, A.: Multiple UAV cooperative searching operation using polygon area decomposition and efficient coverage algorithms. In: Alami, R., Chatila, R., Asama, H. (eds.) Distributed Autonomous Robotic Systems 6, pp. 221–230. Springer, Tokyo (2007). https://doi.org/10.1007/978-4-431-35873-2_22
18. Shi, Y., et al.: Adaptive informative sampling with environment partitioning for heterogeneous multi-robot systems. In: 2020 IEEE/RSJ International Conference on Intelligent Robots and Systems (IROS), pp. 11718–11723 (2020). https://doi.org/10.1109/IROS45743.2020.9341711. ISSN 2153-0866
19. Srinivas, N., Krause, A., Kakade, S.M., Seeger, M.: Gaussian process optimization in the bandit setting: no regret and experimental design. IEEE Trans. Inf. Theory **58**(5), 3250–3265 (2012). https://doi.org/10.1109/TIT.2011.2182033. http://arxiv.org/abs/0912.3995

20. Ravikanna, R., Hanheide, M., Das, G., Zhu, Z.: Maximising availability of transportation robots through intelligent allocation of parking spaces. In: Fox, C., Gao, J., Ghalamzan Esfahani, A., Saaj, M., Hanheide, M., Parsons, S. (eds.) TAROS 2021. LNCS (LNAI), vol. 13054, pp. 337–348. Springer, Cham (2021). https://doi. org/10.1007/978-3-030-89177-0_34

21. Fentanes, J.P., Gould, I., Duckett, T., Pearson, S., Cielniak, G.: Soil compaction mapping through robot exploration: a study into kriging parameters. IEEE, Brisbane, Australia (2018). https://eprints.lincoln.ac.uk/id/eprint/32171/

22. Choi, T., Cielniak, G.: Adaptive selection of informative path planning strategies via reinforcement learning. In: 2021 European Conference on Mobile Robots (ECMR), pp. 1–6 (2021). https://doi.org/10.1109/ECMR50962.2021.9568796

23. Koenig, S., et al.: The power of sequential single-item auctions for agent coordination. In: Proceedings of the 21st National Conference on Artificial Intelligence, AAAI 2006, Boston, Massachusetts, vol. 2, pp. 1625–1629. AAAI Press (2006)

24. Welch, B.L.: The significance of the difference between two means when the population variances are unequal. Biometrika **29**(3/4), 350–362 (1938). https://doi. org/10.2307/2332010. https://www.jstor.org/stable/2332010

A-EMS: An Adaptive Emergency Management System for Autonomous Agents in Unforeseen Situations

Glenn Maguire[1]([✉]), Nicholas Ketz[2], Praveen K. Pilly[3],
and Jean-Baptiste Mouret[1]

[1] Inria, CNRS, Université de Lorraine, Nancy, France
{glenn.maguire,jean-baptiste.mouret}@inria.fr
[2] Colossal Biosciences, Madison, Wisconsin, USA
nick@colossal.com
[3] Proficient Autonomy Center, Intelligent Systems Laboratory,
HRL Laboratories, Malibu, USA
pkpilly@hrl.com

Abstract. Reinforcement learning agents are unable to respond effectively when faced with novel, out-of-distribution events until they have undergone a significant period of additional training. For lifelong learning agents, which cannot be simply taken offline during this period, suboptimal actions may be taken that can result in unacceptable outcomes. This paper presents the Autonomous Emergency Management System (A-EMS) - an online, data-driven, emergency-response method that aims to provide autonomous agents the ability to react to unexpected situations that are very different from those it has been trained or designed to address. The proposed approach devises a customized response to the unforeseen situation sequentially, by selecting actions that minimize the rate of increase of the reconstruction error from a variational auto-encoder. This optimization is achieved online in a data-efficient manner (on the order of 30 to 80 data-points) using a modified Bayesian optimization procedure. The potential of A-EMS is demonstrated through emergency situations devised in a simulated 3D car-driving application.

Keywords: Adaptive control · Intelligent robotics · Lifelong learning

1 Introduction

There has been much progress in recent years in machine learning algorithms that enable autonomous agents to learn how to perform tasks in complex environments online based on observations and sensor feedback. Recent advances in Reinforcement Learning (RL) through deep neural networks in particular have shown promising results in developing autonomous agents that learn to effectively interact with their environments in a number of different application domains [3,11], including learning to play games [6,17], generating optimal control policies for robots [20,21], speech recognition and natural language processing [4], as well as making optimal trading decisions given dynamic market conditions [8]. Under the RL paradigm, the agent learns to perform a given task through numerous training episodes involving trial-and-error interactions with its environment. By discovering the consequences of its actions in terms of the rewards obtained through these interactions the agent eventually learns the optimal policy for the given task.

These approaches work well in situations where it can be assumed that all the events encountered during deployment arise from the same distribution on which the agent has been trained. However, agents that must function within complex, real-world environments for an extended period of time can be subjected to unexpected circumstances outside of the distribution they have been designed for or trained on, due to environmental changes that arise. For example: an autonomous driving car may encounter significantly distorted lane-markings that it has never experienced before due to construction or wear, and must determine how to continue to drive safely; or an unaware worker in a manufacturing facility may suddenly place a foreign object, such as their hand, within the workspace of a vision-guided robot-arm that must then react to avoid damage/injury. In such unexpected, novel situations the agent's policy would be inapplicable, causing the agent to perhaps take unsafe actions.

In this paper, we consider scenarios where a trained agent encounters an unforeseen situation during deployment that renders available system or state-transition models highly unreliable, so that any inferences based on such models, as well as any pre-defined safe state/action regions, are no longer valid for safe decision-making. An agent unable to respond effectively to a novel situation when first encountered is vulnerable to take dangerous actions. This is of particular concern in safety-critical applications where sub-optimal actions can lead to damage or destruction of the agent or loss of human life.

We address this problem by developing a data-driven response-generation system that allows an agent to deal with novel situations without reliance on the accuracy of existing models, or the validity of safe states and recovery policies developed offline or from past experiences. The key insight to our approach is that uncertainty in observations from the environment can be used as a driver for the generation of effective, short-term responses online, when necessary, to circumvent dangers, so that the agent can continue to function and learn within its environment.

Increased observation uncertainty has been used in the past to detect novelty (e.g., by measuring out-of-bounds auto-encoder reconstruction errors [23]), indicating situations for which the existing policy is unprepared. It stands to reason, then, that decreasing this uncertainty would decrease novelty and return states to those that the current policy can handle effectively. The work in this paper investigates, therefore, how uncertainty-minimization can be correlated with safe and effective actions in situations where the existing policy would fail. While use of uncertainty to detect potential danger is not new, using it to generate actions in an online manner, customized to the particular never-before-seen emergency as it unfolds, is novel.

In the absence of a reliable model or policy network to make proper action decisions, determination of an appropriate response to a novel situation must be data-driven and sequential. Moreover, in an emergency situation this response must be devised efficiently (i.e., in just a few time-steps), meaning that little data will typically be available for finding the optimal actions to take. This reactive approach, therefore, necessitates a fast, online, optimal decision-making method.

Bayesian Optimization (BO) provides an ideal theoretical framework for this type of problem [18]. BO is a data-efficient, global-optimization method for sequential decision-making where the objective function is expensive to evaluate or is taken to be a black-box. It builds and sequentially improves a probabilistic model of this objective through measurement data obtained online. This model is used to compute the next best action to take in a manner that balances exploration of the unknown regions of the objective and exploitation of regions found to be most likely to contain the optimal value.

Using this framework we devise an emergency-response-generation method that combines a modified BO procedure for efficient sequential optimization, with Gaussian Process (GP) regression for representing the probabilistic model of the objective. The objective function in our approach is a metric designed to capture the uncertainty in the observations obtained by the autonomous agent in a way that facilitates the generation of an effective emergency response. The responses generated by this method are intended to be action-sequences over a short time-span that are only initiated when deemed necessary to circumvent a dangerous situation that the agent is not yet prepared to handle. Our approach is referred to as the Autonomous Emergency Management System (A-EMS).

2   Related Work

Existing works related to safety for autonomous agents typically involve incorporating pre-designed penalties into the reward or cost function for actions deemed unsafe when training a deep neural network to generate policies [2,25], or restricting agent actions to "safe" regions to prevent it from reaching unsafe states [10,27]. Other approaches use examples of dangers in offline training in representative environments to either help identify conservative behaviors to use based on pre-specified rules [23], or to learn recovery policies for specific dangerous scenarios [26]. However, significantly novel events can arise in complex environments that produce dangerous scenarios not accounted for through the above-mentioned mechanisms, thereby requiring a customized response.

An agent must therefore be able to continually learn and adapt to such novel situations. Continual learning approaches in the literature, though, do so through the initiation of a new learning phase [7,19]. Adaptation to the novel situation, then, is not instantaneous, and must happen over an extended period of time dictated by the continual learning method used.

Nevertheless, what existing approaches do show is that deep learning neural networks produce erratic and unreliable predictions when presented with inputs very different from their training scenarios [23,24], but also that uncertainty in predictions from such out-of-distribution inputs can be an effective way to detect novelty [10, 15, 23]. Moreover, trying to jointly optimize for task performance and safety-violation can lead to restrictive, sub-optimal policies [1, 26]. In addition, despite their limitations, these prior works also make it clear (see, for example, [27]) that including a safety mechanism to assist learning agents improves success-rate, constraint satisfaction, and sample efficiency.

3   Problem Description

We consider the A-EMS method to be used as part of an independent module that monitors a trained and deployed agent as it performs a given task. Within this scenario there may be instances where the agent encounters a situation it has never seen before that presents a danger if not acted upon properly. The agent's existing policy is unable to determine an appropriate response without further training, and any environment models become unreliable. Whenever such an unforeseen event is encountered, the agent is considered to be in an emergency situation for which an emergency response is required to mitigate the danger.

It is assumed that an emergency detection method is available that monitors the agent during deployment and can identify a novel situation that the agent is unprepared to handle. Numerous approaches to novelty detection can be found in the literature (e.g., [7, 16, 23]) which can be used for this purpose. Moreover, context-specific information relevant to the given application domain could also be used to further verify that the agent is in imminent danger if it continues with the actions output by its existing policy.

While monitoring, the A-EMS method remains disengaged and the agent is allowed to freely perform its task using its existing policy. Once an emergency situation is found to be imminent, the A-EMS response generation algorithm is engaged (Fig. 1), which takes over the policy's actions by replacing them with a suitable emergency response. Consequently, this necessitates the halting of any updates to the existing policy over the course of the response.

The response devised is a customized action-sequence over the next N timesteps to address the danger. This action-sequence must be generated online as the encounter with the novel situation unfolds.

4   Methodology

The proposed method for generating a response to address an unforeseen situation is based on the idea that taking actions that reduce uncertainty in the observations should correspond to an effective response that guides the agent to a more familiar state, which the existing policy knows how to effectively handle. In our approach, the uncertainty associated with novel situations is represented by the reconstruction errors (i.e., mean squared pixel-value errors) from a Variational Auto-Encoder (VAE) [13] designed to process RGB images from a camera sensor. Its neural network structure was borrowed from that presented in [12].

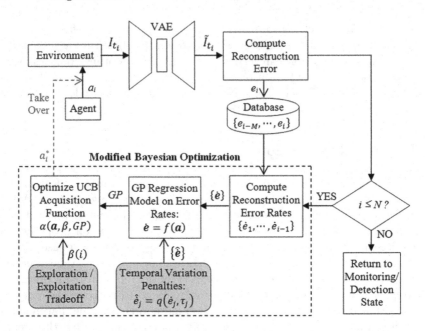

Fig. 1. Workflow of the autonomous emergency management system.

The response devised by A-EMS for an emergency situation is an action-sequence that spans some fixed number of time-steps, N. The generation of actions that reduce observation uncertainty is thus taken to be a sequential optimization process, where each action must ideally be the optimal decision to make given all the data gathered since the initiation of the response.

To perform this online optimization we use BO coupled with GP regression. BO is a data-efficient technique to find the global optimum of a function, $f(\mathbf{x})$, that is significantly expensive to evaluate. It achieves this by building a surrogate, probabilistic model, $G[f(\mathbf{x})]$, of f, which includes a mean function, $\mu(\mathbf{x})$, representing the current best estimate of $f(\mathbf{x})$ over the domain of f, and a variance function, $\sigma^2(\mathbf{x})$, representing the uncertainty in this estimate. We herein employ GP regression to construct this surrogate model [22].

Using this GP model, BO optimizes a corresponding, and relatively simpler, heuristic function, $\alpha(x, G[f(\mathbf{x})])$, termed the acquisition function, which quantifies the utility of any given input, x, in terms of its potential for optimizing $f(\mathbf{x})$. This optimization is achieved by sequentially sampling inputs from the domain of x that have the greatest potential for optimizing f as indicated by the acquisition function. More details on BO can be found in [18].

As shown in Fig. 1, the sequential optimization uses the rate of change of the VAE reconstruction errors to drive the BO loop at each time-step, i, of the response action-sequence. This is because there may be situations where it may not be possible to find actions that reduce the reconstruction errors, and all that can be done is to minimize its increase. This would still be a valid response if that is the best that can be done given the circumstances. An imminent collision with an obstacle is a good example - some situations may simply call for maximum braking as there may not be any way to swerve around the obstacle. In such cases, errors would only rise as the agent approached the obstacle, with braking helping to slow down the rate of increase until it eventually plateaus at a higher but stable value. Minimizing the error-rate would capture the need to slow down the rise of the errors in such situations, but would also be able to keep driving the errors down further (i.e., negative error-rates) if it is indeed possible.

The objective at each time-step, $i \in [1, N]$, of the response is to find an action, a_i^*, that minimizes the error-rate, $\dot{e}_i$, that would result from that action, by conducting one cycle of the BO loop shown in Fig. 1. This optimization will have available data-points containing all the actions, $\mathbf{Pa}_i = \begin{bmatrix} a_1 & a_2 & ... & a_{i-1} \end{bmatrix}_i$, taken in the last $(i-1)$ time-steps of the action-sequence, as well as the corresponding true error-rates, $\mathbf{P\dot{e}}_i = \begin{bmatrix} \dot{e}_1 & \dot{e}_2 & ... & \dot{e}_{i-1} \end{bmatrix}_i$, that resulted.

The last M error data-points are always stored in a database. Once a response generation is triggered, every data-point obtained from the start of the response is also saved ($\mathbf{Pa}_i$ and $\mathbf{P\dot{e}}_i$) for the duration of the response. To compute the error-rate, $\dot{e}_k$, the available (noisy) reconstruction errors, $\mathbf{e}$, are first passed through a smoothing filter, f_s, to compute the smoothed errors, $\tilde{\mathbf{e}}$. The last two smoothed error values can then be used to compute the rate, $\dot{e}_k$, as:

$$\dot{e}_k = \frac{f_s(k) - f_s(k-1)}{\delta i} = \tilde{e}_k - \tilde{e}_{k-1}. \tag{1}$$

BO then proceeds to construct a model of the unknown relationship, $\dot{\mathbf{e}} = f(\mathbf{a})$, between error-rates, $\dot{\mathbf{e}}$, and actions, $\mathbf{a}$, for the given emergency scenario using GP regression. This GP model, $G[f(\mathbf{a})]$, is used to conduct the relatively simpler acquisition-function optimization to find the next best action, a_i^*, to take.

The optimal action, a_i^*, is then applied to the environment. At the subsequent time-step, the resulting error e_i will be obtained, from which $\dot{e}_i$ can be computed. Both $\mathbf{Pa}_i$ and $\mathbf{P\dot{e}}_i$ are then updated accordingly and the above BO loop procedure is repeated, until the response length, N, is reached.

4.1 Acquisition Function

We employ the Upper Confidence Bound (UCB) acquisition function [5], given by Eq. 2. Here, $\mu(\mathbf{a})$ and $\sigma^2(\mathbf{a})$ are the mean and variance of the regression model for the relationship, $\dot{\mathbf{e}} = f(\mathbf{a})$.

$$UCB = \alpha(\mathbf{a}, \beta, G[f(\mathbf{a})]) = \mu(\mathbf{a}) + \sqrt{\beta \cdot \sigma^2(\mathbf{a})}. \tag{2}$$

UCB is chosen since it includes a parameter, β, that allows direct control over the balance between exploration and exploitation, that is, how much the system should try actions that are far from those already sampled versus how much should it focus on the most promising actions found so far. It can be effectively optimized using quasi-Newton methods such as the L-BFGS-B algorithm [14].

4.2   Exploration/Exploitation Trade-Off

Since an emergency response is time-critical, it is important to ensure a transition from an initial exploratory behavior to an exploitative one in a timely manner so that the search converges on an effective solution fast enough to avoid the danger. To accomplish this, the explicit parameter, β, is set to a decreasing function of time, $\beta(t_i)$, $i \in [1, N]$. The initial value, β_0, must be relatively high to encourage the BO to explore the action-space. As the action-sequence progresses, this parameter should decrease to a relatively lower value, β_k, so that the optimization begins to exploit the best solution found so far. These requirements produce the following constraints on the form of the time-varying function chosen for $\beta(t_i)$:

$$\beta(t_1) = \beta_0, \tag{3}$$

$$\beta(t_i \geq t_k) = \beta_k, 1 < k \leq N, \tag{4}$$

$$\beta_0 > \beta_k, \tag{5}$$

$$\frac{d\beta(t_i)}{dt_i} \leq 0, \quad \forall t, \quad t_1 \leq t \leq t_N. \tag{6}$$

In this way, the degree of initial exploration by BO can be controlled by the choice for β_0, and the degree to which it exploits the best solution found so far can be controlled through the choice for β_k.

4.3   Temporal Relevance of Data

A second point of concern in devising the acquisition function is incorporating the influence of time. The underlying relationship between error-rate and actions would, in general, be time-varying. Thus, recent observations will have greater relevance to, and influence on, the decision being made at any given time-step compared to older observations. To account for this temporal variation, we propose a penalty function that discounts the utility of any given observation, based on that observation's "age" within the time-span of the response action-sequence.

The utility of any given action is given by the UCB acquisition function, which depends on the GP model used to obtain $\mu(\mathbf{a})$ and $\sigma^2(\mathbf{a})$ (see Eq. 2). The GP regression model captures the influence of past observations on any other unseen one being estimated based on their relative distances in action-space. Thus, the discounting of action utility must be incorporated into the error-rate data used to compute the GP model. As such, we define a penalty function that operates directly on the set of error-rates available at any given time-step of the response. In particular, at the ith time-step of a response action-sequence, each error-rate, $\dot{e}_j$, in $\mathbf{P}\dot{e}_i$ is transformed to a discounted measure, $\hat{e}_j$, through a penalty function, $q(\dot{e}_j, \tau_j)$, before computing the GP regression, where:

$$\tau_j = i - j, \quad \forall j, \quad 1 \leq j \leq (i - 1), \text{and} \tag{7}$$

$$\frac{dq}{d\tau} \geq 0, \quad \forall \tau \geq 1. \tag{8}$$

Here, τ_j represents the age of the jth error-rate at time-step i, and Eq. 8 indicates that the penalties should increase with age. This user-specified penalty function can be devised under this constraint depending on how strongly and quickly one wishes past data to lose its significance. An example is provided in the experiments presented in Sect. 5.

5   Simulation Experiments

To demonstrate and validate the proposed method, experiments with two differ-ent types of emergency situations were conducted using the open-source CARLA autonomous driving car simulator [9]. In the first situation, the A-EMS method was used to safeguard an agent from unexpected lane-drifting that it has not been designed to detect and correct-for. In the second emergency situation, the proposed response-generation method was used to detect and avoid imminent collisions with obstacles that an agent has never encountered before.

Each simulation run proceeds in discrete time-steps. At the start of each time-step the agent receives an observation corresponding to the current system state in the form of an RGB image from its forward-facing camera sensor. The agent then selects an action, namely, the throttle, brake, and steering inputs. The simulation updates the system state accordingly to the next time-step using the selected action. This process repeats until the end of the simulation run.

The VAE used to compute reconstruction errors is trained offline on images gathered from observations made under nominal conditions. Here, the agent is controlled via the built-in CARLA auto-pilot and made to drive on the same sections of road used in the experiments, but without introducing any emergency situation. A total of 72000 images obtained this way were used to train the VAE.

5.1   Lane-Drifting Experiments

Experimental Setup. In these experiments, a gradual drift to one side is induced in the autonomous car as it drives along a straight section of road simu-lated in CARLA. To ensure no reliance on, or influence from, the agent's policy or learning mechanism on the response generation, the agent was controlled by the built-in auto-pilot software in CARLA, modified to enable only straight driving in the left-hand lane with no action taken to correct drift.

After a period of driving straight unfettered, the steering control inputs are altered so as to cause the car to begin drifting into the right-hand lane. As a result, the incoming observations gradually change to those that are unexpected compared to the nominal driving that the agent has experienced before. An RL agent not trained to deal with such inputs could collide with another vehicle in the right-hand lane, or even drift off the roadway, as it tries to learn the optimal response through its trial-and-error process.

The proposed A-EMS method is triggered to generate a corrective response to curtail this drift with neither any prior experience or training in doing so nor any context-specific information to indicate what exactly the problem is.

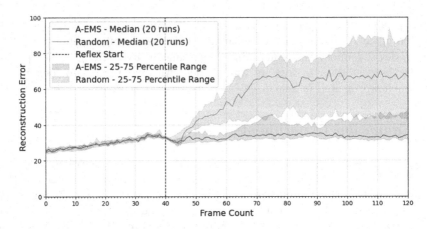

Fig. 2. Comparison of VAE reconstruction errors between the A-EMS and random-response approaches over all experiment runs, from initiation of the drift to completion of the $N = 80$ time-step response. Shaded regions represent the 25th to 75th percentile ranges of the errors over all runs at each time-step.

The response generated by the A-EMS method is used to take-over the actions output by the agent's existing policy over the next $N = 80$ time-steps.

As we are unaware of existing emergency-response methods for novel situations where no prior training or preparation is employed for the scenarios encountered, A-EMS is compared with a random response, where actions are selected at random at each of the next $N = 80$ time-steps. For a fair comparison, both the A-EMS and the random responses are artificially triggered at the same point in time in their respective simulation runs after the drift is initiated. In all experiments, the vehicle maintained an average forward speed of 20 km/h prior to the emergency response. Equations 9 and 10 give the functions used for the trade-off parameter, β, and the time-based penalties on the error data, respectively. These functions were used for illustrative purposes and the user is free to design them as they see fit under the restrictions stipulated by Eqs. 3–8.

$$\beta(ti) = -0.0028t_i^2 + 0.07, \quad i \in [0, N-1], \tag{9}$$

$$q(\dot{e}_j, \tau_j) = 0.02269e^{(0.2293\tau_j)}, \quad i \in [1, N-1], j \in [0, i-1]. \tag{10}$$

Results. A total of 20 runs of the lane-drifting experiments were conducted under each of the response-generation approaches: A-EMS and random-response. Figure 2 shows plots of the VAE reconstruction errors that resulted from all runs for both these methods. Figure 3 shows plots of the 2D position coordinates of the centre-of-mass of the vehicle recorded over all experiment runs, from initiation of the drift to the end of the $N = 80$ time-step response.

Responses that maintained a lateral center-of-mass deviation below 1.5 m relative to the center of the left-lane were considered to be successful. The experimental results showed a 8/20 = 40% success-rate for the random-response approach and a 14/20 = 70% success-rate under the proposed A-EMS method.

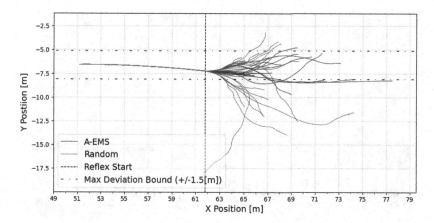

Fig. 3. Comparison of paths traced out by agent over all runs between the A-EMS and random-response approaches.

5.2 Collision-Avoidance Experiments

Experimental Setup. Nine different collision scenarios were setup in CARLA within a simulated urban environment (see Fig. 4), each involving a different, unforeseen, stationary obstacle placed in the path of the autonomous car driving along a section of road in one of 5 different parts of the map. These scenarios simulate a situation where an autonomous driving agent, assumed to have been trained to drive in an obstacle-free urban environment, is suddenly presented with an unforeseen situation involving a stationary obstacle placed in its path. The trial-and-error learning process for an RL agent in such a situation could involve taking dangerous actions, possibly resulting in collisions with the obstacles.

Two sets of experiments were conducted within this emergency situation. In the first, the CARLA auto-pilot maintained an average agent speed of 20 km/h before encountering an obstacle, and the A-EMS method was combined with an example emergency-detection method. In the second set, an average speed of 30 km/h was maintained and response-generation was artificially triggered.

In the first set of experiments a rudimentary, VAE-error-based emergency-detection method was used, only as an example to demonstrate how the A-EMS method could be combined with a detection algorithm to compose a complete, independent, monitoring module that takes over the agent's output with an emergency response only when necessary. This emergency-detection mechanism uses a straightforward approach similar to that presented in [15]. In particular, at each time-step, a second-order polynomial regression fit is computed on the last $M = 15$ VAE reconstruction errors, which are then extrapolated $K = 7$-time-steps into the future and compared against an upper-bound threshold, ULe, to indicate the presence of a novel, unforeseen situation requiring an emergency response. While any mechanism suitable to the application being considered can be used to identify when a dangerous situation is imminent, an auto-encoder-

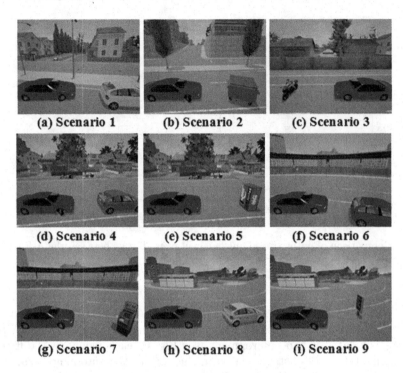

(a) Scenario 1   (b) Scenario 2   (c) Scenario 3

(d) Scenario 4   (e) Scenario 5   (f) Scenario 6

(g) Scenario 7   (h) Scenario 8   (i) Scenario 9

Fig. 4. Simulated stationary-obstacle scenarios used in the collision-avoidance experiments: (a) location A, green car; (b) location B, garbage container; (c) location B, motorcycle; (d) location C, red car; (e) location C, vending machine; (f) location D, blue car; (g) location D, ATM machine; (h) location E, orange car; (i) location E, street-sign. (Color figure online)

based approach presents a natural choice given that the response-generation method employs a VAE as a key part of its input sensor-data processing.

The emergency-detection component monitors the actions of the agent and the observations received from its camera sensor. Upon detecting an imminent collision as the agent approaches a stationary obstacle, the module triggers the A-EMS algorithm to takeover the agent's actions for the pre-specified next $N = 30$ time-steps with a customized action-sequence to attempt to prevent this collision.

In the second set of experiments the emergency-detection mechanism is replaced by an artificial trigger that initiates the different response-generation approaches being compared at the same point in time during each simulation run. Without the additional time-delay caused by a separate emergency-detection component, the simulations could be run at a faster average forward agent speed of 30 km/h. In both sets of experiments a worst-case scenario is simulated where, in the absence of the emergency-response system, the agent takes no action to avoid the obstacle and continues to follow the road.

Results. In the first set of experiments the A-EMS method was compared with a random-response approach. Twenty repetitions for each scenario were conducted and the percent of successful collision-avoidance runs (i.e., success-rate) was computed. Table 1 summarizes the results.

Table 1. Summary of success-rates for simulated collision-avoidance scenarios (note: taking no action resulted in a 0% success-rate in all cases).

Scenario #	Exp. set 1 (20 km/h tests)		Exp. set 2 (30 km/h tests)	
	A-EMS	Random	A-EMS	Random
1	80%	10%	82%	5%
2	65%	20%	90%	25%
3	75%	35%	75%	10%
4	75%	50%	80%	25%
5	75%	25%	85%	70%
6	45%	5%	55%	40%
7	75%	30%	70%	25%
8	70%	25%	25%	7.5%
9	80%	15%	57.5%	17.5%
Avg.	**71%**	**24%**	**68.8%**	**25%**

In the second set of experiments, both the proposed approach and the random-selection approach were triggered manually at the same time for all scenarios. This ensured that the same distance and initial approach speed existed for the approaches compared (see Table 1 for success-rate results). As a representative example for illustration, Fig. 5a shows a plot of the variations in VAE reconstruction errors, and Fig. 5b gives a closer look at the error-rates themselves, over the span of the response action-sequences for Scenario 1 in the second set of experiments where the alternative responses are triggered at the same time for a fair comparison. For reference, Fig. 5 also includes the errors and rates that result from taking no action upon encountering the obstacles.

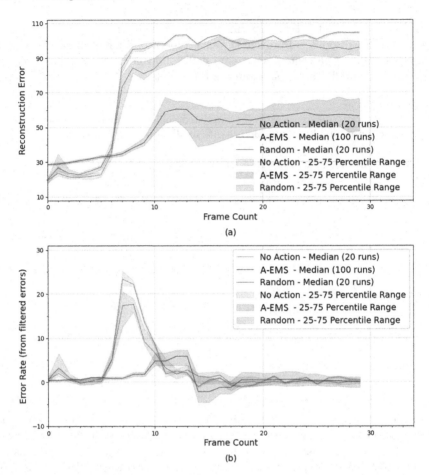

Fig. 5. Comparison of the impact of A-EMS, a random response, and no-action, on (a) VAE reconstruction errors, and (b) VAE reconstruction error-rates, over the Scenario 1 runs in Experiment set 2.

6   Conclusions and Discussion

This paper proposed A-EMS: an emergency-response method that enables an autonomous lifelong-learning agent to safely address unforeseen situations encountered during deployment for which the existing policy becomes unreliable. When triggered, the method generates a response by finding optimal actions sequentially through minimization of VAE reconstruction error rates from the novel observations using a modified BO algorithm. Simulation experiments in an autonomous car-driving domain demonstrate how minimization of observation uncertainty using A-EMS can find safe actions to curtail unexpected lane-drifts and also to avoid collisions with never-before-seen obstacles, despite never having encountered such scenarios before.

The significantly greater average success-rate by A-EMS in controlling lateral drift and in collision-avoidance compared to a random approach indicate that effective, intelligent actions are indeed being selected to avoid the novel dangerous situations, beyond simply what random chance would allow. This demonstrates how minimizing a measure of uncertainty in the observations can be correlated with good actions that help to effectively deal with unforeseen situations. These effective, danger-avoiding behaviors are also reflected in the reconstruction errors themselves (Figs. 2 and 5a), where the errors rise relatively slowly and plateau at a relatively lower final value due to the agent having transitioned to a more familiar state.

Some scenarios from the second emergency situation simulated presented more of a challenge than others. Detection of the imminent collisions in experiment-set 1 was observed to happen when the agent was on average about 8 m away from the obstacle. This left little distance and time to react, and in some cases it was not enough for the final response to avoid the collision, even though it may have been effective had the danger been detected sooner. Qualitative observations of some of the failures under the proposed method show that the agent still tries to make sensible maneuvers to avoid the collision and almost succeeds.

It should be noted that the intention here was not to create the best drift-correction or obstacle-avoidance system for an autonomous car, but rather to demonstrate how minimization of observation uncertainty can be an effective driver to safely address novel situations for which a learning agent would otherwise be unprepared.

Moreover, A-EMS does not require context-specific information either (i.e., understand the significance of lane-markings or know what the obstacle is, or what its presence means in the context of driving). As such, the performance of the method can always be improved by incorporating context-specific mechanisms on top of the basic emergency-response system for the particular application being addressed, if so desired.

References

1. Achiam, J., Amodei, D.: Benchmarking safe exploration in deep reinforcement learning. In: NeurIPS Deep Reinforcement Learning Workshop (2019). https://d4mucfpksywv.cloudfront.net/safexp-short.pdf
2. Achiam, J., Held, D., Tamar, A., Abbeel, P.: Constrained policy optimization. In: Proceedings of the 34th International Conference on Machine Learning, vol. 70, pp. 22–31. JMLR.org, Cambridge (2017)
3. Arulkumaran, K., Deisenroth, M.P., Brundage, M., Bharath, A.A.: Deep reinforcement learning: a brief survey. IEEE Signal Process. Mag. **34**(6), 26–38 (2017)
4. Bengio, S., Vinyals, O., Jaitly, N., Shazeer, N.: Scheduled sampling for sequence prediction with recurrent neural networks. In: Proceedings of the 28th International Conference on Neural Information Processing Systems, vol. 1, pp. 1171–1179. MIT Press, Cambridge (2015)

5. Brochu, E., Cora, M., de Freitas, N.: A tutorial on Bayesian optimization of expensive cost functions, with application to active user modeling and hierarchical reinforcement learning. Technical report TR-2009-023, Department of Computer Science, University of British Columbia (2010)

6. Brown, N., Sandholm, T.: Libratus: the superhuman AI for no-limit poker. In: Proceedings of the Twenty-Sixth International Joint Conference on Artificial Intelligence (IJCAI-17), pp. 5226–5228. IJCAI Organization, Menlo Park (2017)

7. Caselles-Dupré, H., Garcia-Ortiz, M., Filliat, D.: S-TRIGGER: continual state representation learning via self-triggered generative replay. In: International Joint Conference on Neural Networks (IJCNN 2021) (2021, accepted)

8. Deng, Y., Bao, F., Kong, Y., Ren, Z., Dai, Q.: Deep direct reinforcement learning for financial signal representation and trading. IEEE Trans. Neural Netw. Learn. Syst. **28**(3), 653–664 (2017)

9. Dosovitskiy, A., Ros, G., Codevilla, F., Lopez, A., Koltun, V.: CARLA: an open urban driving simulator. In: Proceedings of the 1st Annual Conference on Robot Learning, pp. 3521–3526. PMLR, Bletchley Park (2017)

10. Fisac, J.F., Akametalu, A.K., Zeilinger, M.N., Kaynama, S., Gillula, J., Tomlin, C.J.: A general safety framework for learning-based control in uncertain robotic systems. IEEE Trans. Autom. Control **64**(7), 2737–2752 (2019)

11. Francois-Lavet, V., Henderson, P., Islam, R., Bellemare, M., Pineau, J.: An introduction to deep reinforcement learning. IEEE Signal Process. Mag. **11**(3–4), 219–354 (2018)

12. Ha, D., Schmidhuber, J.: World models. arXiv:1803.10122v4 [cs.LG] (2018)

13. Kingma, D.P., Welling, M.: Auto-encoding variational bayes. arXiv:1312.6114v10 [stat.ML] (2014)

14. Liu, D., Nocedal, J.: On the limited memory BFGS method for large scale optimization. Math. Program. **45**(1), 503–528 (1989)

15. Manevitz, L., Yousef, M.: One-class document classification via neural networks. Neurocomputing **70**(7), 1466–1481 (2007)

16. Marchi, E., Vesperini, F., Eyben, F., Squartini, S., Schuller, B.: A novel approach for automatic acoustic novelty detection using a denoising autoencoder with bidirectional LSTM neural networks. In: 2015 IEEE International Conference on Acoustics, Speech and Signal Processing (ICASSP), pp. 1996–2000. IEEE Press, Piscataway (2015)

17. Mnih, V., et al.: Human-level control through deep reinforcement learning. Nature **518**(7540), 529–533 (2015)

18. Mockus, J. (ed.): Bayesian Approach to Global Optimization: Theory and Applications. Kluwer Academic Publishers, Boston (2013)

19. Nguyen, C.V., Li, Y., Bui, T.D., Turner, R.E.: Variational continual learning. In: Sixth International Conference on Learning Representations, pp. 1–18. iclr.cc, La Jolla (2018)

20. Pan, X., You, Y., Wang, Z., Lu, C.: Virtual to real reinforcement learning for autonomous driving. In: Proceedings of the British Machine Vision Conference (BMVC), pp. 11.1–11.13. BMVA Press, London (2017)

21. Peng, X.B., Berseth, G., Yin, K., Van De Panne, M.: DeepLoco: dynamic locomotion skills using hierarchical deep reinforcement learning. ACM Trans. Graph. **36**(4), 1–13 (2017)

22. Rasmussen, C.E., Williams, C.K.I. (eds.): Gaussian Processes for Machine Learning. MIT Press, Cambridge (2006)

23. Richter, C., Roy, N.: Safe visual navigation via deep learning and novelty detection. In: Proceedings of Robotics: Science and Systems, pp. 1–9. MIT Press, Cambridge (2017)
24. Szegedy, C., et al.: Intriguing properties of neural networks. In: 2nd International Conference on Learning Representations, ICLR 2014, pp. 1–10. iclr.cc, La Jolla (2014)
25. Tessler, C., Mankowitz, D.J., Mannor, S.: Reward constrained policy optimization. arXiv:1805.11074v3 [cs.LG] (2018)
26. Thananjeyan, B., et al.: Recovery RL: safe reinforcement learning with learned recovery zones. IEEE Rob. Autom. Lett. **6**(3), 4915–4922 (2021)
27. Thananjeyan, B., et al.: Safety augmented value estimation from demonstrations (SAVED): safe deep model-based RL for sparse cost robotic tasks. IEEE Rob. Autom. Lett. **5**(2), 3612–3619 (2020)

Towards Scalable Multi-robot Systems by Partitioning the Task Domain

Brendan Devlin-Hill[1]([✉])[iD], Radu Calinescu[1][iD], Javier Cámara[2][iD], and Ipek Caliskanelli[3][iD]

[1] University of York, York, UK
{brendan.devlin-hill,radu.calinescu}@york.ac.uk
[2] ITIS Software, University of Málaga, Málaga, Spain
jcamara@uma.es
[3] UKAEA/RACE, Abingdon, UK
ipek.caliskanelli@ukaea.uk

Abstract. Many complex domains would benefit from the services of Large-scale, Safety-verified, Always-on (LSA) robotic systems. However, existing large-scale solutions often forego the complex reasoning required for safety verification and prescient reasoning in favour of scalability. We propose a method of partitioning the task domain to enable scalability, inspired by a 'problem-first' solution paradigm. Our method decomposes a large, intractable problem into a set of smaller, tractable sub-problems by spatially dividing the task domain into maximally-independent sub-domains. We present experimental evidence of the benefits of this approach in the context of a nuclear maintenance system.

Keywords: Multi-robot systems · Robot teaming · Task partitioning · DEMO · Nuclear fusion · Safety verification · Large-scale systems · Always-on systems · Problem space optimisation · Problem-first paradigm

1 Introduction

There are many application domains that would benefit from the services of robotic systems that are large-scale, safety-verified and always-on (abbreviated herein as 'LSA' systems). For example, large-scale engineering projects such as wind farms and power plants, as well as other domains such as large-scale security, require operation over wide physical areas using many active robots, all while satisfying strict safety parameters as defined by their operators. Furthermore, an appropriate system for such a domain must operate in an 'always-on' regime; that is to say, the constant task-stream necessitates an up-time of the system so long as to be functionally infinite from a planning point of view. The system must therefore be able to handle a dynamic specification and adapt to gradual changes in its environment and its constituent robots.

Supported by RACE/UKAEA.

The research presented here is motivated by the necessity of LSA systems for the nuclear fusion domain. Fusion is an attractive method for energy generation due to its fuel efficiency and cleanliness compared to fission and fossil fuels. DEMO, the DEMOnstration nuclear power plant, is intended to be the first complete nuclear fusion power plant. To that end, it must demonstrate the economic viability of fusion when it opens in the 2050s [1]. Maintenance has been identified as a key concern, as it is the greatest decider of the machine's availability, and thus its economic and power output [2,3].

Constructing an LSA system for such a domain is fundamentally challenging. For instance, there is an innate trade-off between scalability and safety verification. The issue is quality versus quantity; in a scalable system the number of agents makes strict reasoning over all relevant information an intractable problem, and a safety-verified system is likewise limited in scope due to factors related to the computational cost of exhaustive verification tools such as probabilistic model checkers. Likewise, safety verification is complicated by the always-on regime, as the system may evolve out of a safe state into an unsafe one. Maintaining and guaranteeing the safety of the system into the far future therefore requires reasoning with a long time-horizon.

This paper proposes a method of task domain partitioning, inspired by a problem-first design paradigm, which is demonstrated to improve the tractability of large-scale planning problems and thus to enable LSA systems. Section 2 introduces an example problem based on the motivating domain of DEMO which we will use to inform our concept of a nuclear inspection system. Section 3 describes the existing work in the area of large-scale multi-robot systems, discusses relevant literature, and explains how a 'problem-first' paradigm can enable LSA systems. Section 4 presents our method of task partitioning by the k-means algorithm. We also describe the use of the probabilistic model checker PRISM [4] to create a model of the aforementioned nuclear inspection system and synthesise a control policy which satisfies a system specification encoded in Probabilistic Computation Tree Logic (PCTL) [5]. Finally, Sect. 5 presents experiments that corroborate the benefit of the a partitioned approach.

2 Example Problem

The requirements of the nuclear fusion domain are relatively idiosyncratic. Maintenance will be a perpetual task and constant safety verification will be required. Due to its constant operation, the system must be able to handle dynamic incoming tasks and adapt to a gradually changing environment. Robots will also incur damage that impedes their capabilities from environmental factors such as radiation [6,7]; this must be detected and accounted for at runtime. At any one time a large number of robots will be active; therefore, scalability must be a primary concern in designing the system, especially insofar as it allows for strict, safety-critical reasoning over every aspect of operation.

We form an example problem based on continuous inspection tasks. Consider a fusion power plant with a functionally unlimited number of robots. These robots initially reside in an inventory area outside of the main workspace of the plant. The workspace - the plant floor - contains a great many visual inspection tasks in different locations. The plant is radioactive, so the presence of the robots in the workspace causes them to accrue radiation damage, which must be kept below a certain threshold lest they malfunction. Once activated, the inspection system remains on indefinitely, although individual robots may be returned to storage for repairs or recharging when required. Furthermore, although any number of robots may be in operation at once, in practicality only the minimal number of robots should be used so as to reduce the economic cost of maintaining the robots themselves.

Given such a problem, the challenge is to synthesise a control policy for the robotic system that will allow it to fulfil the inspection tasks while upholding the system specification and guaranteeing safety via probabilistic model checking. This problem forms the basis for our model system in Sect. 4.1.

3   Related Work

Although many authors have proposed distributed, scalable systems, no existing approaches support the requirements of a problem such as that outlined in Sect. 2. Decentralised coalition-forming methods such as those proposed by Calinescu *et al.* [8], Scerri *et al.* [9] and Shehory and Kraus [10] demonstrate good scalability but lack points of information aggregation where safety verification can take place. Abdallah and Lesser [11] likewise propose a hierarchical coalition structure that benefits from a strategy of abstracting information moving between layers to lower the computational burden on the latter. This is promising for our purposes, but the formation of the hierarchy is not addressed.

The 'Problem-First' Paradigm

These existing approaches can be categorised as what we term 'agent-first'. In this paradigm of problem solving, the organisation of the agents (robots) is taken as the starting point for optimisation. Although future tasks with complex relationships and uncertainties [12,13] may be considered, the task domain is generally treated as a series of immutable tasks which must be 'dealt with' rather than manipulated to the benefit of the system's operation.

This paper posits that such an agent-first paradigm is fundamentally limited. Naturally, the solution to any problem is constructed from an understanding of the problem itself - an axiom supported by research on human reasoning [14,15] - and as such, optimising one's understanding of the problem is likely to directly optimise the construction of the solution. This is true in human psychology which shows that humans can more easily make valid inferences when provided with logical propositions of certain formats, compared to other propositions which contain the exact equivalent information [16]. The decomposition of problem space as a preliminary to solution is a concept that also appears in the field of design [17].

In this paper we propose an alternative, 'problem-first' paradigm, which we can invoke to create efficient LSA systems. The core tenet of this paradigm is to consider the problem space as a target for manipulation and optimisation to at least the same extent as other commonly-optimised elements such as team composition, path planning, and communication. In fact, the problem space should ideally be optimised first as all planning begins with the problem, and eliminating complexity earlier in the overall solution process has the potential to greatly reduce the complexity of all subsequent stages. However, other forms of optimisation can still be applied after the treatment of the problem space; thus the problem-first paradigm does not preclude the use of powerful, pre-existing optimisation techniques.

4   Proposed Solution

Based on the problem-first paradigm, we propose a method of enabling scalability in LSA systems which works primarily by optimising the problem space for solution. In the nuclear fusion context, the problem space is the systems understanding of the task domain; i.e. the structure and format in which information about maintenance tasks is presented to the planner. The solution to this problem is a control policy that fulfils the task domain while upholding the system specification.

In our approach, the task domain is optimised for solution by partitioning it into sub-domains, reducing the overall planning/safety-verification problem into a series of maximally-independent sub-problems such that each can be solved agnostically of the others. This approach essentially decouples a large, intractable planning problem into a series of smaller, tractable ones.

The approach operates as such. We take as inputs a description of the task domain and the system specification. The task domain is partitioned by the k-means partitioning algorithm [18] into a set of sub-domains. For each sub-domain, we generate a model via python script. Each model is an MDP encoded in the probabilistic model checker PRISM [4]. We then input the specification into PRISM by way of a Probabilistic Computation Tree Logic (PCTL) string. PRISM then generates a set of control policies that satisfy the specification. An summary of the approach is given in Fig. 1 and explained in more detail the following sections.

The effectiveness of the partition will be dependent on the natural organisation of the task domain. In idealised cases, the solution of a partitioned task domain will be no less optimal than the unpartitioned case although in reality some loss of optimality is likely to occur. The structure of DEMO's environment is well-suited to the partitioning due to its inherent organisation; the systems in a fusion power plant (e.g. cryonics, fuel-processing, etc.) will be laid out in a compartmentalised manner so as not to interfere with each other, and as such maximally-independent sub-domains will be more easily extracted than from a completely random distribution of tasks. By choosing a intelligent partitioning algorithm, this loss of optimality can be minimised while also maximising

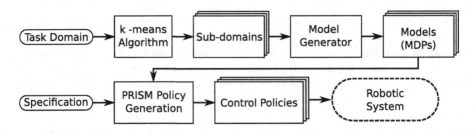

Fig. 1. Summary of our task partitioning approach showing inputs and outputs.

the independence of each sub-domain and thus properly decoupling the sub-problems.

However, a complete LSA system for nuclear fusion is beyond the scope of this paper. Rather, we focus on proposing a preliminary method with which to partition the task domain via the k-means algorithm and to synthesise a control policy to satisfy it.

4.1 System Description and Modelling

Partitioning and probabilistic model checking require a model of the system congruent with the example problem in Sect. 2. To encode our model we used PRISM, a probabilistic model checker that allows formulation of Markov Decision Processes (MDPs) via the high-level PRISM language [4]. PRISM also allows specification of system properties in various logic languages including PCTL [5]. These properties can then be verified or quantified. An optimal control policy will be generated to enforce these properties. A segment of our PRISM model is shown in Listing 1.1.

The model system consists of robots completing inspection tasks in an abstracted environment. The workspace over which the robots operate is abstracted into N_L locales. Each locale represents an area of space such as a room or a segment of one. Each robot is initialised in a special locale L_0 which contains no tasks. This represents the inventory from which robots are recruited.

The model parameters also include N_R robots and N_T tasks. In order to represent the assumption that an unlimited inventory of robots is at hand to accomplish the tasks, we set $N_R = N_T$ in all cases unless specified. Each robot and task may occupy one locale at a time. There is no limit to the total number of tasks or robots in a specific locale. Each task is either active or inactive; a robot may complete an active task if it is in the same locale as it, thus changing the task's status to inactive. Note also that a robot may only move to a locale if it also completes a task there. It is therefore impossible for a robot to move to an empty locale or one in which all tasks are inactive.

A robot will accrue a cost when it moves between locales and completes tasks. Each robot has its own cost structure, and there is also a team cost structure that accrues a cumulative cost from the actions of all robots. The costs are abstract but can represent such factors as energy expense or radiation damage in the individual case or economic cost for robot maintenance in the case of the team cost. Likewise, the specific values of the costs are arbitrary.

Our specification minimises the team cost while restricting each individual robot's cost to be below a threshold. This is encoded in PRISM via a PCTL string of the form:

```
multi(R{"team_cost"}min=? [C], R{"cost_R1"}<=12000 [C],
    R{"cost_R2"}<=12000 [C],... , R{"cost_RN"}<=12000 [C])
```

The model reaches an end-state when all the tasks have been completed. PRISM was used to generate control policies that completed all tasks while upholding the specification.

4.2   Partitioning Method

K-Means Partitioning. We use a partitioning method based on the k-means algorithm, which is a clustering algorithm that divides a set of points into a specified number of clusters (k) based on a distance metric such as Euclidean distance [19]. In the resultant solution, each point belongs to the group whose centroid $\overline{x}$ (the mean position of points in that group) it is closest to. Therefore, k-means can be framed as a problem of the optimal placement of the centroids of k groups.

Taking an input of points $P = \{p_1, \ldots, p_N\}$, the 'naïve' k-means algorithm operates in two steps:

1. Assignment of each point in the set to the group with the nearest centroid.
2. Update of all group centroids.

Steps 1 and 2 repeat until the solution converges upon a stable configuration of groups $S = \{s_1, \ldots, s_k\}$, where each $s = \{p_1, \ldots, p_n\}$ is a cluster containing points p. Effectively, this finds a local minimum of the clustering error σ_k:

$$\sigma_k = \sum_i^k \sum_{x \in s_i} (x - \overline{x}_i)^2 \qquad (1)$$

However, the solution is heavily dependent on the choice of initial centroids around which the solution then converges. To obtain effective solutions, naïve k-means must be run many times with randomised initial conditions to find the most optimal solution. The output of the algorithm is therefore non-deterministic and potentially sub-optimal.

The global k-means algorithm [18] is a modification of the k-means algorithm which is deterministic and optimal. It operates on the basis that if the optimal solution to $i-1$ clusters is known, it is relatively simple to find the optimal placement of the i-th centroid.

```
1   module robot0  // N_R robot modules:
2
3       R0_locale: [0..4] init 0;
4       [R0T0_complete] T0_active = true → (R0_locale' = T0_locale);
5       [R0T1_complete] T1_active = true → (R0_locale' = T1_locale);
6       ...
7   endmodule
8
9   module robot1
10
11      R1_locale: [0..4] init 0;
12      [R1T0_complete] T0_active = true → (R1_locale' = T0_locale);
13      [R1T1_complete] T1_active = true → (R1_locale' = T1_locale);
14      ...
15  endmodule
16  ...
17  module task0  // N_T task modules:
18
19      T0_active : bool init true;
20      [R0T0_complete] true → (T0_active' = false);
21      [R1T0_complete] true → (T0_active' = false);
22      ...
23  endmodule
24  ...
25  rewards "cost_R0"  // costs for each individual robot
26      [R0T0_complete] R0_locale = 1 & T0_locale = 1 : T0_cost;
27      [R0T0_complete] R0_locale = 1 & T0_locale = 2 : dist_L1L2 + T0_cost;
28      ...
29  endmodule
30  ...
31  rewards "team_cost"  //timewide costs
32      [R0T0_complete] R0_locale = 1 & T0_locale = 1 : T0_cost;
33      [R1T0_complete] R1_locale = 1 & T0_locale = 1 : T0_cost;
34      ...
35  endmodule
```

Listing 1.1. Segment of PRISM code showing robot modules, task modules and reward structures. Constants are omitted for brevity. Each robot module defines an action for every task, representing the robot moving to that task's locale. The task modules define corresponding transitions which alter their status from active to inactive, thus representing their completion. Each transition has a unique associated cost based on the locales and tasks involved.

For a set of N points $P = \{p_1, \ldots, p_N\}$, global k-means operates as follows:

1. The optimal solution for $i = 1$ is simply one cluster with the centroid being that of all points in the space.
2. For each solution for i clusters, use the centroids from the $i - 1$ solution as the first $i - 1$ initial centroids.
3. Acquire a set of solutions for i clusters by running naïve k-means for each $p \in P$, each time using p as the initial location of the i-th centroid.
4. The solution with the minimal σ_k is selected as the optimal solution for i clusters.
5. Steps 2–4 are repeated until k clusters are reached.

The output is thus a partition of the system $S = \{s_1, \ldots, s_n\}$ where each $s = \{p_i, \ldots, p_n\}$ is a sub-domain, itself a set of points p.

Partitioning the Task Domain. A partition of the system using simple k-means requires a representation of the model outlined in Sect. 4.1 in Euclidean space. Therefore, we assigned each locale of the system a Cartesian point to represent its general location, and set the transition weight between each two locales to their Euclidean separation. Note that this does not include L_0, which is a special, abstract locale that represents the inventory of robots. To discourage trivial solutions wherein every one robot completes one task, we set the cost of moving from the inventory locale L_0 to any other locale to a relatively high value, thus incentivising the use of as few robots as possible.

The partitioning algorithm takes as input the locations of the locales $L = \{l_1, \ldots, l_{NL}\}$ and the tasks per locale $TPL = \{nt_1, \ldots, nt_{NL}\}$, where nt_i is an integer representing the number of tasks in locale i. It also takes a value $threshold \in \mathbb{Z}^+$ which is the desired mean number of tasks per sub-group in the final partition. Partitioning is executed via global k-means, which terminates upon achieving the condition

$$\frac{\sum_{s \in S}(\text{number tasks in } s)}{|S|} \leq \text{threshold} \qquad (2)$$

This stop condition is useful for specifying the degree of partitioning. Merely relying on a static value of k is unhelpful as one cannot know *a priori* the number of groups that will result from global k-means, nor their sizes. Sole use of k may therefore lead to an over-partitioned system, (leading to highly-suboptimal solutions,) or an under-partitioned system, (leading to long model checking times and intractability). By relying on this stop condition, the resultant group size can be controlled approximately, thus allowing the user to inform the trade-off between tractability and optimality.

Partitioning is relatively fast compared to PRISM's execution time; for the largest model parameters we test ($N_T = 12; N_L = 6; threshold = 3$) the time for global k-means is 0.199 ± 0.004 s whereas the corresponding PRISM time is on the order of 10^6 s.

5   Results and Discussion

5.1   Dependence on Model Parameters

We ran PRISM for a range of model parameters to establish the dependence of the model checking/policy synthesis time and the team cost on N_T and N_L. This was necessary for extrapolation of the unpartitioned times and costs in Sect. 5.2. The results of the experiments are shown in Fig. 2.

Naturally, larger models with larger model parameters required more time for probabilistic model checking. The utility of task partitioning is clear from the exponential relation of the execution time to N_T, as only a small reduction in model parameters can lead to large reductions in execution time. The team cost appears to begin to plateau for higher values of N_T, likely due to a higher number of tasks per locale incentivising the system to complete tasks without accruing the cost of moving between locales.

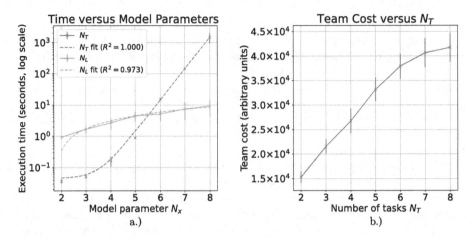

Fig. 2. The response of the model to varying model parameters: a) PRISM execution time versus N_T and N_L. The dashed lines represent an exponential and linear fit, respectively. For the N_T curve $N_L = 6$. For the N_L curve $N_R = 5$; $N_T = 8$. b) The accrued team cost for a range of N_T where $N_L = 6$.

5.2 Partitioning

Partitioning was carried out using the global k-means methods as outlined in Sect. 4.2. The process was repeated for a variety of locale locations and task distributions to encapsulate variance due to environmental factors. The results are displayed in Fig. 3. $N_L = 6$ was selected to allow for interesting partitioning behaviour. However, the algorithm gives uninformative results for cases where $N_L > N_T$ as this can create empty partitions containing no tasks, and the unpartitioned cases became intractable for $N_T > 8$. Therefore, the response of the unpartitioned system had to be extrapolated from the $N_T \leq 8$ data-sets shown in Fig. 2.

The data demonstrate both a reduction in the model checking/policy synthesis time and a reduction in optimality. The mean task-per-group threshold introduced in Eq. 1 proved valuable in maintaining the synthesis time a roughly constant value, several orders of magnitude below the unpartitioned case. As expected, the team cost was greater in the partitioned case then in the unpartitioned case and appears to increase sharply at $N_T = 9$ and $N_T = 12$. This is due to the chosen value of *threshold* = 3 introducing extra groups when N_T passes a multiple of 3. Nonetheless, this decrease of optimality is far below the order of the decrease in synthesis time, which may indicate an attractive trade-off depending on the domain to which the technique is applied.

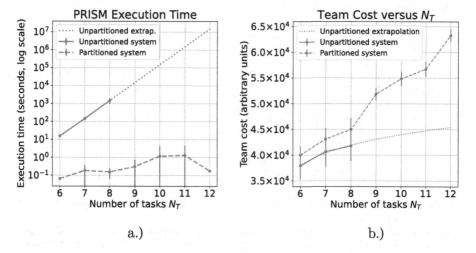

Fig. 3. Comparison of a) PRISM execution time and b) the team cost structure before and after partitioning. The unpartitioned result was extrapolated using a) exponential fit to $N_T \in [2,8]$ ($R^2 = 1.000$) and b) a logarithmic fit to $N_T \in [5,8]$ ($R^2 = 0.997$). In both cases, $N_L = 6$ and *threshold* $= 3$.

6   Conclusion

This paper outlined the 'problem-first' paradigm of problem-solving and utilised it to propose a high-level method of constructing LSA systems. We explained the advantages of this mode of organisation, proposed a basic vector for implementation, and conducting corroborating experiments. The results show a promising improvement in tractability, albeit one coupled with a loss of optimality. Future work should experiment with different partitioning methods which may be able to divide the task domain with less disruption to policy synthesis. It would also be informative to model the effectiveness of this approach for differing environmental parameters; for example, this may involve determining the relation between optimality and the entropy of the task distribution across the workspace. Finally, a practical version of this approach must also take into account a more complex task model which includes the requirements, duration and frequency of the tasks.

Acknowledgement. This work has been carried out within the framework of the EUROfusion Consortium, funded by the European Union via the Euratom Research and Training Programme (Grant Agreement No 101052200—EUROfusion). Views and opinions expressed are however those of the author(s) only and do not necessarily reflect those of the European Union or the European Commission. Neither the European Union nor the European Commission can be held responsible for them.

References

1. Donné, A.J.H.: The European roadmap towards fusion electricity. Philos. Trans. Ser. A Math. Phys. Eng. Sci. **377**, 20170432 (2019)
2. Maisonnier, D., et al.: The European power plant conceptual study. Fusion Eng. Design **75–79**, 1173–1179 (2005). Proceedings of the 23rd Symposium of Fusion Technology
3. Surrey, E.: Engineering challenges for accelerated fusion demonstrators. Phil. Trans. R. Soc. A **377**(2141), 20170442 (2019)
4. Kwiatkowska, M., Norman, G., Parker, D.: PRISM 4.0: verification of probabilistic real-time systems. In: Gopalakrishnan, G., Qadeer, S. (eds.) CAV 2011. LNCS, vol. 6806, pp. 585–591. Springer, Heidelberg (2011). https://doi.org/10.1007/978-3-642-22110-1_47
5. Hansson, H., Jonsson, B.: A logic for reasoning about time and reliability. Form. Asp. Comput. **6**(5), 512–535 (1994)
6. Bachmann, C., et al.: Overview over demo design integration challenges and their impact on component design concepts. Fusion Eng. Design **136**, 87–95 (2018). Special Issue: Proceedings of the 13th International Symposium on Fusion Nuclear Technology (ISFNT-13)
7. George, J.S.: An overview of radiation effects in electronics. AIP Conf. Proc. **2160**(1), 060002 (2019)
8. Calinescu, R., Gerasimou, S., Banks, A.: Self-adaptive software with decentralised control loops. In: Egyed, A., Schaefer, I. (eds.) FASE 2015. LNCS, vol. 9033, pp. 235–251. Springer, Heidelberg (2015). https://doi.org/10.1007/978-3-662-46675-9_16
9. Scerri, P., Xu, Y., Liao, E., Lai, J., Sycara, K.: Scaling teamwork to very large teams. In: Proceedings of the Third International Joint Conference on Autonomous Agents and Multiagent Systems, AAMAS 2004, vol. 2, pp. 888–895. IEEE Computer Society (2004)
10. Shehory, O., Kraus, S.: Methods for task allocation via agent coalition formation. Artif. Intell. **101**(1), 165–200 (1998)
11. Abdallah, S., Lesser, V.: Learning scalable coalition formation in an organizational context. In: Scerri, P., Vincent, R., Mailler, R. (eds.) Coordination of Large-Scale Multiagent Systems, pp. 191–215. Springer, Boston (2006). https://doi.org/10.1007/0-387-27972-5_9
12. Camara, J., et al.: The uncertainty interaction problem in self-adaptive systems. Softw. Syst. Model. **21**(4) (2022)
13. Hezavehi, S.M., Weyns, D., Avgeriou, P., Calinescu, R., Mirandola, R., Perez-Palacin, D.: Uncertainty in self-adaptive systems: a research community perspective. ACM Trans. Auton. Adapt. Syst. **15**(4), 1–36 (2021)
14. Sternberg, R., Smith, E.E.: The Psychology of Human Thought. Cambridge University Press, Cambridge (1988)
15. Simon, H.A., Newell, A.: Human problem solving: the state of the theory in 1970. Am. Psychol. **26**, 145–159 (1971)
16. Johnson-Laird, P.N.: How We Reason, 1st edn. Oxford University Press, Oxford (2008)
17. Alexander, C.: Notes on the Synthesis of Form. Harvard University Press, Cambridge (1964)
18. Likas, A.C., Vlassis, N.A., Verbeek, J.J.: The global K-means clustering algorithm. Pattern Recogn. **36**, 451–461 (2003)
19. Hartigan, J., Wong, M.: Algorithm AS136: a K-means clustering algorithm. Appl. Stat. **28**, 100–108 (1979)

Effectiveness of Brush Operational Parameters for Robotic Debris Removal

Bechir Tabia$^{(\boxtimes)}$ (iD), Ioannis Zoulias(iD), and Guy Burroughes(iD)

Culham Science Centre, United Kingdom Atomic Energy Authority, Abingdon, UK
bechir.tabia@ukaea.uk

Abstract. Surface decontamination is essential in Nuclear Gloveboxes; moving this process from manual to robotic would reduce the risk to operators. Towards the development of robotic and autonomous sweeping systems, brushing debris removal effectiveness is evaluated using visual inspection. In addition, three types of dry simulacrum debris were used: flour, sand, and metallic swarf, each with different particle sizes and friction properties. We evaluate the debris removal effectiveness for each operational brush parameter and debris type. The tested operational brush parameters were the brush angle of attack and the brush penetration with the help of a robotic manipulator arm repeating a slow and steady rectangle sweeping pattern. We found that the brush angle of attack has a higher impact than the brush penetration. Also, flour is fast to remove from a surface and necessitates 80° angle of attack. For sand particles, a 70° angle of attack gives the best configuration to create a contact surface. Regarding debris like metallic swarf, debris particles to bristles bonding must be limited, requiring a 90° angle of attack. These results allowed us to determine that autonomous robotic systems must adapt brushing operative parameters to debris type for an effective debris removal process.

Keywords: Nuclear dismantling · Surface decontamination · Robotic sweeping · Debris collection · Brushing effectiveness

1 Introduction

In nuclear gloveboxes, surface decontamination is essential in the dismantling process. They ensure workers' safety and the glovebox's maintenance by limiting the accumulation on surfaces of hazardous contaminants such as radioactive or toxic material [2,8]. Human operators are currently at considerable risk of performing the cleaning task using tools such as vacuum cleaners, brushes, and wet wipes. The choice of the technique follows the quantity of debris to collect and the complexity of the cleaning operation. In nuclear gloveboxes, dismantling activities are not safe despite the contained area, and accidents involving operator radioactive contamination by cutting have occurred in the past [11]. Thus, robotics are investigated for dismantling activities in nuclear gloveboxes to limit

S. Pacheco-Gutierrez et al. (Eds.): TAROS 2022, LNAI 13546, pp. 293–310, 2022.
https://doi.org/10.1007/978-3-031-15908-4_23

these accidents and increase workers' safety. Consequently, the RAIN hub develops a robot-assisted nuclear glovebox that allows autonomous, semi-autonomous and remote handling operations [15]. The new robot-assisted nuclear glovebox consists of a pair of robotic manipulator arms and sensors replacing/augmenting the human operator in gloveboxes. In the long run, the robot's objective is to perform autonomous dismantling operations. These are size reduction (cutting, drilling), object disassembling, and surface cleaning (vacuuming, brushing, wiping). A typical nuclear glovebox dismantling process involves cutting, drilling, and disassembling contaminated objects and can generate a consequent amount of hazardous debris [8]. Because of these operations, an accumulation of various objects, tools and debris can result in a cluttered environment causing operations disruptions, the accumulation of hazardous debris, and airborne contamination [8].

Three non-abrasive methods are available for the robotic manipulator arm to guarantee the glovebox surface cleanliness from debris [3]. Firstly, vacuum cleaning offers a fast and reliable way to collect large debris on uncluttered surfaces. However, a vacuum cleaner can suck up unwanted or significant objects in a cluttered environment, resulting in tool clogging. Also, vacuum cleaning is a less controlled process undesirable in a Nuclear environment, and this is an expensive option not available in all gloveboxes. Secondly, wet wiping techniques provide a high level of decontamination. However, they are limited to residual quantities of debris collection on clean surfaces. Finally, brushing techniques offer the advantage of removing large debris quantities using brush deflection properties, access to narrow gaps, and safe interaction with surrounding objects. These advantages are thanks to the brush compliance property. The particle removal mechanism involves two forces and one moment, the lifting and sliding forces and the rolling moment [6]. The lifting force allows lifting debris particles from a surface; it must be larger than the adhesion force. The sliding force allows a particle to slide on a surface. The remove a particle, the sliding force must be superior to the difference between adhesion and lifting force multiplied by the coefficient of friction. The rolling moment allows the roll of debris particles on a surface; it depends on the debris particle shape and size. The rolling moment condition can be attained quickly for spherical and small debris. It is more challenging for cubic and large debris to reach the rolling moment debris removal conditions [6]. Also, the contact forces creating the condition of debris removal are located between the brush bristles, the debris and the surface. A theoretical contribution involved using a finite element model for brush debris interaction using a single bristle modelisation [1]. It analysed the influence of brush penetration using bristle deflection properties on debris removal forces and moments. The results indicate that the effective removal mechanisms are the horizontal sliding force and the rolling moment. Also, the brush penetration is beneficial when it is relatively small. Another practical contribution, limited to rotating brushes on road sweepers, indicates that debris removal depends on the interaction of several factors. These factors are the brush angle of attack, the penetration, the rotational speed, coefficient of friction, bristle length, vehicle velocity, and stick-slip friction cycles [16]. Powered brushing tools are inappropriate for the nuclear environment because of airborne contamination risk. They require the development of rad-hard tooling compared to an inexpensive and robust paintbrush. Furthermore, in a complex access environment where the interaction between humans and robots must be limited, DIY paintbrushes offer a good balance between robustness, operational effectiveness and cost-effectiveness.

The long-term goal is to make robots autonomously remove contaminated debris from nuclear gloveboxes. The robotic manipulator must perform compliant and non-prehensile manipulation of a pile of debris from one position to another. The sweeping process requires the manipulator to have the ability to set and control the brushing operative parameters. Several studies have focused on compliant robotic manipulator motion control with a linear brush tool for debris removal [4,7,9,13,14,19]. These studies contributed using conventional or data-driven control and path planning approaches. However, they do not focus on task effectiveness and are not proven effective in our condition. Our operative condition imposes sweeping particles such as Beryllium, dust, sand, concrete, metallic swarf and bits of plastic. Thus, to control the robot and perform effective debris removal, the robot must set the correct operative brush parameters according to debris type. There are significant consequences of setting up the sub-optimal brushing parameters. For example, a high brush penetration increases brush wear and reduce sweeping effectiveness [10,18]. Another challenge in sweeping processes is the "Backward sweeping" effect caused by debris sticking to the brush bristles. Pieces of debris stuck in the brush bristles are reapplied to surfaces at the next sweeping travel, decreasing the sweeping effectiveness and making the cleaning process ineffective [10,18].

The paper builds on the research on robotic debris removal effectiveness by examining the operational brush condition and investigating their effect on debris removal. The sweeping test is performed using a seven degrees-of-freedom robotic manipulator arm equipped with a brush was used to perform the sweeping. The surface to sweep is composed of polished stainless steel to match the actual glovebox condition. Furthermore, the tests are conducted using a 3.8 cm linear nylon brush with three debris sets. The tested debris particles set are flour, sand and metallic swarf. Also, we choose flour for simulating hazardous debris like Beryllium. The surface is smooth, and the debris particles are dry and easy to remove. Thus, we limit the experiment to two operative brush parameters, the brush angle of attack and penetration. The brush angle of attack creates a contact surface between the brush and debris, and the brush penetration creates a bond between the brush and surface. Because the surface is smooth, the friction between the debris and surface is considered low. The sweeping velocity ($0.1 \, m/s$) and travel ($15 \, cm$) are fixed for all the experiments. Also, this focuses the investigation on a slow and long sweeping sliding pattern that limits airborne contamination. This study aims to ascertain whether the tested operational brush parameter affects debris removal effectiveness regarding the type of debris tested. In addition, this study provides data paving the way toward the requirements for an autonomous and robotic sweeping system.

In this paper, Sect. 2 describes the materials and methods used during this experiment. Then in Sect. 2.1 details about the experimental setup is given, followed by the different types of debris components (Sect. 2.2), the debris removal task (Sect. 2.3) and the experimental methodology (Sect. 2.4). Section 3 provides the result of the sweeping experiment for flour (Sect. 3.1), sand (Sect. 3.2) and metallic swarf (Sect. 3.3). Then, Sect. 4 discusses the results of the debris removal experiment. Lastly, Sect. 5 presents the main conclusions from this work.

2   Materials and Methods

2.1   Experimental Setup

Figure 1 represent the experimental setup components. The first component is the glovebox, where the experiment consists of sweeping a 15×10 cm stainless steel flat and horizontal surface. The following components are the robotic manipulator arms (Kinova UltraLigth Gen 3) performing the sweeping task equipped with a 3.8 cm nylon brush. The robot manipulator arm grasps the brush through a rigid mechanical interface (Fig. 2a). Sweeping results pictures are captured with a Digital Single Lens Reflex Camera installed on a fixed tripod (Canon EOS 700D). The camera is installed on top of the sweeping scene with constant and controlled lighting conditions (Fig. 2b).

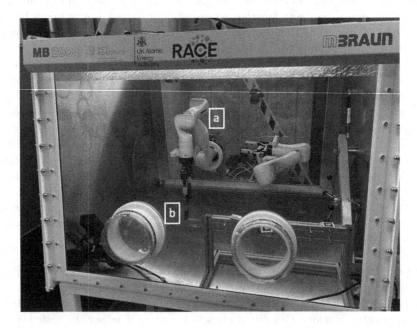

Fig. 1. Robot assisted nuclear glovebox composed of a pair of robotic manipulator (a) holding the brush tool (b)

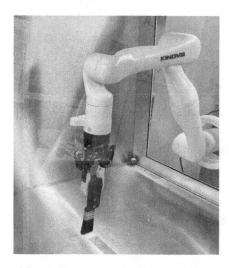

(a) Robotic manipulator holding the brush
in the end effector

(b) DSRL camera used to capture the images

Fig. 2. Robot assisted nuclear glovebox experimental setup

2.2   Debris Components

For this research, the tested piles of debris are flour, sand and metallic swarf (Fig. 3). In addition, for health and safety reasons, the piles of debris tested in this experiment are not the debris collected in actual operational conditions. Beryllium oxide, a toxic material, is replaced with wheat flour as they have both the same colour and particle size despite having different density ($0.59\,g/cm^3$ for wheat flour vs $3.02\,g/cm^3$ for Beryllium) [12,17]. The debris chosen offers various mechanical characteristics and properties regarding debris nature. Flour is a compressible and cohesive product where the friction angle decrease with pressure applied on the surface [5]. In addition, the typical particle size for commercial wheat flour is $20\,\mu m$ [5]. Unlike flour, sand is a non-compressible product and the friction angle increase with the pressure applied to the surface. Sand has a bigger particle size comprised between $20\,\mu m$ to $100\,\mu m$ [5]. The third debris type chosen is metallic swarf, an abrasive and rigid type of debris. We have not assessed the average particle size for this type of debris. However, five samples were measured, showing a particle size comprised between 0.05 to 0.7 cm. For all debris types, we could not determine the precise friction coefficient. The tested debris was dry, and the air relative humidity was 52% during the experiment.

Fig. 3. Debris samples: flour, sand and metallic swarf (from left to right).

2.3   Debris Removal Task

The robotic manipulator arm performs the debris removal task, consisting of a repeated sweeping movement following a vertical rectangle shape (Fig. 4). Also, the robot manipulator control software comprises a sweeping waypoint generator and a cartesian impedance controller (Fig. 6). The sweeping waypoint generator generates the cartesian end-effector position and orientation, allowing a rectangle shape sweeping task to perform. It also offers five parameter settings: sweeping starting point, brush angle of attack, penetration, sweeping velocity, and sweeping travel length. All experiments were carried out using a fixed sweeping velocity of 0.1 m/s and a sweeping travel length of 15 cm; they were chosen to provide a consistent and slow sweeping pattern. A slow and consistent sweeping pattern is needed to limit the energy transferred between the brush bristles and debris particles, thus limiting lifting force and potential airborne contamination. Also, the brush starting point, the brush angle of attack (Fig. 5a), and the brush penetration (Fig. 5b) are set and defined before the experiment run. During the experiment, the brush angle of attack is set to 70, 80 and 90° on the sweeping waypoint generator. As the brush angle of attack modification affects the sweeping pattern and brush penetration, they were adjusted simultaneously to reach the desired starting point and brush penetration value. The brush penetration was set to 0, 0.5 and 1 cm, and the verified a posteriori. The verification of the sweeping starting point end-effector position used a 15 × 3.8 cm frame stuck to the glovebox surface. The control system software performs ten sweeping movements for each experiment set before stopping. To conclude, the sweeping pattern movement is consistent with low velocity (0.1 m/s) during all the sweeping travel. As the piles of debris are pushed, we do not use the dynamical brush property to expel debris from bristles.

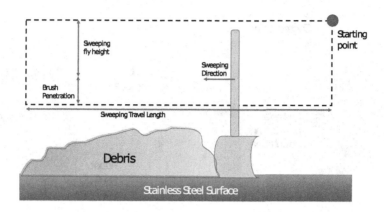

Fig. 4. Debris removal pattern

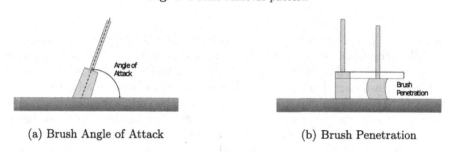

(a) Brush Angle of Attack   (b) Brush Penetration

Fig. 5. Brush operational parameters

2.4 Testing Methodology

In this experiment, sweeping tests were carried out to evaluate whether the brush angle of attack and penetration impact the debris removal rate. Before performing the debris removal test, piles of debris are uniformly and consistently spread to cover all the sweeping test surfaces. The brush of angle attack and penetration was then set and verified using a ruler. Then, an experiment is carried out with the robot performing ten consecutive sweeping movements. After each sweep, a picture of the surface is taken and recorded on a computer. Each experiment is repeated five time to verify the consistency of the sweeping debris removal rate.

The sweeping effectiveness is evaluated using visual inspection with the help of a DSLR camera positioned at the height of 60 cm from the sweeping scene. A picture is taken after each sweeping movement, as shown in Fig. 7a. Then, for an experiment comprising ten sweeping movements, 11 pictures are taken. After the sweeping test, the debris removal effectiveness is calculated. Figure 7b illustrate the image process pipeline allowing us to determine the Debris Removal Effectiveness (DRE). Each image is processed using a Matlab script performing the following action: crop the image to the cleaning frame, perform a greyscale transform (0–255), perform a brightness and contrast adjustment, count the pixel

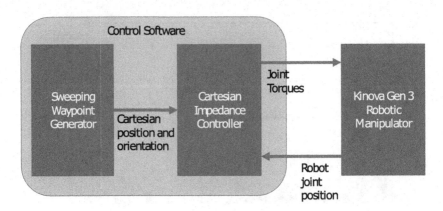

Fig. 6. Debris removal control scheme

considered as part of debris and finally calculate the Debris Removal Effectiveness. The brightness and contrast were adjusted for sand and metallic swarf to render the debris as dark pixels and the surface white. Pixels under a 70 greyscale level were considered debris. The brightness and contrast were adjusted in the flour case to render the flour particle white and the surface darker. Pixel-level above a 200 greyscale level was considered debris. The Matlab script calculates the Debris Removal Effectiveness (DRE, Eq. 1) by calculating the ratio of clean area pixels over the total number of pixels for each picture on an experimental set.

$$DRE = (\frac{TP - DP}{TP}) * 100 \tag{1}$$

Hence all Debris Removal Effectiveness is calculated for all pictures in an experimental set; we want to verify result consistency. Then, we calculate the mean (Eq. 2) and standard deviation (Eq. 3) for each iteration sweep regarding the five experimental repetitions set such:

$$MDRE_i = \frac{1}{n} \sum_{j=1}^{n} DRE_j \tag{2}$$

$$\sigma_i = \sqrt{\frac{1}{n-1} \sum_{j=1}^{n} (DRE_j - MDRE_i)^2} \tag{3}$$

With n corresponding to the number of sweeping tests performed, five times in our case, it corresponds to the sweeping index in a sequence of consecutive sweeping.

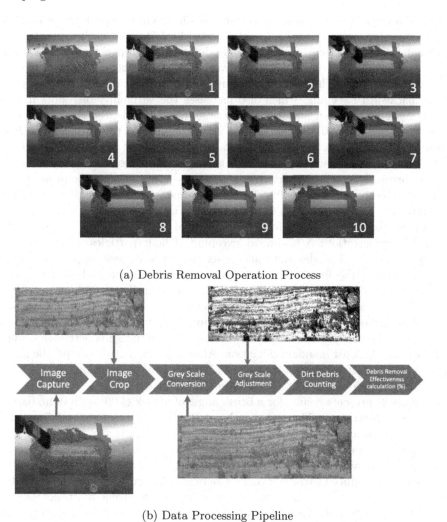

(a) Debris Removal Operation Process

(b) Data Processing Pipeline

Fig. 7. Debris removal operation process and data processing

3   Result and Analysis

3.1   Flour Debris Removal

Figure 8a presents the mean debris removal effectiveness regarding the number of consecutive sweepings for an angle of attack of 70° and with a penetration of 0 cm, 0.5 cm and 1 cm. Despite having different brush penetration, the mean debris removal effectiveness results are very close and fluctuate around an average value of 99.6%. The fluctuation of mean debris removal effectiveness results from backward sweeping, which also increases the variability of results in any case. As a large brush surface is in contact with the debris, the debris particles get caught in the brush bristles and reapplied to the surface. The first sweep catches a large amount of debris on this angle of attack configuration. The metallic swarfs are expelled from the bristles on the next sweeps, thanks to the brush deflection property. After ten consecutive sweeps, the mean debris removal effectiveness attains 99.86% with 1 cm penetration, 99.61% with 0.5 cm penetration, and 99.62% with 0 cm brush penetration.

Figure 8b presents results for a brush angle of attack of 80° with 0 cm, 0.5 cm and 1 cm penetration. A backward sweeping of flour particles appears in any configuration. It degrades the initial sweeping effectiveness despite very high effectiveness at the first sweep. Also, in each configuration and after the first sweep, the Debris Removal Effectiveness decreases until the sixth sweep. After that, it increases as the brush deflection evacuates the debris from the bristles. The standard deviation for the three configurations overlaps, and it is difficult to determine the best configuration. However, the 0.5 cm brush penetration configuration has the least standard deviation. After ten consecutive sweeps, the mean debris removal effectiveness attains 99.84 % with 1 cm penetration, 99.90% with 0.5 cm penetration, and 99.88% with 0 cm brush penetration.

Figure 8c presents results for a brush angle of attack of 90° with 0 cm, 0.5 cm and 1 cm penetration. The best brush penetration results are the 0.5 cm and 1 cm configurations. A performance of 0 cm gives the lower performance as this configuration offers the lower contact between the brush, the surface and debris. The backward sweeping effect is less critical with a brush angle of attack of 90°, thanks to the reduced surface of contact between the brush and the debris. After ten consecutive sweeps, the mean debris removal effectiveness attains 99.85% with 1 cm penetration, 99.86% with 0.5 cm penetration, and 97.12% with 0 cm brush penetration.

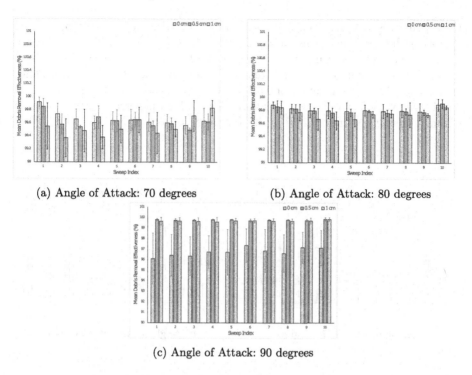

(a) Angle of Attack: 70 degrees   (b) Angle of Attack: 80 degrees

(c) Angle of Attack: 90 degrees

Fig. 8. Mean debris removal effectiveness for flour debris

3.2   Sand Debris Removal

Figure 9a presents results for a brush angle of attack of 70° with 0 cm, 0.5 cm
and 1 cm penetration. In any configuration, the sweeping effectiveness after the
first sweep starts low (around 67% removal effectiveness) as the friction between
the debris and the surface makes the removal challenging. At least three sweeps
are necessary to attain a removal rate of 90%. After ten sweeps, the effectiveness is more than 95% in any case. The backward sweeping effect causes the
performance fluctuation between the fourth and eighth sweeping. This effect
reapplies debris on the surface to clean because the angle of 70° induces a high
surface of contact with the brush. After ten consecutive sweeps, the mean debris
removal effectiveness attains 99.58% with 1 cm penetration, 98.83% with 0.5 cm
penetration, and 97.07% with 0 cm brush penetration.

Figure 9b presents results for a brush angle of attack of 80° with 0 cm, 0.5 cm
and 1 cm penetration. As it seems that the friction coefficient is high between the
building sand and the surface, the least effective configuration is given by a brush
penetration of 0 cm. A better mean debris removal effectiveness is provided by
brush penetration of 0.5 cm and 1 cm. However, the overlap of standard deviation
does not provide enough information to determine which configuration offers the
best outcome. After ten consecutive sweeps, the mean debris removal effective-

ness attains 98.65% with 1 cm penetration, 96.94% with 0.5 cm penetration, and 91.46% with 0 cm brush penetration.

Figure 9c presents results for a brush angle of attack of 90° with 0 cm, 0.5 cm and 1 cm penetration. In this angle of attack configuration, the best performance is given by a brush penetration of 0.5 cm. After ten consecutive sweeps, the mean debris removal effectiveness attains 96.76% with 1 cm penetration, 97.14% with 0.5 cm penetration, and 95.17% with 0 cm brush penetration.

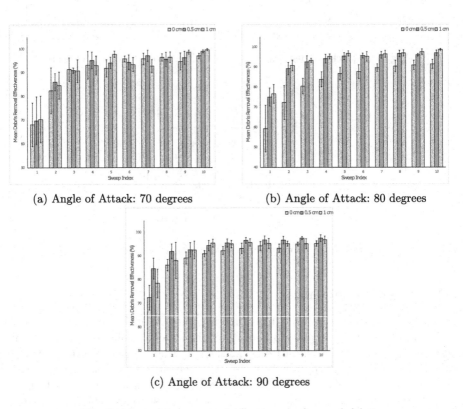

(a) Angle of Attack: 70 degrees

(b) Angle of Attack: 80 degrees

(c) Angle of Attack: 90 degrees

Fig. 9. Mean debris removal effectiveness for sand debris

3.3 Metallic Swarf Debris Removal

Figure 10a presents results for a brush angle of attack of 70° with 0 cm, 0.5 cm and 1 cm penetration. After three sweeps, all penetration configurations make the sweeping removal effectiveness rate fluctuate between 94% and 100% without stabilisation and with a large standard and overlapping standard deviation. This phenomenon is due to backward sweeping, where the metallic swarf particles are firmly caught in brush bristles. The backward sweeping effect is stronger with 1 cm and 0.5 cm brush penetration. After ten consecutive sweeps, the mean debris removal effectiveness attains 99.39% with 1 cm penetration, 99.85% with 0.5 cm penetration, and 99.89% with 0 cm brush penetration. At the end of the testing procedure and for all operational brush configurations, the brush has metallic swarf blocked into the bristles.

Figure 10b presents results for a brush angle of attack of 80° with 0 cm, 0.5 cm and 1 cm penetration. From the first sweep, all penetration configurations make the sweeping removal effectiveness rate fluctuate between 95% and 99% without stabilisation and with a large standard and overlapping standard deviation. The backward sweeping effect is stronger with 1 cm and 0.5 cm brush penetration as the metallic swarf particles are caught within the brush bristles. After ten consecutive sweeps, the mean debris removal effectiveness attains 98.79% with 1 cm penetration, 98.30% with 0.5 cm penetration, and 98.74% with 0 cm brush penetration. At the end of the testing procedure and for all operational brush configurations, the brush has metallic swarf blocked into the bristles.

Figure 10c presents results for a brush angle of attack of 90° with 0 cm, 0.5 cm and 1 cm penetration. After ten consecutive sweeps, the mean debris removal effectiveness attains 98.74% with 1 cm penetration, 98.84% with 0.5 cm penetration, and 95.09% with 0 cm brush penetration. In any configuration, the limitation of surface contact between the brush and debris limits the backward sweeping effect. However, this also affects the sweeping mean debris removal effectiveness, depending on the brush penetration. A higher penetration indicates a better contact between the brush and surface that seal potential debris leak. At the end of the testing procedure and for all operational brush configurations, the brush has metallic swarf blocked into the bristles. The 90° brush angle of attack configuration offers a more consistent result than the 70 and 80° brush angle of attack.

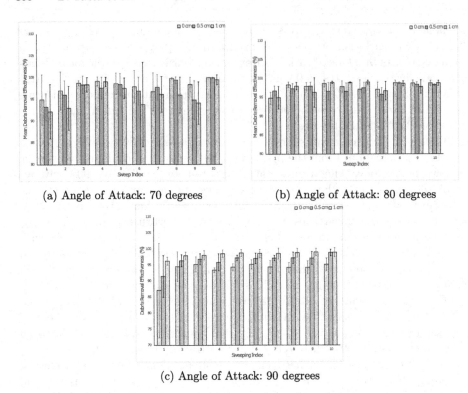

(a) Angle of Attack: 70 degrees   (b) Angle of Attack: 80 degrees

(c) Angle of Attack: 90 degrees

Fig. 10. Mean debris removal effectiveness for metallic swarf debris

4   Discussion

For any debris type, we observe an influence of the brush parameter on the debris
removal effectiveness. Depending on the debris type and the brush configuration
parameter, debris removal effectiveness varies significantly with a more significant influence from the brush angle of attack. In the case of flour, removing large
quantities of debris from a stainless-steel surface is easy as there is low friction
between the debris and surface. For example, an 80° angle of attack and a 0.5 cm
brush penetration offer 99.90% mean debris removal effectiveness after ten consecutive sweeps. This configuration can be considered the best for this debris
type. On the contrary, the lowest performance has been attained with a brush
penetration of 0 cm combined with a brush angle of attack of 90°. Despite removing a 97.12% of debris after ten sweeps, this configuration is the least effective
because it does not create sufficient contact for debris removal. The brush misses
debris particles on the surface to clean. For configuration offering an angle of
attack of 70° or 80°, we can observe the sweeping mean debris removal effectiveness degradation after the first sweep. These degraded performances are due to
backward sweeping resulting from high surface contact between the brush bristle
and the small flour particle size. After the first sweep, flour debris particles are

stuck within the brush bristle. Then, on the following sweep and during brush deflection, the debris particles are released on the surface, causing degradation of debris removal performance.

For sand debris, it appears that the removal of debris is more challenging compared to flour and friction increases when an increasing compression force is applied to the product. For all configurations, the sweeping effectiveness starts lower than other debris types. For example, after the first sweep, the average mean debris removal effectiveness is 73.34% for sand for all operational configurations. Thereby, 70° brush angle of attack offers the best debris removal effectiveness. However, the mean debris removal standard deviation overlaps and does not allow us to evaluate the impact of brush penetration on debris removal effectiveness.

The metallic swarf is the most challenging debris type despite being easy to remove. It has a thread shape combined with abrasiveness and rigid properties. Metallic swarf can quickly get stuck into the brush bristles, resulting in backward sweeping. Unlike debris like flour or sand, the operational condition that offers the best debris removal result is a brush angle of attack of 90° and a brush penetration of 1 cm resulting in 99.89% effectiveness. Indeed, to limit the backward sweeping effect, it is crucial to limit the debris-bristles contact surface. The debris removal effectiveness is degraded in all configurations because of backward sweeping.

Moreover, backward sweeping is a recurring issue met with any debris. Certain operational conditions must be avoided to limit the impact of this effect. Backward sweeping must be considered as it degrades cleaning effectiveness. Therefore, the robot must optimise the brush-debris contact following the debris type. Brush-Debris contact must be maximised for a non-compressible product such as flour, moderate for non-compressible products like sand and minimised for swarf shape debris. Alternative ways to resolve the backward sweeping problem would be to perform movement patterns with small travel lengths and use the brush mechanical properties dynamics. Brush stiffness and compliance properties were not assessed in this study. This way, the brush is deflected to load energy and release the energy resulting in debris expel and less debris stuck in the bristles. The sweeping robot movement limiting backwards sweeping contradicts the airborne limitation requirement. Then, the robot must autonomously find the balance between limiting backwards sweeping and airborne contamination.

The result shows that in all configurations and after ten sweeps, the debris removal effectiveness attains more than 90% for any type of debris. These results indicate that repeating the same sweeping movement multiple times improves the cleanliness of a surface for high friction products. For flour, 95% debris removal effectiveness can be attained after one sweep, where four sweeps are needed in the sand case. The debris removal dynamics attain 95% after the third sweep for the metallic swarf. However, they have more variability because of the swarf caught in brush bristles. Multiple sweeps can decrease the debris removal effectiveness. Within the same condition, the effectiveness of the debris removal dynamic variation could be caused by the debris friction, size and compressibility property.

Effective control for autonomous robots must adapt the number of sweeps to reach a clean surface requirement. This adaptive robot control is essential to avoid brush wear, surface attrition and backward sweeping.

For effective debris removal, the robot must adapt following the brush parameter (bristle length and stiffness), the debris parameter (friction coefficient, particle size, compressibility property) and the surface roughness. Knowing these parameters would allow the robot to adapt to the environment and situation and determine the required task and path planning.

5   Conclusion

This paper studies the effectiveness of operational brush parameters in developing an autonomous and robotic system for sweeping. Debris removal effectiveness has been tested using a robotic manipulator on flour, sand and metallic swarf on stainless steel. Regarding the operational brush conditions, the tested brush angle of attacks were 90°, 80° and 70°, and the tested penetrations were 0 cm, 0.5 cm and 1 cm. The test was performed using a 7 DOF robot manipulator handling a 3.8 cm nylon brush repeating a rectangle shape sweeping pattern with a cartesian impedance controller. Sweeping debris removal effectiveness was evaluated using visual inspection methods.

The results show that the operational brush parameter must be adjusted following the type of debris to remove from the surface. Firstly, for ultra-fine particles such as flour, the best removal effectiveness is given by a moderate angle of attack (80°) and a moderate penetration (0.5 cm). This configuration pressures the debris and limits the backward sweeping effect. Secondly, the best removal effectiveness for fine particles like sand is given by the lowest angle of attack (70°) independently of the brush penetration. As sand seems to have the highest friction coefficient of the tested debris, more pressure is needed to remove the debris particle. Finally, despite being easy to remove, metallic swarf debris necessitates a high angle of attack (90°) with high penetration (1 cm). This type of debris necessitates a little surface of contact between the brush and debris, combined with a high pressure between the brush and the surface.

This preliminary study identifies the performance and issues met during the robotic sweeping process for debris removals in the limit of the debris and operational parameter tested. However, a broader spectrum of particle size distribution and operational brush parameters must be tested in the future. About the particle size distribution, a mix of different types of debris, including a large particle size distribution and a mix of particle size friction, would be essential to observe and analyse the sweeping performance. Future work must focus on two objectives regarding the development of the robotic and autonomous sweeping system for the nuclear glovebox. The first is the autonomous robotic optimisation of brush parameters for debris removal. The second is autonomous path planning for bulk solid non-prehensile manipulation adapted to the nuclear glovebox environment.

Acknowledgements. This project has been supported by the United Kingdom Atomic Energy Authority and the RAIN Hub, funded by the Industrial Strategy Challenge Fund, part of the government's modern Industrial Strategy. The fund is delivered by UK Research and Innovation and managed by EPSRC [EP/R026084/1].

References

1. Abdel Wahab, M.M., Wang, C., Vanegas Useche, L.V., Parker, G.: Finite element models for brush-debris interaction in road sweeping. Acta Mech. **215**(1–4), 71–84 (2010). https://doi.org/10.1007/s00707-010-0304-y
2. Bayliss, C.R., Langley, K.F.: Chapter 11 - dismantling techniques. In: Nuclear Decommissioning, Waste Management, and Environmental Site Remediation, pp. 99–111. Butterworth-Heinemann, Burlington (2003). https://doi.org/10.1016/B978-075067744-8/50014-X, https://www.sciencedirect.com/science/article/pii/B978075067744850014X
3. Bayliss, C., Langley, K.: Decontamination techniques. In: Bayliss, C.R., Langley, K.F. (eds.) Nuclear Decommissioning, Waste Management, and Environmental Site Remediation, pp. 89–97. Butterworth-Heinemann, Burlington (2003). https://doi.org/10.1016/b978-075067744-8/50013-8, https://www.sciencedirect.com/science/article/pii/B9780750677448500138
4. Bormann, R., Hampp, J., Hagele, M.: New brooms sweep clean - an autonomous robotic cleaning assistant for professional office cleaning. In: Proceedings - IEEE International Conference on Robotics and Automation, vol. 2015-June, no. June, pp. 4470–4477 (2015). https://doi.org/10.1109/ICRA.2015.7139818
5. Duroudier, J.P.: Mechanical characteristics of divided solids. Divided Solids Mech. 1–56 (2016). https://doi.org/10.1016/b978-1-78548-187-1.50001-3
6. Kanegsberg, B.: Handbook for Critical Cleaning, vol. 105 (2001). https://doi.org/10.1016/s0026-0576(07)80159-0
7. Leidner, D.S.: Cognitive reasoning for compliant robot manipulation. Doctoral thesis, p. 211 (2019). http://www.springer.com/series/5208
8. Office for Nuclear Regulation: NS-INSP-GD-053 - Criticality Safety, pp. 1–29 (2020)
9. Okada, K., Kojima, M., Sagawa, Y., Ichino, T., Sato, K., Inaba, M.: Vision based behavior verification system of humanoid robot for daily environment tasks. In: Proceedings of the 2006 6th IEEE-RAS International Conference on Humanoid Robots, HUMANOIDS, pp. 7–12 (2006). https://doi.org/10.1109/ICHR.2006.321356
10. Peel, G., Michielen, M., Parker, G.: Some aspects of road sweeping vehicle automation. In: IEEE/ASME International Conference on Advanced Intelligent Mechatronics, AIM, vol. 1, pp. 337–342 (2001). https://doi.org/10.1109/aim.2001.936477
11. Regulation, N.: Investigation into the thermal oxide reprocessing plant (THORP) contamination event (August 2016), pp. 1–15 (2017)
12. Snead, L.L., Zinkle, S.J.: Use of beryllium and beryllium oxide in space reactors. In: AIP Conference Proceedings, vol. 746, pp. 768–775 (2005). https://doi.org/10.1063/1.1867196
13. Sri Vishva, R., Naresh, R., Venkada Krishnan, M.S.: An autonomous cleaning robot. In: Proceedings - International Conference on Artificial Intelligence and Smart Systems, ICAIS 2021, pp. 686–691 (2021). https://doi.org/10.1109/ICAIS50930.2021.9395909

14. Sun, G., et al.: Task-oriented impedance control for integrated autonomous cleaning manipulator. In: IEEE International Conference on Robotics and Biomimetics, ROBIO 2019, pp. 358–363 (2019). https://doi.org/10.1109/ROBIO49542.2019.8961483

15. Tokatli, O., et al.: Robot-assisted glovebox teleoperation for nuclear industry. Robotics **10**(3), 85 (2021). https://doi.org/10.3390/robotics10030085

16. Vanegas-Useche, L.V., Abdel-Wahab, M.M., Parker, G.A.: Effectiveness of oscillatory gutter brushes in removing street sweeping waste. Waste Manag. **43**, 28–36 (2015). https://doi.org/10.1016/j.wasman.2015.05.014, http://dx.doi.org/10.1016/j.wasman.2015.05.014

17. Virji, M.A., et al.: Characteristics of beryllium exposure to small particles at a beryllium production facility. Ann. Occup. Hyg. **55**(1), 70–85 (2011). https://doi.org/10.1093/annhyg/meq055

18. Wang, C.: Brush modelling and control techniques for automatic debris removal during road sweeping. Ph.D. thesis, University of Surrey (2005)

19. Ye, G., Alterovitz, R.: Guided motion planning. In: Christensen, H., Khatib, O. (eds.) Robotics Research. Springer Tracts in Advanced Robotics, vol. 100, pp. 291–307. Springer, Cham (2017). https://doi.org/10.1007/978-3-319-29363-9_17

Automatic, Vision-Based Tool Changing Solution for Dexterous Teleoperation Robots in a Nuclear Glovebox

Joshua Blake[1], Guy Burroughes[2], and Kaiqiang Zhang[2(✉)]

[1] University of Nottingham, Nottingham NG7 2RD, UK
[2] RACE, UK Atomic Energy Authority, Abingdon OX14 3DB, UK
kaiqiang.zhang@ukaea.uk

Abstract. This paper describes a novel automatic solution for tool-changing operations using dexterous teleoperated robots in a nuclear glovebox. This solution can identify and locate tools in the nuclear glovebox by visually tracking augmented reality (AR) tags online at a low computational cost. The solution is designed in a modular manner taking into account different practical constraints, so it can be easily adapted to enormous existing nuclear gloveboxes. In practice, the proposed solution is introduced to an existing robotic system including two teleoperated lightweight manipulators in a nuclear glovebox. The experimental tests have demonstrated the effectiveness of the automated tool-changing solution without any knowledge of the mock-up environment a priori.

Keywords: Nuclear glovebox · Vision-based control · Automation · Teleoperation robot

1 Introduction

The presence of severe risks to human operators is a long-term issue when using gloveboxes to manipulate nuclear materials and wastes. The interior of a glovebox is commonly a highly cluttered environment containing radioactive materials and contaminated tools, including corroded and sharp objects threatening to human operators [5,6]. For instance, gloveboxes being decommissioned often contain exposed wires, cropped cables, pipes or needlesticks, all of which may lead to lethal incidents [15]. Thus, the industry has an increasing interest in developing robotic solutions for replacing manual operations in the nuclear gloveboxes. However, there is not yet an automated system capable of conducting complicated in-glovebox tasks, e.g., repackaging radioactive waste canisters

We would like to thank UK Research and Innovation (UKRI) for their support and funding that has come from the Robotics and Artificial Intelligence in Nuclear (RAIN) grant EP/R026084/1. This work has been part-funded by the EPSRC Energy Programme (grant number EP/W006839/1). To obtain further information on the data and models underlying this paper please contact PublicationsManager@ukaea.uk.

[16], demanding significant dexterity. Also, it is challenging to fit robotic manipulators inside enormous existing gloveboxes, which are originally designed for
manual operations, with limited access, light and visibility (see examples in [15]).
One promising solution is to introduce teleoperated robotic systems that allow
for dexterous human-in-the-loop control. As a prototype, a teleoperated robotic
system has been developed for nuclear-glovebox operations [20]. This robotic
system integrates commercial-off-the-shelf collaborative robots with vision and
haptic feedback systems, i.e., facilitating a teleoperation system in a glovebox.
Thus, skillful human operators can remotely manipulate the robotic systems to
complete tasks in a manner similar to traditional manual operations.

In general, an in-glovebox task needs various specific tools to complete a
series of different operations, such as, radiation inspection, unfastening bolts,
cutting metallic containers, cleaning surfaces, etc., inside the confined, cluttered
interior space [12,20]. For example, an operator may require a powered handheld
cutting tool for size reduction, a near-field scanner for radiation inspection, or a
brush for cleaning surfaces, and switch between different tools in an operation.
Although human operators can easily change manual tools via natural hand
grasping and placing, it is non-trivial and technically challenging to manipulate
teleoperated robots for grasping nuclear-glovebox tools originally designed for
manual operations [13,18,20]. Motivated to achieve high operation efficiency, it
is essential to develop an effective tool changing approach that allows the robots
to easily locate and interface with any required tool with minimum operator
inputs.

Specifically, at the Los Alamos National Lab (LANL), a completely automated line has been developed for processing nuclear material in a glovebox
[10]. In detail, a 5 degree-of-freedom (DOF) robotic manipulator is installed
on an automated Moore lathe, which allows for positioning of the manipulator
above a stationary tool holding rack. The robot has a special flange compatible
with the tools' quick-changer interfaces. Because each tool rests at a predefined
location on the rack, it is possible to preprogamme the robotic system following
fixed trajectories for changing tools automatically. However, this robotic solution
is generally designed as an embedded subsystem of the glovebox. It is neither
cost-effective nor possible to fit such an automated robotic system into common nuclear gloveboxes (genuinely designed for manual operations). Moreover,
regarding a common nuclear glovebox fitted with a highly dexterous teleoperated
system like [20], it is infeasible to introduce quick changers to the robot flanges.
This is because the relatively high weight of quick-changer interfaces will reduce
the manipulation capability of the telemanipulators (each fitted into gloveboxes
via a standard 6 or 8 in. hole [21]) with limited payloads. Also, it is difficult to
fit manual operation tools in various shapes with quick changer interfaces. On
the other hand, clearly, the use of a tool-managing rack is an effective approach
to organise various kinds of tools inside standard gloveboxes.

In the nuclear industry, it is common to add vision-based control functions
into existing robotic manipulation systems, motivated to enable new functionalities, e.g., [1,8,14]. Rather than introducing an additional system (similar to

[10]) into standard gloveboxes, a potential solution for automatic tool-changing is to automatically grasp and place tools via different vision-based approaches. In [8], a surface construction algorithm is developed to use stereo-camera data for building the geometric data of unknown objects in 3D. The constructed 3D models can then be interrogated to find suitable grasp points. This offers an online decision-making approach for an industrial manipulator to grasp nuclear wastes in unknown shapes. However, depending on a series of user-defined criteria, this vision-based approach leads to variable grasp locations for the same grasping task, i.e., yielding a lack of automation and repeatability. Differently, in [1], depth cameras are used to measure the geometric point clouds of objects in a glovebox. The geometric data is then used for classifying the type of each object according to a trained classification database. The robotic manipulator will then grasp an object at specific positions that are predefined for every type of objects. Although this approach guarantees the repeatability of grasping motions, the classification of in-glovebox tools in various shapes is a non-trivial task requiring extensive data-processing to get reliable results from large databases.

An alternative, repeatable vision-based control approach is to use augmented reality (AR) tags to guide automated robotic motions. Specifically, an AR tag is an encoded fiducial marker that can be extracted from live camera feeds at a low computational cost. Thus, a vision-based system can efficiently track the AR tags, which can be attached to landmarks in an environment or objects to be manipulated. For example, an AR tracking method is utilised to track the positional and rotational data of mobile robots accurately in [7]. In a nuclear glovebox application, the position of a hand is AR tracked using the RGB-D data from a fixed camera in [19]. This allows for optimising automated collision-free motions of a robotic manipulator sharing the same workspace with the human hand. It can be seen that AR tracking methods can be used to develop a vision-based control approach for automated grasping and positioning operations, although no similar solution has yet been developed for operations in nuclear gloveboxes.

This paper presents a novel vision-based solution for changing tools automatically at high efficiency using robotic manipulators in nuclear gloveboxes. The primary focuses are to develop the essential mechanical components and robotic system design, taking into account the constraints and considerations in the associated nuclear-industry practice. These considerations lead to the creation of a generic solution suitable for different nuclear gloveboxes. Another focus here is to describe how the functional software modules are adopted, motivated to implement a robust solution at a low-computational demand.

Specifically, a compact mobile tool management rack is designed for organising various tools inside gloveboxes. Two mechanical interfaces are designed to introduce a special kind of mating interfaces to various types of tools for nuclear glovebox operations. The modified tools therefore can be placed on and taken from the management rack using robotic manipulators at ease. Benefiting from these special mechanical designs, a novel vision-based control solution is developed integrating various functions in the robot operating system (ROS) environment. The solution processes the native RGB data from cameras providing fixed views in a glovebox. Each tool loading and unloading position is AR tagged, so they can be located and managed online by the vision-based robotic control system. This allows for automatically planning and manoeuvring of the robotic manipulators in a glovebox for loading and unloading an objective tool. The effectiveness of the proposed automatic solution has been demonstrated in practice using a mock-up nuclear glovebox. The mock-up setup consists of two teleoperated manipulators similar to [20].

2 Practical Design Considerations

In the nuclear industry, gloveboxes vary dramatically in size and shape as well as in intended applications. Motivated to develop a generic solution compatible with different gloveboxes, it is essential to design the automatic tool changing system with high flexibility. The system design needs to take into account a variety of important practical considerations as follows.

The first major consideration is that gloveboxes likely contain a variety of semi-permanent objects inside that are being stored or broken down (see [12] for example). Depending on the space required for specific operations in certain gloveboxes, there may be limited options for where the tools can be placed and organised inside the gloveboxes. Here, a tool management rack is adopted to host tools efficiently, inspired by the concept of using a tool rack in [10]. Motivated to guarantee high flexibility of the solution, the management rack needs to be mobile and able to be positioned freely inside different gloveboxes. Therefore, the rack can be moved to any position resulting in maximum operation efficiency.

Secondly, the size and shape of the mobile tool rack need to be designed carefully, because there are very limited approaches for transferring equipment into and out of the glovebox's interior workspace. The common approach for posting tools into or from a glovebox is through one or several antechamber ports located on the glovebox sides. An antechamber is typically designed with small, well-sealed doors in order to isolate the hazardous interior from the external ambient environment. This means that the tools and the associated management rack need to be small enough for being transferred through the standard antechambers.

Considering the size limitations of the glove ports or the antechambers, it is also challenging to accommodate robotic manipulators that can fit inside gloveboxes. This constrains the choices of robotic manipulators that can be introduced via standard glovebox ports (originally designed for manual operations). Despite the size limitation, the robotic manipulators need to be dexterous enough to undertake a vast series of operations, i.e., enabling remote operations inside gloveboxes. As a result, the dimensions and kinematic constraints of the suitable robotic manipulators naturally imply the limitation of the manipulators' payload. Motivated to retain high dexterity, it is necessary to maximise the operational payload of the robotic manipulators and avoid attaching accessories. Thus, heavy end-effectors and common industrial tool-changing interfaces (such as electromagnetic [2] or pneumatic [11] tool changers) are not suggested, because they would take up a significant proportion of the available payload. Because a teleoperated robotic arm with a two-finger gripper has been a well-proven design successful in teleoperation missions for thousands of hours [4], a lightweight two-finger gripper is adopted as the end-effector. As electromagnetic or pneumatic tool-changers are not recommended, it is infeasible to develop an automated solution relying on quick-changer interfaces similar to [10].

In addition, the teleoperated manipulators need to be capable of interfacing with (for instance grasping) the existing manual tools that are specifically designed for processing nuclear materials. As a result, manual operations can be easily replaced by teleoperations using the existing tools in a cost-effective manner, rather than investing to develop new bespoke tools purely for teleoperations. Helpfully, numerous tools have been designed for teleoperations over decades [3,9], motivated to maintain nuclear-fusion reactors. These tools are designed with special kinematic mating interfaces that are naturally radiation hardened and capable of ensuring consistently robust tool-grasping. Because such mating interfaces are implemented via mechanical designs, it is easy to introduce the same interfaces to the existing in-glovebox manual tools with minimal modifications. This beneficial design concept is adopted here by using a gripper finger design (see Fig. 4) and a gripping block design (see Fig. 2a).

Overall, the automatic tool changing solution needs a mobile tool management rack of which the size is customisable according to the constrained access via glovebox ports, and robotic manipulators that employ two-finger grippers with special mechanical interfaces. The associated interfaces can be easily introduced to existing manual tools for in-glovebox operations. Thus, the robotic system can grip either the manual tools (designed for standard nuclear glovebox operations) or the remote handling tools (developed for nuclear-fusion operations) for teleoperations. Alongside this should be an automatic control system which allows for the changing of the gripped tool using the robotic manipulators. This tool should be selected from a range of tools hosted on a tool management rack in a robust and repeatable manner.

3   Tool Management Rack and Interfaces

This section presents the design of the mechanical components, as aforementioned, which are designed to facilitate the automatic tool changing solution. Specifically, these mechanical components include a) a tool management rack for storing teleoperation tools in a glovebox, b) remote-handling grip blocks with special kinematic mating interfaces, and c) two kinds of tool interfaces allowing for adding grip blocks onto different manual tools. Note that all the mechanical components are designed according to a specific glovebox as a representative demonstration similar to [20].

Tool Management Rack
The tool management rack (see Fig. 1a) is designed primarily following two design considerations. Firstly, different teleoperation tools need to be stored on the rack that could be placed anywhere inside the glovebox. Secondly, the rack

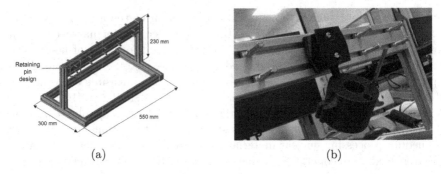

Fig. 1. Tool rack design (a) and a photo showing a remote-handling grip hosted at a tool rack (b).

could also be easily fed into and out of the glovebox through pre-existing transfer ports, specifically, an antechamber in this paper. Here, aluminium extrusions are adopted to construct a strong but lightweight supporting structure. As a result, the structure is light enough for robotic manipulators with limited payloads to lift and manoeuvre the rack. The use of extrusions also ensures the possibility of customising the size of the rack, depending on the dimensional limitations of the glovebox and its access antechamber.

The other design element is the retaining pins as highlighted in Fig. 1a. There are pairs of retaining pins in parallel designed on the horizontal primary beam of the rack. Each tool or grip block has one or several pairs of holes. By mating the pair of pins and holes, it realises a stable way of hosting a tool on the tool rack as Fig. 1b shows. This figure demonstrates how a remote-handling grip block (see Fig. 2a and the design details below) is stably attached to a management rack. Once a tool is gripped by a robotic manipulator successfully, the manipulator can take/put the tool from/onto a management rack via a linear motion parallel to the pins. Such a linear motion can easily be carried out in either a teleoperated or automated way.

Remote-Handling Grip Block

Here, a remote-handling grip block is designed as an interface between the teleoperated robot with different tools. Motivated to maximise the compatibility with nuclear fusion tools, the blocks are designed following the grip design principles that have been well established through years of teleoperation in [9]. Note that the grip blocks here require slight modifications to be compatible with the tool management rack. An essential modification is the addition of a pair of through holes with lead-in angles. The chamfered holes can passively guide a grip block being inserted into a pair of retaining pins, following the design principles in [3,9]. This design therefore effectively reduces the required accuracy in the robotic manipulation. As a result, the design of remote-handling grip blocks is given in Fig. 2a. Figure 1b shows a grip block is firmly put onto a tool management rack. Here, the bottom of the grip block is attached with a tool interface,

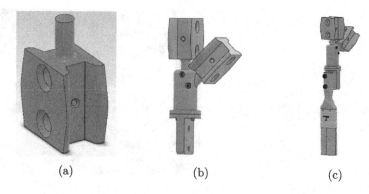

(a)   (b)   (c)

Fig. 2. Gripper block design (a), tool interface design with a bolting feature (a) and an example of using the tool interface to make a manual brush compatible with remote handling operations (b).

which makes a manual tool compatible with remote handling operations. The design of two kinds of tool interfaces is described as follows.

Tool Interfaces

Two types of tool interfaces are designed to introduce remote-handling grip blocks to manual tools in different ways. Thus, various manual tools can be converted to be compatible with teleoperated manipulators.

One tool interface design is with a bolting feature shown in Fig. 2b. One part of this interface design contains two holes where two grip blocks can be inserted and secured (see Fig. 2b). The other part of this interface primarily is a flat plate with two bolting holes. Such a feature allows for bolting any manual tool with a handle firmly. For example, a manual brush (presented as the coloured model in Fig. 2c) is installed to a tool interface of this type.

This interface design realises a simple, reliable method of providing manual tools with standardised grasp points for robotic manipulators. In Fig. 2b, the two grip blocks can be attached separately for single-robot manipulation or as a pair for collaborative manipulation. Furthermore, the rotation of these grip blocks can be easily customised, depending on the required angle of operations or tool configurations. However, sometimes modifications are needed for installing such a tool interface to a manual tool. As an example in Fig. 2c, a brush with a long handle would require the shortening of its handle and drilling of through-holes for installing such a tool interface. Although such a modification is acceptable for simple tools (e.g., manual brushes) with handles, this would not be possible for complex manual tools (such as the manual cutting tool highlighted in Fig. 3b). Also, once a tool is mounted below the interface, the assembly is often significantly long. This may lead to spatial difficulties in operational dexterity and storage, considering the limited space in gloveboxes.

The other type of tool interfaces includes a clamping feature as Fig. 3a shows. This tool interface design includes a hinged clamp consisting of two halves. The internal surface of each half is rubberised filling, which provides pliancy and extra

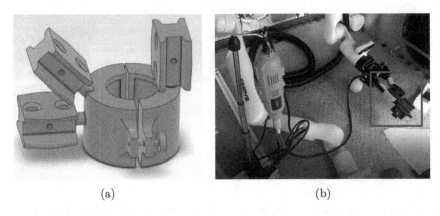

(a)   (b)

Fig. 3. Tool interface design with a clamping feature (a) and a teleoperated manipulator holding a rotary cutting tool with this type of tool interface (b).

friction, ensuring secure clamping of the tools. This design allows for clamping tools in various complex shapes without the need for any physical modifications. There are three holes designed for installing remote-handling grip blocks (see Fig. 3a). In practice, a specific tool can be clamped by such a tool interface with one or more grip blocks, enabling efficient tool configurations. Specifically, a manual hand cutting tool is held by a robotic manipulator as marked in Fig. 3b as an example.

Such an interface design allows for fitting grip blocks with a wide range of tools, such as sanders, screwdrivers, cutters and so on, which could hardly be attached to the aforementioned bolting feature due to the presence of electronics in their handles. Similar to the tool interface with a bolting feature, there are a number of positions where remote-handling grip blocks can be installed at any rotation depending on the use case of the tool. Also, it is possible to adjust the clamping tightness and the rubber filling to change the clamping friction and damping, i.e., resulting in stable and effective use of different tools for telemanipulations. The drawback of having this clamp, however, is that it contains moving parts and joints which could be potential points of failure. Additionally, the need for components, such as hinges and spaces for installing grip blocks, results in a broad tool assembly.

On the tool management rack (see Fig. 4), an AR tag is stuck onto each tool hosting position, where a remote-handling grip block installed on an operation tool is to be placed. Because a tool can be secured on the tool management rack by inserting an associated grip block into the retaining pins, this yields the position and orientation of a grip block are relatively consistent w.r.t. its hosting position as shown in Fig. 1b. Therefore, by tracking the hosting position of an objective tool, the position and orientation of the hosted grip block can be calculated accordingly online. As the grasping points at each grip block are known a priori, it is straightforward to control a robotic manipulator to grasp and then move any objective tool (hosted at the tool rack) that is always tracked by a robot control system.

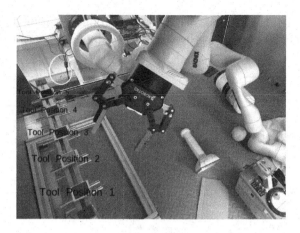

Fig. 4. Tool hosting positions are tracked online using AR tags in the experimental glovebox (overlaid by coloured markers in this figure). A tool hosting position is where a pair of retaining pins matches with a remote-handling grip block. In practice, a tool with a tool interface will have one or more grip blocks.

4   Integrated System for Automatic Tool Changing

The automatic tool changing solution is designed in a modular, highly compatible manner. Thus, the integrated system can be deployed to different systems consisting of different hardware and running in different operating system environments. The system is integrated using the Docker software platform, which allows for deploying software as packages in different operating systems. By designing each function in the integrated system as an independent container (i.e., a functional module), the integrated system can be developed and built up in a modular way. Thus, it is possible to easily adopt suitable software for efficiently use of specific hardware in practice, i.e., facilitating a highly flexible system.

Here, the system is integrated using a network-based architecture as shown in Fig. 5. The network is hosted by a ROS master, which enables and manages the communications between interconnected hardware and containers. The overall system primarily consists of four containers realising different functions, including: a) a **camera container** to process vision-data from cameras and then publish the data to the ROS master, b) an **AR-tag tracking container** to process vision-data for calculating the position and orientation information of the tracked AR tags attached to different tool hosting positions (at the tool management rack), c) a **control system container** to capture the operator inputs and use the AR-tracked data to compute the demand positions for loading/unloading tools, and d) a **MoveIt container** to compute the manipulation trajectories based on the demand positions and then communicate with the manipulators for motion execution. In this ROS-network-based design, the interfaces between the containers are implemented to exchange data in fixed formats. Thus, as long as the same design is retained, each of these containers can be distributed and updated independently without the need for modifying other containers.

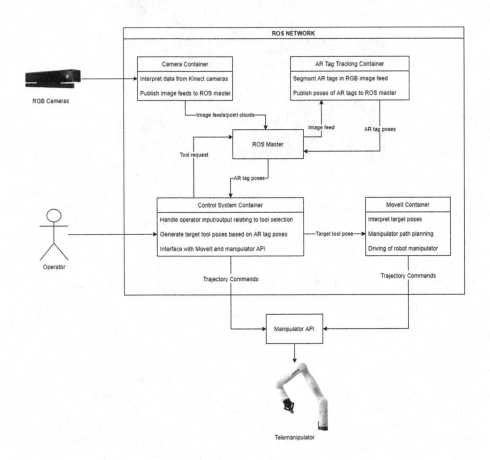

Fig. 5. Modular control system architecture.

This system integration design is applied to the experimental set-up in a glovebox tested in this paper. Specifically, to provide a clear view of the workspace, two Kinect 2 cameras are placed in two top corners of the glovebox. These cameras provide essential RGB-D data that are used for enabling teleoperation processes in the glovebox (, for example, to realise image segmentation and grasp pose synthesis in [20]). The provided RGB-D data can also be used for implementing the AR-tag tracking function for changing the teleoperation tool automatically. This avoids the need for introducing additional camera hardware dedicated to realising the AR-tag tracking function. Although it is challenging to introduce cameras into harsh glovebox environments, the use of cameras is common in the nuclear industry [1, 8, 14]. Thus, the installation and calibration of cameras are not a focus here and are not necessarily discussed in this paper.

The RGB-D vision data fed from the cameras is then integrated with the control system via the camera container. In practice, the camera container has been tested running with different computation hardware. Here, a JETSON Xavier System on a Module (SOM) produced by NVIDIA is recommended, guaranteeing a stable online image processing performance. This SOM consists of an 8-core ARM CPU and 32 GB of memory running a Linux distribution. Thus, the camera vision can be easily processed and transmitted as multiple image feeds and point clouds via standard Ethernet communications (see the multiple live image feeds in Fig. 6 as an example). Note that the SOM is able to process the camera data and provide high fidelity point clouds at improved speed and performance, when it takes the advantage of GPU hardware acceleration.

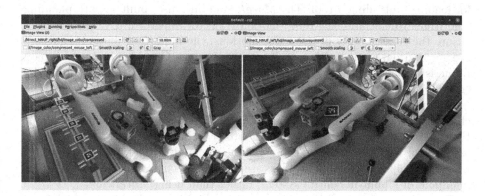

Fig. 6. Live image feeds from glovebox cameras accessed through a ROS network.

The AR-tag tracking container is mainly implemented using a ROS package called *ar-track-alvar*. Through pure image processing, the position and rotation of any number of AR tags in the camera view can be tracked and published online to a network for use by other functional modules. Specifically, the AR-tag tracking function can be achieved by using either RGB-D segmentation or RGB information only. It was assumed that using the RGB-D data could improve the reliability of tracking AR-tags rather than using the RGB vision only, as a result of introducing the additional depth information. However, using RGB-D data for tracking AR tags results in highly unstable tracking performance, because the reflections of the cluttered in-glovebox environment lead to erroneous depth data being produced. In contrast, the software achieves a robust, stable AR-tag tracking performance using the RGB vision data after optimising the border sizes of the tags and configuring the certainty tolerances in the processing software.

In experimental tests, it is found that the AR-tag tracking container can track the tags effectively online as shown in Fig. 4. Here, in the user interface, coloured overlays are automatically generated to highlight the identified AR tags, motivated to assist the operator to verify the tracking performance at ease. Also, each AR tag is assigned with an ID number, which is overlaid online on the AR tags as Fig. 4 shows. The software, therefore, could distinguish different tags in the environment, i.e., identifying the ID of different tool hosting locations at the management rack. It shows that these highlighted boxes match the actual positions and orientations of the tags well, and the tracking information agrees with the true positions of the AR tags in practice. Note that it is trivial to adopt a different AR-tag tracking library, as a result of the presented modular system design. This paper focuses on proposing such a robotic control system design, so the performance of different AR-tag tracking libraries is not investigated and evaluated here.

The tracked tool hosting positions are then used by the *MoveIt* container for planning the robot motions. After the operator gives a command, the control system container creates a sequence of motions which move the robot gripper for loading/unloading a tool. The *MoveIt* container uses built-in path planning algorithms to calculate the robot-motion trajectories accordingly. Motivated to ensure the repeatability of the robot motions, the important motion sequences are all pre-programmed with respect to a relative base Cartesian frame. This base frame is associated with the tool management rack, which can be identified by tracking the AR tags. Therefore, the same motion sequences can be applied, no matter how the specific position and orientation of the tool management rack are changed in operations. These important motion sequences are the linear motions that are to insert or extract grip blocks into or from the tool rack. Alternatively, the control system container can send the demand gripper positions directly to each manipulator's API. In this case, the robot paths are computed by the manipulator's built-in control system, rather than using *MoveIt*.

In practice, it is found that using the manipulator's built-in control functions can provide a robust, smooth robot-motion performance. This is because the *MoveIt* container may command the robot joints to move at a speed or acceleration exceeding the hardware limitations. Such a problem can be resolved by configuring the hardware limitations in the *MoveIt* container. The software limits need to be carefully adjusted w.r.t. specific manipulator set-ups or any changes affecting the associated dynamics limitations. In summary, the flowchart Fig. 7 gives a brief overview presenting the process of how the *MoveIt* container and the manipulator API are used in conjunction.

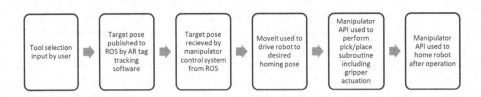

Fig. 7. Flowchart presenting how the robotic control system realises an automatic tool-changing process.

As a part of the integrated system, a user interface (UI) has been developed for testing the implemented control functions. The integrated system only requires two types of commands from an operator in operations. One type of commands is to select the objective tool to be loaded. The other type is to specify the hosting position to return a loaded tool, if there is any. This enables a simple, efficient human-robot-interaction workflow to change tools in a nuclear glovebox. It requires very little time and no operational experience to complete the tool-changing motions automatically. In contrast, it often takes a skilful operator significant attention and time to change a tool via human-in-the-loop teleoperations.

5 Results and Discussions

The performance of the proposed vision-based tool-changing solution has been tested using an experimental glovebox as a part of the RAIN project. Specifically, the experimental test rig was primarily a standard glovebox with two glove ports and one antechamber. In the glovebox, two manipulators were fed through the glove ports that normally were for operator hand access. The manipulators can be teleoperated via haptic feedback (enabled by two control robots) and vision (provided by two Kinect 2 cameras as discussed in Sect. 4) feedback. The tool management rack was placed inside the glovebox, and it hosted various tools with the designed tool interfaces.

In practice, the bolting interfaces were introduced to a cleaning brush, a scoop and a vacuum tube. The clamping interfaces were applied to different manual tools, such as rotary cutting devices, glass scrapers and a radiation scanner. The proposed solution has succeeded in loading and unloading these tools automatically. As the test rig included two manipulators, it was also possible to test how the automatic tool-changing solution could be used in a dual-robot collaboration mission. Specifically, one manipulator succeeded in changing its loaded tool automatically, whilst the other manipulator was teleoperated to hold the tool management rack. The effectiveness of the developed solution has been tested in the live demonstration [17] as an example.

Note that the performance of the proposed automated solution is not yet evaluated nor validated quantitatively. Specifically, for instance, the camera systems have been calibrated via a manual procedure so far. The calibration accuracy clearly affected the positioning error of the AR-tracking function. Here, an automated camera calibration procedure is recommended as a part of future work. Further in-depth analysis, which evaluates the proposed solution's robustness against the calibration errors, needs to be carried out afterwards.

Significantly, this novel tool changing solution can improve the operation efficiency of teleoperated systems designed for nuclear gloveboxes. Such an improvement is realised by automating specific operations, which are challenging and time-consuming to be carried out by human-in-the-loop teleoperations. Automatically generated manipulator movements are more effective than the movements generated by teleoperations, i.e., potentially resulting in a reduction of time, energy and joint wearing in the manipulators. Also, the automatic solution can be integrated into operational routines, which need little human intervention and change tools frequently in sequences. For example, an automatic cleaning routine may use brushes, vacuum cleaners, and radiation scanners to clean a fixed workspace surface after operations. A robotic system will need to change different tools for multiple times to complete such a routine. By introducing the proposed tool-changing solution, it is possible to automate such a cleaning routine in a completely automated manner, whereas the tool-changing operations are typically carried out by human-in-the-loop control nowadays.

Nevertheless, the integrated system is implemented in a highly flexible and modular way, using Docker containers and network-based structures. This makes it easy to introduce additional devices or features to the system. For example, when the AR-tag tracking performance using RGB-D data was tested, an additional function was used for compressing the point clouds measurements. Adding such a new function reduces the network bandwidth spent on transmitting the vision-data, without the need for changing any other containers. Also, the modular design allows for expanding this tool-changing solution to applications at large scales, e.g., facilitating automatic tool management in parallel glovebox operations employing multiple collaborating robotic arms. As a result of the highly flexible design, the integrated system can be easily modified to adapt to different legacy gloveboxes that already exist in nuclear facilities.

6   Conclusions

This paper presents the mechanical design and a robotic system design that enable changing operation tools in nuclear gloveboxes. Two types of tool interfaces are designed to make conventional manual tools compatible with remote handling operations. A mobile tool management rack is designed for storing tools considering the limitations of nuclear gloveboxes. These mechanical designs allow for robotic manipulators to automatically grasp a tool at ease and securely manoeuvre a gripped tool. AR tags are introduced to the mechanical set up, so that the developed integrated system can track the mechanical components and control robotic manipulators changing tools automatically. The effectiveness of this novel automatic tool changing solution has been demonstrated in practice. The future work will begin with investigating the influences of different camera calibration methods and AR-tracking algorithms on the overall efficiency and performance.

References

1. Allevato, A., Lu, T., Pryor, M.: Using a depth camera for object classification in nuclear gloveboxes. In: American Nuclear Society Student Conference (2015)
2. Ambrosio, H., Karamanoglu, M.: Design and development of an automatic tool changer for an articulated robot arm. In: IOP Conference Series: Materials Science and Engineering, vol. 65, p. 012023 (2014)

3. Buckingham, R., Authority, U.A.E.: Towards a remote handling toolkit for fusion: lessons learnt and future challenges-17360. In: Proceedings, Waste Management Conference (WM2017) (2017)
4. Buckingham, R., Loving, A.: Remote-handling challenges in fusion research and beyond. Nat. Phys. **12**(5), 391–393 (2016)
5. Cournoyer, M.E., Kleinsteuber, J.F., Garcia, V.E., Wilburn, D.W., George, G.L., Blask, C.L.: Safety observation contributions to a glovebox safety program. J. Chem. Health Saf. **18**(5), 43–55 (2011)
6. Cournoyer, M.E., Lee, S., Grundemann, R.F.: An independent analysis of a glovebox glove failure incident. In: International Conference on Radioactive Waste Management and Environmental Remediation, vol. 80173, pp. 745–749. American Society of Mechanical Engineers (2001)
7. Cybulski, B., Wegierska, A., Granosik, G.: Accuracy comparison of navigation local planners on ROS-based mobile robot. In: 2019 12th International Workshop on Robot Motion and Control (RoMoCo), pp. 104–111. IEEE (2019)
8. Grasz, E., Huber, L., Horvath, J., Roberson, P., Wilhelmsen, K., Ryon, R.: Advanced robotics handling and controls applied to mixed waste characterization, segregation and treatment. Technical report, Lawrence Livermore National Laboratory (1994)
9. Haist, B., Mills, S., Loving, A.: Remote handling preparations for JET EP2 shutdown. Fusion Eng. Des. **84**(2–6), 875–879 (2009)
10. Harden, T.A., Lloyd, J.A., Turner, C.J.: Robotics for nuclear material handling at LANL: capabilities and needs (2009)
11. Iqbal, Z., Pozzi, M., Prattichizzo, D., Salvietti, G.: Detachable robotic grippers for human-robot collaboration. Front. Robot. AI **8**(174) (2021). https://doi.org/10.3389/frobt.2021.644532
12. Kitamura, A., Watahiki, M., Kashiro, K.: Remote glovebox size reduction in glovebox dismantling facility. Nucl. Eng. Des. **241**(3), 999–1005 (2011)
13. Li, H., Zhang, L., Kawashima, K.: Operator dynamics for stability condition in haptic and teleoperation system: a survey. Int. J. Med. Robot. Comput. Assist. Surg. **14**(2), e1881 (2018)
14. Marturi, N., et al.: Towards advanced robotic manipulation for nuclear decommissioning: a pilot study on tele-operation and autonomy. In: 2016 International Conference on RAHA, pp. 1–8. IEEE (2016)
15. National Nuclear Laboratory: Challenge seeks safer glovebox gauntlets (2020). https://www.gamechangers.technology/news/Challenge_seeks_safer_glovebox_gauntlets
16. Nuclear Decommissioning Authority, Sellafield: Successful start for sellafield repackaging mission (2020). https://www.gov.uk/government/news/successful-start-for-sellafield-repackaging-mission
17. RAIN Hub: Working in a nuclear glovebox: a remote handling system demonstration event (2021). https://www.youtube.com/watch?v=eAIQN0wCUzs
18. Selvaggio, M., Cognetti, M., Nikolaidis, S., Ivaldi, S., Siciliano, B.: Autonomy in physical human-robot interaction: a brief survey. IEEE Robot. Autom. Lett. **6**(4), 7989–7996 (2021)
19. Sharp, A., Hom, M.W., Pryor, M.: Operator training for preferred manipulator trajectories in a glovebox, pp. 1–6. IEEE (2017)
20. Tokatli, O., et al.: Robot-assisted glovebox teleoperation for nuclear industry. Robotics **10**(3), 85 (2021)
21. UK Nuclear Ventilation Forum: An aid to the design of ventilation for glove boxes issue 01 (2021)

Author Index

Printed in the United States
by Baker & Taylor Publisher Services